Fulfilling the FOUNDING

A Reader for American Heritage

Gary Daynes, General Editor

Printed in the United States of America

10 9 8 7 6 5 4 3 2 1

Please visit our website at www.pearsoncustom.com

ISBN 0–536–02728–5

BA 990379

PEARSON CUSTOM PUBLISHING
160 Gould Street/Needham Heights, MA 02494
A Pearson Education Company

COPYRIGHT ACKNOWLEDGMENTS

Grateful acknowledgment is made to the following sources for permission to reprint material copyrighted or controlled by them:

"1882 Sharecrop Contract," reprinted from *The Grimes Family Papers*, Vol. 58, No. 3357, edited by Robert D. Marcus and David Burner, 1992, by permission of the Southern Historical Collection, Wilson Library, The University of North Carolina at Chapel Hill.

"Letter to Eleanor Roosevelt, 1934," by Mrs. L.K.S., reprinted from *Down and Out in the Great Depression: Letter from the Forgotten Man*, edited by Robert S. McElvaine, 1983. Copyright © 1983 by the University of North Carolina Press.

"Unforgettable John Wayne," by Ronald Reagan, reprinted by permission from *Reader's Digest*, October 1979. Copyright © 1979 The Reader's Digest Association, Inc.

Selections by Robert A. Collinge and Ronald M. Ayers, reprinted from *Economics By Design: Principles and Issues*, 1997, by permission of Prentice-Hall, Inc.

CONTENTS

INTRODUCTION TO *FULFILLING THE FOUNDING*

Since the ink dried on the Declaration of Independence, Americans have been trying to fulfill the founding. It has not been a tidy process. Federalists and Anti-federalists accused each other of treason in the debates over the Constitution. Thomas Jefferson and John Adams destroyed their lifelong friendship in a fight about the meaning of freedom (they later made up). Half a million soldiers died in a war over whether American principles permitted slavery. The nation then spent a century fighting about the Civil War's legacy of racial equality. Today the foes and friends of abortion wrap themselves in the Constitution. Senators and Representatives did the same as they sought to impeach (or not impeach) the President of the United States.

Fulfilling the founding has been messy for many reasons. The founders were not a unified bunch. Some favored more liberty, others stronger government. Some liked local perspectives, others preferred the national view. So they bent their ideas together into a system that included bits and pieces of many beliefs. The founders did not predict many of the issues that would confront the nation in the future. The Constitution was silent on political parties and judicial review. It did not contemplate that women would demand the vote, that Americans would speak hundreds of languages, that the atomic bomb would give humanity the ability to destroy itself, or that the global marketplace could make national boundaries obsolete. People concerned about these issues have had to extrapolate from the founding to find positions both constitutional and wise. Finally, the founding set up a political system that was, by nature, messy. Create a nation that values personal liberty, found a government on the voice of the people, and you can expect debate, disagreement, and anger as an everyday part of public life.

But for all of its messiness, the founding has provided a remarkable coherence for Americans. Even the nation's harshest critics use the standards of the founding to criticize America. When abortion protesters disagree about the right to an abortion they agree to the significance of the Constitution in determining what is right and wrong. In short, the founding established a context for American life that has lasted through two centuries and dozens of disputes that would have torn apart other nations.

This book is a chronicle of American efforts to fulfill the founding. It aims to describe both the messiness and the coherence of American life. In it you will read about the efforts of everyday Americans to reform American government and enjoy American life. This book is also an attempt to emulate the messiness and coherence of the American political system. Instead of reading chapters written by a single author with a single point of view, you will read chapters that incorporate a variety of viewpoints on American life. You will also read documents written by the people who lived through the events the book describes—everything from letters to the President of the United States written during the Great Depression, to a first hand account of the violence of the Civil War, to Ronald Reagan's tribute to John Wayne's patriotism. But while the book is full of different perspectives, each section of the book focuses on a few basic questions: What influence did the founding have on people at this time? How did Americans use the founding to make sense of their problems? How did they expand or shrink the vision of the founders in the face of success and failure?

Because this is an unusual book, a few tips for using it are in order. First, pay close attention to the syllabus for your American Heritage class. Some professors may assign you to read everything in this book. Others will assign only portions. Second, be sure to attend the lectures that go along with the readings. On some occasions your professor may agree with the perspectives in the book, on others she may not. Third, read carefully. Not every part of this book is easy reading. You may find the language of Supreme Court decisions confusing, or you may find the length of some chapters daunting. Do not be dismayed. Make an outline of what you are reading. Take good notes in class. Work. Ask questions! A devoted effort to understand the variety and unity of American life will pay great rewards.

My thanks go out to the authors of these chapters, to Alison Whiting, Todd Welker, and Kent Okeson for their help in compiling primary documents, and to Barbara Sherry, the best editor I've ever known. And, as always, to my wife Kristine, the fire and love of my life.

Gary Daynes
Provo, Utah
June 1999

THE RULE OF LAW

Noel B. Reynolds
Department of Political Science

The Problem of Tyranny

Tyranny and liberty are words which came easily to the lips of the Founders. Their writings teem with appeals and polemics based on these twin concepts. Furthermore, these ideas extended far beyond the pages of newspapers and the halls of the Philadelphia convention. In hamlets and villages up and down the Atlantic coast, citizens designated "liberty trees" around which they would gather for meetings and rallies. "Tyrants," such as George III's chief minister Lord North, were often burned in effigy. Yet what do these terms actually mean? What are liberty and tyranny?

They can perhaps be best understood with an example. Atop a beautiful mountain in western Virginia sits Monticello, the home of Thomas Jefferson. Just below the brow of the hill once stood the shacks where Jefferson's slaves lived. The kinds of lives in these two houses exemplify what is meant by liberty and tyranny.

Jefferson's life at Monticello was the life of liberty. He magnificently designed the house to fulfill his personal aims. Its beautiful library accommodated his love of books and learning. Its halls were filled with the objects amassed by his curiosity. Its dining room, guest rooms, and kitchens accommodated Jefferson's love of good food and good society (preferably enjoyed together). In short, at Monticello Jefferson lived a life in pursuit of his own goals and tastes. And that is the essence of liberty.

In stark contrast to Jefferson's life stood that of his slaves. Their condition exemplified life under tyranny. Almost everything in the slaves' lives was organized to satisfy the ends of someone else: Thomas Jefferson. They worked in fields to produce crops which enriched and supported Jefferson's life. They worked in kitchens to produce food for Jefferson's table. They cared for horses and carriages which existed for Jefferson's use.

Although it is true that they also produced food and goods for their own consumption, this was not to satisfy any personal goal. Rather it was to ensure that they remained alive, healthy, and available to work for ends defined by their master.

The difference between liberty and tyranny doesn't lie in the material status of Jefferson and his slaves. Beneath the apparent opulence of Jefferson's lifestyle were debts and financial demands he could never satisfy. The slaves almost certainly enjoyed a higher standard of living than many of the white settlers on the frontier beyond Monticello. The fundamental difference lies in the ends pursued by either side. Jefferson pursued ends of his own choosing. The slaves pursued ends largely defined by someone else. In that difference lies the distinction between liberty and tyranny.

For the Founders, government presented a profound risk of tyranny. If a person or faction wants to control and organize the lives of others for some personal end, government is the perfect tool. In 1975, communists under the leadership of Pol Pot came to power in Cambodia. They proceeded to use the power of the state to reorganize society according to their ideology. Private property was abolished, educated people were persecuted or executed, and the cities were emptied in an attempt to make Cambodia into a self-sufficient, agrarian society. In the end millions of Cambodians dies at the hands of their own government. Yet ultimately the tyranny of the communist regime lay not only in its deplorable violence, but also in the fact that it kept Cambodians from pursuing their own personal ends, demanding instead that they pursue ends defined by the state. For the Founders preventing tyranny was one of the chief aims of the art of government. Their solution to this problem was the rule of law.

Rule of Law to the Rescue

John Adams wrote in 1776 that "good government is an empire of laws." By making this announcement Adams reaffirmed an ancient political ideal. More than two thousand years before, Plato had declared, "Let not Sicily nor any city anywhere be subject to human masters–such is my doctrine–but to laws." Under the rule of law the government cannot act on the whim of the sovereign whether it be a single person or faction. In short, the government cannot be arbitrary. It can only act in accordance with law.

To understand the rule of law better, we should first understand what the rule of law is not. The rule of law is not simply rule by official edicts. An empire of laws demands more than simply putting rules and regulations on the books. On September 15, 1935, the German Reichstag or parliament passed what became known as the Nuremburg laws. Although these "laws" took the form of regular statutes, they violently ruptured the underlying agreement that gives laws their authority—the agreement that valid laws will treat citizens equally. The Nuremburg laws laid the foundation for the mass murder of six million people in the holocaust which followed. They stripped all Jews of legal citizenship, deprived them of full legal protection by making them "subjects" of the German state, and imposed a host of professional and personal restrictions. Nazi laws excluded Jews from public office, the civil service, journalism, radio, farming, teaching, theater, and film. Marriage between Aryans and Jews became a crime. The Nazis violated all the social agreements that make rule of law possible, and established the most blatant and ominous forms of discrimination through what appeared to be formally valid laws. In so doing the Nazi party handed an anti-Semitic population what proved to be an adequate rationale that subverted the emerging tradition of German law.

The American Founders also had first-hand experience with a government that excused itself in gross lapses of attention to the requirements of the law and the protections it provides to citizens. In the decades leading up to the Revolution, the British Parliament passed a series of acts relating to the American colonies. In form they looked like any other laws, but in substance they amounted to what Jefferson called "a history of repeated injuries and usurpations, all having in direct object the establishment of an absolute Tyranny over these States." For example in 1774, Parliament passed a series of laws designed to punish the people of Massachusetts for the Boston Tea Party. They closed the port of Boston which meant financial ruin for the colony and stripped the town and provincial governments of much of their power. All of this was done through nominally legal means, but to the colonists it smacked of tyranny and arbitrariness. The Intolerable Acts, as they were called, sparked resentment throughout the colonies and ultimately led directly to the Revolutionary War.

Thus the rule of law demands more than the appearance of law. Put another way, not just any act of the government can be law in the full sense. To achieve its purpose of enabling extensive social cooperation while protecting the people from tyranny, law must conform to certain principles that have been recognized in all regimes that have achieved liberty under law. It is these principles of the rule of law which distinguish a society in which government is limited and liberty protected.

Principles of the Rule of Law: Consent

For the Founders, the first principle of the rule of law was consent. Jefferson wrote about the "consent of the governed," and for decades leading up to the Revolution, American patriots struggled under the motto of "taxation without representation is tyranny!" Both of these statements point to a central tenet of the rule of law: people can only be bound by laws to which they agree.

There are several ways in which people give their consent to the legal system and give consent to particular laws. For the Founders, all governments were based on an original contract where men in the state of nature agreed to form civil society. This basic social contract is the underlying agreement between government and governed upon which all law rests. These moments of original, voluntary agreement are unanimous and occur only rarely. Thus there are other, more periodic ways in which people signal their consent to give consent to particular laws. Periodic elections ensure that laws to which the majority of people do not agree cannot last for long. Finally, the Founders believed in a right to revolution which ensured that if a regime ignored the laws and lost the voluntary support of the people, it could be overturned. Thus the Declaration of Independence asserts, "That whenever any Form of Government becomes destructive of these ends [i.e. protecting inalienable rights], it is the Right of the People to alter or to abolish it, and to institute a new Government." Although it isn't practical to insist on unanimous agreement for every law, through these various kinds of consent, the law, or at least the law-making institutions, will always rest on a foundation of significant agreement.

Principles of the Rule of Law: Generality

Because equal citizens should not be favored or discriminated against by the law, the rule of law requires that the law must take the form of general rules rather than commands, benefits, or punishments aimed at specific individuals or groups. This requirement makes it difficult for public officials to persecute or discriminate against some and favor others. Perhaps an example can illustrate this concept. For many centuries the English Parliament could pass a special kind of "law" called a bill of attainder. A bill of attainder is an act of the legislature which declares a specific person guilty of a crime and then declares a punishment for him or her. One of the most famous cases of bill of attainder involved the Earl of Strafford. During the 1630s, King Charles I and Parliament fought an increasingly bitter battle for political supremacy. Eventually this conflict would end in the English Civil War and the execution of the king. In its early years, the Earl of Strafford was one of the king's closest advisers and one of Parliament's most hated enemies. After repeatedly failing to "get" Strafford, Parliament hit on the idea of a bill of attainder. In a 1641 statute, they declared Strafford guilty of treason and had him executed. When the American Founders wrote the Constitution in 1787, they explicitly forbade bills of attainder. Thus, the idea of generality means that laws should be written so that they are directed at certain kinds of acts, rather than specific individuals. The provisions in many state constitutions forbidding "special, local, or private laws" embody this principle.

Because all citizens are equal before the law, none is above it. Law is supreme, even over the rulers themselves. Consider two examples: one ancient and one modern. After the fall of Rome in 455, the eastern half of the Roman Empire, called Byzantium, continued for another thousand years. A Byzantine Emperor named Justinian authored a legal code which became one of the standard legal models for the next thousand years. Under Justinian's Code the sovereign or emperor occupies a special place. Unlike regular citizens, the emperor is completely above and outside of the laws. They simply don't apply to him. In modern times, under the laws of the Soviet Union, the Communist Party occupied a similar position. All other organizations in the USSR were strictly controlled by the laws of the Soviet Union. However, none of these laws applied to the Communist Party. Like the emperor in Justinian's Code, the Party occupied a special place completely outside the law.

For the Founders, if the rule of law meant anything, it meant that special exceptions in the law were unacceptable. When John Adams spoke of the "empire of laws," he had in mind an empire in which everyone, even the king's troops, was subjected to the same rules. The trial of the soldiers after the Boston Massacre was important not only because they received a fair trial, but because there was no question that they were accountable to the laws for their actions.

Principles of the Rule of Law: Knowability

In order for citizens to obey the law, they must first know what the law is. For this reason, vague and unknowable "laws" are incompatible with the rule of law. For example, during the last half of the fifteenth century, England was engulfed in the War of the Roses between competing claimants to the throne. Eventually the Tudors won, and Henry VII crowned himself king of England in 1485. Yet Henry and his Tudor descendants were never easy on the throne and they frequently used the charge of treason to eliminate potential threats. They could do this because what actually constituted treason was conveniently vague. Despite a long line of statutes stretching back to 1352 "defining" treason, friendly judges could always find new meanings for the law, allowing the crown to "legally" eliminate its enemies. In a twist of irony, the same vagueness about what was meant by the word treason allowed Parliament to execute King Charles I on the same charge a century later. Given this history, it's hardly surprising that the Founders carefully defined treason in the Constitution.

Vagueness is not the only way the law can be made unknowable and tyrannical. The Constitution includes a provision forbidding congress from making "ex post facto law." "Ex post facto" is a Latin phrase meaning "after the fact." The Founders wanted to ensure that all law would be prospective or forward looking. Government should not be able to make action which was legal at the time it was carried out suddenly become illegal. Citizens shouldn't be punished tomorrow for actions committed yesterday which were only today made illegal. For example, in the wake of the Russian Revolution a civil war broke out among the various factions which had overthrown the czar. By the 1920s the communists had won and taken control of the entire country. Lenin decided to stage a show trial to punish the Socialist Revolutionaries, one of the parties which had opposed the communists. Despite the fact that there had been no law against the Socialist Revolutionaries' activities when they were carried out, as well as the fact that the communists themselves granted a general amnesty in 1919, the Soviets passed Articles of Law criminalizing the Socialist Revolutionaries' past activities. In 1922 a trial was held in which the leaders of the party were found guilty of breaking a law several years before it was passed.

Finally, the law must be made public. People have to have some set of rules to which they can refer. For example, after World War II the Soviet Army occupied much of Eastern Europe. Local communists immediately began cooperating with the Red Army to suppress political opponents and take control of the state. By 1949, Hungary was a single party country. The new regime turned its attention immediately to the courts. New judges loyal to the communists began referring to the "revolutionary legal awareness of the working people" as the authority for their actions. Thus the necessity of deriving legal decisions from any body of formal, written law was abolished. As a result, over the next four years the Hungarian government issued some 280,000 judgements on the basis of "political considerations." There was no way people could know enough to avoid violating these future laws.

Principles of the Rule of Law: Doability

The final principle of the rule of law seems a bit strange. It is the simple idea that citizens should be able to obey the laws their government makes. If governments make laws which citizens cannot obey, then there is no way in which the people can avoid committing "crime." When everyone is "guilty," it is possible for government to act arbitrarily in punishing those they wish while maintaining the appearance of legality.

Due Process of Law

The rule of law, in addition to laying out criteria to which laws must conform, provides an array of procedures determining how the law should be administered. Over the centuries a wide range of legal devices have developed to ensure that the law is applied justly. This array of checks are what the Founders called "due process of law."

Independent Judiciary

The first principle of due process is that the law should be administered by an impartial judiciary. Alexander Hamilton wrote of the need for "a steady, upright and impartial administration of the laws." Long before the American Revolution, the English had sought to provide for such administration by making judges independent of both king and Parliament. The Founders adopted this principle when they provided for an independent judiciary in Article III of the Constitution.

Habeas Corpus

"Habeas Corpus" is a Latin phrase which literally means "produce the body," and something called a writ of habeas corpus is one of the most basic safeguards of due process. Under the English law if the king imprisoned one of his subjects, a court could issue a writ of habeas corpus which was a demand that the king "produce the body" of the prisoner and offer proof that he or she had committed some crime. If the king didn't have any proof, then the prisoner walked free.

Government without habeas corpus means that at any moment the police may imprison a citizen and throw away the key, without providing a scrap of evidence that he or she is actually guilty of any crime. Thus habeas corpus provides one of the chief safeguards against arbitrary, tyrannical power. The Founders adopted this protection, providing explicitly in the Constitution that "the Privilege of the Writ of Habeas Corpus shall not be suspended, unless when in Cases of Rebellion or Invasion the public Safety may require it." During the Civil War, Abraham Lincoln suspended habeas corpus, throwing hundreds of suspected Confederate sympathizers in prison without trial. Southerners loudly proclaimed this as evidence of Lincoln's tyranny, at least until Jefferson Davis and the Confederate government also suspended habeas corpus.

Speedy and Public Trial

The Bill of Rights states that "in all criminal prosecutions, the accused shall enjoy the right to a speedy and public trial." If the government wants to accuse one of its citizens of a crime, it may not hold him or her indefinitely while awaiting trial. It has to bring a case, prove its accusations, or let the citizen go. This principle has led to one of the central rules in our court system. During the late 1960s and early 1970s, crime rates had increased to the point where many people arrested were not tried for months because of backlogs in the court system. Because of the Bill of Rights the government could not hold these people until trial, yet when they were released before their trials many of them continued to commit crimes. Congress responded by passing the Speedy Trial Act of 1974. The act stated that the government must bring a criminal case against anyone it arrests within thirty days of an indictment (a formal accusation that someone has committed a crime). If they don't the case is "dismissed with prejudice," which means it will be difficult, if not impossible, to reopen. Since its passage the Speedy Trial

Act has worked. In 1995, only two cases were dismissed under the act in the entire country. Every other accused person in the federal court system received a speedy trial.

The government should not be able to try its own citizens in secret. During Stalin's purges many people accused of "crimes" were "tried" in secret by the regime. As a result Stalin and the Communist Party were able to murder tens of thousands of people they found bothersome or threatening. When it became public that someone had been executed for crimes there was no way of finding out if they were really guilty and thus hold the government accountable. All of the "evidence" had been produced and evaluated in secret.

Trial by Jury

In the Declaration of Independence the Founders charged that King George III had "depriv[ed] us in many cases of the benefits of trial by jury." For the Founders this was an outright accusation of tyranny. In 1215, the barons of England forced King John Lackland to sign a document called Magna Carta. It contained a list of sixty limits on royal power and formed the foundation of what the Founders considered their inherent "rights as Englishmen." Among these was clause thirty-nine which stated that "no free man shall be seized or imprisoned. . . except by the lawful judgement of his equals or by the laws of the land."

Juries are the fact finders in a trial. The judge applies the law to the facts, but it is the jury which determines what the facts are. By making a group of the accused's "equals" the fact finders, trial by jury ensures that the government cannot manufacture "facts" to suit its own ends. Rather, it must convince a group of regular, uninterested citizens before it can take an action.

Right to Counsel

Since Shakespeare declared "first thing, let's kill all the lawyers," and most probably since long before, people have often held a low opinion of attorneys. Yet they are an important part of due process. Law, unavoidably, is a complicated thing. It may be public, but that doesn't mean that everyone understands everything about it. Without lawyers who have the expertise to understand law, there is nothing that protects citizens when the government tries to use their own ignorance against them.

Consider the example of John Adams and the trial of the British soldiers in the Boston Massacre. There was no doubt that the soldiers had fired their muskets and killed some of the Boston rowdies. The question was whether or not they could be executed for their action. Ultimately, their defense turned on distinctions in the law between manslaughter, homicide justifiable, homicide excusable, and homicide felonious. These distinctions, in turn, rested on a maze of ancient statutes and legal precedents. Without a lawyer they couldn't have understood the law, let alone invoked it for their protection. During the trial John Adams, by all accounts the most skilled and learned lawyer in Massachusetts, carefully explained and relentlessly hammered home the legal distinctions to the Boston jury. As a result the soldiers enjoyed the full protection of the law. It was to ensure that citizens could thus invoke the law to protect themselves that the Founders included the right to legal counsel in the Bill of Rights.

Right to Confront Accusers and to Compel Friendly Testimony

In October and November of 1770, there were probably no less popular persons in the town of Boston than the soldiers accused in the Boston Massacre. Since March, Boston newspapers, Boston politicians, and (perhaps most importantly) Boston pastors had been thundering the words of the Old Testament: "Whoso sheddeth Man's blood, by Man shall his Blood be shed." Ninety-six Bostonians had sworn statements to the effect that the accused redcoats had fired on the Boston crowd without the least provocation. Against such a mass of evidence and public opinion, the case of the soldiers appeared hopeless. Fortunately, they had the benefits of due process, specifically the right to confront their accusers and the right to compel friendly testimony.

Ninety-six Bostonians may have signed affidavits, but for their evidence to mean anything it had to be presented in open court where the soldiers could confront it through their counsel. And their counsel knew his business. Under the relentless cross-examination of John Adams and his associates, the inconsistencies, exaggerations, and falsehoods of the ninety-six statements emerged. The evidence against the soldiers crumbled.

Many other people had seen what really happened on March 3, 1770. However much they may have feared the Boston mob or hated the British soldiers, they had no choice but to appear and testify on behalf of the accused. Failure to do so would have resulted in a prison term. Thus the soldiers, because of due process of law, were able to mount a defense in court, regardless of outside circumstances.

Freedom from Torture and Self-incrimination

When Henry VIII wanted to get rid of his second wife, Anne Boleyn, he had her accused of infidelity, which in the case of the queen amounted to treason. There was one problem: Henry had no evidence that his wife had actually been unfaithful. Henry's prosecutors got around this inconvenience by torturing several likely suspects until they implicated the queen, repeating what the prosecutors told them to say. Both they and the queen were eventually executed.

This is not the kind of trial the Founders liked. Concentration camps and gulags have become our symbols of tyranny in the twentieth century. For the Founders this kind of royal manipulation of trials and the law was synonymous with tyranny. For them due process of law meant that evidence could not be manufactured, especially with torture. Nor would they allow the government to put one of its citizens on the stand and make him or her testify against him or herself. If the government was to prove its case, it had to do it without the forced cooperation of its intended victim.

Preconditions of the Rule of Law

The rule of law is much more than a system of principles or a list of procedural protections. It is certainly more than an abstract philosophy of government. During the French Revolution, politicians, drawing on the ideas of pre-revolutionary intellectuals known as the *philosophes,* sought to completely break their ties with the past and rebuild French society from the ground up. Ultimately their attempt ended in what English observer Edmund Burke called "a cart load of headless corpses and a tyrant."

In contrast, the rule of law is a way of thinking and set of attitudes which were deeply embedded in the traditions of the Founders. Far from being an abstract philosophy culled from the works of theorists, rule of law rests on a long history of legal experiment, development and tradition. Its success in America, in contrast to its failure in other parts of the world, can be traced at least in part to the presence or absence of such a tradition.

Locating the precise beginnings of the rule of law is impossible, but the Bible is probably the best candidate. After the Israelites fled Egypt, God delivered a set of laws to His people. For the rest of their history, the idea of the supremacy and wisdom of God's law sank deep into the minds of the Israelites. "Whoso keepeth the law is a wise son" (Prov. 28:7) declares the author of Proverbs. This ideal of respect for law was not lost on the later generations who revered and studied the Bible.

The Bible is not the only ancient source of the rule of law. An important element of Greek political thought was the concept of *isonomia. Isonomia* literally means "equality of law," and stands for the ideal that every citizen of a polis (Greek city-state) should be subject to the same laws. Greeks revered their great law givers such as Solon the Great of Athens and Lycurgus of Sparta. Plato even equated disobedience to law with impiety.

The Roman Empire succeeded Greek civilization in the ancient world, and they too had a legal tradition which would influence the development of rule of law. The Romans were perhaps the greatest organizers and administrators in history, and they applied those talents to the law. The Romans codified various ancient laws into a unified whole and then disseminated it throughout their empire. For centuries Roman law was a legal standard and model for dozens of countries. Even today, law schools around the world have courses on Roman law.

Later historians have often called the period from the fall of the Roman Empire in the fifth century to the rise of the Italian Renaissance in the fifteenth century the Dark Ages. Yet this "dark" period produced some very important legal traditions. During the Middle Ages parliaments developed throughout Europe. Yet they didn't legislate in the modern sense. Rather, it was thought that law could not be created. The purpose of parliaments was to discover and publish pre-existing law. This created a powerful bias against arbitrary action and for preexisting rules.

All of these traditions converged on England which would provide the basis for the Founders' thought. England had its own rich legal tradition. In 1066, William Duke of Normandy (an area of western France) invaded and conquered England. The Norman conquerors set out on an ambitious program of centralization and consolidation which transformed the patchwork of local customs and laws into a single, national legal system. This "common law" took several centuries of trial, error, adaptation, and improvisation to develop but in the end it formed the backbone of the Founders' legal tradition.

The seventeenth century saw a series of conflicts between the Stuart kings of England and Parliament. The two most important of these were the English Civil War (1642–46) and the Glorious Revolution of 1688. The Civil War ultimately ended with the beheading of King Charles I and an abortive attempt at a republic which ended in the military dictatorship of Oliver Cromwell. After Cromwell's death, Charles' son returned to the throne. However, conflict continued and in 1688 Parliament finally expelled the Stuarts once and for all and raised William of Orange, the prince of the Netherlands, to the English throne.

These seventeenth century conflicts had a decisive influence on the Founders. The Glorious Revolution of 1688 produced many of the political and legal theories they would incorporate into the Declaration of Independence and the Constitution. In addition, these conflicts settled once and for all that the king was subject to the law as written by Parliament. The lesson in the supremacy of law was not lost on the Founders a century later.

Finally, the immediate colonial experience of the Founders reinforced their commitment to the rule of law. The American colonists seemed to have been particularly fond of settling disputes with lawsuits. The agrarian economy of the south led to endless litigation over boundaries and real estate, while the commercial economies farther north produced suits dealing with contracts and commerce. The result was the Americans, in general, were far more familiar with law than their European counterparts. American lawyers were numerous and many of them, such as John Adams and George Wythe, were learned and subtle legal thinkers. Even gentlemen planters like Thomas Jefferson and James Madison had received formal legal training.

All of these factors meant that the American experiment with the rule of law rested on a tradition extending back centuries. To Americans in the 1770s and 1780s the principles of rule of law were familiar and widely accepted. Citizens expected their government to obey the law, and by and large they did as well.

The American experience can be contrasted to new nations without a strong rule of law tradition. After World War II, Korea, which had been occupied for the previous forty years by the Japanese, was divided between a communist north and a nominally democratic south. In 1950, North Korea invaded South Korea and a military stalemate a few years later ensured the continued survival of the South. Yet the South Korean government under Sigmuhn Rhee regularly trampled on the rule of law.

Rhee passed vague anti-communist laws which allowed him to use police to suppress and occasionally torture his political opponents as "spies." This was done despite the fact that on paper South Korea had a constitution devoted to the rule of law. Although it had a history which reached back well over two thousand years, Korea had little or no experience with the western concept of rule of law. Not surprisingly, paper commitment unbacked by historical tradition was unable to compete with the fear brought on by war and an omni-present foe to the immediate north. As the countries of the former Soviet Union attempt to establish the rule of law, they also struggle with the lack of such traditions.

Civic Virtue

The Founders felt that Providence had given them a situation uniquely suited for beginning a new political experiment. Much of their sense of optimism and opportunity can be traced to what is known as civic virtue. This quality is another important prerequisite for the rule of law.

Civic virtue refers to a certain attitude towards public life. For example, although by late 1774 war had not yet broken out, royal government in Massachusetts had pretty much ceased to exist. Boston, lying under the guns of British warships and occupied by British troops remained under royal control, but in the countryside, for all practical purposes, the government of the colony of Massachusetts did not exist. The courts of justice were closed and no royal tax collector dared show his face. Yet what was the result? Anarchy? Far from it. Citizens came together in town meetings and voted representatives to a provincial congress at the town of Watertown, safely beyond the range of British guns. People even continued to pay their taxes, although now they went to the provincial militia (soon to be the beginning of the United States Army) rather than the royal governor. Nor did lawlessness result. Courts and law enforcement may have ceased, but the citizens of Massachusetts continued to live orderly, law-abiding lives. In short, even in the absence of government, Massachusetts maintained its civic life. This commitment to orderliness and basic civic morality is what is meant by civic virtue.

Civic virtue is vital to the success of rule of law because it relieves law of the responsibility for providing all public order. When people possess an internal commitment to order, they do not require that the law be constantly keeping them in line. Law is free to deal with those who are exceptions to the rule. This means that society can allow the delay and inefficiency of due process. When civic virtue declines, the law must take up the slack in social ordering, the pressure to use other more "efficient" methods mounts.

Civic virtue affects the law in two other important ways. If people share a basic set of moral beliefs, it is unlikely that they will agree to laws that fundamentally oppose their beliefs. Furthermore, such beliefs also facilitate agreement on laws. For example, common beliefs that child abuse and rape are morally wrong have an important effect on the law. They make it impossible for people to agree to laws sanctioning such actions and make it much easier to agree on laws prohibiting it. Second, when the law more or less follows a shared sense of morality, people are more likely to obey it. Most people abstain from rape and child abuse, not because they fear the force of the law, but because they think rape and child abuse are wrong. As a result the government uses much less force than it otherwise would. If you imagine a state in which everyone needed a policeman with them all the time to keep them from breaking the law, you can get some idea of how important civic virtue is.

The Blessings of Liberty

The Founders declared in the Preamble to the Constitution that one of its purposes was to "secure the Blessings of Liberty to ourselves and our Posterity." The rule of law is one of the ways in which those blessings are secured. But what exactly are they? What is the nature of the liberty secured by the rule of law and what are its advantages?

First, the rule of law removes the fear or arbitrary government action. Under the rule of law, the government can only move against a citizen when he or she breaks the law. Furthermore, the law must be prospective, known, and obeyable. All of this means that citizens can avoid government coercion. This being the case, they can pursue their own goals without fear of government interference, provided they obey the law. It also means that government cannot usually force citizens to pursue some end defined by the state.

Second, rule of law provides the context for what the Founders called "the enjoyment of property." This means more than simply the protection of property rights. It refers to the arrangements which allow markets to occur. Rule of law stabilizes expectations about the behavior of others. Without law, people wishing to come to an agreement and sign a contract must constantly renegotiate the form of a valid agreement. Furthermore, once the bargain is struck they have no way of knowing whether

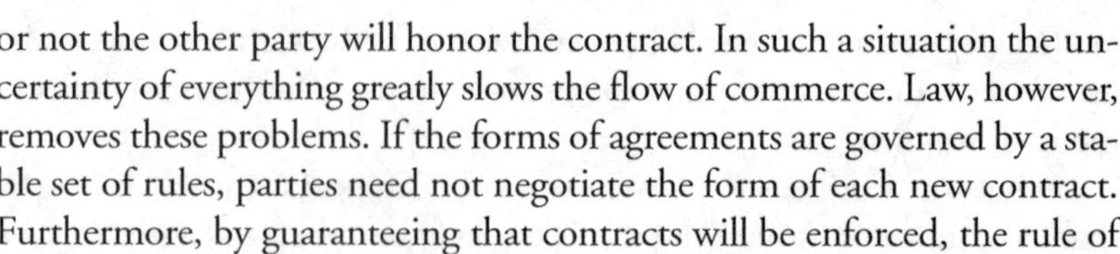

or not the other party will honor the contract. In such a situation the uncertainty of everything greatly slows the flow of commerce. Law, however, removes these problems. If the forms of agreements are governed by a stable set of rules, parties need not negotiate the form of each new contract. Furthermore, by guaranteeing that contracts will be enforced, the rule of law creates a certainty which allows people to proceed with their business.

The rule of law also diminishes uncertainty about the future. It diminishes the chance that people will fall victim to the tyranny of either the government or their neighbors. As a result they will save and invest because they believe they will be able to enjoy the fruits of such investment in the future.

The Pursuit of Happiness

Rule of law creates the framework which allows markets to generate wealth and prosperity, but it does more than simply allow for the accumulation of money. By removing the fear of arbitrary government action and providing a basis for material prosperity, the rule of law allows for what Thomas Jefferson called "the pursuit of happiness." What is meant by this?

The answer is liberty. The rule of law won't make people happy, but it will provide a context in which they can pursue happiness for themselves. It frees them from the fear of becoming means to someone else's end. Rather, under the rule of law people can define their own ends. They can have a faith in the future which allows them to improve themselves. Education and self-improvement make much more sense in the context of a stable future. Rule of law provides such a future. Under it, people can determine for themselves what will bring them happiness. Then they are ensured the freedom to pursue it.

On to Philadelphia

The rule of law creates a kind of society in which everyone, government and governed, agrees to abide by the same set of rules in pursuit of their own ends. The Founders were acutely aware that such a society will not spring into being from nothing. It requires a commitment to law born of history, practice, and civic virtue. They also realized that it wouldn't maintain itself without careful precautions.

Government had to be carefully structured and limited to ensure that it followed the rule of law. For the Founders this would be accomplished by creating a constitution, a document that established frequent elections, the separation of powers, a bicameral legislature, a complex system of checks and balances, and basic legal procedures. These constitutional devices are procedures and distributions of authority that make it difficult for the government to ignore principles of rule of law. They make it unlikely that all the powers of government can be controlled by one group of people. This strategy of dividing and limiting authority is known as constitutionalism.

The delegates who converged on Philadelphia in the muggy summer of 1787 had a free society, a society under the rule of law, as their goal. The document they produced—despite crisis and change—has emerged as one of the most successful political experiments in the history of the world.

RIGHTS AND REVOLUTION: A COMPARISON OF THE FRENCH AND AMERICAN REVOLUTIONS

Ralph Hancock
Department of Political Science

With the forming of a new government the Americans effectively resolved a crisis that had threatened to dash the hopes and discredit the principles of their revolution, principles expressed in the Declaration of Independence of 1776. They held up their new constitution to the world as proof that freedom need not be an enemy to order, that men were truly capable of self-government. Our appreciation of this achievement may be enhanced by widening our view to encompass events in France. For just as America's elected representatives were drafting a Bill of Rights intended in part to reconcile many moderate Anti-federalists to the Constitution, a decrepit Bourbon dynasty was collapsing before a gathering insurrection. The meeting of the estates-general that Louis XVI had called in an attempt to fend off the crisis thanked him by declaring themselves a Constituent Assembly, in effect claiming an authority more fundamental than that of the monarchy. And the world was convinced of the seriousness of these claims when, on July 14, 1789, a mob of their supporters stormed a Parisian prison and armory called the Bastille, symbol of royal power. Thus, just as the world learned of the successful outcome of the American revolution, another rebellion had erupted—but this was not an uprising of a few million colonials on the periphery of civilization, but a cataclysm in the heart of Europe. Friends and enemies of the new revolution alike sensed almost immediately that the very course of Western civilization was implicated in the events in Paris.

It is in fact hard to assign a date to the end of the French Revolution. The fall of Robespierre in July, 1794 marked the end of the most violent and radical phase of the revolution. The "Thermidorians" who then assumed power pledged loyalty to the revolution but did what they could to recover stability. In 1795 a new Constitution replaced that of 1793—which really hadn't been used, anyway. This Constitution of the "Directory" established in effect the rule of a five executives called directors, who managed to retain power until General Bonaparte's coup d'etat in 1799. Some would end the revolution here, but Napoleon himself claimed, not entirely without warrant, to be the savior of the new republic. He ruled until 1814, first as consul, then (after 1804) as Emperor. The fall of Napoleon, followed by a restoration of a limited monarchy, did not so much conclude the revolution as give birth to a second revolutionary cycle of regimes from monarchy (Bourbon then Orleanist) to republic (1848–1852) to a new dictatorship with a new Napoleon (1852–1870). Only with the establishment of the Third French Republic is it clear that the turmoil unleashed by the revolution, including the succession of about fifteen distinct regimes, has come to a halt. Thus the leading contemporary historian of the revolution, Francois Furet of the Ecole des Hautes Etudes, has recently published a large volume on *La Revolution* that covers the whole period up to the Third Republic.

These chronological difficulties would of course be of minor interest if they did not point to a deeper problem: what, exactly, is to be celebrated? One must sympathize with the eagerness of the French to pass over much of their revolution in silence. The events no one seems eager to celebrate can be summed up in the image that comes forcibly to mind as soon as the Revolution is mentioned, an image that haunts the bicentennial celebration: the guillotine. We first find this tall, stark and efficient implement on the center stage of the Revolution in January 1793, above the crouched figure of Louis Capet, formerly Louis XVI. But this is not the Revolutionary event the French are most eager to forget (though a telephone poll following a recent television dramatization of the King's trial discovered a large majority of viewers in sympathy with the defense). However irregular were the trial and execution of the king from a juridical point of view, many are prepared to argue that they were politically necessary, the most vivid and irrevocable affirmation of the new sovereignty of the People against the living symbol of the Old Regime.

Other executions are harder to stomach. The worst specters of the revolution hover around the guillotines of 1793–1794, when it became the most visible instrument of the infamous "Terror"—a label for the period first applied not by contemporary or retrospective opponents of the regime but by the revolutionary leaders themselves. Robespierre and his associates brandished the word proudly as an arm of republican virtue, boldly proclaiming Terror as the "order of the day." The repressed memory of these years haunts the present because their violence was not merely the random or incidental effect of a society reduced to chaos (though there was surely plenty of that), but the deliberate, systematic, institutionalized policy of the Jacobins, the revolutionary faction then ascendant. From their positions on the Committee on Public Safety and the Committee on General Security these zealots oversaw the creation of numerous special tribunals and committees, experimenting with ever more efficient institutional means of discovering and exterminating all possible enemies of the People that is, whomever the ruling revolutionary faction found it convenient to accuse. The systematic liquidation of the perceived enemies of the dominant faction was by no means confined to Paris; Terror was the arm of Revolution throughout the land.

This harvest of heretics went on steadily, and generally with ever-increasing ferocity and efficiency from the spring of 1793 until the blood of Robespierre himself seemed to quench the most violent thirst of the revolutionary guillotine in July of 1794.

The savage character of the revolutionary Terror is evident enough in considering just the famous names: one is struck by how remorselessly a Danton or a Robespierre calls for the heads of an entire circle of former allies. But to form a sense of the pervasiveness of the Terror one must multiply the deaths by tens of thousands and the arrests by hundreds of thousands. For revolutionary work on this scale, of course, the individualized efficiency of the revolutionary tribunal and the guillotine proved inadequate; to carry out the Convention's orders of total liquidation of anti-revolutionary populations, commanders such as Carrier in the Vendee (a western province including the city of Nantes) resorted to mass shootings and drownings of men, women, and children. Here, it seems, technology failed to keep pace with the Revolutionary spirit; if the Jacobins had possessed the gas chamber, a French scholar has remarked, there is no reason to doubt they would have used it. Clearly a cheerful celebration of the French Revolution requires more than the usual measure of forgetfulness.

Just what, then, is to be celebrated in the French Revolution? The French have settled on what appears to be a satisfactory answer to this question. The dominant, indeed practically the only theme of their commemorations has been the revolutionary idea of "human rights," and especially the first and most famous Declaration of the Rights of Man and Citizen, adopted by the Assembly on the 26th of August, 1789. This recommends itself as a non-partisan, consensual approach, fitting for a national celebration. The core vocabulary of the Revolution is now the common heritage not only of all French parties but of all western democracies. Indeed, in a way, the common heritage of practically the whole world, since Eastern bloc "people's republics" are as ready as third world insurgents to appropriate the vocabulary of 18th century European rationalism.

Of course, one might want to distinguish between genuine and deceitful uses of this vocabulary, but there can be no denying that the language of rights is peculiarly elastic. Everyone is for human rights, because everyone reads into them what he wants—from the protection of private property to the government's responsibility to the needy to rights of national self-determination to the dream of collectively transforming the human condition. But to recognize this is to see that the inoffensive, ecumenical quality of "human rights" calls for reflection as much as celebration. The problem is that what appears to make human rights inoffensive—their elasticity—is precisely what links them with the great offenses of the Terror. The problem is a troubling kinship between what we find is easiest to remember and what we are most eager to forget.

Much to their credit, the French have themselves taken the lead in recent years in exploring this kinship. French scholars such as Furet and Mona Ozouf have been busy excavating the meaning of the revolution as it emerges from the stated intentions of the revolutionaries. While they have shown little inclination to oppose the official, celebratory view of the Revolution of Human Rights in the political arena, as scholars they have not shrunk before the most unsettling questions. To state the problem in chronological terms, one may say that everything hangs on the link between 1789 and 1793–94. For much as we would like, it may not be possible to sustain the view that these were separate revolutions within the revolution, distinct movements based upon dissimilar principles. Consistently to repudiate the Terror while celebrating Human Rights may thus not be so easy as first appears.

A first step in coming to terms with the Revolution as a whole is to see that the systematic terrorizing and sometimes decimation of whole populations was the natural outcome of a certain way of thinking. There is a logic to the Terror, a pattern of thought and deed traceable to a definite set of ideas. Robespierre and his soulmates certainly craved power, but their characters and conduct cannot be grasped by viewing them simply as the kind of ruthless egoists who have plagued human society from the beginning.

These were rogues of a new kind, true believers who sometimes seem almost as ready to sacrifice themselves as their countrymen to the bloodthirsty gods of the Revolution. It seems clear that the "incorruptible" Robespierre (to take the clearest and most representative case) toiled and killed not for personal gain in any ordinary sense, but for the sake of an ideal which dominated his own self-understanding, for the cause that he called "La Justice." Alexis de Tocqueville provides a key to the meaning of this peculiar sense of justice when he observes that "the French Revolution was a political revolution that proceeded in the manner of religious revolutions." It promised by political means to accomplish an end formerly thought to be beyond politics: the regeneration of mankind. New institutions and new policies were mere instruments in the creation of new human beings, beings who would escape all the limitations, troubles, and perplexities that earlier ages had assumed to inhere necessarily in the human condition. Such a creation clearly requires a radical repudiation of the beliefs, habits, and institutions of the past; these must be destroyed in order to allow the emergence of regenerate humanity.

The attempt to effect such a rupture is nicely summarized in the introduction of a new, rationalized calendar: the new age would not accept the burden of 1792 years from the Christian calendar, but would start afresh in the year I. The logic of the Terror can be seen to follow from this radical project of destroying the past and creating a new humanity.

In the first place, the past is a hard thing to kill. The "people," who are supposed to be eager to be reborn as free and equal, find it hard to break old habits; they require more and more aggressive midwives to bring them forth. Second, "regeneration" is by its nature a difficult thing to define, and thus to limit. It can have no public and settled meaning until a new public is created; the aims of the revolution must thus of necessity be entrusted to a visionary vanguard. Such a vanguard must refuse all accountability to allegedly higher authorities, whether religious, moral, or political. The prospect of universal human regeneration supercedes all ordinary human concerns; the agents of this regeneration must despise all traditional restraints. There is, then, a certain consistency in the Revolution's appeal to the authority of "the People" to justify violence against the population. For the people evoked as sovereign are not the actual, concrete human beings who supply grist for the mills of the Terror, but the regenerate people which does not yet exist, except germinally in the revolutionary vanguard. In the last analysis the Revolution recognizes no authority but that of a "humanity" it proposes to create.

This is of course not to say that the French people (in the ordinary, concrete sense) play no role in the revolution. In fact winning the support of a critical mass of the population, and particularly the Parisian mob, was essential to the calculations of all revolutionary factions. It is in fact precisely the ambiguity of the "people" in the revolutionary vocabulary that enables the vanguard to appeal to real popular interests and prejudices in creating the institutional machinery necessary for social regeneration. The masses are the engine of the revolution, but only an elite revolutionary corps can provide engineers and drivers. The people must be fed and flattered to provide the power to create the People.

With all traditional institutional and moral restraints reduced to dust and ashes, there is nothing to check the dynamics of demagoguery. Whatever party, faction, or individual can best manipulate the people can claim to speak for the People. Whoever rides the tiger of popular favor at a given moment possesses not only the keys to power but the only recognized touchstone of Truth. The support of the mob becomes the foundation of power, and power the only available criterion of truth. Thus Robespierre's "justice" is not contaminated by any residue of traditional morality: any act that advances the revolution (as defined by those empowered to define it) is by that very fact a just act: "To punish the oppressors of humanity is mercy; to pardon them is barbarism." It follows that "evil" is embodied in the enemies of the revolution, a category designated by whoever is empowered at a given time to define the revolutionary categories. The French revolutionary mentality did not assume that all people could be held to the same moral standards. Instead it supposed a dualistic vision of society—we embody the Good, and everyone who is not with us is Evil. The vision of a new humanity erases all moral distinctions except that between those who have the power to define themselves as friends of Humanity and those who find themselves defined as its enemies. "Between the people and their enemies, there is nothing left in common but the sword," declared Saint-Just, Robespierre's most loyal disciple. The winners of each struggle for power are entitled, indeed called to treat the losers as devils to be vanquished or insects to be crushed.

Since the purity of the Revolution itself cannot be questioned, there is no choice but to enlarge the search for devils, for counterrevolutionary conspirators hidden among the people or disguised among the very elite.

Without new enemies to feed upon, the Revolution cannot sustain itself; precisely because the dream is indefinite, almost spiritual, it can assert its reality only in consuming flesh and blood. Thus the distinctive features of the terror—concentration of power "of the people" in the hands of a few, merciless liquidation of enemies real or perceived, construction of a new moral vocabulary, irresistible radicalization—can be seen to issue from a fundamental commitment to the regeneration of humanity by human means. The question then arises, was this commitment distinctive of the period dominated by the Jacobins, or was it characteristic of the revolution from the beginning?

The answers provided by Furet and others make it clear that the faction dominant in 1793–4 does not differ essentially in its objectives and self-understanding from its predecessors. The practice of terror may have reached new extremes in that period, but its logic was present much earlier. The revolutionary "mechanism of interpretation, of action, and of power . . . is in place already in 1789. . . ." In particular, the core idea of regeneration figures prominently in revolutionary rhetoric from the very beginning. Indeed, ten years before the fall of the Bastille a French ideologue gave voice to the all-too-common dream: "Let us institute laws for wisdom and for happiness, and surely we will see on earth only wise and happy men . . . then all will be accomplished: mankind will have but to rejoice in life. . . ."

Once the spirit of '89 is implicated in the most notorious events of the Revolution, the possibilities of celebration are narrowed indeed. The only remaining hope for joining the French Revolution with good historical conscience would appear to lie in the possibility of severing the principles set forth in the Declaration of the Rights of Man and Citizen from the extravagant dreams of its authors. To celebrate the Declaration without condoning the Terror, it must be possible to distinguish the principle of human rights from the radical aspiration to human regeneration.

Clearly Americans have an interest in such a distinction. For our own revolution appealed to rights inherent in all human beings; the Declaration of 1789 indeed appears in many respects a close relation if not a twin to our Declaration of 1776. The attempt to save the Rights of Man from association with the unlimited politics of regeneration, to prove such rights compatible with a moderate, decent, and stable form of government, suggests a comparative reflection on our own "inalienable rights" in relation to our constitutional tradition.

The most well-known passages of the 1776 document, proclaiming the "self-evident" truths that all men are created equal, that they possess inalienable rights, including rights to life, liberty, and the pursuit of happiness, and that popular consent is the source of political authority organized to secure these rights, find clear echoes in 1789. The first article of the French declaration proclaims that human beings are born free and equal in rights; the second makes the goal of political association the preservation of these rights, including liberty and property. It is clear that both the French and American statements speak the basic political vocabulary of the Enlightenment of the 18th century, which in turn may be traced to the central ideas of John Locke's political treatises of 1690.

The two declarations appear to derive from a common program: religious and aristocratic prejudices are to be stripped away in order to reveal and to liberate human nature. The differences are, however, important, indeed, decisive.

The framers of the French declaration, though ready to acknowledge the value of American precedents, including the declarations of rights published by various states, were eager to surpass them, to produce what they believed to be a more purely rational and universalistic statement. In particular, they found that the Americans did not break radically enough with their English past. Despite the ringing statements of abstract principles of equality and freedom in the Declaration of Independence, the former colonists revealed a willingness to appeal as well to traditional norms and guarantees; their lapses included references to the King George's imposition of "a jurisdiction foreign to our constitution" as well as his "abolishing the free system of English laws in a neighboring province." More generally, the Declaration of 1776 and the state declarations which followed it seemed to the French to betray a tendency to focus on concrete, procedural guarantees; they confused abstract rights and particular, institutional protections and remedies. From the French point of view, the Americans tended to lose sight of the grandeur and purity of the new political philosophy as they focused on certain legal forms which had proved useful in their particular experience. In some respects, one could almost accuse the Americans of claiming to be more English than the Empire from which they were separating. In sum, the French were persuaded that, whereas the Americans were preoccupied with specific legal forms and limitations, they owed it to themselves and to the world to address with full clarity the question of the essence of law.

Their answer is best represented in articles 3–6 of the 1789 Declaration. These articles appear in certain respects consonant with the American statements; they seem to bespeak a commitment to a liberal individualist social order and to a rather restrictive notion of the scope of legitimate government: "Freedom consists in being able to do anything that is not harmful to others. Thus, the exercise of natural rights . . . has no other limits than those that guarantee to other members of society the enjoyment of these same rights. . . . (Art. 4) Law has the right to forbid only those actions harmful to society. . . ." (Art. 5) But these individualistic themes are embedded in a framework quite foreign to our Declaration of Independence and to the American political tradition as a whole: "The principle of all sovereignty resides essentially in the nation. . . ." (Art. 3) The limits of rights "can only be determined by law." (Art. 4) "Law is the expression of the general will . . ." (Art. 6) In the last analysis, the People or Nation, a collective entity, must be regarded as absolutely superior in right to the individual, for the rights of individuals are in fact determined by Law, the voice of the General Will. The individual can appeal to no authority higher than that of actual statutes legislated by "all the citizens or by their representatives" (Art. 6). In the French formulation, the effectual truth of the sovereignty of the people is the sovereignty of the legislative power.

This commitment to absolute legislative sovereignty lies behind French impatience with the American doctrine of separation of powers. The economist Turgot attacked the Americans on this point for what he regarded a thoughtless imitation of English institutions; he could not see the point of checks and balances in a system where privilege had been abolished in favor of the equal rights of all citizens. Likewise, the philosopher Condorcet found that in the American constitutions the luster of the new political science was tainted by "prejudices that those who drafted them had imbibed in their youth"; thus "their simplicity was impaired by a determination to preserve a balance of power within the state." All this inelegant limiting and balancing made no sense to the French; it only served unnecessarily to obstruct the simple truth which philosophy had discovered: that the will of the people as expressed in legislation is sovereign.

It may be, however, that the difference between American and French principles is greater than that between theoretical consistency and hesitation. For the Declaration of Independence represents an alternative to the French view that the legislature, as representative of the People, is sovereign. Thus, whereas a certain "Supreme Being" is present in the French declaration only as a passive witness mentioned in the preamble, the American declaration holds the Creator to be the very source of man's natural equality and liberty. Moreover, the American claim to unalienable rights is set within a framework defined by "the laws of nature and of nature's God." Human rights are not, at the deepest level, simply human assertions to be sanctioned by human power alone, but claims of moral beings within an ordered universe.

Americans have succeeded in doing without a theory of a unitary sovereign because they believe in an authority higher than any created by human beings. The rule of law in America is not reducible to the rule of the legislative (or judicial) power for the simple reason that human laws are presumed to be subordinate to the laws of nature and of nature's God. More precisely, ordinary legislation (as well as execution and judgment) is measured against a Constitution which is in turn understood to embody the permanent principles announced in the Declaration of Independence. The sovereignty of the people can be effectively focused in a written Constitution without being uniquely represented by any political body because the people constitute themselves as a whole by reference to an authority beyond human power. The most fundamental difference between the American Declaration of 1776 and the French Declaration of 1789 is the willingness of the former to ground human rights in the laws of nature and of nature's God.

Insofar as both declarations and both revolutions appeal to "nature", to a ground of understanding presumed to be accessible to all rational human beings, rather than to some particular revelation or ancient custom, both may be said to owe much to the philosophy of the Enlightenment. But it must be said that the Americans' understanding of "nature," particularly human nature, was considerably richer, more subtle, and more informed by experience than that which guided the French. It gave place, notably, to largely traditional conceptions of honor, both political and "sacred." An appeal to nature was held to be compatible with the moral standards of a humanity that already existed, and did not have to be created. If American ideals of liberty and equality have been relatively effective in practice, if they have proved compatible with a decent and stable social and political order, it is because they rest on a moderate theory.

This difference over the interpretation of "nature" provides a key for sorting out other comparisons between the French and American traditions. The idea of liberty associated with the American Founding may appear more "materialistic" than the French version precisely, in a sense, because it is less so. American liberty generates a way of life that is more prosaic, more "bourgeois," more respectful of the ordinary interests and ambitions of ordinary people, because it makes no claim to realizing the full and final meaning of human existence. The individual's right to pursue his own happiness can only be safe when founded upon a common recognition of ends beyond human mastery and thus beyond the limits of political and social authority. On the other hand, the human nature upon which the French founded their political theories was a nature stripped of all inherently social and transcendent dimensions. Their theories founded respect for no humanity except that which they proposed to create. In order to liberate mankind from tradition, the revolutionaries were ready to make him altogether the creature of a new society, to reconstruct his very humanity to meet the demands of the General Will.

This is not at all to say, of course, that the French revolutionaries showed no concern for honor and virtue. On the contrary, they showed an extreme concern for the duties of the individual to The Republic and to Humanity; they relished a high-minded rhetoric imitative of classical antiquity, and seemed to speak of nothing but noble ideals and self-sacrifice. But they subordinated it all to the demands of radical Revolution, to political regeneration. The morality of the Revolution abolishes the distinction between the public and the private, between political utility and individual character.

The meaning of this new virtue may be illustrated by contrasting the characters of the two men most representative of their respective revolutions, Robespierre and Washington. The virtue claimed by Robespierre was an altogether public virtue; it was exhausted in his revolutionary zeal, his total commitment to social transformation. His devotion to a new deity called The People completely eclipsed all concern for conventional restraints or standards of character. Washington, on the other hand, was not only governed by traditional ideals of individual character but also quite aware that his usefulness to the new republic depended upon his embodiment of a kind of greatness that the people could be expected to admire. French revolutionary virtue proved harsh towards the people in practice because it was identified with the People in theory. Whereas Washington's virtue may be said to represent the best of the standards of character that already informed American society, Robespierre's virtue was identical only with his vision of some future Humanity.

A similar point may be made with respect to religion: it is not enough to say that the American Revolution was friendly to religion and the French Revolution hostile. Rather, one might say that America religion was in a sense both more closely associated with revolutionary politics and more distinct from it than was the case in France. The American people's understanding of the revolution and of its motivating principles was embedded in a broadly Protestant worldview; their enthusiasm for liberty was not cordoned off in their minds from their understanding of man's spiritual destiny. Providence was believed to be friendly to the revolutionary cause, and many indeed were given to associating the rise of America with the millennium prophesied in scripture. And of course the evocation of a new dawn of history was not a rhetorical form employed only by evangelicals; the more philosophically minded had their own version of a New Order of the Ages. Still, the relative moderation of the American revolution is represented in the fact that, however religious and political ends may have been allied, they were not simply fused; religion maintained a place outside and above politics. But the French dream of political regeneration eliminated all loyalties not reducible human autonomy. Only a God whose very being was defined by the Revolution could meet the requirements of the revolution.

The disconcerting conclusion of this reflection on the theoretical core of the French Revolution is that idea of human rights that informs the Declaration of the Rights of Man and Citizen of 1789 cannot be altogether severed from the logic of the Terror. The potential for tyranny in the name of the People exists from the moment the rights of man are extracted from a framework defined by the laws of nature and nature's God. The germ of the Terror, the dream of the regeneration of humanity by political means, is present in the idea of sovereignty that informs the Declaration of the Rights of Man and Citizen. The denial of an authoritative realm of meaning beyond politics is barely separable from the absorption of all meaning into the political realm. If politics is all there is, then politics must be everything, it must hold the key to fulfilling not only the ordinary needs but even the deepest longings of humanity.

If I am right that the largely similar vocabularies of 1776 and 1789 concealed fundamentally different self-understandings, then we may not understand ourselves until we understand this difference. If we cannot distinguish human rights that are divinely endowed from those that are merely asserted and defined by human beings, then we will not know which legacy to claim.

AN AMERICAN TRAGEDY: SLAVERY IN A LAND OF LIBERTY

Mary Stovall Richards
Department of History

> *This, for the purpose of this celebration, is the 4th of July. It is the birthday of your National Independence, and of your political freedom. This, to you, is what the Passover was to the emancipated people of God. . . .*
>
> *But, I am not included within the pale of this glorious anniversary! Your high independence only reveals the immeasurable distance between us. The blessings in which you, this day, rejoice, are not enjoyed in common. The rich inheritance of justice, liberty, prosperity and independence, bequeathed by your fathers, is shared by you, not by me. The sunlight that brought forth life and healing to you, has brought stripes and death to me. This Fourth [of] July is* yours, *not* mine. *(Frederick Douglass, "What to the Slave Is the Fourth of July?" speech of 5 July 1852 in Rochester, New York, in John W. Blassingame et al., eds.,* The Frederick Douglass Papers *[New Haven: Yale University Press, 1979–], vol. 2, 360, 368.)*

Beginnings

The Virginia summer of 1619, twelve years after initial settlement at Jamestown, heralded two events of immense, and ironic, import: the first meeting of the colony's elected assembly and the arrival of twenty black Africans on a Dutch slave ship. No commentators at the time perceived the paradox inherent in the juxtaposition of the two milestones; most Virginians were too busy trying to get rich growing tobacco to see portents of the conflict between freedom and slavery. Certainly, they had no premonition of what would become the tragic irony of American history—that freedom for some would be secured at the cost of slavery for others. In fact, more than a century and a half would pass before the inherent contradictions of "Life, Liberty and the pursuit of Happiness" and the holding of human beings in hereditary lifelong bondage would be recognized by large numbers of persons. Even then it took a bloody civil war to eradicate slavery as a legal institution and the quasi-slavery of sharecropping, debt peonage, segregation, and disfranchisement persisted until the second half of the twentieth century. Slavery and its aftermath stand as challenges to the American experiment.

Slavery is as old as human history, though its specific form has varied. The Old Testament, as Southern pro-slavery theorists liked to emphasize, allowed the Hebrews to enslave the heathen, yet those same apologists disregarded the Biblical injunction that slaves were to be freed during the jubilee year, which occurred every fifty years. Greece and Rome both depended on slavery to supply part of their workforces. Classical slavery was not based on race, but on captivity in war, and as Rome expanded, so did the numbers of slaves. One authority has estimated that upwards of 250,000 slaves were imported to the Italian peninsula during the half century from 220 to 150 B.C. So harsh was Roman slavery that slave revolts (including one involving 70,000 slaves in 135 B.C.) rocked the country from time to time.

In the modern era, the Portuguese in the 1400s were among the first to exploit the advantages of black Africans as slaves both in Portugal and in the Azores and Madeira Islands. By the early 1500s Portuguese traders sold slaves in the Portuguese and Spanish outposts in the New World.

The English were more tentative. While English trading in African slaves began with John Hawkins in 1562, it was not until the seventeenth century that Englishmen began enslaving Africans in their own colonies. The English Caribbean islands first adopted slavery on a large scale to meet their labor needs. In the 1640s as the English West Indies turned away from tobacco to the horrendously demanding sugar culture, which required work almost around the clock during harvest and processing, the number of white indentured servants—who sold their labor for a fixed number of years in exchange for passage to the new world—dropped, and the demand for labor tripled. The result was predictable: a large enslaved black population ruled by an oligarchy of planters, who had few qualms against exploiting their workforce to achieve higher profits. Indeed, so great were those profits that some planters simply worked their slaves to death and then bought more. From 1640 to 1699, the mortality rate of those Africans transported to the English West Indies was approximately 62 percent.

By contrast, the beginnings of slavery in Virginia remain ambiguous. The surviving evidence is too meager to determine definitively the status of those twenty Africans sold in 1619 or to analyze with any precision their fate or that of the relatively small number of other Africans who came to Virginia in the next two decades. In the 1620s apparently some Africans were slaves, some were free, and yet others were treated as indentured servants, becoming free after a few years. Unlike English men and women who served indentures, however, not all the twenty-two blacks counted in the census of 1624 were given a personal name. Clearly, Africans were differentiated in some fashion as contemporary records make distinctions between *English* and *Negroes*. Yet, in the 1640s an Anthony Johnson, who was black and free, not only had two names but owned property and even other Africans.

Beginning in that latter decade the records reveal sales of blacks, not for a term of service—as was the case for indentured servants—but for life; such purchases could include the slave's potential offspring. One transaction incorporated the future children of a ten-year-old girl. Thus, slavery was being defined as a lifelong, inheritable condition applicable to blacks, but not to whites. By the 1660s slavery was recognized and protected by law in Virginia and Maryland. Significantly, the legal status of a child as free or slave followed that of the mother. In 1705 Virginia articulated its views of slaves in its first slave code.

What factors led to this acceptance of slavery—a practice that had no foundation in English common law? The paucity and equivocal nature of the surviving evidence have led to differing opinions among historians. Whether the establishment of slavery was, in Winthrop Jordan's phrasing, an "unthinking decision" by the colonists or if it arose, to use Kenneth Stampp's words, from their "deliberate choice," both views emphasize that the *colonists* made a decision or choice of some nature; slavery was not foisted upon them by the mother country. Further, it is evident that at least two elements were requisite for slavery to be embraced and to flourish: economic necessity and the view of black Africans as "other," different and apart from the English. While some historians have advanced one or the other hypothesis, in recent years the two have been joined.

Tobacco culture, the staple-crop economy of the Chesapeake region, required some form of coercive labor—either indenture or slavery—

since profitable large-scale production simply demanded too much work for a single farmer. Slaves cost as much as double the price of indentured servants because one bought a slave for life but purchased the labor of an indentured servant for only four to seven years. As the historian Edmund Morgan has argued, in the early 1600s, catastrophic mortality rates exacerbated the price differential. If one's own life or that of his workers could not be guaranteed, it was far better to buy the short-term labor of a servant than to invest in an expensive slave who might die shortly after his acquisition. However, as mortality rates declined by the mid-1600s, slaves became relatively cheaper since their cost could be averaged over their lifetimes. Not surprisingly, few slaves were acquired before 1660, when blacks constituted only 3.5 percent of Virginia's population. As the number of white indentured servants decreased, mainly from a drop in the English population coupled with increased economic opportunity in England, and the number of slaves rose in the latter decades of the seventeenth century, blacks' proportion in the population soared. By 1680 that percentage had risen to 7 percent, and by 1700 it stood at 27 percent.

Yet, if slavery were simply a matter of economics, then why not keep English indentured servants in lifelong bondage? The answer, according to the extensive research of Winthrop Jordan, is that black Africans were viewed as enslavable where English men and women were not. Precedent had been set by the Portuguese and the Spanish and by the English in the West Indies, who enslaved blacks in ever-increasing numbers. Equally essential were the perceptions of black Africans held by the English. The most readily apparent difference between the two groups was skin color. To the English who esteemed their whiteness as symbolic of their goodness and purity, the very blackness of sub-Saharan Africans was indicative of sinfulness and evil. Some English commentators attributed black skin to the intense rays of the sun near the equator; others, however, argued that blacks had dark skin because they were inheritors of the curse of Ham placed on his son Canaan to be a "servant of servants," although the Bible makes no mention of skin color as part of the curse. Proponents of the idea that blacks were recipients of the curse on Ham saw additional support for their opinion in blacks' supposed savage condition. Since black Africans were clearly not Christians, they were characterized as heathens. Nor did their cultures indicate civilization to the English, who viewed the tropical scarcity of clothing as evidence of blacks' licentiousness.

A racially-based slavery offered other advantages to Chesapeake elites. By replacing white indentured servants with black slaves, planters removed the threat of an uprising by the increasing numbers of freed white indentured servants, who wanted land and power within society. (Ironically, however, as the numbers of black slaves rose, they generated their own brand of terror among owners fearful of slave revolts.) Perhaps most important, slavery based on race created over time a powerful unity among whites; by the simple possession of a white skin, the most abased white stood higher than the most cultured black. It is not surprising, then, that even nonslaveholding Southerners, who became increasingly disadvantaged economically by slavery as the centuries passed, nevertheless continued their support for the institution.

Nor is it astonishing that American society still has to deal with the legacy of slavery based on race. Many of the invidious distinctions between whites and blacks made by persons of previous centuries have been passed along, almost unthinkingly, to the present generation. There are still those who see blacks as less "civilized" or more lascivious than other groups or as cursed by God. The recognition that these attitudes arose first among those who knew little about black Africans and then were reinforced and explicated by those who wanted to justify holding human beings in perpetual slavery underscores their baselessness.

This discussion raises the question, if slavery became based upon race, why not enslave Native Americans? Certainly, the attempt was made, but Native American slavery never succeeded on a large scale. First, Native Americans knew the surrounding countryside better than white immigrants and could escape from their bondage to their homes; this option was not open to those who had been transported across the ocean. Second, among the eastern North American native societies, men were warriors and hunters, not agricultural workers. Male Native Americans resisted performing what they considered to be women's work. Third, enslaving the natives destroyed them as trading partners. Further, the population of Native Americans declined dramatically from the time of European contact; the surviving numbers could not satisfy the labor needs of the colonies. There was a final ideological reason. The English views of Native Americans were complex and contradictory but generally more favorable than their attitudes toward Africans. As the historian Betty Wood has noted, while Africans were seen as inheritors of the curse of Ham, some Englishmen saw Native Americans as descendants of the lost tribes of Israel. On a Biblical scale of honor and esteem, the two perceptions were polar opposites.

The precedents for black slavery established in the seventeenth century were embraced wholeheartedly in the eighteenth century by inhabitants of the Chesapeake and especially of the lowcountry of South Carolina, which echoed the slavery of Barbados, as the numbers of slaves imported into the colonies escalated. Vast rice and tobacco plantations that used slave labor led to the accumulation of immense fortunes for the elite, who ratified their position in society by building replicas of the great houses of England as seats of their power. Few questioned the rightness, or righteousness, of this process.

Nor was slaveholding confined to the South. With the exception of Georgia, which was initially founded in 1732 as an experiment in humanitarianism that banned slavery and sought to create a society of small yeoman farmers, all the colonies recognized and permitted slavery. Even Georgia, however, readily capitulated to the lure of slave labor as soon as its plans proved economically unsuccessful. While slavery never flourished in the rocky soil of New England, the Middle Colonies of New Jersey, New York, and even Pennsylvania had slaves in the thousands, although their numbers were slight compared to those in the South.

Slave Trade

Fortunes were also being made by those who dealt in slaves—the British and the New England slavers that now dominated the slave trade. Despite the losses incurred through high mortality rates, the trade was remarkably lucrative. Some traders in the late eighteenth century made profits of 100 percent per voyage. They and their Portuguese, Dutch, and French predecessors transported an estimated 10 to 12 million Africans from their homeland to the new world from the sixteenth to the nineteenth centuries. It is hardly necessary to add that these persons, unlike the vast majority of other immigrants to America, had been ripped away from their homes and families without their consent.

The process was horrific. Tribes were attacked, persons killed, and families broken apart to satisfy new world labor needs. After capture, slaves were shackled together and marched the many miles to the holding areas on the coast. There, still chained together, slaves were placed in pens to await their fate. Bereft of everything they held dear and in fear for their lives, many died from ill treatment or gave up hope in the face of so much psychological trauma.

But their ordeal had just begun. The infamous "Middle Passage" aboard ship demanded that the captives be packed like sardines in the ship's hold for four to six weeks. So many persons were placed on the ship that they had little room to move. Sanitation was appalling, seasickness common, and disease rampant. As the historian John Hope Franklin has noted, high mortality rates combined with often permanent impairments from illness or physical abuse in those still alive meant that probably only one-half of those who left Africa became fully productive laborers.

Upon arrival, the captives faced more indignities. Those who landed at the South Carolina port of Charleston (the point of entry for more than 40 percent of Africans brought to America during the first three-quarters of the eighteenth century) were taken to the pest house, where they were quarantined to ensure that no diseases had been imported along with them. Those still alive at the end of the period were sold on the auction block to the highest bidder, who had been granted the right prior to bidding to examine the "merchandise."

Slavery in the Revolution and the Constitution

Apart from the opposition of some Quakers, few persons in the colonies in the first half of the eighteenth century objected to slavery. Ironically, the first questioning of the institution arose not because of any recognition of its inherent inhumanity but because white colonists in the mid-eighteenth century began to see themselves as slaves to England. George Grenville's imposition of various taxes on the colonies in the 1760s to pay England's debt from the Seven Years' War quickly became a cause celebre. Underlying the protests against taxation without representation was the recognition that far more was at stake than mere taxes. The natural rights triumvirate of life, liberty, and property linked the three so closely that a threat to one affected all. Colonial protestors, following natural rights philosophy, insisted that one should be able to possess property without interference. Taxation without representation was tyranny because it, by illegally confiscating property, deprived one of a necessary part of one's liberty. And, to complete the syllogism, if one lost liberty, he was a slave.

Grievances against the crown focused not only on the notion of natural human rights but also challenged entrenched ideas of hierarchy. It was only a small logical step, then, to wonder if all persons were equally entitled to the rights white colonists claimed. How could one simultaneously protest England's usurpation of the colonists' rights and yet hold other human beings in bondage? Those who affirmed the incompatibility of slavery with natural rights reads like a who's who of the American Revolution: James Otis, Benjamin Franklin, Benjamin Rush, Thomas Jefferson, George Mason, Patrick Henry, and Richard Henry Lee, among others. Surprisingly, included in this group were slaveholders who never freed their slaves, even in their wills. Some, like Henry and Jefferson, found slavery so personally advantageous that even their moral aversion to the institution did not translate into personal sacrifice. Many other slaveholders, however, were inspired by the revolution to give their slaves their freedom. In other cases, slaves liberated themselves either through buying their freedom or running away.

Despite his failure to emancipate his slaves (he freed only a few in his will), Jefferson's antipathy to the institution was genuine. In an accusation against King George III never incorporated into the Declaration of Independence, Jefferson charged that "he has waged cruel war against human nature itself, violating its most sacred rights of life and liberty in the persons of a distant people who never offended him, captivating and carrying them into slavery in another hemisphere. . . ." While Jefferson had conveniently foisted a shared sin onto the king alone, his indictment was impassioned. He strongly believed that natural rights were shared by all persons created by God; because of that, slavery was morally wrong.

Yet, Jefferson and many of his Virginia contemporaries wrestled with a dilemma: their repugnance toward slavery was coupled with a belief in the inherent inferiority of blacks. No civilized society, they argued, could contain both free blacks and whites. Those supposed characteristics of black Africans, first identified by the English upon initial contact, had hardened into a folk faith, whose tenets stressed blacks' essential barbarism. Thus, for Jefferson and many others, freedom for blacks had to be coupled with deportation from America. Blacks' arrival in Jamestown a year before the Pilgrims landed at Plymouth made no difference in validating their claim to be seen as Americans; America was a white man's country.

The predicament of Jefferson and the upper South was not shared by the sections to the south or to the north. South Carolina and Georgia, with their large slave populations, never entertained much antislavery sentiment at all. Conversely, the Northern states, where slavery had never been as intertwined with the economy and where the black population was smaller, were much more influenced by the republican sentiments of the revolution. Antislavery societies grew in number, and the Northern states began to pass legislation providing for the gradual emancipation of those held in bondage. Usually such laws stipulated that children would be freed when they reached a certain age. For example, in 1780 Pennsylvania provided that those slaves born after March of that year would have to serve until they reached twenty-eight, but the law did not emancipate those already in slavery.

The growing division of the country between North and South was reinforced during the Constitutional Convention of 1787. There, to retain the allegiance of the states of the lower South, the delegates not only refrained from disallowing slavery generally but included three carefully-worded provisions that safeguarded slavery while never mentioning that institution by name.

Perhaps the most bizarre was the so-called three-fifths compromise. Both Georgia and South Carolina believed that slaves should be counted as part of the population to determine the numbers of representatives of each state in the House of Representatives. Such a provision would obviously not only inflate the number of representatives for each slave state but also strengthen the comparative weight of each Southern white man's vote since slaves were property and had no right to the franchise. The North refused to consider the idea. Finally, a compromise was struck: each slave would be counted as three-fifths of a person for the purposes of representation and direct taxation. Property was thus given representation in the national government.

A second compromise focused on the slave trade. Even those who supported slavery often felt moral compunctions about the trade itself. Yet, once again the lower South threatened a rupture, insisting that no barriers be placed upon the slave trade. As a result, the Constitution specified that the trade could not be prohibited for twenty years. In 1807 Congress passed a law to take effect the following year to end the trade, but as W. E. B. DuBois has shown, enforcement was lax and slave smuggling continued, despite subsequent strengthening legislation, down to the Civil War.

Lastly, the document included a fugitive slave provision that declared both that slaves who escaped to other states were not made free thereby and required the return of slaves to their owners across state lines.

While the inclusion of the first two provisions into the Constitution was accepted by many of the delegates under sufferance only to keep the states united (the third met little debate), the cumulative effect of the document was to recognize and legitimate slavery. Little wonder, then, that abolitionists like William Lloyd Garrison saw the Constitution as a "covenant with death and an agreement with hell," or that a John C. Calhoun could erect a political theory based on the Constitutional legitimation of slavery. Or, that modern African-American historians have stressed the essentially conservative nature of the document, particularly in its recognition of property rights in slaves. As John Hope Franklin has commented, "Ironically enough, America's freedom was the means of giving slavery itself a longer life than it was to have in the British empire," which ended slavery in 1833. Similarly, former Supreme Court justice Thurgood Marshall declared in 1987 that the Constitution "gave African Americans . . . little about which to cheer."

However, such an assessment minimizes the effect of the great genius of the document—its ability to grow with the moral awareness of the nation. By making the amendment process sufficiently difficult to lessen the possibility of frivolous alterations yet allowing modifications, the Constitution developed. The Thirteenth, Fourteenth, and Fifteenth Amendments eventually outlawed slavery, provided grounds for citizenship, and ensured the extension of the franchise to black males. While the full implementation of the latter two amendments took almost one hundred years, they nevertheless remained for that century a part of the Constitution and an implicit challenge to racial discrimination and denial of basic rights to black citizens.

Of the founding documents, the Declaration of Independence was probably most important in asserting the basic rights of all persons. While by the 1850s many influential Southerners believed that Jefferson's stirring "all men are created equal" referred to white men only, the plain language of the document made no such qualifications. Further, as the black historian Benjamin Quarles has pointed out, "The unfree never read the fine print." Throughout the post-revolutionary and antebellum periods, free blacks petitioned state legislatures and Congress to live up to the ideals of the Declaration—to little avail. With its expansive aspirational language, the Declaration became an inspiration to oppressed peoples not only in the United States but all over the world. Even Vietnam's Ho Chi Minh quoted Jefferson in Vietnam's 1945 declaration of independence.

Although slavery had been questioned by the republican rhetoric of the revolution and was moving toward extinction in the North, it remained a vital force, particularly in the lower South, and, with the new century, gained fresh life. Antislavery discourse in the upper South had, according to the historian Ira Berlin, focused more on the harm slavery caused whites in destroying their virtue than on its effects on blacks. Not surprisingly, then, when white society felt itself threatened by slave rebellion, its enthusiasm for the eradication of slavery quickly waned. Most frightening was the slave rebellion in Saint Domingue beginning in 1791, during which numerous whites were killed or forced off the island. Those who settled in the South brought tales of bloody horror. In the first year of the new century, Gabriel Prosser in Virginia led approximately one thousand slaves in an armed march on Richmond. while Gabriel's rebellion failed and he and thirty-five others were executed, the insurrection reaffirmed whites' paranoia. Occurring in such proximity, the two rebellions dramatically reduced Southerners' interest in antislavery; their efforts now were directed toward control of the slaves and free blacks in their midst.

Cotton Kingdom

Further diminishing antislavery sentiment was the importance of slavery to the Southern economy. By the late eighteenth century, the lands of the upper South were wearing out, and slavery was declining in the region. Yet, in one of the great ironies of history, technological advance came at probably the worst possible moment to spread slavery throughout the Old Southwest and entrench the institution even more firmly within the economic, social, and cultural world of the South.

That invention was the cotton gin, developed by Eli Whitney in 1793. Up to this time, cotton had been a marginal crop, grown on the Sea Islands off the coasts of Georgia and South Carolina. The so-called Sea Island, or long staple, cotton produced elegant cloth (one still pays a premium price for such fabric), but it was a temperamental plant that refused to thrive in other Southern areas. Another variety, green seed, or short staple, cotton would grow almost everywhere there were 200 days of frost-free weather. It, however, was not economically viable since its short fibers and sticky seeds formed a tangled mass that took hours to separate. Whitney's genius was to invent a machine to separate the seeds from the fibers and thus allow cotton to be grown commercially. The timing of his invention meant that as settlers moved west onto the expanding frontier during the next decades, they could take cotton culture and slavery with them. The cotton kingdom was born.

Crucial to the success of cotton was slavery. While cotton could be successfully cultivated on small plots of land, it flourished on large plantations, and those plantations needed laborers. For the upper South, which found itself with a surplus of slaves, the cotton lands of the lower South provided a ready market. As the figures ascertained by historian Ulrich B. Phillips document, the economic incentive for selling slaves south was powerful. In 1820, a slave that would have brought $700 in Virginia sold for $1000 in New Orleans; by 1860, profits of 50 percent was not unusual. A prime field hand who sold for $1200 in Virginia commanded $1800 in New Orleans. Not surprisingly, during the first half of the nineteenth century, large numbers of slaves (upwards of one million, according to one estimate) were brought from the upper to the lower South—a small proportion by their owners, who were also moving, but the majority were sold away from family.

Antebellum Slavery

Antebellum slavery has been studied extensively by historians, particularly in the past thirty years. This monumental research has shown that generalizations about slavery are exceedingly precarious. Seemingly common sense notions, such as that small slaveholders were less cruel than large slaveholders, do not hold up under the evidence, nor does the view that women were necessarily kinder than men to their slaves. About the only generalization that does seem to have some universality is that slaves who lived on plantations held by absentee masters were treated the worst since there was no owner to counteract the drive of the overseer to make profits. In addition, even the notion of cruelty has come under reexamination. If, as some ex-slaves pointed out, the ownership of persons constituted cruelty in itself, by definition there was no such creature as a kind master.

The failure of generalizations seems to stem from the ambiguous nature of slavery. Slaves were legally property, but only a moral monster would deny that they were also human beings. The inherent tension between the two visions of slaves created a dilemma for slaveholders. As John Hope Franklin has argued, masters found themselves caught between their consciences and their pocketbooks. If slaveholders treated slaves as property without regard to the slaves' humanity, they violated their vision of themselves as Christians; however, if they stressed the humanity of their slaves over economics, they often lost money. Each slaveholder made a different determination of the weight he placed on each variable; over a lifetime, the balance could change. Thus historians find it difficult to generalize about the same person, much less a system that in 1860 included approximately 384,000 slaveholders (out of a white population of about eight million) and roughly four million slaves.

These statistics indicate an important point: most Southerners were not slaveholders. Further, those who held large numbers of slaves constituted a distinct minority; only 46,000 owned the minimum of twenty slaves to be considered planters. Of those, fewer than 8,000 had fifty or more. A minuscule eleven had 500 slaves. Conversely, 275,000 slaveholders held ten to nineteen slaves, while another 62,000 had fewer than ten. The assumption that all antebellum Southerners lived on huge plantations that were replicas of Margaret Mitchell's Tara is contradicted by the data.

Yet, ironically, most slaves lived on plantations. Three-quarters of agricultural slaves lived on large farms or plantations that held ten or more slaves. There, they found their lives highly circumscribed by the labor requirements of staple-crop production: tobacco in Maryland and Virginia (where it was increasingly supplemented by wheat) and in Middle Tennessee and Kentucky; rice in the South Carolina lowcountry; sugar in Louisiana; and cotton from the South Carolina upcountry to Texas.

All these crops required the supervision of slaves by masters or overseers to be productive. Tobacco was so labor intensive that one worker could not cultivate more than a couple of acres. Work in the rice fields necessitated that the slaves stand in mosquito and snake-infested water; sugar production proved so arduous that women and children were often incapable of performing the work. While cotton was less labor intensive than tobacco, it involved back-breaking exertion. Slaves stooped to pick cotton from the sharp bolls while dragging a sack filled with cotton from one end of the often mile-long rows to the other. The deep South's cotton fields, baked hard by the summer sun, reflected the sun's rays so well that temperatures could easily reach over 110 degrees in the moisture-laden air that pressed down like a hot, wet blanket.

Exacerbating the physical toil was the mind-numbing monotony of the work. Slaves on most plantations worked from dawn to dusk—from "can't see to can't see," to use the vernacular. Those in the rice fields were on the task system, which required that a set number of jobs, or tasks, be performed each day; when those were finished, the slave could stop. All other plantations used the so-called gang system of labor, in which slaves were herded to the fields in the morning and returned in the evening. During the interim, they worked under the watchful eye of the overseer or of the driver, if the plantation was sufficiently large to divide the workers into separate groups. All field workers, however, found much of their waking lives defined by the endless rows of crops that demanded their attention year in and year out with little variation.

Because such work was intrinsically dull, masters had to employ a wide range of techniques to get the slaves to work. These included positive incentives, such as holidays, gifts for meeting certain quotas, or trips to town or nearby plantations. One master allowed an individual slave to have a half-acre plot on which all the slaves would work if that worker had toiled industriously in the master's fields. If the carrot did not work, there was the stick, which encompassed everything from revocation of privileges to whippings and confinement in irons.

While most slaves felt that they had little choice other than to obey, others were able to use passive aggression and trickery, what Gilbert Osofsky has called "puttin' on old massa," to expand the boundaries of their world or to get back at their masters. Such devices could not be employed too often, but their judicious use in specific circumstances gave slaves a surprising amount of leverage. Slow or careless work, damaging property, faking illness, theft, and even running away for a time were strategies slaves utilized. Because all these behaviors ratified racist notions about blacks' supposed inherent laziness, negligence, or lack of honesty, masters could never be sure if slaves were just exhibiting "expected" conduct or were deliberately misbehaving.

Some slaves learned how to use these stereotypes held by whites for their own advantage. For example, planters complained that they had to buy heavy "Negro hoes," because slaves were supposedly so careless that they broke normal ones. Similarly, there are accounts of slaves hiding out in the woods to escape a beating; when the master cooled off, the slave returned—not to a whipping but to an uneasy truce between the two. While this was far from the usual outcome of so flagrant a violation of plantation discipline, that it occurred at all shows the ways a canny slave could sometimes exploit the cracks in the system.

For slaves whose situations were intolerable, there were more drastic measures. A few slaves were in such extremity that they mutilated themselves to render themselves less valuable to their owners. Some slaves resorted to arson—burning barns, especially—or to other violence, including murder, against their owner. In a famous 1861 case the slaves of Betsey Witherspoon smothered her because they were afraid they would he punished for the theft of some of her belongings.

The most feared tactic of slaves was insurrection. From the beginnings of slavery in the colonies, slaveowners trembled at the thought of large numbers of slaves massing to attack whites. The most famous rebellions—Stono in South Carolina in 1739, Saint Domingue in the 1790s, Gabriel's in Virginia in 1800, Denmark Vesey's abortive attempt in South Carolina in 1822, and Nat Turner's rebellion in Virginia in 1831—increased Southern paranoia. Especially in the wake of Turner's uprising, during which sixty whites were killed, the South tightened its grip on its slaves, toughening slave codes and prohibiting slaves from learning to read and write. Vigilante bands of whites attacked free blacks.

The foregoing has not made major demarcations between male and female slaves because these generalizations apply to a great extent to both sexes. As many historians of black women's experiences have pointed out, the gender considerations extended to white women in the antebellum South were absent for black women, who hoed, picked cotton, and even dug ditches—tasks that would have been unthinkable for all but the poorest white women. Yet, at day's end, black women were considered women again, since they were the ones expected to cook and perform domestic tasks in the slave cabin. Even pregnancy and childbirth did not always garner better treatment for slave women. While many masters gave pregnant women lighter tasks and allowed them to recuperate after giving birth, others worked them until delivery and marched them back into the fields soon after. There are even accounts of pregnant women being whipped; holes were dug in the earth so the woman could lie prone without hurting her baby.

There is little evidence that white women interceded for slave women when they were mistreated; in fact, abuse also came at the hands of white women themselves. As Elizabeth Fox-Genovese has pointed out, there was no overarching gender solidarity that bound women together just because of their sex. While there were close and affectionate relationships between mistresses and slave women, these attachments were not between equals. More frequently race and class proved far more divisive than gender proved unifying.

Further, sexual jealousy over the master's attentions drove wedges between white and black women. Although definite statistics on the extent of miscegenation are not available, the rape, sexual exploitation, or—in a small minority of cases—willing involvement of slave women happened frequently enough that a large mulatto population existed in both the North and the South. Such sexual abuse threatened both the black family and the white family. Slave families found it impossible to protect their female members from violation. White wives often found it too threatening to their world to confront their husband directly and instead displaced their anger onto slave women, who became double victims.

Black families were greatly affected by slavery. Because slaves were personal property, they could not make contracts or own anything. Thus, slave marriages had no legal standing; any marriage existed solely at the sufferance of the master, who also held legal claims on the children of the family. While many masters recognized family ties and refused to separate families through sale, even the most beneficent master could not guard against debt or death. In either case, slave family members could be sold as individuals to satisfy creditors or to settle an estate. Indeed, it was common for slaveowners' children to inherit slaves and to carry them off to their plantation—often in another state. One historian has calculated that, over a lifetime, a slave had a 50 percent chance of being sold. Because of the substantial threat of forced separation, Herbert Gutman has argued that all slave marriages were vulnerable. No matter how long a couple had been married or how docile they were or how well the white folks liked them, there was no guarantee that when slave prices became sufficiently attractive or some calamity befell the master that they too would not be sold.

Slave children also faced a precarious existence. Because of the lack of prenatal care and placement of children in the plantation nursery at an early age, the infant mortality rate among slave children was approximately 33 percent. As the historian John Blassingame has documented, a slave's childhood was a series of psychological shocks. Favored young slave children often played with the master's children and even received gifts from the master when he returned from trips. It was easy to live in denial—to believe that slavery did not apply to oneself. Soon, however, even indulged slave children were put to work. As the former slave Lunsford Lane recalled, "When I began to work, I discovered the difference between myself and my master's white children. They began to order me about, and were told to do so by my master and mistress. . . . Indeed all things now made me *feel*, what I had before known only in words, that *I was a slave.*"

Despite the threats to the stability of black families posed by slavery, family life and the black community offered slaves perhaps their only sense of security. John Blassingame has shown that the bonds formed among the slaves constituted their "primary environment." Here they held their own religious meetings apart from the white-dominated services that stressed submission and obedience, told stories such as the Brer Rabbit tales that focused on overcoming physically stronger animals through shrewdness and trickery, and played their own music. Women, according to Deborah Gray White, established ties by helping each other through pregnancy, childbirth, tending children, and domestic tasks. Indeed, so important was the community to their psychic survival that slaves established, in the words of Herbert Gutman, "fictive kin"—a whole network of aunts and uncles—to aid each other.

Not all slaves in the antebellum South resided on plantations. Approximately one-quarter of agricultural slaves were scattered on the farms of masters whose holdings ranged from one to nine slaves, while a significant minority of slaves lived in cities (where black women—either slave or free—outnumbered black men) and worked either as domestics, artisans, or in industry. Robert Starobin, the foremost historian of industrial slavery, found that 25,000 slaves toiled in Southern industry in 1850 and that such enterprises were generally economically successful. One of the most famous was the Tredegar Iron Works of Richmond, Virginia, whose production would prove crucial to the Confederacy in the Civil War. Perhaps one reason industrial slavery prospered was that owners did not expend vast resources on the care of slaves, who were worked hard and yet given only the minimum in the way of housing, food, and clothing. Starobin found a "tragic incidence of disease and fatality" among slaves in industry.

Such conditions tore at the consciences of those who saw a contradiction between the rhetoric of the Revolution, the tenets of Christianity, and slavery. Included in this group from the latter part of the eighteenth century until about 1830 were both Northerners and Southerners. Many Southerners saw slavery as an evil, an inheritance from previous generations, which was destructive to both whites and blacks. Yet, because of racist notions about the nature of blacks, they and many Northerners could not conceive of a bi-racial society founded on freedom.

Pro-Slavery Arguments

However, the willingness of Southerners to see slavery as an evil, albeit in the eyes of many a necessary one, lessened significantly in the 1830s. Attacks on slavery during the Missouri debates, Denmark Vesey's 1822 revolt, the appearance in 1829 of David Walker's *Appeal . . . to the Colored Citizens of the World,* which advocated that slaves destroy the institution, and, most frightening, in 1831 the combination of the publication of William Lloyd Garrison's *The Liberator* and Nat Turner's revolt (though there was no cause and effect between the first and the second) destroyed Southern enthusiasm for antislavery. In the 1830s the thrust of the defense of slavery turned from the apologetic "necessary evil" argument to the defiant "positive good" proposition.

In 1837 South Carolina Senator John C. Calhoun avowed on the Senate floor that "the relation now existing in the slaveholding States between the two [races], is, instead of an evil, a good—a positive good." Southerners built on Calhoun's statement and erected an elaborate defense of the peculiar institution, which argued that the South was the epitome of culture and learning—a recreation of Greek democracy built on slavery. According to these arguments religion, history, ethnology, and sociology all pointed to the superiority of Southern society over that of the North.

As Biblical literalists, Southerners proclaimed scriptural sanction for slavery in both the old and New Testaments. The Israelites had been allowed by God to enslave the heathen; Christ did not denounce slavery during His ministry, and Paul was the source of their favorite quotation: "Servants, obey in all things your masters according to the flesh; . . . in singleness of heart, fearing God" (Colossians 3:22). Further, apologists affirmed, slavery was God's plan for Christianizing the slaves, who would otherwise be lost as heathens. This Biblical justification paralleled the historical argument since the Bible was evidence for slavery's longevity; further, slavery had been an integral part of the great ancient civilizations of Egypt, Greece, and Rome.

Southerners also expended much effort on scientific experiments to "prove" blacks' inherent difference and inferiority. In the twentieth century, science has shown that there is far more difference among persons of the same race than between races, but the nineteenth century saw a hierarchy of racial groups, with whites at the top. Southerners conveniently found that blacks' skin color allowed them to work in the sun more easily than whites could, and they contended that blacks were naturally suited for such work because their brains were smaller and lighter than those of whites. Dr. Samuel Cartwright of New Orleans believed that a black person was a natural slave, "almost void of reflective faculties, and consequently unable to provide for and take care of himself." (Cartwright performed some phrenological experiments on Mormons and found them "defective" as well.)

Blacks provided the manual labor in society so that others, supposedly more gifted, could devote themselves to high culture. This point was famously articulated in 1858 by South Carolina planter and senator James Henry Hammond: "In all social systems there must be a class to do the menial duties, to perform the drudgery of life. That is, a class requiring but a low order of intellect and but little skill. . . . Such a class you must have, or you would not have that other class which leads (to] progress, civilization, and refinement. It constitutes the very mud-sill of society and of political government. . . ." Further, slaves were well-treated, according to George Fitzhugh, who contrasted their status with that of the "wage slaves" of the North who found themselves discarded by their employer when they could no longer perform their jobs.

Finally, as Jefferson Davis argued in 1850, slavery allowed all white men to "stand upon the broad level of equality with the rich man . . . because the distinction between the classes throughout the slaveholding states, is a distinction of color," not of economic class. In other words, slavery based on race constructed a hierarchy in which all whites were considered above all blacks—irrespective of their character or wealth.

Not surprisingly such pro-slavery arguments fell on the deaf ears of the relatively small group of abolitionists, who saw slaveholders as evil, not just as inheritors of an evil system. Imbued with religious zeal, abolitionists called for the immediate end of slavery without colonization since they sought a bi-racial society in which blacks enjoyed the privileges of citizenship. This does not mean that white abolitionists had no racial prejudice; black abolitionists complained that they were often treated as children by their white colleagues, who were equivocal about social equality. Yet, abolitionists were in the forefront of radical change and thus elicited violent opposition, even in the North.

Their arguments centered on natural rights and religion. Slavery contradicted the theory of natural rights, especially as phrased in the Declaration of Independence—life, liberty, and the pursuit of happiness. Abolitionists also stressed the "spirit of the law" in scripture, countering the slavery apologists' literal readings with a focus on the gospel of Christ, which taught that all persons were children of God.

In a final argument, the abolitionists found a shared view with the so-called free-soilers, who wanted to exclude slavery from the territories but were willing to allow slavery to exist in the South. While they disagreed on the continuance of Southern slavery, both groups argued that the peculiar institution was unprofitable since it was based on coerced labor. Free labor was economically superior because it was morally superior.

By the middle decades of the nineteenth century, the South had wedded itself firmly to slavery. Its economic, intellectual, social, and cultural life centered on the institution. And, much of its political life from the Missouri Compromise focused on maintaining its power in the face of ever greater opposition from the North. Little wonder, then, that when the South felt slavery—and thus itself—threatened with the events of the 1850s that culminated in Lincoln's election, it believed it had no choice but to secede. Not surprisingly, the deep South, most bound to slavery, was the first to go. The upper South, where slavery had less force, left the union after Fort Sumter and Lincoln's call for troops.

In secession, the South continued to insist on liberty for white men while denying it to four million black persons held in bondage. The contradictions of a nation founded on freedom that, nevertheless, recognized and even implicitly encouraged slavery in its constitution could no longer stand. From the horrific conflagration of civil war came its one redeeming aspect—the legal end of chattel slavery.

THE RISE OF DEMOCRACY

Gary Daynes

The early nineteenth century was the "age of the common man," so called for its political and cultural celebration of democratic values. This "celebration" of the ordinary ushered in a new definition of Democracy, quite different from that of the Founders, who had hoped to limit the direct influence of the common man in national government. By 1835, the right to vote was available to nearly all white males. The expansion of suffrage changed the way politics worked in America.The party system developed and became an important medium which served to link the people and the National Government. Congressional caucuses were replaced by popular parties, and electors were chosen directly by the people. Finally, the "gentleman politics" associated with the Founders dissolved as Andrew Jackson initiated the applied use of patronage, and insisted that "to the victor belong the spoils." American democracy would never be the same.

The "new" democracy, in addition to political changes, would also initiate significant social change. Women began to play a more pronounced role in society. Industrialization opened jobs to some women. Others formed clubs that worked to reform society. Efforts at reform often led to calls for women's suffrage. Ethnic minorities both gained and lost ground with the rise of democracy. In the North, abolitionists demanded an end to slavery, reasoning that if all men were created equal, then slavery was an abomination. The American Indian, on the other hand, suffered greatly when a number of eastern tribes were forced to relocate west of the Mississippi in accordance with the wishes of white voters. The Democratic transformation had an effect on nearly every aspect of society.

The following selections are primary sources that help to tell the story of the Democratic transformation and evaluate its political and social effects. The first two, "A Legal Scholar Opposes Spreading the Vote, 1821," and an excerpt from *The Life of Colonel David Crockett,* demonstrate different aspects of the issue involving the extension of voting rights to "men of no property." The former is a speech by the first professor of law at Columbia College, James Kent. Kent, like many, "opposed broadening voting rights and desired to restrict the electoral rights to property holders." In this article he defends his position at the 1821 New York constitutional convention. The latter selection, taken from the autobiography of Davy Crockett, describes the beginning of Crockett's political career. From the perspective of a man who knew little of politics, Crockett's story illustrates exactly how common-man participation changed the electoral system. Notice the central argument of Kent's speech. What might men such as Kent have gained by limiting the vote? What might politicians have gained by extending the vote? Does the story of Davy Crockett demonstrate a step in a positive direction? Why or why not? With whom might the Founders agree and why?

The next few selections illustrate both the political and social effects of increased extension of the vote and the rise of democracy. Each deals with three important groups directly affected by the democratic transformation. The first involves women in the early nineteenth century and is entitled, "Sarah Grimke on the Condition of Women in the United States." Grimke was born into a wealthy slaveholding family and yet became deeply involved in the anti-slavery movement in the 1830s. In 1838, in the form of a series of letters written to a friend, she published her first book in which she argues in favor of slave's rights and also the rights of women. Notice the specific changes she advocates and the justification for such changes. How might the political democratic transformation have influenced her argument?

The next two selections deal with ethnic minority groups—the African-American slave and the Native American Indian. The slaves gained increased support during the early nineteenth century as democracy gave the abolitionist movement more life. One source of the strength came from the formation of the Anti-Slavery Society, created in Philadelphia in December 1833. One of the principal leaders of the society was William Lloyd Garrison. "Declaration of the National Anti-Slavery Convention" is Garrison's manifesto setting forth the aims and goals of the newly formed society. By making reference to the rule of law and God-given rights as set forth in the Declaration of Independence, Garrison argues that it is the duty of Congress to abolish slavery. Notice both his appeal to "the Good" and the implications concerning the concept of Federalism. How might the Founders have reacted to his arguments?

Unlike women and slaves, the rise of democracy affected adversely the rights of the American Indian. In May of 1830, under the leadership of President Andrew Jackson, Congress approved the Indian Removal Act. The Act called for the relocation of several Indian tribes living on their own lands between the Appalachian Mountains and the Mississippi River. Although it prohibited the use of force, many of the tribes were literally driven out. Among these was the Choctaw, who ceded the last of their lands to the American government in 1830, and were moved to the Indian Territory in what is now Oklahoma. George Harkins, a chief of the Choctaws, wrote this "Farewell Letter to the American People," in 1832. Notice his people's reasons for leaving and arguments against the state of Mississippi. Also, look for the irony in his appraisal of the American government in relation to the situation. How might the democratic transformation have played a role in limiting the rights of Native Americans?

Excerpt from *Life of David Crockett*

Davy Crockett

I offered my name [for election] in the month of February, and started about the first of March with a drove of horses to the lower part of the State of North Carolina. This was in the year 1821, and I was gone upwards of three months. I returned, and set out electioneering, which was a bran-fire new business to me. It now became necessary that I should tell the people something about the government, and an eternal sight of other things that I knowed nothing more about than I did about Latin and law, and such things as that. I have said before that in those days none of us called General Jackson the government, nor did be seem in as fair a way to become so as I do now; but I knowed so little about it, that if any one had told me he was "the government," I should have believed it, for I had never read even a newspaper in my life, or anything else, on the subject. But over all my difficulties, it seems to me I was born for luck, though it would be hard for any one to guess what sort. I will, however, explain that hereafter.

I went first into Heckman county, to see what I could do among the people as a candidate. Here they told me that they wanted to move their town nearer to the center of the county, and I must come out in favor of it. There's no devil if I knowed what this meant, or how the town was to be moved; and so I kept dark, going on the identical same plan that I now find is called "*non-committal.*" About this time there was a great squirrel hunt on Duck river, which was among my people. They were to hunt two days; then to meet and count the scalps, and have a big barbecue, and what might be called a tip-top country frolic. The dinner, and a general treat, was all to be paid for by the party having taken the fewest scalps. I joined one side, taking the place of one of the hunters, and got a gun ready for the hunt. I killed a great many squirrels, and when we counted scalps, my party was victorious.

The company had everything to eat and drink that could be furnished in so new a country, and much fun and good humor prevailed. But before the regular frolic commenced, I mean the dancing, I was called on to make a speech as a candidate; which was a business I was as ignorant of as an outlandish negro.

A public document I had never seen, nor did I know there were such things; and how to begin I couldn't tell. I made many apologies, and tried to get off, for I know'd I had a man to run against who could speak prime, and I know'd, too, that I wasn't able to shuffle and cut with him. He was there, and knowing my ignorance as well as I did myself, he also urged me to make a speech. The truth is, he thought my being a candidate was a mere matter of sport; and didn't think for a moment, that he was in any danger from an ignorant backwoods bear bunter. But I found I couldn't get off, and so I determined just to go ahead, and leave it to chance what I should say. I got up and told the people I reckoned they know'd what I had come for, but if not, I could tell them. I had come for their votes, and if they didn't watch mighty close I'd get them too. But the worst of all was, that I could not tell them anything about government. I tried to speak about something, and I cared very little what, until I choaked up as bad as if my mouth had been jamm'd and cramm'd chock full of dry mush. There the people stood, listening all the while, with their eyes, mouths, and ears all open, to catch every word I would speak.

At last I told them I was like a fellow I had heard of not long before. He was beating on the head of an empty barrel near the roadside, when a traveler, who was passing along, asked him what be was doing that for? The fellow replied that there was some cider in that barrel a few days before, and he was trying to see if there was any then, but if there was he couldn't get at it. I told them that there had been a little bit of a speech in me a while ago, but I believed I couldn't get it out. They all roared out in a mighty laugh, and I told some other anecdotes, equally amusing to them, and believing I had them in a first-rate way, I quit and got down, thanking the people for their attention. But I took care to remark that I was as dry as a powder-horn, and that I thought it was time for us all to wet our whistles a little; and so I put off to the liquor-stand, and was followed by the greater part of the crowd.

I felt certain this was necessary, for I knowed my competitor could talk government matters to them as easy as he pleased. He had, however, mighty few left to bear him, as I continued with the crowd, now and then taking a horn, and telling good-humored stories, till he was done speaking. I found I was good for the votes at the hunt, and when we broke up I went on to the town of Vernon, which was the same they wanted me to move. Here they pressed me again on the subject, and I found I could get either party by agreeing with them. But I told them I didn't know whether it would be right or not, and so couldn't promise either way.

A Legal Scholar Opposes Spreading the Vote, 1821

James Kent

These are some of the fruits of our present government; and yet we seem to be dissatisfied with our present condition, and we are engaged in the bold and hazardous experiment of remodelling the constitution. Is it not fit and discreet: I speak as to wise men; is it not fit and proper that we should pause in our career, and reflect well on the immensity of the innovation in contemplation? Discontent in the midst of so much prosperity, and with such abundant means of happiness, looks like ingratitude, and as if we were disposed to arraign the goodness of Providence. Do we not expose ourselves to the danger of being deprived of the blessings we have enjoyed? . . .

The senate has hitherto been elected by the farmers of the state-by the free and independent lords of the soil, worth at least $250 in freehold estate, over and above all debts charged thereon. The governor has been chosen by the same electors, and we have hitherto elected citizens of elevated rank and character. Our assembly has been chosen by freeholders, possessing a freehold of the value of $50, or by persons renting a tenement of the yearly value of $5, and who have been rated and actually paid taxes to the state. By the report before us, we propose to annihilate, at one stroke, all those property distinctions and to bow before the idol of universal suffrage. That extreme democratic principle, when applied to the legislative and executive departments of the government, has been regarded with terror, by the wise men of every age, because in every European republic, ancient and modern, in which it has been tried, it has terminated disastrously, and been productive of corruption, injustice, violence, and tyranny. And dare we flatter ourselves that we are a peculiar people, who can run the career of history, exempted from the passions which have disturbed and corrupted the rest of mankind. If we are like other races of men, with similar follies and vices, then I greatly fear that our posterity will have reason to deplore in sackcloth and ashes, the delusion of the day. . . .

Now, sir, I wish to preserve our senate as the representative of the landed interest. I wish those who have an interest in the soil, to retain the exclusive possession of a branch in the legislature, as a strong hold in which they may find safety through all the vicissitudes which the state may be destined, in the course of Providence, to experience. I wish them to be always enabled to say that their freeholds cannot be taxed without their consent. The men of no property, together with the crowds of dependents connected with great manufacturing and commercial establishments, and the motley and undefinable population of crowded ports, may, perhaps, at some future day, under skilful management predominate in the assembly, and yet we should be perfectly safe if no laws could pass without the free consent of the owners of the soil. That security we at present enjoy; and it is that security which I wish to retain.

The apprehended danger from the experiment of universal suffrage applied to the whole legislative department, is no dream of the imagination. It is too mighty an excitement for the moral constitution of men to endure. The tendency of universal suffrage, is to jeopardize the rights of property, and the principles of liberty. There is a constant tendency in human society, and the history of every age proves it; there is a tendency in the poor to cover a share in the plunder of the rich; in the debtor to relax or avoid the obligation of contracts; in the majority to tyrannize over the minority, and trample down their rights; in the indolent and profligate, to cast the whole burthens of society upon the industrious and the virtuous; and *there is a tendency in ambitious and wicked men, to inflame these combustible materials.* It requires a vigilant government, and a firm administration of justice, to counteract that tendency. Thou shalt not covet; thou shalt not steal; are divine injunctions induced by this miserable depravity of our nature. Who can undertake to calculate with any precision, how many millions of people, this great state will contain in the course of this and the next century, and who can estimate the future extent and magnitude of our commercial ports? The disproportion between the men of property, and the men of no property, will be in every society in a ratio to its commerce, wealth, and population. We are no longer to remain plain and simple republics of farmers, like the New-England colonists, or the Dutch settlements on the Hudson. We are fast becoming a great nation, with great commerce, manufactures, population, wealth, luxuries, and with the vices and miseries that they engender. One seventh of the population of the city of Paris at this day subsists on charity, and one third of the inhabitants of that city die in the hospitals; what would become of such a city with universal suffrage? France has upwards of four, and England upwards of five millions of manufacturing and commercial labourers without property. Could these Kingdoms sustain the weight of universal suffrage? The radicals in England, with the force of that mighty engine, would at once sweep away the property, the laws, and the liberties of that island like a deluge.

The growth of the city of New-York is enough to startle and awaken those who are pursuing the IGNIS FATUUS of universal suffrage.

On the Condition of Women in the United States

Sarah M. Grimke

During the early part of my life, my lot was cast among the butterflies of the *fashionable* world; and of this class of women, I am constrained to say, both from experience and observation, that their education is miserably deficient; that they are taught to regard marriage as the one thing needful, the only avenue to distinction; hence to attract the notice and win the attentions of men, by their external charms, is the chief business of fashionable girls. They seldom think that men will be allured by intellectual acquirements, because they find, that where any mental superiority exists, a woman is generally shunned and regarded as stepping out of her 'appropriate sphere,' which, in their view, is to dress, to dance, to set out to the best possible advantage her person, to read the novels which inundate the press, and which do more to destroy her character as a rational creature, than any thing else. Fashionable women regard themselves, and are regarded by men, as pretty toys or as mere instruments of pleasure; and the vacuity of mind, the heartlessness, the frivolity which is the necessary result of this false and debasing estimate of women, can only be fully understood by those who have mingled in the folly and wickedness of fashionable life; and who have been called from such pursuits by the voice of the Lord Jesus, inviting their weary and heavy laden souls to come unto Him and learn of Him, that they may find something worthy of their immortal spirit, and their intellectual powers; that they may learn the high and holy purposes of their creation, and consecrate themselves unto the service of God; and not, as is now the case, to the pleasure of man.

There is another and much more numerous class in this country, who are withdrawn by education or circumstances from the circle of fashionable amusements, but who are brought up with the dangerous and absurd idea, that *marriage* is a kind of preferment; and that to be able to keep their husband's house, and render his situation comfortable, is the end of her being. Much that she does and says and thinks is done in reference to this situation; and to be married is too often held up to the view of girls as the sine qua non of human happiness and human existence. For this purpose more than for any other, I verily believe the majority of girls are trained. This is demonstrated by the imperfect education which is bestowed upon them, and the little pains taken to cultivate their minds, after they leave school, by the little time allowed them for reading and by the idea being constantly inculcated, that although all household concerns should be attended to with scrupulous punctuality at particular capacities is only a secondary consideration, and may serve as an occupation to fill up the odds and ends of time. In most families, it is considered a matter of far more consequence to call a girl off from making a pie, or a pudding, than to interrupt her whilst engaged in her studies. This mode of training necessarily exalts, in their view, the animal above the intellectual and spiritual nature, and teaches women to regard themselves as a kind of machinery, necessary to keep the domestic engine in order, but of little value as the *intelligent* companions of men.

Let no one think, from these remarks that I regard a knowledge of housewifery as beneath the acquisition of women. Far from it: I believe that a complete knowledge of household affairs is an indispensable requisite in a woman's education,—that by the mistress of a family, whether married or single, doing her duty thoroughly and *understandingly,* the happiness of the family is increased to an incalculable degree, as well as a vast amount of time and money saved. All I complain of is, that our education consists so almost exclusively in culinary and other manual operations. I do long to see the time, when it will no longer be necessary for women to expend so many precious hours in furnishing 'a well spread table,' but that their husbands will forego some of their accustomed indulgences in this way, and encourage their wives to devote some portion of their time to mental cultivation, even at the expense of having to dine sometimes on baked potatoes, or bread and butter.

I believe the sentiment expressed by the author of 'Live and let Live,' is true:

> 'Other things being equal, a woman of the highest mental endowments will always be the best housekeeper, for domestic economy, is a science that brings into action the qualities of the mind, as well as the graces of the heart. A quick perception, judgment, discrimination, decision and

order are high attributes of mind, and are all in daily exercise in the well ordering of a family. If a sensible woman, an intellectual woman, a woman of genius, is not a good housewife, it is not because she is either, or all of those, but because there is some deficiency in her character, or some omission of duty which should make her very humble, instead of her indulging in any secret self-complacency on account of a certain superiority, which only aggravates her fault.'

The influence of women over the minds and character of *children* of both sexes, is allowed to be far greater than that of men. This being the case by the very ordering of nature, women should be prepared by education for the performance of their sacred duties as mothers and as sisters. A late American writer,* speaking of this subject, says in reference to an article in the Westminster Review:

> 'I agree entirely with the writer in the high estimate which he places on female education, and have long since been satisfied, that the subject not only merits, but imperiously demands a thorough reconsideration. The whole scheme must, in my opinion, be reconstructed. The great elements of usefulness and duty are too little attended to. Women ought, in my view of the subject, to approach to the best education now given to men, (I except mathematics and the classics,) far more I believe than has ever yet been attempted. Give me a host of educated, pious mothers and sisters, and I will do more to revolutionize a county, in moral and religious taste, in manners and in social virtues and intellectual cultivation, than I can possibly do in double or treble the time, with a similar host of educated men. I cannot but think that the miserable condition of the great body of the people in all ancient communities, is to be ascribed in a very great degree to the degradation of women.'

There is another way in which the general opinion, that women are inferior to men, is manifested, that bears with tremendous effect on the laboring class, and indeed on almost all who are obliged to earn a subsistence, whether it be by mental or physical exertion—I allude to the disproportionate value set on the time and labor of men and of women. A man who is engaged in teaching, can always, I believe, command a higher price for tuition than a woman—even when he teaches the same branches, and is not in any respect superior to the woman. This I know is the case in boarding and other schools with which I have been acquainted, and it is so in every occupation in which the sexes engage indiscriminately. As for example, in tailoring, a man has twice, or three times as much for making a waistcoat or pantaloons as a woman, although the work done by each may be equally good. In those employment's which are peculiar to women, their time is estimated at only half the value of that of men. A woman who goes out to wash, works as hard in proportion as a wood sawyer, or a coal heaver, but she is not generally able to make more than half as much by a day's work. The low remuneration which women receive for their work, has claimed the attention of a few philanthropists, and I hope it will continue to do so until some remedy is applied for this enormous evil. I have known a widow, left with four or five children, to provide for, unable to leave home because her helpless babes demand her attention, compelled to earn a scanty subsistence, by making coats shirts at 12 1-2 cents a piece, or by taking in washing, for which she was paid by some wealthy persons 12 1-2 cents per dozen. All these things evince the low estimation in which woman is held. There is yet another and more disastrous consequence arising from this unscriptual notion—women being educated, from earliest childhood, to regard themselves as inferior creatures, have not that self-respect which conscious equality would engender, and hence when their virtue is assailed, they yield to temptation with facility, under the idea that it rather exalts than debases them, to be connected with a superior being.

There is another class of women in this country, to whom I cannot refer, without feelings of the deepest shame and sorrow. I allude to our female slaves. Our southern cities are whelmed beneath a tide of pollution; the virtue of female slaves is wholly at the mercy of irresponsible tyrants, and women are bought and sold in our slave markets, to gratify the brutal lust of those who bear the name of Christians. In our slave States, if amid all her degradation and ignorance, a woman desires to preserve her virtue unsullied, she is either bribed or whipped into compliance, or if she dares resist her seducer, her life by the laws of some of the slave States may be, and has actually been sacrificed to the fury of disappointed passion. Where such laws do not exist, the power which is necessarily vested in the master over his property, leaves the defenseless slave entirely at his mercy, and the sufferings of some females on this account, both physical and mental, are intense. Mr. Gholson, in the House of Delegates of Virginia, in 1832, said, 'He really had been under the impression that he owned his slaves. He had lately purchased four women and ten children, in whom he thought he had obtained a great bargain; for he supposed they were his own property, *as were his brood mares.'* But even if any laws existed in the United States, as in Athens formerly, for the protection of female slaves, they would be null and void, because the evidence of a colored person is not admitted against a white, in any of our Courts of Justice in the slave States. 'In Athens, if a female slave had cause to complain of any want of respect to the laws of modesty, she could seek the protection of the temple, and demand a change of owners; and such appeals were never discountenanced, or neglected by the magistrate.' In Christian America, the slave has no refuge from unbridled cruelty and lust.

S. A. Forrall, speaking of the state of morals at the South, says, 'Negresses when young and likely, are often employed by the planter, or his friends, to administer to their sensual desires. This frequently is a matter of speculation, for if the offspring, a mulatto, be a handsome female, 800 or 1000 dollars may be obtained for her in the New Orleans market. It is an occurrence of no uncommon nature to see a Christian father sell his own daughter, and the brother his own sister.' The following is copied, by the N. Y. Evening Star from the Picayune, a paper published in New Orleans. 'A very beautiful girl, belonging to the estate of John French, a deceased gambler at New Orleans, was sold a few days since for the round sum of $7,000. An ugly-looking bachelor named Gouch, a member of the Council of one of the Principalities, was the purchaser. The girl is a brunette; remarkable for her beauty and intelligence, and there was considerable contention, who should be the purchaser. She was, however, persuaded to accept Gouch, he having made her princely promises.' I will add but one more from the numerous testimonies respecting the degradation of female slaves, and the licentiousness of the South. It is from the Circular of the Kentucky Union, for the moral and religious improvement of the colored race. 'To the female character among our black population, we cannot allude but with feelings of the bitterest shame. A similar condition of moral pollution and utter disregard of a pure and virtuous reputation, is to be found *only without the pale of Christendom.* That such a state of society should exist in a Christian nation, claiming to be the most enlightened upon earth, without calling forth any *particular attention* to its existence, though ever before our eyes and *in our* families, is a moral phenomenon at once unaccountable and disgraceful.' Nor does the colored woman suffer alone: the moral purity of the white woman is deeply contaminated. In the daily habit of seeing the virtue of her enslaved sister sacrificed without hesitancy or remorse, she looks upon the crimes of seduction and illicit intercourse without horror, and although not personally involved in the guilt, she loses that value for innocence in her own, as well as the other sex, which is one of the strongest safeguards to virtue. She lives in habitual intercourse with men, whom she knows to be polluted by licentiousness, and often is she compelled to witness in her own domestic circle, those disgusting and heart-sickening jealousies and strifes which disgraced and distracted the family of Abraham. In addition to all this, the female slaves suffer every species of degradation and cruelty, which the most wanton barbarity can inflict; they are indecently divested of their clothing, sometimes tied up and severely whipped, sometimes prostrated on the earth, while their naked bodies are torn by the scorpion lash.

> 'The whip on WOMAN'S shrinking flesh!
> Our soil yet reddening with the stains
> Caught from her scourging warm and fresh.'

Can any American woman look at these scenes of shocking licentiousness and cruelty, and fold her hands in apathy, and say, 'I have nothing to do with slavery'? *She cannot and be guiltless.*

I cannot close this letter, without saying a few words on the benefits to be derived by men, as well as women, from the opinions I advocate relative to the equality of the sexes. Many women are now supported, in idleness and extravagance, by the industry of their husbands, fathers, or brothers, who are compelled to toil out their existence, at the counting house, or in the printing office, or some other laborious occupation, while the wife and daughters and sisters take no part in the support of the family, and appear to think that their sole business is to spend the hard bought earnings of their male friend. I deeply regret such a state of things, because I believe that if women felt their responsibility, for the support of themselves, or their families it would add strength and dignity to their characters, and teach them more true sympathy for their husbands, than is now generally manifested—a sympathy which would be exhibited by actions as well as words. Our brethren may reject my doctrine, because it runs counter to common opinions, and because it wounds their pride; but I believe they would be 'partakers of the benefit' resulting from the Equality of the Sexes, and would find that woman, as their equal, was unspeakably more valuable than woman as their inferior, both as a moral and an intellectual being.

Thine in the bonds of womanhood.

Note

* Thomas S. Grimke.

Declaration of the National Anti-Slavery Convention

The Convention, assembled in the City of Philadelphia to organize a National Anti-Slavery Society, promptly seize the opportunity to promulgate the following DECLARATION OF SENTIMENTS, as cherished by them in relation to the enslavement of one-sixth portion of the American people.

More than fifty-seven years have elapsed since a hand of patriots convened in this place, to devise measures for the deliverance of this country from a foreign yoke. The cornerstone upon which they founded the TEMPLE OF FREEDOM was broadly this—'that all men are created equal; that they are endowed by their Creator with certain inalienable rights; that among these are life, LIBERTY, and the pursuit of happiness.' At the sound of their trumpet-call, three millions of people rose up as from the sleep of death, and rushed to the strife of blood; deeming it more glorious to die instantly as freemen, than desirable to live one hour as slaves. They were few in number—poor in resources; but the honest conviction that TRUTH, JUSTICE, and RIGHT were on their side, made them invincible.

We have met together for the achievement of an enterprise, without which, that of our fathers is incomplete, and which, for its magnitude, solemnity, and probable results upon the destiny of the world, as far transcends theirs, as moral truth does physical force.

In purity of motive, in earnestness of zeal, in decision of purpose, in intrepidity of action, in steadfastness of faith, in sincerity of spirit, we would not be inferior to them.

Their principles led them to wage war against their oppressors, and to spill human blood like water, in order to be free. *Ours* forbid the doing of evil that good may come, and lead us to reject, and to entreat the oppressed to reject, the use of all carnal weapons for deliverance from bondage—relying solely upon those which are spiritual, and mighty through God to the pulling down of strong holds.

Their measures were physical resistance—the marshalling in arms—the hostile array—the mortal encounter. *Ours* shall be such only as the opposition of moral purity to moral corruption—the destruction of error by the potency of truth—the overthrow of prejudice by the power of love—and the abolition of slavery by the spirit of repentance.

Their grievances, great as they were, were trifling in comparison with the wrongs and sufferings of those for whom we plead. Our fathers were never slaves—never bought and sold like cattle—never shut out from the light of knowledge and religion—never subjected to the lash of brutal taskmasters.

But those, for whose emancipation we are striving,—constituting at the present time at least one-sixth part of our countrymen,—are recognized by the laws, and treated by their fellow beings, as marketable commodities—as good and chattels—as brute beasts;—are plundered daily of the fruits of their toil without redress;—really enjoy no constitutional nor legal protection from licentious and murderous outrages upon their persons;—are ruthlessly torn asunder—the tender babe from the arms of its frantic mother—the heart-broken wife from her weeping husband—at the caprice or pleasure of irresponsible tyrants;—and, for the crime of having a dark complexion, suffer the pangs of hunger, the infliction of stripes, and the ignominy of brutal servitude. They are kept in heathenish darkness by laws expressly enacted to make their instruction a criminal offence.

These are the prominent circumstances in the condition of more than TWO MILLIONS of our people, the proof of which may be found in thousands of indisputable facts, and in the laws of the slaveholding States.

Hence we maintain—

That in view of the civil and religious privileges of this nation, the guilt of its oppression is unequalled by any other on the face of the earth;—and, therefore,

That it is bound to repent instantly, to undo the heavy burden, to break every yoke, and to let the oppressed go free.

We further maintain—

That no man has a right to enslave or imbrute his brother—to hold or acknowledge him, for one moment, as a piece of merchandise—to keep back his hire by fraud—or to brutalize his mind by denying him the means of intellectual, social and moral improvement.

The right to enjoy liberty is inalienable. To invade it, is to usurp the prerogative of Jehovah. Every man has a right to his own body—to the products of his own labor—to the protection of law—and to the common advantages of society. It is piracy to buy or steal a native African, and subject him to servitude. Surely the sin is as great to enslave an AMERICAN as an AFRICAN.

Therefore we believe and affirm—

That there is no difference, in *principle,* between the African slave trade and American slavery;

That every American citizen, who retains a human being in involuntary bondage, as his property, is [according to Scripture] a MAN-STEALER.

That the slaves ought instantly to be set free, and brought under the protection of law;

That if they had lived from the time of Pharaoh down to the present period, and had been entailed through successive generations, their right to be free could never have been alienated, but their claims would have constantly risen in solemnity;

That all those laws which are now in force, admitting the right of slavery, are therefore before God utterly null and void; being an audacious usurpation of the Divine prerogative, a daring infringement on the law of nature, a base overthrow of the very foundations of the social compact, a complete extinction of all the relations, endearments and obligations of mankind, and a presumptuous transgression of all the holy commandments—and that therefore they ought to be instantly abrogated.

That all persons of color who possess the qualifications which are demanded of others, ought to be admitted forthwith to the enjoyment of the same privileges, and the excercise of the same prerogatives, as others; and that the paths of preferment, of wealth, and of intelligence, should be opened as widely to them as to persons of a white complexion.

We maintain that no compensation should be given to the planters emancipating their slaves—

Because it would be a surrender of the great fundamental principle, that man cannot hold property in man;

Because SLAVERY IS A CRIME, AND THEREFORE IT IS NOT AN ARTICLE TO BE SOLD;

Because the holders of slaves are not the just proprietors of what they claim;—freeing the slaves is not depriving them of property, but restoring it to the right owner;—it is not wronging the master, but righting the slave—restoring him to himself;

Because immediate and general emancipation would only destroy nominal, not real property; it would not amputate a limb or break a bone of the slaves, but by infusing motives into their breasts, would make them doubly valuable to the masters as free laborers; and

Because if compensation is to be given at all, it should be given to the outraged and guiltless slaves, and not to those who have plundered and abused them.

We regard, as delusive, cruel and dangerous, any scheme of expatriation which pretends to aid, either directly or indirectly, in the emancipation of the slaves, or to be a substitute for the immediate and total abolition of slavery.

We fully and unanimously recognise the sovereignty of each State, to legislate exclusively on the subject of the slavery which is tolerated within its limits. We concede that Congress, *under the present national compact,* has no right to interfere with any of the slave States, in relation to this momentous subject.

But we maintain that Congress has a right, and is solemnly bound, to suppress the domestic slave trade between the several States, and to abolish slavery in those portions of our territory which the Constitution has placed under its exclusive jurisdiction.

We also maintain that there are, at the present time, the highest obligations resting upon the people of the free States to remove slavery by moral and political action, as prescribed in the Constitution of the United States. They are now living under a pledge of their tremendous physical force to fasten the galling fetters of tyranny upon the limbs of millions in the southern States;—they are liable to be called at any moment to suppress a general insurrection of the slaves;—they authorise the slave owner to vote for three-fifths of his slaves as property, and thus enable him to perpetuate his oppression;—they, support a standing army at the south for its protection;—and they seize the slave who has escaped into their territories, and send him back to be tortured by an enraged master or a brutal driver.

This relation to slavery is criminal and full of danger: IT MUST BE BROKEN UP.

These are our views and principles—these our designs and measures. With entire confidence in the overruling justice of God, we plant ourselves upon the Declaration of our Independence, and upon the truths of Divine Revelation, as upon the EVERLASTING ROCK.

We shall organize Anti-Slavery Societies, if possible, in every city, town and village in our land.

We shall send forth Agents to lift up the voice of remonstrance, of warning, of entreaty and rebuke.

We shall circulate, unsparingly and extensively anti-slavery tracts and periodicals.

We shall enlist the PULPIT and the PRESS in the cause of the suffering and the dumb.

We shall aim at a purification of the churches from all participation in the guilt of slavery.

We shall encourage the labor of freemen over that of the slaves, by giving a preference to their productions;—and

We shall spare no exertions nor means to bring the whole nation to speedy repentance.

Our trust for victory is solely in GOD. *We* may be personally defeated, but our principles never. TRUTH, JUSTICE, REASON, HUMANITY, must and will gloriously triumph. Already a host is coming up to the help of the Lord against the mighty, and the prospect before us is full of encouragement.

Submitting this DECLARATION to the candid examination of the people of this country, and of the friends of liberty all over the world, we hereby affix our signatures to it;—pledging ourselves that, under the guidance and by the help of Almighty God, we will do all that in us lies, consistently with this Declaration of our principles, to overthrow the most execrable system of slavery that has ever been witnessed upon earth—to deliver our land from its deadliest curse—to wipe out the foulest stain which rests upon our national oscutcheon—and to secure to the colored population of the United States, all the rights and privileges which belong to them as men and as Americans—come what may to our persons, our interests, or our reputations—whether we live to witness the triumph of JUSTICE, LIBERTY and HUMANITY, or perish untimely as martyrs in this great, benevolent and holy cause.

A Choctaw Chief Bids Farewell, 1832

George W. Harkins

To the American People.

It is with considerable diffidence that I attempt to address the American people, knowing and feeling sensibly my incompetency; and believing that your highly and well improved minds could not be well entertained by the address of a Choctaw. But having determined to emigrate west of the Mississippi river this fall, I have thought proper in bidding you farewell, to make a few remarks of my views and the feelings that actuate me on the subject of our removal.

Believing that our all is at stake and knowing that you readily sympathize with the distressed of every country, I confidently throw myself on your indulgence and ask you to listen patiently. I do not arrogate to myself the prerogative of deciding upon the expediency of the late treaty, yet I feel bound as a Choctaw, to give a distinct expression of my feelings on that interesting, (and to the Choctaws) all important subject.

We were hedged in by two evils, and we chose that which we thought least. Yet we could not recognize the right that the state of Mississippi had assumed to legislate for us. Although the legislature of the state were qualified to make laws for their own citizens, that did not qualify them to become law makers to a people who were so dissimilar in manners and customs as the Choctaws are to the Mississippians. Admitting that they understood the people, could they remove that mountain of prejudice that has ever obstructed the streams of justice, and prevented their salutary influence from reaching my devoted countrymen? We as Choctaws rather chose to suffer and be free, than live under the degrading influence of laws, where our voice could not be heard in their formation.

Much as the state of Mississippi has wronged us, I cannot find in my heart any other sentiment than an ardent wish for her prosperity and happiness.

I could cheerfully hope that those of another age and generation may not feel the effects of those oppressive measures that have been so illiberally dealt out to us; and that peace and happiness may be their reward. Amid the gloom and honors of the present separation, we are cheered with a hope that ere long we shall reach our destined home, and that nothing short of the basest acts of treachery will ever be able to wrest it from us, and that we may live free. Although your ancestors won freedom on the fields of danger and glory, our ancestors owned it as their birthright, and we have had to purchase it from you as the vilest slaves buy their freedom.

Yet it is said that our present movements are our own voluntary acts—such is not the case. We found ourselves like a benighted stranger, following false guides, until he was surrounded on every side, with fire or water. The fire was certain destruction, and feeble hope was left him of escaping by water. A distant view of the opposite shore encourages the hope; to remain would be utter annihilation. Who would hesitate, or would say that his plunging into the water was his own voluntary act? Painful in the extreme is the mandate of our expulsion. We regret that it should proceed from the mouth of our professed friend, and for whom our blood was commingled with that of his bravest warriors, on the field of danger and death.

But such is the instability of professions. The man who said that he would plant a stake and draw a line around us, that never should be passed, was the first to say he could not guard the lines, and drew up the stake and wiped out all traces of the line. I will not conceal from you my fears, that the present grounds may be removed—I have my foreboding—who of us can tell after witnessing what has already been done, what the next force may be.

I ask you in the name of justice, for repose for myself and my injured people. Let us alone—we will not harm you, we want rest. We hope, in the name of justice, that another outrage may never be committed against us, and that we may for the future be cared for as children, and not driven about as beasts, which are benefitted by a change of pasture.

Taking an example from the American government, and knowing the happiness which its citizens enjoy, under the influence of mild republican institutions, it is the intention of our countrymen to form a government assimilated to that of our white breathern in the United States, as nearly as their condition will permit.

We know that in order to protect the rights and secure the liberties of the people, no government approximates so nearly to perfection as the one to which we have alluded. As east of the Mississippi we have been friends, so west we will cherish the same feelings with additional fervor; and although we may be removed to the desert, still we shall look with fine regard, upon those who have promised us their protection. Let that feeling be reciprocated.

Friends, my attachment to my native land is strong—that cord is now broken; and we must go forth as wanderers in a strange land! I must go—let me entreat you to regard us with feelings of kindness, and when the hand of oppression is stretched against us, let me hope that every part of the United States, filling the mountains and valleys, will echo and say stop, you have no power, we are the sovereign people, and our friends shall no more be disturbed. We ask you for nothing that is incompatible with your other duties.

We go forth sorrowful, knowing that wrong has been done. Will you extend to us your sympathizing regards until all traces of disagreeable oppositions are obliterated, and we again shall have confidence in the professions of our white brethern.

Here is the land of our progenitors, and here are their bones; they left them as a sacred deposit, and we have been compelled to venerate its trust; it is dear to us yet we cannot stay, my people are dear to me, with them I must go. Could I stay and forget them and leave them to struggle alone, unaided, unfriended, and forgotten by our great father? I should then be unworthy the name of a Choctaw, and be a disgrace to my blood. I must go with them, my destiny is cast among the Choctaw people. If they suffer, so will I; if they prosper, then I will rejoice. Let me again ask you to regard us with feelings of kindness.

THE CIVIL WAR AND RECONSTRUCTION

Gary Daynes

The debate over slavery had been escalating for decades as abolitionists gained strength in the North and the defense of slavery became tangled with the self-image of the South. The conflict came to a head as the frontier pushed further west. Should the newly created territories and states allow for slavery? Could the new states decide for themselves or did the federal government have the right to decide for them? Such questions only heightened the tensions between those in favor and those against the "peculiar institution." The Constitution provided little concrete help because of its ambiguous position on slavery. By the time Abraham Lincoln was sworn into office on March 4, 1861, seven southern states had seceded from the union. A month later, the first shots were fired at Fort Sumner and the Civil War began.

For four long years the nation's bloodiest conflict ensued under the leadership of President Lincoln. In 1861 many people North and South expected the war to end within a year. By 1863 Americans wondered if it would ever end. That year two events turned the tide. In January President Lincoln issued the Emancipation Proclamation, freeing the slaves in Southern territory controlled by the Union. Then, in July, the Union Army repulsed the Confederate Army at the Battle of Gettysburg, PA. From Gettysburg on, the South was in retreat. The war drew to a close in April 1865, but not before it claimed the lives of more Americans than any other war before or since.

The end of the war did not mean the end of conflict. Neither the status of freed slaves nor that of their former masters had been decided. The effort to reunite the nation and turn slaves into citizens became known as Reconstruction. With Lincoln's assassination, congressional Republicans led Reconstruction. They pushed the passage of the 13th and 14th Amendments to the Constitution. When southern states would not ratify the 14th Amendment (which grants due process and equal protection of the laws to freedmen), congress disbanded those states. Their re-admission to the Union could come only when they had accepted both the 14th and 15th Amendments (which granted black men the right to vote). Reconstruction thus represents an extension of rights to the freedmen and an extension of federal power over the states.

The fight for black enfranchisement led to some success in gaining greater social and economic prominence. However, the South quickly fought back with what they called the "Redemption." By the 1870s, the Democratic Party regained control of most of the southern states. As a result, Southern states began again to restrict the political rights of African-Americans. Moreover, economic programs such as the crop-lien/sharecropping system served to further inhibit the spread of freedom. By the end of the decade, Redemption proved an effective method of ensuring social control in the post-Reconstruction South, which sealed the fate of the African-American citizen for nearly a century.

The following are primary documents that help tell the story of the Civil War and Reconstruction and evaluate their respective political and social effects. We begin with "The Declaration of the Causes of Secession" issued by the state of South Carolina. This declaration, issued on December 24, 1860, sought to explain why South Carolina should secede. Shortly following, President Lincoln took his presidential oath on March 4, 1861. The next primary document includes a portion of his first inaugural address in which he made a last effort to "reconcile the differences between the states" and discourage a resort to war. Notice the references in both documents to constitutional law. In what ways do each appeal to the Constitution? What was at stake for South Carolina? For President Lincoln? How would the ideas of both affect the war and its outcome?

The next two documents describe important acts made by President Lincoln during the course of the war. The first includes a portion of Lincoln's "Emancipation Proclamation" issued on January 1, 1863. In November 1863, Lincoln addressed a crowd assembled to mark the dedication of a national cemetery following what was likely the most destructive and decisive battle of the Civil War. "The Gettysburg Address" was significant not only for its sincere tribute to those who died while fighting for our nation's freedom, but also for its defense of popular government based on correct principles. What connection, if any, can be made between the two documents? Is the Gettysburg Address in any way a reflection of the Emancipation Proclamation? If so, how? What effects did each document have on the war and its outcome?

The final three documents associated with the section on the Civil War help to portray the images of war from the battlefield's perspective, as related by eye-witnesses. Views from both the North and South are represented as the war progresses to an eventual northern victory. Scenes of blood, destruction and strategy are vividly described in the next two documents by Clara Barton and David Conyngham, respectively. Barton, who had become a battlefield nurse in response to the war crisis in Virginia later became the principal founder of the American Red Cross. Conyngham was both an officer in Sherman's Army of the Republic, and a newspaper correspondent for the New York Herald. Both writers offer interesting accounts of typical life on the Civil War battlefields. The document by Constance Harrison, on the other hand, includes a civilian account of the fall of Richmond in 1865. A member of the plantation aristocracy, Harrison tells of the take-over of Union forces on April 4. Notice the attitude of each writer. How might the different purposes and aims of each side (north and south) have affected the attitudes and actions of each? In what way would these attitudes and actions affect post-war America? Just how devastating was the battlefield scene and how might this have affected society after the war?

The remaining documents are associated with the post-war reconstruction period of American history. The first two tell of events that took place as the war was coming to a close. The first selection includes a letter written by Cornelia Hancock. Hancock, like many other women, volunteered as a nurse during the war, and worked for a time in the Contraband Hospital near Washington D.C. treating recently freed slaves. There she encountered the realities of black freedom. She noted a sharp contrast between the rhetoric of abolitionists and the actual way of life for the African-American following the Emancipation Proclamation. The next document is "Lincoln's Second Inaugural Address" given in 1865. Lincoln's address was brief yet memorable. According to the first document, what problems did former slaves face once they were freed? In what ways does Hancock appeal to the government for solutions? To what extent does Lincoln outline a plan for Reconstruction?

The next three documents provide a general outline describing the handling of Reconstruction on a political level. The Republican party was key in influencing much of the legislation that followed the Civil War. The first document includes Constitutional Amendments 13, 14, and

15. Along with new amendments, Radical Republicans drew up a series of laws, two of which are included here. The first is known as "The Civil Rights Act of 1866." The first major act to pass over a president's veto (that of the Democrat Andrew Johnson, who, because he was Lincoln's Vice President, took office after Lincoln's assassination), the Civil Rights Act provided a definition of American Citizenship and proposed that the federal government "guarantee the principle of equality before the law, regardless of race" (233). The second is known as "The First Reconstruction Act, 1867." In response to President Johnson's veto attempts to override radical legislation, and in light of the South's overall rejection of the Fourteenth Amendment, the Republican Congress passed this law outlining the main principles and ideas concerning Reconstruction. What role did each piece of legislation play during the Reconstruction period? Which laws were truly effective in providing African-Americans with greater freedom and opportunity? Which laws were ultimately ineffective and why? How did each contribute to the democratic backlash of the 1870s?

The remaining selections tell the story of how the South began to regain its strength and influence on the both the political and social stage. With restored power in the hands of the Democratic party on the state level, and the introduction of the plan of "Redemption," Southerners were determined to reassert themselves and their principles. In fact, as early as 1865, some southern states began enacting "black codes" in hopes of restricting rights and freedoms of former slaves. The next selection, "The Black Code of Mississippi, 1865," provides one such example. In reaction to the Emancipation Proclamation, the state of Mississippi sought to control the lives, and especially the labor, of the newly freed people. Furthermore, under the leadership of former Confederate General Nathan Bedford Forrest, the Ku Klux Klan was organized in 1866. Strongest in rural areas, the Klan consisted mostly of members from elite Southern society. The next selection outlines the organization and its principles. Because of the Klan and other efforts at voter intimidation, blacks began to lose the political influence they had only recently gained. Blanche Bruce, the first black man elected to the U. S. Senate, describes some of the challenges facing black voters in his 1876 speech to the Senate. The last document includes a typical sharecrop contract issued in 1882. Such contracts were common in the 1870s and 1880s and were nothing more than economic agreements which forced blacks and poor whites into a position of long-term dependency. Why and how was it possible for the South to get away with such acts? What long-term effects would these codes, organizations and programs have on American politics and society in general?

Lincoln Is Elected and Southern Secession Begins in 1860

An Ordinance to Dissolve the Union between the State of South Carolina and other States united with her under the compact entitled the Constitution of the United States of America:

We, the people of the State of South Carolina, in Convention assembled, do declare and ordain, and it is hereby declared and ordained, that the ordinance adopted by us in Convention, on the 23d day of May, in the year of our Lord 1788, whereby the Constitution of the United States of America was ratified, and also all Acts and parts of Acts of the General Assembly of this State ratifying the amendments of the said Constitution, are hereby repealed, and that the union now subsisting between South Carolina and other States under the name of the United States of America is hereby dissolved.

The people of the State of South Carolina in Convention assembled, on the 2d day of April, A.D. 1852, declared that the frequent violations of the Constitution of the United States by the Federal Government, and its encroachments upon the reserved rights of the States, fully justified this State in their withdrawal from the Federal Union; but in deference to the opinions and wishes of the other Slaveholding States, she forbore at that time to exercise this right. Since that time these encroachments have continued to increase, and further forbearance ceases to be a virtue.

And now the State of South Carolina having resumed her separate and equal place among nations, deems it due to herself, to the remaining United States of America, and to the nations of the world, that she should declare the immediate causes which have led to this act.

In 1787, Deputies were appointed by the States to revise the articles of Confederation; and on 17th September, 1787, these Deputies recommended, for the adoption of the States, the Articles of Union, known as the Constitution of the United States.

. . . Thus was established by compact between the States, a Government with defined objects and powers, limited to the express words of the grant. . . . We hold that the Government thus established is subject to the two great principles asserted in the Declaration of Independence; and we hold further, that the mode of its formation subjects it to a third fundamental principle, namely, the law of compact. We maintain that in every compact between two or more parties, the obligation is mutual; that the failure of one of the contracting parties to perform a material part of the agreement, entirely releases the obligation of the other; and that, where no arbiter is provided, each party is remitted to his own judgment to determine the fact of failure, with all its consequences.

In the present case, that fact is established with certainty. We assert that fourteen of the States have deliberately refused for years past to fulfil their constitutional obligations, and we refer to their own statutes for the proof.

The Constitution of the United States, in its fourth Article, provides as follows:

"No person held to service or labor in one State under the laws thereof, escaping into another, shall, in consequence of any law or regulation therein, be discharged from such service or labor, but shall be delivered up, on claim of the party to whom such service or labor may be due."

This stipulation was so material to the compact that without it that compact would not have been made. The greater number of the contracting parties held slaves, and they had previously evinced their estimate of the value of such a stipulation by making it a condition in the Ordinance for the government of the territory ceded by Virginia, which obligations, and the laws of the General Government, have ceased to effect the objects of the Constitution. The States of Maine, New Hampshire, Vermont, Massachusetts, Connecticut, Rhode Island, New York, Pennsylvania, Illinois, Indiana, Michigan, Wisconsin and Iowa, have enacted laws which either nullify the acts of Congress, or render useless any attempt to execute them. In many of these States the fugitive is discharged from the service of labor claimed, and in none of them has the State Government complied with the stipulation made in the Constitution. The State of New Jersey, at an early day, passed a law in conformity with her constitutional obligation; but the current of Anti-Slavery feeling has led her more recently to enact laws which render inoperative the remedies provided by her own laws and by the laws of Congress. In the State of New York even the right of transit for a slave has been denied by her tribunals; and the States of Ohio and Iowa have refused to surrender to justice fugitives charged with murder, and with inciting servile insurrection in the State of Virginia. Thus the constitutional compact has been deliberately broken and disregarded by the non-slaveholding States; and the consequence follows that South Carolina is released from her obligation. . . .

We affirm that these ends for which this Government was instituted have been defeated, and the Government itself has been destructive of them by the action of the non-slaveholding States. Those States have assumed the right of deciding upon the propriety of our domestic institutions; and have denied the rights of property established in fifteen of the States and recognized by the Constitution; they have denounced as sinful the institution of Slavery; they have permitted the open establishment among them of societies, whose avowed object is to disturb the peace of and eloin the property of the citizens of other States. They have encouraged and assisted thousands of our slaves to leave their homes; and those who remain, have been incited by emissaries, books, and pictures, to servile insurrection.

For twenty-five years this agitation has been steadily increasing, until it has now secured to its aid the power of the common Government. Observing the *forms* of the Constitution, a sectional party has found within that article establishing the Executive Department, the means of subverting the Constitution itself. A geographical line has been drawn across the Union, and all the States north of that line have united in the election of a man to the high office of President of the United States whose opinions and purposes are hostile to Slavery. He is to be intrusted with the administration of the common Government, because he has declared that "Government cannot endure permanently half slave, half free," and that the public mind must rest in the belief that Slavery is in the course of ultimate extinction.

This sectional combination for the subversion of the Constitution has been aided, in some of the States, by elevating to citizenship persons who, by the supreme law of the land, are incapable of becoming citizens; and their votes have been used to inaugurate a new policy, hostile to the South, and destructive of its peace and safety.

On the 4th of March next this party will take possession of the Government. It has announced that the South shall be excluded from the common territory, that the Judicial tribunal shall be made sectional, and that a war must be waged against Slavery until it shall cease throughout the United States.

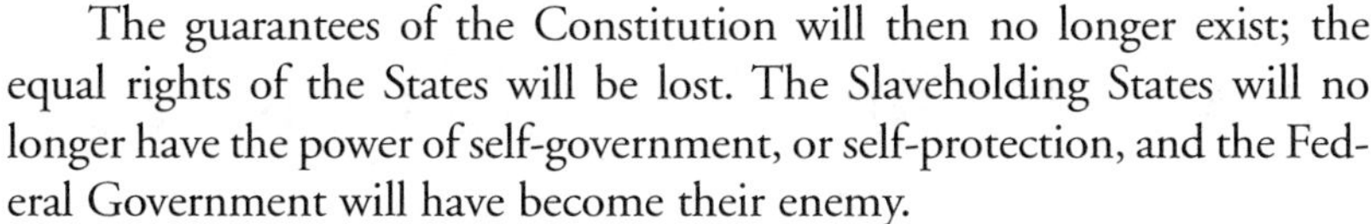

The guarantees of the Constitution will then no longer exist; the equal rights of the States will be lost. The Slaveholding States will no longer have the power of self-government, or self-protection, and the Federal Government will have become their enemy.

Sectional interest and animosity will deepen the irritation; and all hope of remedy is rendered vain, by the fact that the public opinion at the North has invested a great political error with the sanctions of a more erroneous religious belief.

We, therefore, the people of South Carolina, by our delegates in Convention assembled, appealing to the Supreme Judge of the world for the rectitude of our intentions, have solemnly declared that the Union heretofore existing between this State and the other States of North America is dissolved, and that the State of South Carolina has resumed her position among the nations of the world, as a separate and independent state, with full power to levy war, conclude peace, contract alliances, establish commerce, and to do all other acts and things which independent States may of right do.

A New President Is Sworn In, in 1861

. . . Apprehension seems to exist among the people of the Southern States that by the accession of a Republican Administration their property and their peace and personal security are to be endangered. There has never been any reasonable cause for such apprehension. Indeed, the most ample evidence to the contrary has all the while existed and been open to their inspection. It is found in nearly all the published speeches of him who now addresses you. I do but quote from one of those speeches when I declare that—

I have no purpose, directly or indirectly, to interfere with the institution of slavery in the States where it exists. I believe I have no lawful right to do so, and I have no inclination to do so. . . .

. . . Before entering upon so grave a matter as the destruction of our national fabric, with all its benefits, its memories, and its hopes, would it not be wise to ascertain precisely why we do it? Will you hazard so desperate a step while there is any possibility that any portion of the ills you fly from have no real existence? Will you, while the certain ills you fly to are greater than all the real ones you fly from, will you risk the commission of so fearful a mistake?

All profess to be content in the Union if all constitutional rights can be maintained. Is it true, then, that any right plainly written in the Constitution has been denied? I think not. . . .

No organic law can ever be framed with a provision specifically applicable to every question which may occur in practical administration. No foresight can anticipate nor any document of reasonable length contain express provisions for all possible questions. Shall fugitives from labor be surrendered by national or by State authority? The Constitution does not expressly say. *May* Congress prohibit slavery in the Territories? The Constitution does not expressly say. *Must* Congress protect slavery in the Territories? The Constitution does not expressly say.

From questions of this class spring all our constitutional controversies, and we divide upon them into majorities and minorities. If the minority will not acquiesce, the majority must, or the Government must cease. There is no other alternative, for continuing the Government is acquiescence on one side or the, other. If a minority in such case will secede rather than acquiesce, they make a precedent which in turn will divide and ruin them, for a minority of their own will secede from them whenever a majority refuses to be controlled by such minority. For instance, why may not any portion of a new confederacy a year or two hence arbitrarily secede again, precisely as portions of the present Union now claim to secede from it? All who cherish disunion sentiments are now being educated to the exact temper of doing this.

Is there such perfect identity of interests among the States to compose a new union as to produce harmony only and prevent renewed secession?

Plainly the central idea of secession is the essence of anarchy. A majority held in restraint by constitutional checks and limitations, and always changing easily with deliberate changes of popular opinions and sentiments, is the only true sovereign of a free people. Whoever rejects it does of necessity fly to anarchy or to despotism. Unanimity is impossible. The rule of a minority, as a permanent arrangement, is wholly inadmissible; so that, rejecting the majority principle, anarchy or despotism in some form is all that is left. . . .

One section of our country believes slavery is *right* and ought to be extended, while the other believes it is *wrong* and ought not to be extended. This is the only substantial dispute. . . .

Physically speaking, we can not separate. We can not remove our respective sections from each other nor build an impassable wall between them. A husband and wife may be divorced and go out of the presence and beyond the reach of each other, but the different parts of our country can not do this. They can not but remain face to face, and intercourse, either amicable or hostile, must continue between them. Is it possible, then, to make that intercourse more advantageous or more satisfactory *after* separation than *before*? Can aliens make treaties easier than friends can make laws? Can treaties be more faithfully enforced between aliens than laws can among friends? Suppose you go to war, you can not fight always; and when, after much loss on both sides and no gain on either, you cease fighting, the identical old questions, as to terms of intercourse, are again upon you. . . .

Why should there not be a patient confidence in the ultimate justice of the people? Is there any better or equal hope in the world? In our present differences, is either party without faith of being in the right? If the

Almighty Ruler of Nations, with His eternal truth and justice, be on your side of the North, or on yours of the South, that truth and that justice will surely prevail by the judgment of this great tribunal of the American people.

By the frame of the Government under which we live this same people have wisely given their public servants but little power for mischief, and have with equal wisdom provided for the return of that little to their own hands at very short intervals. While the people retain their virtue and vigilance no Administration by any extreme of wickedness or folly can very seriously injure the Government in the short space of four years.

My countrymen, one and all, think calmly and *well* upon this whole subject. Nothing valuable can be lost by taking time. If there be an object to *hurry* any of you in hot haste to a step which you would never take *deliberately*, that object will be frustrated by taking time; but no good object can be frustrated by it. Such of you as are now dissatisfied still have the old Constitution unimpaired, and, on the sensitive point, the laws of your own framing under it; while the new Administration will have no immediate power, if it would, to change either. If it were admitted that you who are dissatisfied hold the right side in the dispute, there still is no single good reason for precipitate action. Intelligence, patriotism, Christianity, and a firm reliance on Him who has never yet forsaken this favored land are still competent to adjust in the best way all our present difficulty.

In *your* hands, my dissatisfied fellow-countrymen, and not in *mine,* is the momentous issue of civil war. The Government will not assail *you.* You can have no conflict without being yourselves the aggressors. *You* have no oath registered in heaven to destroy the Government, while *I* shall have the most solemn one to "preserve, protect, and defend it."

I am loath to close. We are not enemies, but friends. We must not be enemies. Though passion may have strained it must not break our bonds of affection. The mystic chords of memory, stretching from every battlefield and patriot grave to every living heart and hearthstone all over this broad land, will yet swell the chorus of the Union, when again touched, as surely they will be, by the better angels of our nature.

President Abraham Lincoln Issues the Emancipation Proclamation on January 1, 1863

By the President of the United States of America: *A Proclamation.*

Whereas on the 22d day of September, A.D. 1862, a proclamation was issued by the President of the United States, containing, among other things, the following, to wit:

"That on the 1st day of January, A.D. 1863, all persons held as slaves within any State or designated part of a State the people whereof shall then be in rebellion against the United States shall be then, thenceforward, and forever free; and the executive government of the United States, including the military and naval authority thereof, will recognize and maintain the freedom of such persons and will do no act or acts to repress such persons, or any of them, in any efforts they may make for their actual freedom.

"That the executive will on the 1st day of January aforesaid, by proclamation, designate the States and parts of States, if any, in which the people thereof, respectively, shall then be in rebellion against the United States; and the fact that any State or the people thereof shall on that day be in good faith represented in the Congress of the United States by members chosen thereto at elections wherein a majority of the qualified voters of such States shall have participated shall, in the absence of strong countervailing testimony, be deemed conclusive evidence that such State and the people thereof are not then in rebellion against the United States."

Now, therefore, I, Abraham Lincoln, President of the United States, by virtue of the power in me vested as Commander-in- Chief of the Army and Navy of the United States in time of actual armed rebellion against the authority and government of the United States, and as a fit and necessary war measure for suppressing said rebellion, do, on this 1st day of

January, A.D. 1863, and in accordance with my purpose so to do, publicly proclaimed for the full period of one hundred days from the first day above mentioned, order and designate as the States and parts of States wherein the people thereof, respectively, are this day in rebellion against the United States the following, to wit:

Arkansas, Texas, Louisiana (except the parishes of St. Bernard, Plaquemines, Jefferson, St. John, St. Charles, St. James, Ascension, Assumption, Terrebonne, Lafourche, St. Mary, St. Martin, and Orleans, including the city of New Orleans), Mississippi, Alabama, Florida, Georgia, South Carolina, North Carolina, and Virginia (except the forty-eight counties designated as West Virginia, and also the counties of Berkeley, Accomac, Northhampton, Elizabeth City, York, Princess Anne, and Norfolk, including the cities of Norfolk and Portsmouth), and which excepted parts are for the present left precisely as if this proclamation were not issued.

President Abraham Lincoln Delivers the Gettysburg Address in 1863

Four score and seven years ago our fathers brought forth on this continent, a new nation, conceived in Liberty, and dedicated to the proposition that all men are created equal.

Now we are engaged in a great civil war, testing whether that nation, or any nation so conceived and so dedicated, can long endure. We are met on a great battle-field of that war. We have come here to dedicate a portion of that field, as a final resting place for those who here gave their lives that that nation might live. It is altogether fitting and proper that we should do this.

But, in a larger sense, we can not dedicate—we can not consecrate—we can not hallow—this ground. The brave men, living and dead, who struggled here, have consecrated it, far above our poor power to add or detract. The world will little note, nor long remember what we say here, but it can never forget what they did here. It is for us the living, rather, to be dedicated here to the unfinished work which they who fought here have thus far so nobly advanced. It is rather for us to be here dedicated to the great task remaining before us—that from these honored dead we take increased devotion to that cause for which they gave the last full measure of devotion—that we here highly resolve that these dead shall not have died in vain—that this nation, under God, shall have a new birth of freedom—and that government of the people, by the people, for the people, shall not perish from the earth.

A Nurse Writes of the Destruction on the Battlefields of Virginia in 1863

At 10 o'clock Sunday (August 31) our train drew up at Fairfax Station. The ground, for acres, was a thinly wooded slope—and among the trees on the leaves and grass, were laid the wounded who were pouring in by scores of wagon loads, as picked up on the field under the flag of truce. All day they came and the whole hillside was covered. Bales of hay were broken open and scattered over the ground like littering for cattle, and the sore, famishing men were laid upon it.

And when the night shut in, in the mist and darkness about us, we knew that standing apart from the world of anxious hearts, throbbing over the whole country, we were a little band of almost empty handed workers literally by ourselves in the wild woods of Virginia, with 3000 suffering men crowded upon the few acres within our reach.

After gathering up every available implement or convenience for our work, our domestic inventory stood 2 water buckets, 5 tin cups, I camp kettle, 1 stewpan, 2 lanterns, 4 bread knives, 3 plates, and a 2-quart tin dish, and 3000 guests to serve. . . .

You generous thoughtful mothers and wives have not forgotten the tons of preserves and fruits with which you filled our hands. Huge boxes of these stood beside that railway track. Every can, jar, bucket, bowl, cup or tumbler, when emptied, that instant became a vehicle of mercy to convey some preparation of mingled bread and wine or soup or coffee to some helpless famishing sufferer who partook of it with the tears rolling down his bronzed cheeks and divided his blessings between the hands that fed him and his God. I never realized until that day how little a human being could be grateful for and that day's experience also taught me the utter worthlessness of that which could not be made to contribute directly to our necessities. The bit of bread which would rest on the surface of a gold eagle was worth more than the coin itself.

But the most fearful scene was reserved for the night. I have said that the ground was littered with dry hay and that we had only two lanterns, but there were plenty of candles. The wounded were laid so close that it was impossible to move about in the dark. The slightest misstep brought a torrent of groans from some poor mangled fellow in your path.

Consequently here were seen persons of all grades from the careful man of God who walked with a prayer upon his lips to the careless driver hunting for his lost whip,—each wandering about among this hay with an open flaming candle in his hands.

The slightest accident, the mere dropping of a light could have enveloped in flames this whole mass of helpless men.

How we watched and pleaded and cautioned as we worked and wept that night! How we put socks and slippers upon their cold, damp feet, wrapped your blankets and quilts about them, and when we had no longer these to give, how we covered them in the hay and left them to their rest!" . . .

The slight, naked chest of a fair-haired lad caught my eye, and dropping down beside him, I bent low to draw the remnant of his torn blouse about him, when with a quick cry he threw his left arm across my neck and, burying his face in the folds of my dress, wept like a child at his mother's knee. I took his head in my hands and held it until his great burst of grief passed away. "And do you know me?" he asked at length, "I am Charley Hamilton, who used to carry your satchel home from school!" My faithful pupil, poor Charley. That mangled right arm would never carry a satchel again. . . .

A Union Captain Describes Sherman's March to the Sea in 1864

It was no unusual thing to see our pickets and skirmishers enjoying themselves very comfortably with the rebels, drinking bad whiskey, smoking and chewing worse tobacco, and trading coffee and other little articles. The rebels had no coffee, and our men plenty, while the rebels had plenty of whiskey; so they very soon came to an understanding. It was strange to see these men, who had been just pitted in deadly conflict, trading, and bantering, and chatting, as if they were the best friends in the world. They discussed a battle with the same gusto they would a cock-fight, or horse-race, and made inquiries about their friends, as to who was killed, and who not, in the respective armies. Friends that have been separated for years have met in this way. Brothers who parted to try their fortune have often met on the picket line, or on the battle-field. I once met a German soldier with the head of a dying rebel on his lap. The stern veteran was weeping, whilst the boy on his knee looked pityingly into his face. They were speaking in German, and from my poor knowledge of the language, all I could make out was, that they were brothers; that the elder had come out here several years before; the younger followed him, and being informed that he was in Macon, he went in search of him, and got conscripted; while the elder brother, who was in the north all the time, joined our army. The young boy was scarcely twenty, with light hair, and a soft, fair complexion. The pallor of death was on his brow, and the blood was flowing from his breast, and gurgled in his throat and mouth, which the other wiped away with his handkerchief. When he could speak, the dying youth's conversation was of the old home in Germany, of his brothers and sisters, and dear father and mother, who were never to see him again.

In those improvised truces, the best possible faith was observed by the men. These truces were brought about chiefly in the following manner. A rebel, who was heartily tired of his crippled position in his pit, would call out, "I say, Yank!"

"Well, Johnny Reb," would echo from another hole or tree.

"I'm going to put out my head; don't shoot."

"Well, I won't."

The reb would pop up his head; the Yank would do the same.

"Hain't you got any coffee, Johnny?"

"Na'r a bit, but plenty of rot-gut."

"All right; we'll have a trade."

They would meet, while several others would follow the example, until there would be a regular bartering mart established. In some cases the men would come to know each other so well, that they would often call out, —

"Look out, reb; we're going to shoot," or "Look out, Yank, we're going to shoot," as the case may be.

On one occasion the men were holding a friendly *rèunion* of this sort, when a rebel major came down in a great fury, and ordered the men back. As they were going back, he ordered them to fire on the Federals. They refused, as they had made a truce. The major swore and stormed, and in his rage he snatched the gun from one of the men, and fired at a Federal soldier, wounding him. A cry of execration at such a breach of faith rose from all the men, and they called out, "Yanks, we couldn't help it." At night these men deserted into our lines, assigning as a reason, that they could not with honor serve any longer in an army that thus violated private truces. . . .

A Southern Lady Recounts the Fall of Richmond in 1865

Grace Street, Richmond, April 4, 1865.

My Precious Mother and Brother:

I write you this jointly, because I can have no idea where Clarence is. Can't you imagine with what a heavy heart I begin it—? The last two days have added long years to my life. I have cried until no more tears will come, and my heart throbs to bursting night and day. When I bade you good-bye, dear, and walked home alone, I could not trust myself to give another look after you. All that evening the air was full of farewells as if to the dead. Hardly anybody went to bed. We walked through the streets like lost spirits till nearly daybreak. My dearest mother, it is a special Providence that has spared you this! Your going to nurse poor Bert at this crisis has saved you a shock I never can forget. With the din of the enemy's wagon trains, bands, trampling horses, fifes, hurrahs and cannon ever in my ears, I can hardly write coherently. As you desired, in case of trouble, I left our quarters and came over here to be under my uncle's wing. In Aunt M.'s serious illness the house is overflowing; there was not a room or a bed to give me, but that made no difference, they insisted on my staying all the same. Up under the roof there was a lumber-room with two windows and I paid an old darkey with some wrecks of food left from our housekeeping, to clear it out, and scrub floor and walls and windows, till all was absolutely clean. A cot was found and some old chairs and tables—our own bed linen was brought over, and here I write in comparative comfort, so don't bother about me!

Hardly had I seemed to have dropped upon my bed that dreadful Sunday night—or morning rather—when I was wakened suddenly by four terrific explosions, one after the other, making the windows of my garret shake. It was the blowing up, by Admiral Semmes, by order of the Secretary of the Navy, of our gunboats on the James, the signal for an all-day carnival of thundering noise and flames. Soon the fire spread, shells in the burning aresenals began to explode, and a smoke arose that shrouded the whole town, shutting out every vestige of blue sky and April sunshine. Flakes of fire fell around us, glass was shattered, and chimneys fell, even so far as Grace Street from the scene.

By the middle of the day poor Aunt M.'s condition became so much worse in consequence of the excitement, the doctor said she positively could not stand any further sudden alarm. His one comfort is that you, his dear sister, are taking care of his wounded boy of whom his wife has been told nothing. It was suggested that some of us should go to head-quarters and ask, as our neighbors were doing, for a guard for the house where an invalid lay so critically ill. Edith and I were the volunteers for service, and set out for the Capitol Square, taking our courage in both hands. Looking down from the upper end of the square, we saw a huge wall of fire blocking out the horizon. In a few hours no trace was left of Main, Cary, and Canal Streets, from 8th to 18th Streets, except tottering walls and smouldering ruins. The War Department was sending up jets of flame. Along the middle of the streets smouldered a long pile, like street-sweepings, of papers torn from the different departments' archives of our beloved Government, from which soldiers in blue were picking out letters and documents that caught their fancy. The Custom House was the sole building that defied the fire amongst those environing the Square. The marble Statesman on the Monument looked upon queer doings that day, inside the enclosure from which all green was soon scorched out, or trampled down by the hoofs of cavalry horses picketted at intervals about it. Mr. Reed's Church, Mrs. Stanard's house, the Prestons' house, are all burned; luckily the Lee house and that side of Franklin stand uninjured. General Lee's house has a guard camped in the front yard.

We went on to the head-quarters of the Yankee General in charge of Richmond, that day of doom, and I must say were treated with perfect courtesy and consideration. We saw many people we knew on the same errand as ourselves. We heard stately Mrs.—and the—'s were there to ask for food, as their families were starving. Thank God, we have not fallen to that! Certainly, her face looked like a tragic mask carved out of stone.

A courteous young lieutenant, . . . was sent to pilot us out of the confusion, and identify the house, over which a guard was immediately placed. Already the town wore the aspect of one in the Middle Ages smitten by pestilence. The streets filled with smoke and flying fire were empty of the respectable class of inhabitants, the doors and shutters of every house tight closed. . . .

The ending of the first day of occupation was truly horrible. Some negroes of the lowest grade, their heads turned by the prospect of wealth and equality, together with a mob of miserable poor whites, drank themselves mad with liquor scooped from the gutters. Reinforced, it was said, by convicts escaped from the penitentiary, they tore through the streets, carrying loot from the burnt district. (For days after, even the kitchens and cabins of the better class of darkies displayed handsome oil paintings and mirrors, rolls of stuff, rare books, and barrels of sugar and whiskey.) One gang of drunken rioters dragged coffins sacked from undertakers, filled with spoils from the speculators' shops, howling so madly one expected to hear them break into the Carmagnole. Thanks to our trim Yankee guard in the basement, we felt safe enough, but the experience was not pleasant.

Through all this strain of anguish ran like a gleam of gold the mad vain hope that Lee would yet make a stand somewhere—that Lee's dear soldiers would give us back our liberty.

Dr. Minnegerode has been allowed to continue his daily services and I never knew anything more painful and touching than that of this morning when the Litany was sobbed out by the whole congregation.

A service we went to the same evening at the old Monumental I never shall forget. When the rector prayed for 'the sick and wounded soldiers and all in distress of mind or body,' there was a brief pause, filled with a sound of weeping all over the church. He then gave out the hymn: 'When gathering clouds around I view.' There was no organ and a voice that started the hymn broke down in tears. Another took it up, and failed likewise. I, then, with a tremendous struggle for self-control, stood up in the corner of the pew and sang alone. At the words, 'Thou Savior see'st the tears I shed,' there was again a great burst of crying and sobbing all over the church. I wanted to break down dreadfully, but I held on and carried the hymn to the end. As we left the church, many people came up and squeezed my hand and tried to speak, but could not. Just then a splendid military band was passing, the like of which we had not heard in years. The great swell of its triumphant music seemed to mock the shabby broken-spirited congregation defiling out of the gray old church buried in shadows, where in early Richmond days a theatre with many well-known citizens was burned! That was one of the tremendous moments of feeling I experienced that week. . . .

A Civil War Nurse Writes of Conditions of Freed Slaves, 1864

Cornelia Hancock
Jan. 1864

Dear William[1]

Where are the people who have been professing such strong abolition proclivity for the last thirty years?—certainly not in Washington laboring with these people whom they have been clamoring to have freed. They are freed now or at least many of them, and herded together in filthy huts, half clothed. And, what is worse than all, guarded over by persons who have not a proper sympathy for them.

I have been in the Washington Contraband Hospital for the past two months—it is in close proximity to the Camp of Reception—and I have had ample opportunity to see these people, the persons in charge of them, and the whole mode of proceeding with them. Their wants are great and appeal in every way for aid from the North. Their idea of freedom is exemption from labor. And those who are industrious and do labor we find much neglected on the part of employers in paying. Consequently there is much less inducement for them to labor than there otherwise would be. To get them to labor is the earnest desire of everyone working for the interest of these people—for they *must* be self-supporting—they should not remain paupers upon the government as they now are. They are totally ignorant of the mere rudiments of learning, not one in one hundred can read so as to be understood. The laws were very stringent in the slave states on that subject. . . .

The situation of the Camp is revolting to a degree, 12 or 14 persons occupy a room not 15 ft. square, do all their cooking, eating, etc. therein. The Camp has but one well of water and that out of order most of the time. All the water used by nearly 1,000 persons is carted from Washington so one can judge of the cleanliness of the Camp.

In "the hall," consisting of nothing conducive to comfort, neither light nor beds, probably some fifty sleep and the consequence is in a few days several of these people are seized with some aggravated disease and have to be carried to the hospital on stretchers and lay there to be supported by this same government that the authorities here say refuses to give them better accommodations when they first arrive. Now, I maintain an ounce of preventative would be worth a pound of cure, if the object is to save the government expense.

. . . The order now is to remove all contrabands south of the Potomac. It may be better there than here, but we remain under the same authority and let me state emphatically that nothing for the permanent advancement of these people can be effected until the whole matter is removed from the military authority and vested in a separate bureau whose *sole object* is that protection and elevation of these people.

. . . And the only way to ever get justice done to these people is to separate the whole matter from the military authority, make a separate bureau, have men at the head of this bureau with living souls in them large enough to realize that a contraband is a breathing *human being* capable of being *developed,* if not so now. Let them have the power to appoint officers to have charge of these camps, good energetic, anti-slavery persons who will take an interest in the improvement of those under their charge. I feel this to be the duty of every individual to urge upon every senator and congressman that this step be taken, but meanwhile as we stand at our present, our needs are very pressing and any contributions of any kind of clothing, old or new, shoes and stockings especially, both men's and women's, will prevent much immediate suffering. There is much charity being extended to our poor soldiers and I would not that any one should withhold one mite from them, but I maintain that persons living in their comfortable homes in the North should give liberally to those so sadly situated as these forlorn contrabands, as well as to the soldiers. A national Sanitary Commission for the Relief of Colored Persons of this class would save lives and a great deal of suffering. The slaves generally get free when our army advances; they come into our lines several hundred at a time, follow the army for a while, then come into Washington, some probably having walked 50 miles. One woman carried one child in her arms and dragged two by her side. Judge of the condition of that woman when she arrives. Should not some comfortable quarters await her weary body?

Thy sister,
Cornelia H.

Lincoln's Second Inaugural Address, 1865

FELLOW-COUNTRYMEN:—At this second appearing to take the oath of the presidential office there is less occasion for an extended address than there was at the first. Then a statement somewhat in detail of a course to be pursued seemed fitting and proper. Now, at the expiration of four years, during which public declarations have been constantly called forth on every point and phase of the great contest which still absorbs the attention and engrosses the energies of the nation, little that is new could be presented. The progress of our arms, upon which all else chiefly depends, is as well known to the public as to myself, and it is, I trust, reasonably satisfactory and encouraging to all. With high hope for the future, no prediction in regard to it is ventured.

On the occasion corresponding to this four years ago all thoughts were anxiously directed to an impending civil war. All dreaded it, all sought to avert it. While the inaugural address was being delivered from this place, devoted altogether to *saving* the Union without war, insurgent agents were in the city seeking to *destroy* it without war-seeking to dissolve the Union and divide effects by negotiation. Both parties deprecated war, but one of them would *make* war rather than let the nation survive, and the other would *accept* war rather than let it perish, and the war came.

One eighth of the whole population was colored slaves, not distributed generally over the Union, but localized in the southern part of it. These slaves constituted a peculiar and powerful interest. All knew that this interest was somehow the cause of the war. To strengthen, perpetuate, and extend this interest was the object for which the insurgents would rend the Union even by war, while the Government claimed no right to do more than to restrict the territorial enlargement of it. Neither party expected for the war the magnitude or the duration which it has already attained. Neither anticipated that the cause of the conflict might cease with or even before the conflict itself should cease. Each looked for an easier triumph, and a result less fundamental and astounding. Both read the same Bible and pray to the same God, and each invokes His aid against the other. It may seem strange that any men should dare to ask a just God's assistance in wringing their bread from the sweat of other men's faces, but let us judge not, that we be not judged. The prayers of both could not be answered. That of neither has been answered fully. The Almighty has His own purposes. "Woe unto the world because of offenses; for it must needs be that offenses come, but woe to that man by whom the offense cometh." If we shall suppose that American slavery is one of those offenses which, in the providence of God, must needs come, but which, having continued through His appointed time, He now wills to remove, and that He gives to both North and South this terrible war as the woe due to those by whom the offense came, shall we discern therein any departure from those divine attributes which the believers in a living God always ascribe to Him? Fondly do we hope, fervently do we pray, that this mighty scourge of war may speedily pass away. Yet, if God wills that it continue until all the wealth piled by the bondsman's two hundred and fifty years of unrequited toil shall be sunk, and until every drop of blood drawn with the lash shall be paid by another drawn with the sword, as was said three thousand years ago, so still it must be said, "The judgments of the Lord are true and righteous altogether."

With malice toward none, with charity for all, with firmness in the right as God gives us to see the right, let us strive on to finish the work we are in, to bind up the nation's wounds, to care for him who shall have borne the battle and for his widow and his orphan, to do all which may achieve and cherish a just and lasting peace among ourselves and with all nations.

The Constitution of the United States

Amendment 13

(Ratified December 6, 1865)

Section 1. Neither slavery nor involuntary servitude, except as a punishment for crime whereof the party shall have been duly convicted, shall exist within the United States, or any place subject to their jurisdiction.

Section 2. Congress shall have power to enforce this article by appropriate legislation.

Amendment 14

(Ratified July 9, 1868)

Section 1. All persons born or naturalized in the United States, and subject to the jurisdiction thereof, are citizens of the United States and of the State wherein they reside. No State shall make or enforce any law which shall abridge the privileges or immunities of citizens of the United States; nor shall any State deprive any person of life, liberty, or property, without due process of law; nor deny to any person within its jurisdiction the equal protection of the laws.

Section 2. Representatives shall be apportioned among the several States according to their respective numbers, counting the whole number of persons in each State, excluding Indians not taxed. But when the right to vote at any election for the choice of electors for President and Vice President of the United States, Representatives in Congress, the Executive and Judicial officers of a State, or the members of the Legislature thereof, is denied to any of the male inhabitants of such State, being twenty-one years of age, and citizens of the United States, or in any way abridged, except for participation in rebellion, or other crime, the basis of representation therein shall be reduced in the proportion which the number of such male citizens shall bear to the whole number of male citizens twenty-one years of age in such State.

Section 3. No person shall be a Senator or Representative in Congress, or elector of President and Vice President, or hold any office, civil or military, under the United States, or under any State, who, having previously taken an oath, as a member of Congress, or as an officer of the United States, or as a member of any State legislature, or as an executive or judicial officer of any State, to support the Constitution of the United States, shall have engaged in insurrection or rebellion against the same, or given aid or comfort to the enemies thereof. But Congress may by a vote of two-thirds of each house, remove such disability.

Section 4. The validity of the public debt of the United States, authorized by law, including debts incurred for payment of pensions and bounties for services in suppressing insurrection or rebellion, shall not be questioned. But neither the United States nor any State shall assume or pay any debt or obligation incurred in aid of insurrection or rebellion against the United States, or any claim for the loss or emancipation of any slave; but all such debts, obligations and claims shall be held illegal and void.

Section 5. The Congress shall have power to enforce, by appropriate legislation, the provisions of this article.

Amendment 15

(Ratified February 3, 1870)

Section 1. The right of citizens of the United States to vote shall not be denied or abridged by the United States or by any State on account of race, color, or previous condition or servitude.

Section 2. The Congress shall have power to enforce this article by appropriate legislation.

The Civil Rights Act of 1866

An Act to protect all Persons in the United States in their Civil Rights, and furnish the Means of their Vindication.

Be it enacted, That all persons born in the United States and not subject to any foreign power, excluding Indians not taxed, are hereby declared to be citizens of the United States; and such citizens, of every race and color, without regard to any previous condition of slavery or involuntary servitude, except as a punishment for crime whereof the party shall have been duly convicted, shall have the same right, in every State and Territory in the United States, to make and enforce contracts, to sue, be parties, and give evidence, to inherit, purchase, lease, sell, hold, and convey real and personal property, and to full and equal benefit of all laws and proceedings for the security of person and property, as is enjoyed by white citizens, and shall be subject to like punishment, pains, and penalties, and to none other, any law, statute, ordinance, regulation, or custom, to the contrary notwithstanding.

Sec. 2. *And be it further enacted,* That any person who, under color of any law, statute, ordinance, regulation, or custom, shall subject, or cause to be subjected, any inhabitant of any State or Territory to the deprivation of any right secured or protected by this act, or to different punishment, pains or penalties on account of such person having at any time been held in a condition of slavery or involuntary servitude, except as a punishment for crime whereof the party shall have been duly convicted, or by reason of his color or race, than is prescribed for the punishment of white persons, shall be deemed guilty of a misdemeanor, and, on conviction, shall be punished by fine not exceeding one thousand dollars, or imprisonment not exceeding one year, or both, in the discretion of the court.

Sec. 3. *And be it further enacted,* That the district courts the United States, . . . shall have, exclusively of the courts of the several States, cognizance of all crimes and offences committed against the provisions of this act, and also, concurrently with the circuit courts of the United States, of all causes, civil and criminal, affecting persons who are denied or cannot enforce in the courts or judicial tribunals of the State or locality where they may be any of the rights secured to them by the first section of this act. . . .

Sec. 4. *And be it further enacted,* That the district attorneys, marshals, and deputy marshals of the United States, the commissioners appointed by the circuit and territorial courts of the United States, with powers of arresting, imprisoning, or bailing offenders against the laws of the United States, the officers and agents of the Freedmen's Bureau, and every other officer who may be specially empowered by the President of the United States, shall be, and they are hereby, specially authorized and required, at the expense of the United States, to institute proceedings against all and every person who shall violate the provisions of this act, and cause him or them to be arrested and imprisoned, or bailed, as the case may be, for trial before such court of the United States or territorial court as by this act has cognizance of the offence. . . .

Sec. 8. *And be it further enacted,* That whenever the President of the United States shall have reason to believe that offences have been or are likely to be committed against the provisions of this act within any judicial district, it shall be lawful for him, in his discretion, to direct the judge, marshal, and district attorney of such district to attend at such place within the district, and for such time as he may designate, for the purpose of the more speedy arrest and trial of persons charged with a violation of this act; and it shall be the duty of every judge or other officer, when any such requisition shall be received by him, to attend at the place and for the time therein designated.

Sec. 9. *And be it further enacted,* That it shall be lawful for the President of the United States, or such person as he may empower for that purpose, to employ such part of the land or naval forces of the United States, or of the militia, as shall be necessary to prevent the violation and enforce the due execution of this act.

Sec. 10. *And be it further enacted,* That upon all questions of law arising in any cause under the provisions of this act a final appeal may be taken to the Supreme Court of the United States.

The First Reconstruction Act, 1867

An Act to provide for the more efficient Government of the Rebel States

WHEREAS no legal State governments or adequate protection for life or property now exists in the rebel States of Virginia, North Carolina, South Carolina, Georgia, Mississippi, Alabama, Louisiana, Florida, Texas, and Arkansas; and whereas it is necessary that peace and good order should be enforced in said States until loyal and republican State governments can be legally established: Therefore,

Be it enacted, That said rebel States shall be divided into military districts and made subject to the military authority of the United States as hereinafter prescribed, and for that purpose Virginia shall constitute the first district; North Carolina and South Carolina the second district; Georgia, Alabama, and Florida the third district; Mississippi and Arkansas the fourth district; and Louisiana and Texas the fifth district.

Sec. 2. That it shall be the duty of the President to assign to the command of each of said districts an officer of the army, not below the rank of brigadier-general, and to detail a sufficient military force to enable such officer to perform his duties and enforce his authority within the district to which he is assigned.

Sec. 3. That it shall be the duty of each officer assigned as aforesaid, to protect all persons in their rights of persons and property, to suppress insurrection, disorder, and violence, and to punish, or cause to be punished, all disturbers of the public peace and criminals; and to this end he may allow local civil tribunals to take jurisdiction of and to try offenders, or, when in his judgment it may be necessary for the trial of offenders, he shall have power to organize military commissions or tribunals for that purpose, and all interference under color of State authority with the exercise of military authority under this act, shall be null and void.

Sec. 4. That all persons put under military arrest by virtue of this act shall be tried without unnecessary delay, and no cruel or unusual punishment shall be inflicted, and no sentence of any military commission or tribunal hereby authorized, affecting the life or liberty of any person, shall be executed until it is approved by the officer in command of the district, and the laws and regulations for the government of the army shall not be affected by this act, except in so far as they conflict with its provisions: *Provided,* That no sentence of death under the provisions of this act shall be carried into effect without the approval of the President.

Sec. 5. That when the people of any one of said rebel States shall have formed a constitution of government in conformity with the Constitution of the United States in all respects, framed by a convention of delegates elected by the male citizens of said State twenty-one years old and upward, of whatever race, color, or previous condition, who have been resident in said State for one year previous to the day of such election, except such as may be disfranchised for participation in the rebellion or for felony at common law, and when such constitution shall provide that the elective franchise shall be enjoyed by all such persons as have the qualifications herein stated for electors of delegates, and when such constitution shall be ratified by a majority of the persons voting on the question of ratification who are qualified as electors for delegates, and when such constitution shall have been submitted to Congress for examination and approval, and Congress shall have approved the same, and when said State, by a vote of its legislature elected under said constitution, shall have adopted the amendment to the Constitution of the United States, proposed by the Thirty-ninth Congress, and known as article fourteen, and when said article shall have become a part of the Constitution of the United States said State shall be declared entitled to representation in Congress, and senators and representatives shall be admitted therefrom on their taking the oath prescribed by law, and then and thereafter the preceding sections of this act shall be inoperative in said State: *Provided,* That no person excluded from the privilege of holding office by said proposed amendment to the Constitution of the United States, shall be eligible to election as a member of the convention to frame a constitution for any of said rebel States, nor shall any such person vote for members of such convention.

Sec. 6. That, until the people of said rebel States shall be by law admitted to representation in the Congress of the United States, any civil governments which may exist therein shall be deemed provisional only, and in all respects subject to the paramount authority of the United States at any time to abolish, modify, control, or supersede the same; and in all elections to any office under such provisional governments all persons shall be entitled to vote, and none others, who are entitled to vote, under the provisions of the fifth section of this act; and no persons shall be eligible to any office under any such provisional governments who would be disqualified from holding office under the provisions of the third article of said constitutional amendment.

Black Code of Mississippi, 1865

1. Civil Rights of Freedmen in Mississippi

Sec. 1. *Be it enacted,* That all freedmen, free negroes, and mulattoes may sue and be sued, implead and be impleaded, in all the courts of law and equity of this State, and may acquire personal property, and choses in action, by descent or purchase, and may dispose of the same in the same manner and to the same extent that white persons may: *Provided,* That the provisions of this section shall not be so construed as to allow any freedman, free negro, or mulatto to rent or lease any lands or tenements except in incorporated cities or towns, in which places the corporate authorities shall control the same. . . .

Sec. 3. . . . All freedmen, free negroes, or mulattoes who do now and have herebefore lived and cohabited together as husband and wife shall be taken and held in law as legally married, and the issue shall be taken and held as legitimate for all purposes; that it shall not be lawful for any freedman, free negro, or mulatto to intermarry with any white person; nor for any white person to intermarry with any freedman, free negro, or mulatto; and any person who shall so intermarry, shall be deemed guilty of felony, and on conviction thereof shall be confined in the State penitentiary for life; and those shall be deemed freedmen, free negroes, and mulattoes who are of pure negro blood, and those descended from a negro to the third generation, inclusive, though one ancestor in each generation may have been a white person. . . .

Sec. 6. . . . All contracts for labor made with freedmen, free negroes, and mulattoes for a longer period than one month shall be in writing, and in duplicate, attested and read to said freedman, free negro, or mulatto by a beat, city or county officer, or two disinterested white persons of the county in which the labor is to be performed, of which each party shall have one; and said contracts shall be taken and held as entire contracts, and if the laborer shall quit the service of the employer before the expiration of his term of service, without good cause, he shall forfeit his wages for that year up to the time of quitting.

Sec. 7. . . . Every civil officer shall, and every person may, arrest and carry back to his or her legal employer any freedman, free negro, or mulatto who shall have quit the service of his or her employer before the expiration of his or her term of service without good cause; and said officer and person shall be entitled to receive for arresting and carrying back every deserting employe aforesaid the sum of five dollars, and ten cents per mile from the place of arrest to the place of delivery; and the same shall be paid by the employer, and held as a set-off for so much against the wages of said deserting employe: *Provided,* that said arrested party, after being so returned, may appeal to the justice of the peace or member of the board of police of the county, who, on notice to the alleged employer, shall try summarily whether said appellant is legally employed by the alleged employer, and has good cause to quit said employer; either party shall have the right to appeal to the county court, pending which the alleged deserter shall be remanded to the alleged employer or otherwise disposed of, as shall be right and just; and the decision of the county court shall be final. . . .

Sec. 9. . . . If any person shall persuade or attempt to persuade, entice, or cause any freedman, free negro, or mulatto to desert from the legal employment of any person before the expiration of his or her term of service, or shall knowingly employ any such deserting freedman, free negro, or mulatto, or shall knowingly give or sell to any such deserting freedman, free negro, or mulatto, any food, raiment, or other thing, he or she shall be guilty of a misdemeanor, and, upon conviction, shall be fined not less than twenty-five dollars and not more than two hundred dollars and the costs; and if said fine and costs shall not be immediately paid, the court shall sentence said convict to not exceeding two months' imprisonment in the county jail and he or she shall moreover be liable to the party injured in damages: P*rovided,* if any person shall, or shall attempt to, persuade, entice, or cause any freedman, free negro, or mulatto to desert from any legal employment of any person, with the view to employ said freedman, free negro, or mulatto without the limits of this State, such person, on conviction, shall be fined not less than fifty dollars, and not more than five hundred dollars and costs; and if said fine and costs shall not be immediately paid, the court shall sentence said convict to not exceeding six months imprisonment in the county jail. . . .

2. Mississippi Apprentice Law
(Laws of Mississippi, 1865, p. 86*)*

Sec. 1. . . . It shall be the duty of all sheriffs, justices of the peace, and other civil officers of the several counties in this State, to report to the probate courts of their respective counties semi-annually, at the January and July terms of said courts, all freedmen, free negroes, and mulattoes, under the age of eighteen, in their respective counties, beats or districts, who are orphans, or whose parent or parents have not the means or who refuse to provide for and support said minors; and thereupon it shall be the duty of said probate court to order the clerk of said court to apprentice said minors to some competent and suitable person, on such terms as the court may direct, having a particular care to the interest of said minor: P*rovided,* that the former owner of said minors shall have the preference when, in the opinion of the court, he or she shall be a suitable person for that purpose. . . .

Sec. 3. . . . In the management and control of said apprentice, said master or mistress shall have the power to inflict such moderate corporal chastisement as a father or guardian is allowed to inflict on his or her child or ward at common law. *Provided,* that in no case shall cruel or inhuman punishment inflicted.

Sec. 4. . . . If any apprentice shall leave the employment of his or her master or mistress, without his or her consent, said master or mistress may pursue and recapture said apprentice, and bring him or her before any justice of the peace of the county, whose duty it shall be to remand said apprentice to the service of his or her master or mistress; and in the event of a refusal on the part of said apprentice so to return, then said justice shall commit said apprentice to the jail of said county, on failure to give bond, to the next term of the county court; and it shall be the duty of said court at the first term thereafter to investigate said case, and if the court shall be of opinion that said apprentice left the employment of his or her master or mistress without good cause, to order him or her to be punished, as provided for the punishment of hired freedmen, as may be from time to time provided for by law for desertion, until he or she shall agree return to the service of his or her master or mistress: . . . if the court shall believe that said apprentice had good cause to quit his said master or mistress, the court shall discharge said apprentice from said indenture, and also enter a judgment against the master or mistress for not more than one hundred dollars, for the use and benefit of said apprentice. . . .

3. Mississippi Vagrant Law

(Laws of Mississippi, 1865, p. 90*)*

Sec. 1. *Be it enacted,* etc., . . . That all rogues and vagabonds, idle and dissipated persons, beggars, jugglers, or persons practicing unlawful games or plays, runaways, common drunkards, common night-walkers, pilferers, lewd, wanton, or lascivious persons, in speech or behavior, common railers and brawlers, persons who neglect their calling or employment, misspend what they earn, or do not provide for the support of themselves or their families, or dependents, and all other idle and disorderly persons, including all who neglect all lawful business, habitually misspend their time by frequenting houses of ill-fame, gaming-houses, or tippling shops, shall be deemed and considered vagrants, under the provisions of this act, and upon conviction thereof shall be fined not exceeding one hundred dollars, with all accruing costs, and be imprisoned at the discretion of the court, not exceeding ten days.

Sec. 2. . . . All freedmen, free negroes and mulattoes in this State, over the age of eighteen years, found on the second Monday in January, 1866, or thereafter, with no lawful employment or business, or found unlawfully assembling themselves together, either in the day or night time, and all white persons so assembling themselves with freedmen, free negroes or mulattoes, or usually associating with freedmen, free negroes or mulattoes, on terms of equality, or living in adultery or fornication with a freed woman, free negro or mulatto, shall be deemed vagrants, and on conviction thereof shall be fined in a sum not exceeding, in the case of a freedman, free negro or mulatto, fifty dollars, and a white man two hundred dollars, and imprisoned at the discretion of the court, the free negro not exceeding ten days, and the white man not exceeding six months. . . .

4. Penal Laws of Mississippi

*(Laws of Mississippi, 1*865, p. 165*)*

Sec. 1. *Be it enacted,* . . . That no freedman, free negro, or mulatto, not in the military service of the United States government, and not licensed so to do by the board of police of his or her county, shall keep or carry fire-arms of any kind, or any ammunition, dirk or bowie knife, and on conviction thereof in the county court shall be punished by fine, not exceeding ten dollars, and pay the costs of such proceedings, and all such arms or ammunition shall be forfeited to the informer; and it shall be the duty of every civil and military officer to arrest any freedman, free negro, or mulatto found with any such arms or ammunition, and cause him or her to be committed to trial in default of bail.

2. . . . Any freedman, free negro, or mulatto committing riots, routs, affrays, trespasses, malicious mischief, cruel treatment to animals, seditious speeches, insulting gestures, language, or acts, or assaults on any person, disturbance of the peace, exercising the function of a minister of the Gospel without a license from some regularly organized church, vending spirituous or intoxicating liquors, or committing any other misdemeanor, the punishment of which is not specifically provided for by law, shall, upon conviction thereof in the county court, be fined not less than ten dollars, and not more than one hundred dollars, and may be imprisoned at the discretion of the court, not exceeding thirty days.

Sec. 3. . . . If any white person shall sell, lend, or give to any freedman, free negro, or mulatto any firearms, dirk or bowie knife, or ammunition, or any spirituous or intoxicating liquors, such person or persons so offending, upon conviction thereof in the county court of his or her county, shall be fined not exceeding fifty dollars, and may be imprisoned, at the discretion of the court, not exceeding thirty days. . . .

Sec. 5. . . . If any freedman, free negro, or mulatto, convicted of any of the misdemeanors provided against in this act, shall fail or refuse for the space of five days, after conviction, to pay the fine and costs imposed, such person shall be hired out by the sheriff or other officer, at public outcry, to any white person who will pay said fine and all costs, and take said convict for the shortest time.

Organization and Principles of the Ku Klux Klan, 1868

Appellation

This Organization shall be styled and denominated, the Order of the * * *

Creed

We, the Order of the * * *, reverentially acknowledge the majesty and supremacy of the Divine Being, and recognize the goodness and providence of the same. And we recognize our relation to the United States Government, the supremacy of the Constitution, the Constitutional Laws thereof, and the Union of States thereunder.

Character and Objects of the Order

This is an institution of Chivalry, Humanity, Mercy, and Patriotism; embodying in its genius and its principles all that is chivalric in conduct, noble in sentiment, generous in manhood, and patriotic in purpose; its peculiar objects being

First: To protect the weak, the innocent, and the defenseless, from the indignities, wrongs, and outrages of the lawless, the violent, and the brutal; to relieve the injured and oppressed; to succor the suffering and unfortunate, and especially the widows and orphans of Confederate soldiers.

Second: To protect and defend the Constitution of the United States, and all laws passed in conformity thereto, and to protect the States and the people thereof from all invasion from any source whatever.

Third: To aid and assist in the execution of all constitutional laws, and to protect the people from unlawful seizure, and from trial except by their peers in conformity to the laws of the land.

Titles

Sec. 1. The officers of this Order shall consist of a Grand Wizard of the Empire, and his ten Genii; a Grand Dragon of the Realm, and his eight Hydras, a Grand Titan of the Dominion, and his six Furies; a Grand Giant of the Province, and his four Goblins; a Grand Cyclops of the Den, and his two Night Hawks; a Grand Magi, a Grand Monk, a Grand Scribe, a Grand Exchequer, a Grand Turk, and a Grand Sentinel.

Sec. 2. The body politic of this Order shall be known and designated as "Ghouls."

Territory and Its Divisions

Sec. 1. The territory embraced within the jurisdiction of this Order shall be coterminous with the States of Maryland, Virginia, North Carolina, South Carolina, Georgia, Florida, Alabama, Mississippi, Louisiana, Texas, Arkansas, Missouri, Kentucky, and Tennessee; all combined constituting the Empire.

Sec. 2. The Empire shall be divided into four departments, the first to be styled the Realm, and coterminous with the boundaries the several States; the second to be styled the Dominion and to be coterminous with such counties as the Grand Dragons of the several Realms may assign to the charge of the Grand Titan. The third to be styled the Province, and to be coterminous with the several counties; provided the Grand Titan may, when he deems it necessary, assign two Grand Giants to one Province, prescribing at the same time, the jurisdiction of each. The fourth department to be styled the Den, and shall embrace such part of a Province as the Grand Giant shall assign to the charge of a Grand Cyclops. . . .

Interrogations to be Asked

1st . Have you ever been rejected, upon application for membership in the * * *, or have you ever been expelled from the same?

2d. Are you now, or have you ever been, a member of the Radical Republican party, or either of the organizations known as the "Loyal League" and the "Grand Army of the Republic?"

3d. Are you opposed to the principles and policy of the Radical party, and to the Loyal League, and the Grand Army of the Republic, so far as you are informed of the character and purposes of those organizations?

4th. Did you belong to the Federal army during the late war, and fight against the South during the existence of the same?

5th. Are you opposed to negro equality, both social and political?

6th. Are you in favor of a white man's government in this country?

7th. Are you in favor of Constitutional liberty, and a Government of equitable laws instead of a Government of violence and oppression?

8th. Are you in favor of maintaining the Constitutional rights of the South?

9th. Are you in favor of the reenfranchisement and emancipation of the white men of the South, and the restitution of the Southern people to all their rights, alike proprietary, civil, and political?

10th. Do you believe in the inalienable right of self-preservation of the people against the exercise of arbitrary and unlicensed power? . . .

. . . 9. The most profound and rigid secrecy concerning any and everything that relates to the Order, shall at all times be maintained.

10. Any member who shall reveal or betray the secrets of this Order, shall suffer the extreme penalty of the law.

Blanche K. Bruce, Speech in the Senate, 1876

The conduct of the late election in Mississippi affected not merely the fortunes of partisans—as the same were necessarily involved in the defeat or success of the respective parties to the contest—but put in question and jeopardy the sacred rights of the citizen; and the investigation contemplated in the pending resolution has for its object not the determination of the question whether the offices shall be held and the public affairs of that State be administered by democrats or republicans, but the higher and more important end, the protection in all their purity and significance of the political rights of the people and the free institutions of the country. . . .

The evidence in hand and accessible will show beyond peradventure that in many parts of the State corrupt and violent influences were brought to bear upon the registrars of voters, thus materially affecting the character of the voting or poll lists; upon the inspectors of election, prejudicially and unfairly thereby changing the number of votes cast; and, finally, threats and violence were practiced directly upon the masses of voters in such measures and strength as to produce grave apprehensions for their personal safety and as to deter them from the exercise of their political franchises. . . .

It will not accord with the laws of nature or history to brand colored people a race of cowards. On more than one historic field, beginning in 1776 and coming down to this centennial year of the Republic, they have attested in blood their courage as well as a love of liberty. I ask Senators to believe that no consideration of fear or personal danger has kept us quiet and forbearing under the provocations and wrongs that have so sorely tried our souls. But feeling kindly toward our white fellow-citizens, appreciating the good purposes and offices of the better classes, and, above all, abhoring a war of races, we determined to wait until such time as an appeal to the good sense and justice of the American people could be made. . . .

The sober American judgment must obtain in the South as elsewhere in the Republic, that the only distinctions upon which parties can be safely organized and in harmony with our institutions are differences of opinion relative to principles and policy of government, and that differences of religion, nationality, or race can neither with safety nor propriety be permitted for a moment to enter into the party contests of the day. The unanimity with which the colored voters act with a party is not referable to any race prejudice on their part. On the contrary, they invite the political co-operation of their white brethren, and vote as a unit because proscribed as such. They deprecate the establishment of the color line by the opposition, not only because the act is unwise and wrong in principle, but because it isolates them from the white men of the South, and forces them, in sheer self-protection and against their inclination, to act seemingly upon the basis of a race prejudice that they neither respect nor entertain. As a class they are free from prejudices, and have no uncharitable suspicions against their white fellow-citizens, whether native born or settlers from the Northern States. They not only recognize the equality of citizenship and the right of every man to hold, without proscription any position of honor and trust to which the confidence of the people may elevate him; but owing nothing to race, birth, or surroundings, they, above all other classes in the community, are interested to see prejudices drop out of both politics and the business of the country, and success in life proceed only upon the integrity and merit of the man who seeks it. . . . But withal, as they progress in intelligence and appreciation of the dignity of their prerogatives as citizens, they, as an evidence of growth begin to realize the significance of the proverb, "When thou doest well for thyself, men shall praise thee;" and are disposed to exact the same protection and concession of rights that are conferred upon other citizens by the Constitution, and that, too, without the humiliation involved in the enforced abandonment of their political convictions. . . .

I have confidence, not only in my country and her institutions, but in the endurance, capacity, and destiny of my people. We will, as opportunity offers and ability serves, seek our places, sometimes in the field of letters, arts, sciences, and the professions. More frequently mechanical pursuits will attract and elicit our efforts; more still of my people will find employment and livelihood as the cultivators of the soil. The bulk of this people—by surroundings, habits, adaptation, and choice—will continue to find their homes in the South, and constitute the masses of its yeomanry. We will there probably, of our own volition and more abundantly than in the past, produce the great staples that will contribute to the basis of foreign exchange, aid in giving the nation a balance of trade, and minister to the wants and comfort and build up the prosperity of the whole land. Whatever our ultimate position in the composite civilization of the Republic and whatever varying fortunes attend our career, we will not forget our instincts for freedom nor our love of country.

A Sharecrop Contract, 1882

To every one applying to rent land upon shares, the following conditions must be read, and *agreed to.*

To every 30 or 35 acres, I agree to furnish the team, plow, and farming implements, except cotton planters, and I *do not* agree to furnish a cart to every cropper. The croppers are to have half of the cotton, corn and fodder (and peas and pumpkins and potatoes if any are planted) if the following conditions are compiled with, but—if not—they are to have only two fifths (2/5). Croppers are to have no part or interest in the cotton seed raised from the crop planted and worked by them. No vine crops of any description, that is, no watermelons, muskmelons, . . . squashes or anything of that kind, except peas and pumpkins, and potatoes, are to be planted in the cotton or corn. All must work under my direction. All plantation work to be done by the croppers. My part of the crop to be *housed* by them, and the fodder and oats to be hauled and put in the house. All the cotton must be topped about 1st August. If any cropper fails from any cause to save all the fodder from his crop, I am to have enough fodder to make it equal to one half of the whole if the whole amount of fodder had been saved.

For every mule or horse furnished by me there must be 1000 good sized rails . . . hauled, and the fence repaired as far as they will go, the fence to be torn down and put up from the bottom if I so direct. All croppers to haul rails and work on fence whenever I may order. Rails to be split when I may say. Each cropper to clean out every ditch in his crop, and where a ditch runs between two croppers, the cleaning out of that ditch is to be divided equally between them. Every ditch bank in the crop must be shrubbed down and cleaned off before the crop is planted and must be cut down every time the land is worked with his hoe and when the crop is "laid by," the ditch banks must be left clean of bushes, weeds, and seeds. The cleaning out of all ditches must be done by the first of October. The rails must be split and the fence repaired before corn is planted.

Each cropper must keep in good repair all bridges in his crop or over ditches that he has to clean out and when a bridge needs repairing that is outside of all their crops, then any one that I call on must repair it.

Fence jams to be done as ditch banks. If any cotton is planted on the land outside of the plantation fence, I am to have *three fourths* of all the cotton made in those patches, that is to say, no cotton must be planted by croppers in their home patches.

All croppers must clean out stables and fill them with straw, and haul straw in front of stables whenever I direct. All the cotton must be manured, and enough fertilizer must be brought to manure each crop highly, the croppers to pay for one half of all manure bought, the quantity to be purchased for each crop must be left to me.

No cropper to work off the plantation when there is any work to be done on the land he has rented, or when his work is needed by me or other croppers. Trees to be cut down on Orchard, House field & Evanson fences, leaving such as I may designate.

Road field to be planted from the *very edge of the ditch to the fence,* and all the land to be planted close up to the ditches and fences. *No stock of any kind* belonging to croppers to run in the plantation after crops are gathered.

If the fence should be blown down, or if trees should fall on the fence outside of the land planted by any of the croppers, any one or all that I may call upon must put it up and repair it. Every cropper must feed, or have fed, the team he works, Saturday nights, Sundays, and every morning before going to work, beginning to feed his team (morning, noon, and night *every day* in the week) on the day he rents and feeding it to and including the 31st day of December. If any cropper shall from any cause fail to repair his fence as far as 1000 rails will go, or shall fail to clean out any part of his ditches, or shall fail to leave his ditch banks, any part of them, well shrubbed and clean when his crop is laid by, or shall fail to clean out stables, fill them up and haul straw in front of them whenever he is told, he shall have only two-fifths (2/5) of the cotton, corn, fodder, peas and pumpkins made on the land he cultivates.

If any cropper shall fail to feed his team Saturday nights, all day Sunday and all the rest of the week, morning/noon, and night, for every time he so fails he must pay me five cents.

No corn nor cotton stalks must be burned, but must be cut down, cut up and plowed in. Nothing must be burned off the land except when it is *impossible* to plow it in.

Every cropper must be responsible for all gear and farming implements placed in his hands, and if not returned must be paid for unless it is worn out by use.

Croppers must sow & plow in oats and haul them to the crib, but *must have no part of them.* Nothing to be sold from their crops, nor fodder nor corn to be carried out of the fields until my rent is all paid, and all amounts they owe me and for which I am responsible are paid in full.

I am to gin & pack all the cotton and charge every cropper an eighteenth of his part, the cropper to furnish his part of the bagging, ties, & twine.

The sale of every cropper's part of the cotton to be made by me when and where I choose to sell, and after deducting all they owe me and all sums that I may be responsible for on their accounts, to pay them their half of the net proceeds. Work of every description, particularly the work on fences and ditches, to be done to my satisfaction, and must be done over until I am satisfied that it is done as it should be.

No wood to burn, nor light wood, nor poles, nor timber for boards, nor wood for any purpose whatever must be gotten above the house occupied by Henry Beasley—nor must any trees be cut down nor any wood used for any purpose, except for firewood, without my permission.

THE MOVEMENT FOR BLACK CIVIL RIGHTS—1896 TO 1968

Gary Daynes
History Department

In the seventy three years between 1792 and 1865, only two amendments were added to the Constitution, the 11th which clarified the role of the federal courts and the 12th which refined the process by which electors chose the President and Vice President. Then, in a five year period, three amendments raced to ratification. The 13th Amendment ended slavery, the 14th guaranteed due process and equal protection to all citizens, and the 15th ensured that black men could vote. These amendments are testament both to the rapid changes brought on by the Civil War and to the stubborn refusal of many Americans to believe that all citizens deserve equal treatment by their government. The Civil War destroyed the South and slavery, but it did not end prejudice against the freedmen. The 13th, 14th, and 15th Amendments were meant to do that. But in this case, the Constitution was not strong enough to withstand the racist traditions of the past.

By 1900, the rights described in the 13th, 14th, and 15th Amendments had been taken from blacks, by law in the South and by practice in much of the North. The Civil Rights Movement was the effort to regain them. Though there were always white people involved in this work, the movement was mostly made up of regular black women and men who refused to be mistreated because of their race. The movement was born in the first half of the twentieth century, and made its greatest strides between 1945 and 1968. The movement was never completely unified. It was divided by geography, religious beliefs, protest tactics, and definitions of equality. Nonetheless, by the end of that period, blacks had regained equality under the law. That equality did not guarantee an end to the grievances of minorities in America. And so, the legacy of the Civil Rights Movement has two parts. It is first an example of how dedicated citizens can change the nation's laws. But it is also a reminder that all men being "created equal" has not guaranteed that all men equally share the benefits of freedom.

Setting the Stage, 1896–1945

Segregation

When the Supreme Court ruled in *Plessy v. Ferguson* (1896) that states could legally segregate on the basis of race, it was accepting an already-common practice. Since at least the end of Reconstruction, Southerners had been voluntarily practicing certain forms of segregation. Whites and blacks attended different churches, ate at different restaurants, and got hair cuts in different barber shops. But *Plessy v. Ferguson* marked a landmark date in the history of the United States, for it extended segregation to public, state-sponsored institutions, such as schools, parks, and transportation. And because it granted state and local government the right to segregate, it granted to the white majority the power to make decisions about segregation. *Plessy v. Ferguson* thus allowed segregation to become equivalent to discrimination. Black schools received less money than their white counterparts, black parks were less well maintained, blacks rode at the back of the bus.

Legalized discrimination in the South joined three other trends that defined the political life of blacks at the end of the nineteenth and beginning of the twentieth centuries: the disenfranchisement of black voters, the migration of blacks from the rural South to cities in the South and industrialized North, and the increasing strength of black institutions. These trends would combine, sixty years later, to inspire and shape the Civil Rights Movement.

Disenfranchisement

The Fifteenth Amendment to the Constitution (1867) granted black men the right to vote. This right was important for both practical and symbolic reasons. Using the vote, black men worked with Southern members of the Republican Party during Reconstruction to elect state and local governments sympathetic to the cause of the freedmen. These governments, staffed with white and black elected officials, strengthened the public school systems, reformed the tax system, and began to rebuild the roads and riverways of the South. Reconstruction governments were not perfect—they were prone to mismanagement and open to corruption, as are all elected governments. But they marked the first time in the history of the United States where large numbers of blacks and whites worked together in elected positions.

Perhaps even more important than the ability to elect sympathetic governments (which lasted, after all, only until the mid-1870s in most of the South), was the symbolic power of the franchise. In a democracy, the right to vote is a potent symbol of citizenship. For the freedmen, the end of slavery marked the birth of their freedom, but the right to vote demonstrated their equality. Black voter turnout in the South remained high long after their ability to determine the outcome of elections disappeared.

While the vote was an inspiration for blacks, for many whites it was an affront. They argued that people who only a few years before had been slaves had no place determining the outcome of elections. Their position was inspired by equal parts racism and elitism. The elitists of the day fretted over the thought of unlearned men voting. The racists shuddered at the thought that those voters were black. Together they conspired to prevent black men from exercising their constitutional rights.

Efforts to block the black vote started well before *Plessy v. Ferguson.* Several southern states passed laws requiring voters to be literate and pay a poll tax before voting. These laws disenfranchised thousands of black *and* white voters who either couldn't read or were too poor to pay for the ballot. (Many of them left the Republican and Democratic parties for the populist movement.) Other tactics were more brutal. Racist organizations like the Knights of the White Camellia and the Ku Klux Klan terrorized potential black voters. In one instance a freedman reported that the Klan had rousted him out of bed just before the elections of 1871. They took him into the woods, stripped off his shirt, and began to whip him. After hitting him with "ten or fifteen licks, pretty keen," the torturers stopped and told him "You must promise to vote the democratic ticket, or you go dead before we leave you." (*Report to the Joint Select Committee to Inquire into the Condition of Affairs in the Late Insurrectionary States* (Washington, GPO, 1872), Vol. 1, p. 436).

Plessy v. Ferguson hastened the pace of disenfranchisement. Because it permitted racial segregation, political parties were free to admit only white members, thus ensuring that major party candidates for the general election would have been selected only by whites. And because it granted power to the states to make determinations about race relations, blacks knew that they could not count on the federal government to preserve their constitutional rights. In 1896, 130,344 blacks were registered to vote in Louisiana. In 1898, Louisiana amended its constitution to limit the black vote. In 1900, only 5,320 blacks remained on the registration lists. By 1910, Mississippi, South Carolina, North Carolina, Alabama, Virginia, Georgia, and Oklahoma had joined Louisiana in disenfranchising their black citizens.

Migration

The Civil War broke the ties that bound slaves to a particular spot of land. And so during Reconstruction the freedmen moved about the South searching for family members, work, and greater freedom. As Reconstruction ended and opportunities in the South constricted, black migrations increasingly stretched beyond the borders of the Confederacy.

The first wave of migrants, numbering somewhere between forty and sixty thousand, left the South for Kansas in the 1870s. They, like the hundreds of thousands who would follow them north in the next fifty years, left for many reasons. Discrimination was always a cause, but a dismal Southern economy contributed as well. Cotton prices fell through the 1870s and 80s. At the same time a boll weevil infestation spread throughout the South, ruining thousands of acres of cotton. Southern farmers turned increasingly to loans to finance their failing farms, but these loans led many farmers into inescapable debt, or forced them to abandon their hopes of owning a farm and turn to sharecropping to survive. These economic trials weighed heaviest on the poorest farmers, and so blacks bore the brunt of the burden.

Today Kansas may seem an unlikely destination for emigrants from the Deep South, but in the late 1870s it was a perfect place to settle. Open land was still available there. Railroads connected Kansas to the South and East. And Kansas had been the home of John Brown, the abolitionist who tried to inspire a war against slavery at Harper's Ferry, Virginia in 1859. Black entrepreneurs traveled the South encouraging emigration to Kansas. The most effective of these agents was Henry "Pap" Singleton. Singleton journeyed from town to town, speaking in black churches. There he described his vision of a movement following him, the "Moses of the Colored Exodus" to Kansas, "The Land That Gives Birth to Freedom" (as a popular hymn of the day put it). When in Kansas, blacks would colonize certain parts of the state, establishing towns where they could farm without fear.

The migration to Kansas was a qualified success. The migrants who arrived with money, tools, and seed did fairly well. Exodusters founded Baxter Springs, Nicodemus, Morton City, and Singleton, Kansas—all-black towns on the Kansas prairie. And thousands of other travelers ended up in Kansas' growing cities. But for the poorest migrants, Kansas was no promised land. Thousands eventually returned to the South, while those who stayed faced poverty and segregation in a new state.

Segregation remained a common theme in the other major migration from the South—the Great Migration of the 1910s and 20s. The outbreak of World War I, coupled with an upsurge in lynchings in the South inspired approximately 700,000 blacks to leave for the North and Midwest. But as with the Kansas exodus, members of the Great Migration were not just forced out of the South. They were also pulled to the North, encouraged especially by jobs advertised in black newspapers. The *Chicago Defender* ran the following ad on 10 February 1917.

> The Defender invites all to come North. Plenty of room for the good, sober industrious man. Plenty of work. For those who will not work, the jails will take care of you. When you have served your 90 days at hard labor you will then have learned how to work. . . . Come join the ranks of the free. Cast the yoke from around your neck. See the light. When you have crossed the Ohio River, breathe the fresh air and say, "Why didn't I come before?" (Quoted in Daniel M. Johnson and Rex R. Campbell, *Black Migration in America: A Social Demographic History* (Durham: Duke University Press, 1981), 81).

The *Defender* received dozens of responses from blacks in the South, some thanking the paper for its efforts, others describing the difficulties of raising enough money to make the trip. One correspondent from Daphne, Alabama wrote in a letter dated 20 April 1917:

> Sir: I am writing to let you know that there is 15 or 20 families wants to come up there at once but cant come on account of money to come with and we cant phone you here we will be killed and they don't want us to leave here and say if we don't go to war and fight for our country they are going to kill us and wants to get away if we can if you send 20 passes there is no doubt that every one will come at once. (Quoted in Johnson and Campbell, p.82).

When people like the *Defender's* readers in Daphne came North, they usually settled in major industrial cities. Los Angeles, Chicago, Detroit, New York, and Gary, Indiana all experienced huge upswings in their black populations (Gary's grew by 1280%). When the migrants arrived they tended to live around other blacks, either by choice or because the city fathers wanted to keep them apart from whites. As a result these cities soon developed black neighborhoods—Chicago's South Side, Watts in Los Angeles, Harlem in New York City. These neighborhoods were both impediments to black progress and sources of that progress. The ghettoes of the North faced poverty and poor public service. They were constant reminders that blacks were second-class citizens. They bred discontent. Race riots rocked Chicago's black neighborhoods in 1919 and Detroit's in 1943. Each riot left dozens of blacks dead. Anger at the conditions of northern ghettoes made them fertile ground for black nationalism. Marcus Garvey's Universal Negro Improvement Association (UNIA), which called for blacks to return to Africa, found a wealth of supporters in Harlem in the 1920s, as did Elijah Muhammed's Nation of Islam in the decades following World War II.

But the discontent in black ghettoes was often matched by creativity. Blues music traveled with the Great Migration from the Mississippi Delta to Chicago, while Jazz left New Orleans for Kansas City and then Harlem. There it became the unofficial music of the Harlem Renaissance—an outpouring of black music, literature, poetry, and art that attempted to blend the folk life of the rural South with the urgent rhythms of the urban North and the cultural practices of Africa. Of the creativity in Harlem, the philosopher Alain Locke (himself a participant in the Harlem Renaissance) wrote:

> Here in Manhattan is not merely the largest Negro community in the world, but the first concentration in history of so many diverse elements of Negro life. It has attracted the African, the West Indian, the Negro American; has brought together the Negro of the North and the Negro of the South. . . . Proscription and prejudice have thrown these dissimilar elements into a common area of contact and interaction. Within this area, race sympathy and unity have determined a further fusing of sentiment and experience. So what began in terms of segregation becomes more and more, as its elements mix and react, the laboratory of a great race-welding. . . . In Harlem, Negro life is seizing upon its

first chances for group expression and self-determination. (Alain Locke, "The New Negro" in Alain Locke, ed. *The New Negro* (NY: Albert and Charles Boni, 1925), 6–7).

Institutions

The "chances for group expression and self-determination" that Locke noted can be clearly seen in the black institutions that arose between Reconstruction and World War II. These institutions—black schools, newspapers, civil rights organizations, and churches—served several important purposes. They trained black leaders, protested injustice, and preserved the black community. From these institutions sprang the Civil Rights Movement.

When the Civil War destroyed slavery it created the need for schools. The South's educational system had never distinguished itself, and it was certainly incapable of embracing hundreds of thousands of newly freed students. Missionaries from the North, with financial aid from the federal government, raced south to meet that need. As the decades passed, missionary schools were joined by segregated public schools. By 1920 a full range of educational opportunities—from first grade through the university—was available to black students.

This is not to say that black students were overwhelmed with educational opportunities. Segregated public schools owed their existence to all-white local school boards, which guaranteed that they would struggle financially even as they faced strict oversight. Missionary schools often treated their students paternalistically—as if they were incapable of rising to the same level as their white teachers. Still, for a black man or woman, an education was a way to greater prosperity.

One man who grasped the power of education was Booker T. Washington. Washington was born a slave in Franklin County, Virginia in 1856. Washington did not know his father (who was rumored to be a white man). And so when freedom came, the Washington's set out to make a life. Booker Washington ended up working in the coal mines of Virginia. There he heard about Hampton Institute, a school for freedmen in Hampton, Virginia. The idea of getting a practical education inspired Washington. He worked and saved until in 1872 he was able to set out for the school.

Washington's trip was 500 miles long, and when he arrived at Hampton he was dirty and bedraggled. The headmistress, uncertain about admitting a man in such a state, asked Washington to clean an adjoining room. He scrubbed it so clean that the headmistress not only admitted him but gave him a job as a janitor. In his memoir, *Up From Slavery,* Washington described his reaction:

> I was one of the happiest souls on earth. The sweeping of that room was my college examination, and never did any youth pass any examination for entrance into Harvard or Yale that gave him more genuine satisfaction. I have passed several examinations since then, but I have always felt that this was the best one I ever passed. (Booker T. Washington, *Up From Slavery* (NY: Penguin Books, 1986), 53).

Hard work would become Washington's trademark. It carried him through Hampton and then became the centerpiece of the curriculum at the Tuskegee Institute, a school he founded in Alabama. Washington had no patience for "elitist" education. At Tuskegee, students learned good hygiene and practical skills. They built the buildings on campus and grew much of the food they ate. When they graduated, Washington hoped they would be prepared to work along whites to rebuild the South. It would be this hard work, not political agitation, that Washington hoped would guarantee blacks their rights.

By many measures, Washington was a success. His efforts won the attention of philanthropic Northerners who opened their pocketbooks for Tuskegee. He became the most powerful black man in America, advising Theodore Roosevelt during his presidency. Washington dispensed jobs to his supporters and laid obstacles for his opponents. All the while, he ran Tuskegee, turning it into one of the most prestigious black colleges in the United States.

But Washington's success came at a cost for himself and Southern blacks. In order to maintain his influence and Tuskegee's funding, Washington had to blunt his calls for justice. In private he worked to block discrimination, but in public he told blacks and whites that hard work, not legal reform, was the path towards equality. Until blacks demonstrated their worth through labor, they should accept segregation, Washington taught. In his most famous speech, at the Atlanta Exposition in 1895, Washington put it this way:

> The wisest among my race understand that the agitation of questions of social equality is the extremist folly, and that progress in the enjoyment of all the privileges that will come

> to us must be the result of severe and constant struggle rather than of artificial forcing. No race that has anything to contribute to the markets of the world is long in any degree ostracized. It is important and right that all privileges of the law be ours, but it is vastly more important that we be prepared for the exercises of these privileges. The opportunity to earn a dollar in a factory just now is worth infinitely more than the opportunity to spend a dollar in an opera house. (Washington, *Up From Slavery,* 223-4).

Washington's willingness to accept segregation at exactly the time that Southern whites were legalizing it has made Washington a controversial figure. But his call for blacks to help themselves instead of relying on whites has resonated through the decades, inspiring figures as diverse as Malcolm X and Clarence Thomas.

Not all graduates of black schools ended up accepting the racial status quo in the south. Ida B. Wells, like Washington born into slavery, attended Rust College in Mississippi. There she studied to be a school teacher, one of the only middle-class jobs available to black women. At age 16 she graduated from Rust and headed North by train. In Tennessee the conductor asked her to leave the first class car due to the state's newly passed segregation laws. She refused, and when the conductor forcibly removed her from the train, she sued. The case took its time moving through the court system. By the time it was over (Wells won the original case, but the appeals court overturned the verdict), she had settled in Memphis, Tennessee. There she took up journalism, writing at first about her own case. The *Memphis Free Speech,* a black paper, published her account. That paper became her main literary outlet in the late 1880s and early 1890s, especially once she purchased part ownership of it.

Wells' focus soon turned to lynchings. In the *Free Speech* she reported case after case where mobs had killed black men whom they accused of raping white women. Wells' investigations discovered that the accusation of rape was usually a cover for simple terrorism against blacks who challenged white supremacy. Her forceful reporting on the lynching of three men in Memphis who had dared to open a grocery store across the street from a white-owned store led to threats on her life. That year (1892) she left Memphis for Chicago.

Though the *Free Speech* died when Wells left Memphis, black newspapers flourished throughout the United States. Black journalism has a long tradition in America, beginning well before the Civil War with the works of black abolitionists like Frederick Douglass. After the war, black newspapers sprang up in most major cities. They, like all newspapers, provided information, entertainment, and advertising. But they also maintained the tradition and variety of protest that inspired their pre-war counterparts. The *Amsterdam (New York City) News,* the *Chicago Defender,* and the *Pittsburgh Courier* were only three of the best-known black papers. Because their audiences and advertisers were overwhelmingly black, these papers were free to report on bigotry and call for reforms that mainstream papers would never have mentioned.

A measure of the influence of black papers was the speed with which newly founded civil rights organizations began publishing them. Marcus Garvey's UNIA published a widely read paper called the *Negro World.* That paper was routinely criticized by the *Messenger,* the New York City paper of the Brotherhood of Sleeping Car Porters, and both the *Messenger* and the *Negro World* drew attacks from *The Crisis,* the publication of the National Association for the Advancement of Colored People (NAACP).

The vitriol spilled among the three is a sign of the deep disagreements on how the civil rights movement should proceed in the first decades of the twentieth century. The NAACP, founded in 1910 as an integrated civil rights organization (and as a rejection of Booker Washington's accommodation to segregation), urged legislative and judicial action. The NAACP's lawyers traveled the United States looking for cases that could advance the cause of civil rights. Walter White, the NAACP's director, encouraged blacks to establish branches around the nation. And W. E. B. DuBois, the editor of *The Crisis,* worked to build black pride while uncovering injustice. In a particularly memorable editorial at the end of World War I, DuBois demonstrated both the pride and anger that characterized the NAACP. After listing the ways in which the United States mistreated blacks (lynching, disenfranchisement, poor education, theft), DuBois called for action.

> This is the country to which we soldiers of Democracy return. This is the fatherland for which we fought! But it is our fatherland. It was right for us to fight. The faults of our country are our faults. Under similar circumstances, we would fight again. By the God of Heaven, we are cowards and jackasses if now that the war is over, we do not marshal every ounce of our brain and brawn to fight a sterner, longer, more unbending battle against the forces of hell in

> our own land. We *return.* We *return from fighting.* We *return fighting.* Make way for democracy! We saved it in France, and by the Great Jehovah, we will save it in the United States of America, or know the reason why. (W. E. B. DuBois, "Returning Soldiers," *The Crisis,* May, 1919: 13–4).

The NAACP quickly became the largest, most effective civil rights organization in America. But its emphasis on gaining equality through the law left room for other types of activism. That space was filled by dozens of civil rights groups. Among them, the two most important were the National Urban League and the Congress on Racial Equality (CORE). The Urban League, which focused on improving living and working conditions in American cities, combined protest with social services for blacks. CORE pioneered the use of non-violent direct action, including sit-ins and boycotts, to encourage integration. By 1945, then, civil rights groups in American were actively using all of the tactics that would bring them success in the 1950s and 1960s.

Neither the NAACP, Urban League, nor CORE had huge payrolls. Instead their tiny paid staffs recruited volunteers to do most of the day-to-day work. Some of the volunteers came from the black colleges across the South. But most came from black churches. These churches ranged in size from tiny storefronts to massive cathedrals, and in style from the emotionalism of the Holiness sect to the staid traditionalism of Episcopalianism. Not all of them were friendly to civil rights activists—the National Baptist Convention, for one, preferred to focus on salvation instead of segregation. But all black churches shared two qualities that made them a powerful source of protest. First, they had developed a theology that identified their suffering with that of God's people in the Bible. The assurance that God stood on their side would bolster many a faltering activist. Second, they trained all of their members, both women and men, to help and support each other. These organizational skills made protest movements possible in the smallest towns and poorest ghettoes.

Portions of the black church (as well as some white liberal Protestant sects) also developed a religious commitment to nonviolence. The belief that Christians were required to bring about change without violence had its origins in Christ's teachings. But it made particular sense for minorities who could not hope to defend themselves from armed evil or win change at the ballot box. The theology department of Howard University, a black university in Washington, D. C., was an especially important source of nonviolent Christian activism. Howard Thurman, a professor there, trained dozens of divinity students in nonviolence. Those students fanned out across the United States, spreading nonviolence from the pulpit and in the classroom. Thurman inspired the young activists who founded CORE. Mordecai Johnson, president of Howard, traveled to India, spent time studying Gandhi's nonviolent activism, and then returned to the American lecture circuit. Martin Luther King, Jr. first took nonviolence seriously after hearing Johnson lecture about his visit with Gandhi.

World War II

Though nonviolence drew an increasing number of activists in the 1930s and 40s, it was the violence of World War II that began the destruction of segregation. One million black men and women served in the U. S. military during the war. They fought with bravery (and occasionally cowardice) equal to that of their white counterparts. They suffered through the heat of the Pacific war and shivered through European winters. They saw skeletons, living and dead, in Germany's concentration camps. They rejoiced at the power of the atom bomb and mourned the deaths of their friends. But while blacks saw the same war as whites, they saw it from an entirely different perspective. America's military was still segregated, white officers oversaw black divisions (just as they had in the Civil War), black soldiers did more dangerous work and were more severely punished for mistakes than their white counterparts. For white soldiers the battle against Hitler was a clear battle of good against evil. For black soldiers the event was more complicated. They delighted in defeating Hitler's racist Reich. But they couldn't help seeing a certain hypocrisy in a segregated army denouncing Hitler for racism.

Many black soldiers reasoned that if they were being asked to give their lives for their country, then they ought to work to make their country better. At military bases around the world, black soldiers challenged segregation. Some defied a ban on reading black newspapers. At Freeman Field in Indiana, 100 black officers were arrested for trying to integrate the officers club. And at Port Chicago, California, black soldiers were charged with mutiny after refusing to perform dangerous work assigned to them because they were black.

Blacks who did not join the military noted a similar hypocrisy. The war brought a boom in employment, but that boom did not extend equally to whites and blacks. Whites received higher-paying jobs, while blacks were relegated to unskilled labor. Blacks were almost entirely excluded from some of the most prosperous industries and most powerful unions. In January 1941, A. Philip Randolph, president of the Brotherhood of Sleeping Car Porters, called for a march on Washington to demand an end to such discrimination. Randolph's call had an electrifying effect on America. The Roosevelt administration immediately tried to discourage Randolph, urging him to consider the effect such a protest would have in Berlin. Randolph would not reconsider. Nor could he, given the groundswell of public support for the march. Thousands of blacks from around the United States began to make preparations to go to Washington, D. C. in July. Finally in late June, President Roosevelt summoned Randolph to the White House. Roosevelt promised to do something substantial to end discrimination if Randolph would call off the march. Randolph agreed, and on 25 June 1941 Roosevelt issued Executive Order 8802. The order required that there be

> no discrimination in the employment of workers in defense industries or Government because of race, creed, color, or national origin. . . . And it is the duty of employers and of labor organizations . . . to provide for the full and equitable participation of all workers in defense industries, without discrimination because of race, creed, color, or national origin. (Franklin Delano Roosevelt, "Executive Order 8802", quoted in John Hope Franklin and Alfred A. Moss, Jr. *From Slavery to Freedom* (NY: McGraw-Hill, 1994), 437).

By the end of World War II, two trends had combined to ignite the civil rights movement. The black experience in World War II encouraged increased activism. And the executive branch of the federal government responded by beginning to revise its racial policies. These trends never fit easily together. Activists pushed for changes more sweeping than the government would accept. But the uneasy alliance of activism and federal reform led, over the next 25 years, to an end to legal segregation and a beginning of racial equality.

It is impossible to discuss all of the major efforts of the civil rights movement. In fact, most of them, run by small, local groups of citizens, have been lost to history. But in retrospect, the period of reform stretching from the early 1950s to the late 1960s can be divided into three main categories: ending segregation, regaining the franchise, and seeking equality. Of course civil rights efforts did not divide themselves so neatly—after all, ending segregation on buses was a step towards equality. But these categories do allow a simple division of this very complex period in American history.

Ending Segregation—1945–1962

The blows against segregation that began with Executive Order 8802 continued after World War II. In 1949 the Army began to desegregate its forces and the rest of the military followed. Federally owned housing was increasingly integrated after 1950. These government efforts were accompanied by local activism—a CORE-led sit-in desegregated a restaurant in Chicago in 1945; in 1948 protesters in Baton Rouge, Louisiana boycotted the city's segregated bus lines.

These limited efforts got a huge boost in 1954 when the Supreme Court outlawed segregation in public schools in *Brown v. Board of Education.* The *Brown* case was brought by several black families in Topeka, Kansas whose children were forced to attend black schools across town in spite of the fact that other (white) schools were much closer to their homes. The NAACP, looking for a case with which to challenge segregation, argued the case before the Court. In its unanimous decision the Court ruled that segregated schools were inherently unequal, and thus violated the "equal protection" clause of the 14th Amendment. School desegregation was painfully slow. In Mississippi the state closed its public schools rather than integrate. The governor of Alabama swore that he would block integration with his own body. And as late as 1996 some school districts involved in the Brown decision were still under court supervision to ensure that their schools remained desegregated.

The *Brown* case energized activists to attack other forms of segregation. For the black citizens of Montgomery, Alabama, the most obvious sign of segregation was their seats in the back of public buses. Since the Supreme Court had ruled segregation on interstate bus lines illegal in the mid-1940s, the NAACP had been looking for an opportunity to challenge segregation on local bus routes. Two times before December 1955 the NAACP had thought it had good test cases in Montgomery, only to have them fall apart at the last minute. But when Rosa Parks, the secretary of the local NAACP, was arrested on 1 December 1955 for failing to give up her seat to a white man, the NAACP had its case.

Even before the NAACP could defend Parks in court, the black citizens of Montgomery began defending her in the streets. As in many other places, women began the effort. JoAnn Robinson, a professor of English at Montgomery's black Alabama State University, gathered her friends for a marathon session at the ditto machine on the night of 1 December. On 2 December they copied and distributed 50,000 leaflets calling on blacks to boycott the buses starting the following Monday. That night, black ministers met at Dexter Avenue Baptist Church, and selected the 26 year old Martin Luther King, Jr. as the spokesman of the boycott. The choice of King was entirely practical. Because he was new to Montgomery, he had yet to offend any of the powerful black ministers. His wife, Coretta, a college graduate and professional singer, made the King family an appealing public face for the boycott.

Monday morning, Montgomery's buses were empty. Monday afternoon Rosa Parks was convicted; the NAACP lawyers filed an immediate appeal. Monday night King stood at the pulpit of the largest black church in Montgomery, filled to overflowing with women and men ready to sacrifice to end segregation. King laid out the justification for the boycott. He started by calling for nonviolence. "Now let us say that we are not here advocating violence. We have overcome that," he exclaimed. "The only weapon that we have in our hands this evening is the weapon of protest," and that weapon would lead to peaceful but powerful protests, in contrast to the brutality that many blacks had faced. "There will be no white persons pulled out of their homes and taken out on some distant road and murdered. There will be nobody among us who will stand up and defy the Constitution of this nation."

King continued in this vein, mixing Christian doctrine and respect for just American laws. In a series of thundering sentences, King made his vision clear:

> My friends, I want it to be known that we're going to work with grim and bold determination to gain justice on the buses in this city. And we are not wrong. We are not wrong in what we are doing. If we are wrong—the Supreme Court of this nation is wrong. If we are wrong—God Almighty is wrong! If we are wrong—Jesus of Nazareth was merely a utopian dreamer and never came down to earth! If we are wrong—justice is a lie. (Quoted in Taylor Branch, *Parting the Waters: America in the King Years, 1954–1963* (N.Y.: Simon and Schuster, 1988), 140–1).

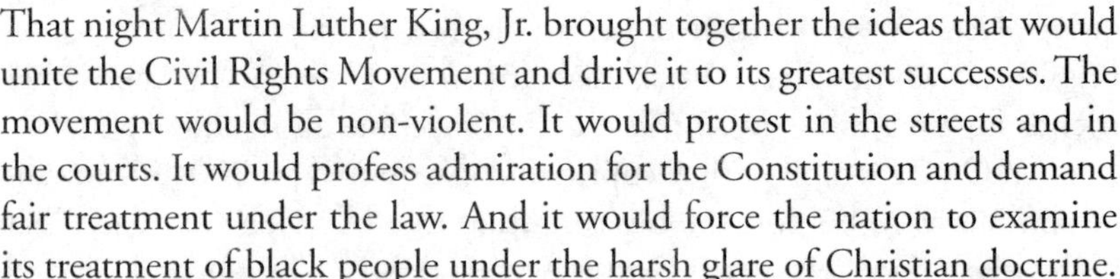

That night Martin Luther King, Jr. brought together the ideas that would unite the Civil Rights Movement and drive it to its greatest successes. The movement would be non-violent. It would protest in the streets and in the courts. It would profess admiration for the Constitution and demand fair treatment under the law. And it would force the nation to examine its treatment of black people under the harsh glare of Christian doctrine.

The boycott lasted over a year. During that time, blacks who owned cars drove blacks who did not to work. King and the other ministers negotiated at length with the city. The NAACP pursued its case to the Supreme Court. The national media descended on Montgomery. The police looked for excuses to harass boycotters. (Giving tickets for burned out tail lights was a favorite.) Local thugs blew up the front half of King's house while Coretta and her infant daughter were in the back, part of a city-wide terror effort. And throughout it all, King preached nonviolence from the pulpit (even as activists from CORE and other peace organizations taught him what it was). Finally, on 20 December the Supreme Court ruled that Montgomery's system of segregated buses was unconstitutional. The boycott ended the next day. On December 23rd King's house was strafed with shotgun fire. On December 24th a fifteen year old black girl was pulled from a bus stop and beaten. On Christmas night, fifteen sticks of dynamite destroyed the home of one of King's closest friends, the Reverend Fred Shuttlesworth.

King was quick to learn the lessons of Montgomery. Black people, organized and united in nonviolence, could triumph over racist laws, even in the deepest South. But those triumphs did not guarantee safety. Therefore the movement needed an organization dedicated to nonviolent protest in the South and it needed the backing of the federal government. King started by calling together black ministers to form the Southern Christian Leadership Conference (SCLC) in 1957. That same year the leaders of the NAACP, SCLC, and Urban League, among others, met with President Dwight Eisenhower seeking more active federal support for civil rights. They were disappointed.

The next major action against segregation came not from King or the NAACP, but instead from the black colleges of the South. For months Ezell Blair, Jr., David Richmond, Franklin McCain, and Joseph McNeil, freshmen at North Carolina A&T, had talked about segregation in Greensboro, N. C. The target of their frustration were the businesses in Greensboro that denied equal service to blacks. On February 1, 1960, when they could talk no more, they went to the whites-only lunch counter at Woolworth's, sat down, and ordered coffee. Woolworth's refused them service; they refused to leave. The next day they returned, with twenty other A&T students. By the fourth day of protest, white students at the University of North Carolina Women's College joined the Woolworth's protest. By the end of the month, it seemed that every town with a black college and a whites-only business was home to a sit-in.

The sit-ins differed from King's boycott in two ways. First, they attacked segregation in privately owned businesses, not state-run facilities. Second, the students were younger and more impatient than the preachers in the SCLC. Nevertheless, King tried to organize the students. The college protesters found King a bit annoying (they called him "Da Lawd"—a reference to his occupation and healthy ego). But they found Ella Baker, a SCLC staff member, much more congenial. Baker encouraged students to establish their own organization, one that would work with the SCLC but not be a part of it. After several days of discussion and nonviolence training, the students agreed. They formed a new organization—the Student Nonviolent Coordinating Committee (SNCC). SNCC adopted nonviolence, but as a tactic, not a religious philosophy. And they had little patience for negotiation, hoping instead to overturn segregation by attacking it head-on. SNCC began local organizing efforts in 1961 and 1962. SNCC field workers moved into communities facing the harshest racism and began the process of encouraging black resistence to segregation.

CORE made similar efforts to face down the ugliest racism. In 1961 CORE organized a series of "freedom rides" in the South. White and black college students rode buses through the South to see if bus facilities were integrated as the Supreme Court had demanded. In Rock Hill, South Carolina, one of the riders, John Lewis (now a U. S. representative from Georgia), entered a white restroom, explained his constitutional rights to a group of men there, who proceeded to beat him. When the bus reached Aniston, Alabama, a mob stopped it. A man threw a burning bundle of rags into the bus. Riders rushed off the bus. The mob beat them as the bus burned to the ground. Another bus pulled into the bus station in Birmingham, Alabama on Mother's Day 1961. They were met there by 30 armed members of the KKK. The police gave the Klan 15 minutes to attack before the police would arrive on the scene. The Klan wasted no time, bloodying all of the riders. When John Seigenthaler, the Kennedy administration's representative on the scene, tried to stop the beating of two women, the Klan beat him too. Photos of the carnage ran in papers across the United States. Within a year, almost all interstate bus facilities were integrated.

The freedom rides mark an important point in the history of the Civil Rights Movement. Protesters had learned the power of media coverage in rallying public support for civil rights. And the Kennedy administration, rather than have the world see racial strife in the United States, was willing to help the movement. This is not to say that Kennedy was an activist—he was much more concerned with the Soviet Union than with the SCLC. But after the sluggardly behavior of the Eisenhower administration, Kennedy's involvement was a real improvement.

The role of the media and the Kennedy administration is clear in the major civil rights events of 1963. That spring, the SCLC, SNCC, and local activists began protests in Birmingham, Alabama. Several weeks into a stand-off between protesters and city officials over public and private segregation, activists provoked the police by recruiting protesters from local high schools. The police responded by spraying protesters with water from fire hoses. Television carried footage of teenagers being blown over by the force of the water. The national outrage shamed the city into ending segregation and encouraging the employment of blacks in jobs previously reserved for whites.

The civil rights organizations responded to their hard won success by calling for a march on Washington to lobby for federal legislation guaranteeing integration. The Kennedy administration originally opposed the march; Kennedy feared that a protest in the nation's capital would scare legislators who might support his civil rights proposals. But when the administration saw it could not block the march, it gave its support. Federal support came with strings—the organizing committee would have to be integrated, and the administration could veto any speech given at the march if it was too inflammatory. On 28 August 1963, an integrated crowd of 250,000 gathered on the steps of the Lincoln Memorial to demand freedom and jobs. Several people spoke, including John Lewis, the freedom rider beaten in Rock Hill, South Carolina. (Lewis was the only person whose remarks were censored by the government.)

Martin Luther King, Jr. was the final speaker. The crowd had endured late-August heat and generally dull speeches for six hours. He began his remarks reminding the audience that Lincoln had promised freedom and government support to blacks, but that neither had come for almost 100 years. He applauded the spirit of nonviolent activism that had overtaken the South and begun to win that freedom. He encouraged the people in attendance to stay true to nonviolence. Then he departed from his prepared remarks and improvised the greatest lines of American oratory since the Gettysburg Address. King spoke of his dream of an integrated nation. It was a dream "deeply rooted in the American dream," he said. It was a dream that the nation would be true to its creed: "We hold these truths to be self-evident, that all men are created equal." It was a dream of legal and social equality, a dream of a place where "all God's children, black men and white men, Jews and gentiles, Protestants and Catholics, will be able to join hands and sing in the words of the old Negro spiritual, 'Free at last, free at last, thank God almighty we are free at last.'" The crowd erupted in cheers. The national media gave the march front page coverage.

The success of the march energized the federal government. The Kennedy administration threw its weight behind civil rights legislation. Congressmen who had wavered on the anti-segregation bill began to support it. After President Kennedy was assassinated, his replacement, Lyndon Baines Johnson, urged passage of the Civil Rights Act as a tribute to Kennedy. Within a year of the march, Congress had passed the first major civil rights legislation in 90 years, legislation that forbade discrimination on the basis of race, creed, or color. Legalized segregation was no more.

Seeking Power Through the Ballot—1960–1965

Ending segregation did not guarantee black access to political power. Nor did it grant blacks full citizenship. Civil rights leaders recognized by 1960 what the Reconstruction congress had realized in 1870—citizens without the freedom to vote were not full citizens. And so while the most public protests in the South had been to end segregation, the most painstaking work had been to register blacks to vote. For the civil rights workers of the NAACP, CORE, and SNCC, voter registration was doubly challenging. First they had to persuade blacks to make the effort to register. Then they had to contend with local officials who blocked those registrations. These obstacles made voter registration slow work. As late as 1964, only 40% of the South's voting-age blacks were registered to vote. In certain parts of the South, the numbers were even more dismal. Only 32% of Louisiana blacks and 6% of the black citizens of Mississippi were registered. In Selma, Alabama, 335 black citizens out of a population of 15,000 could go to the polls.

In 1963 SNCC began a voter registration drive in Selma. SNCC's workers immediately faced hostility from the local sheriff, Jim Clark.

Clark had deputized hundreds of local residents who traveled the South "discouraging" civil rights efforts. The posse turned its efforts to Selma, harassing workers and helping to arrest protesters. All through 1964 tensions grew in Selma. Delays in voter registration made blacks impatient while black impatience made Jim Clark ever more resentful. By January 1965 everyone knew that Selma was set to explode. Martin Luther King figured that such tensions made Selma the perfect site for the SCLC's next round of protests, which were aimed at getting the federal government to pass voting rights legislation. On his first day in Selma, King was attacked as he tried to register for his hotel room. The attack signaled the course the Selma protests would follow. Clark arrested blacks who arrived at the courthouse to register, his posse herding them to jail with cattle prods. By the middle of February more blacks were in jail than on the voter lists. In rural areas around Selma, white vigilantes attacked blacks. Then, on 7 March 1965, with the cameras of the world media watching, 600 black protesters began a march from Selma to Montgomery, the state capital. As they crossed the Edmund Pettis Bridge on the outskirts of Selma, Alabama state troopers waded into the crowd, firing tear gas and swinging their night sticks. When the attack ended, 75 blacks were in the hospital, John Lewis' skull was fractured, marauding whites had destroyed a section of Selma's black neighborhood, and film of the protest again filled America's television screens. Within the week President Lyndon Johnson presented the Voting Rights Act of 1965 to Congress and federalized the Alabama National Guard to protect black marchers on the way to Montgomery. The marchers got to Montgomery before the bill got through Congress, but by August 1965 the United States government was finally pledged to protect the voting rights guaranteed black men in the 15th Amendment.

Seeking Equality, 1965 to 1968

The Selma protest and the Voting Rights Act that grew out of it were the high point of the Civil Rights Movement. At no time since have local civil rights activists, the federal government, and the American public been in such close agreement. This agreement dissolved, in part because of pressures from outside the movement—particularly the Vietnam War and the protests that accompanied it. But it also fell apart because the next phase in the movement—the push for real equality—divided black protesters, challenged the deeply held beliefs of many Americans, and discouraged the federal government from supporting further protests.

On 11 August 1965, police officers in Watts, California tried to arrest a black man for drunken driving. Watts was Los Angeles' black ghetto. The poverty there was deep and persistent. Two-thirds of Watts' residents received welfare; 34% of the men were unemployed. Though the population was 98% black, the police force was 97% white. When Marquette Frye resisted arrest and white officers tried to manhandle him into the squad car in the midst of a bored and angry crowd, Watts exploded. Six days of riots destroyed 150 blocks, killed 34 people, and destroyed 45 million dollars worth of property.

The Watts riots also destroyed the assumption that the civil rights gains of the previous years had solved the nation's racial problem. Instead, Watts demonstrated that legal equality did not guarantee peace or progress. Blacks in Watts already enjoyed the rights that protesters had fought for in the South. Yet those rights seemed useless in a ghetto. After the Watts riot, one young man predicted that riots would continue because "I, as a Negro, am immediately considered to be a criminal by police, and if I have a woman with me, she is a tramp even if she is my wife or mother." (Quoted in Weisbrot, *Freedom Bound,* 160). An Urban League worker in Harlem noted that equal rights did not respond to poverty. "The black cat in Harlem wasn't worried about [freely riding] no damn bus—he'd been riding for fifty years. What he didn't have was the fare." (Quoted in Weisbrot, *Freedom Bound,* 169).

The civil rights movement responded to the Watts riot in two ways. The Rev. King moved his operations to Chicago and worked for fair housing and economic equality. His tactics continued to rely on nonviolent protest and negotiation, while he tried to expand his constituency to include all poor people. Younger activists in CORE and SNCC rejected both King's tactics and his audience. Instead they urged black people to reject nonviolence and negotiation with those in power. Watts had shown them that all the nonviolence in the world would not end economic inequality and that powerless people would always suffer at the hands of the powerful. This world view became known as Black Power—a movement that promised to return violence for violence while building up self-sufficient black communities.

Neither King's efforts nor those of Black Power advocates proved immediately successful. King proposed to end economic inequality by providing all Americans with an annual minimum income—a proposal that smacked of socialism to many Americans. In Chicago his protests drew angry crowds (after a march through one Chicago suburb where he had been pelted with bricks and bottles King said he had never seen such angry racism in the South) and meaningless concessions from the city government. King pressed on, calling on the government to end poverty and the war in Vietnam. To push these two goals he called on poor people from around the country to occupy Washington D. C. in August 1968, shutting down the government. His call met with scorn from President Johnson, who saw it as an attack on the very institution that had best supported the cause of civil rights.

Meanwhile, Black Power advocates managed to win followers in some ghettoes and on some college campuses. But the prospects of armed black resistance to power did little to help ghetto dwellers. Riots continued through the summer of 1967. The rhetoric of black power also alienated white liberals who had previously supported the movement. They began to slip away from civil rights activism and towards the anti-war and women's movements. A part of the movement that only recently had tried to end segregation now segregated itself.

In March and April 1968 King led a protest against unfair wages being paid to trashmen in Memphis, Tennessee. King, ever the coalition builder, invited local black power advocates and gang members to join his marches. Some did, and the result was a series of protests that were non-violent around King, but violent on the fringes. After one particularly disturbing march, where young black men had fought with white thugs and looters damaged some Memphis stores, King called for a halt to the protests. During the day on April 4 he met with his closest advisors at the Lorraine Motel, trying to find a way to win their dispute with the City of Memphis without losing control of the protests. Just before dinner, King stepped out onto the balcony of his room. A bullet smashed into his jaw. He was dead before the ambulance could get him to the hospital. Police arrested James Earl Ray, a white man. King's associates called for peace, his wife and father called for peace, the president called for peace. But there was no peace to be found. Riots convulsed every major American city. Tanks rolled through the streets of Washington, DC. The National Guard patrolled Newark, New Jersey for six weeks. Congress passed the Civil Rights Act of 1968, which helped guarantee equal treatment of blacks wanting to buy homes, but also expanded federal power to prosecute rioters. King's planned occupation of Washington, D. C.

went ahead, but only a few thousand dispirited protesters arrived. They sensed that the era of mass protest on behalf of racial equality had reached its end.

The Legacy of the Civil Rights Movement

Though it ended in discouragement, the Civil Rights Movement left an important legacy for the United States. It forced the federal government and most Americans to abandon the belief that blacks are inferior to whites. It inspired the government to live up to its constitutional responsibilities, not only to blacks, but to other minorities. It taught a generation of Americans that peaceful protest could lead to meaningful change, that democracy could work, and that citizens could successfully mix religion and political action. These grassroots efforts spread across the political and racial spectrum. The women's movement and anti-Vietnam protests used the Civil Rights Movement as a model. More recently conservative groups such as the Christian Coalition and Operation Rescue have adopted both the tactics and the willingness to blend political and moral beliefs that characterized protests for black civil rights.

In addition to its successes, the movement raised a host of questions that still trouble the nation. Most of them deal with the meaning of equality and freedom. The civil rights movement won equality under the law, but that did not lead to other sorts of equality. While there is a growing black middle class, blacks on average still earn less than whites, still face higher unemployment rates, and are more frequently poor. Black men compose a disproportionately large portion of the prison population and a disproportionately small portion of the college population. Since the 1960s, income inequality has continued to grow. Today there is a larger gap between rich and poor than at any time in this century. Martin Luther King argued that these facts were a sign that the government should do more to guarantee economic equality. That argument won only lukewarm popular support in the 1960s, and, in an era where the trend is toward smaller, less active government, gets even less today. Does liberty from too-powerful government leave us powerless to respond to poverty and discrimination?

Nor is the nonviolence of the Civil Rights Movement much in vogue today. For many activists, violence was never an acceptable choice for Christians. But today violence permeates American life—it fills our homes, movies, and games; it afflicts our schools and streets. But the tools of violence are legal, and the language of violence receives its protection from the Constitution. How then do we respond to a culture that favors the right to hurt over love?

The Civil Rights Movement suggests an answer to both questions—bold, patient, persuasive citizens can change the laws and the lives of Americans.

Suggested Readings

Taylor Branch, *Parting the Waters: America in the King Years, 1954–1963* (NY: Simon and Schuster, 1988).

James H. Cone, *Martin and Malcolm and America: A Dream or a Nightmare* (NY: Orbis Books, 1992).

John Hope Franklin and Alfred A. Moss, *From Slavery to Freedom: A History of African Americans,* 7th ed. (NY: McGraw Hill, 1994).

Hugh Pearson, *The Shadow of the Panther: Huey Newton and the Price of Black Power in America* (Reading, MA: Addison-Wesley, 1994).

Robert Weisbrot, *Freedom Bound: A History of America's Civil Rights Movement* (NY: Penguin, 1991).

Cary D. Wintz, ed., *African American Political Thought, 1890–1930* (Armonk, NY: M. E. Sharpe, 1996).

AGRICULTURAL AND INDUSTRIAL DEMOCRACY: "REPUBLICAN" REACTIONS IN THE GILDED AGE

Richard Kimball
Department of History

Whatever the root causes, a large number of Americans in the last decades of the nineteenth century sought a radical redefinition of the founder's republican ideals. Still acutely interested in freedom, democracy, and individual virtue, farmers and industrial workers in the 1890s promoted a new vision of the American "city on a hill." "Populist" social groupings—including farmer groups and labor unions among others—reworked the traditional version of American republicanism and offered Americans a cooperative alternative to the economic and social world founded on the principles of laissez-faire economics.

Several related but divergent strands of populism, usually defined as a social or political movement designed to meet the needs of common people, emerged to address conditions at the end of the century. Although society and the economy had changed vastly in the century since the constitutional convention, Americans still clung to the core concepts of consent, representation, and personal virtue. Agricultural and labor populist ideologies, however, revised the republican ideas to include cooperation and a labor theory of value. Where Jefferson, Madison, and others had posited the independent yeoman farmer as the key to American prosperity, workers in the Gilded Age believed that abundance would flow not from individual virtue alone but from all producers working together as a unified whole. The principles of personal morality and self-abnegation continued to influence populist thought; however, as nineteenth century workers realized, one farmer or one worker alone could have no impact on the industrial giants that had come to dominate

American society. Since industrialization (both on the farm and in the factory) had changed the face of America, populists sought to revise republicanism to fit the emerging social and economic context as the nineteenth century closed.

To farmers and workers in the 1890s, the American "city on a hill" had fallen on hard times. By the end of the century, freehold farmers—thought to be the backbone of Jeffersonian republicanism—found themselves in dire economic straits while skilled workers in American cities were being replaced by unskilled operatives running industrial machines. The apex of the farmer-led movement to make society more just and equitable was reached with the creation of a viable third political party in the 1890s. When American industrial workers faced similar threats to their livelihoods, they likewise sought control over part of the industrial process through cooperative involvement in labor unions. Instead of focusing on grass-roots political organizations, however, American workers turned to collective bargaining to ensure their viability in a changing American economy.

In the years following the Civil War, American farmers faced one crisis after another. Beset by banks that refused to operate on terms favorable to agriculturists and cornered by the exorbitant rates charged by monopolistic railroads, farmers in the American hinterlands always seemed to be traveling uphill, against the wind. Despite these formidable obstacles, farmers pushed their annual production levels to unprecedented heights. New devices like the combine, mower, seeder, barbed wire, and improved water drilling techniques brought mass production to the farm. In a sense, farmers became too good at growing foodstuffs. The increase in production was nothing less than miraculous. Before agricultural mechanization, a single farmer could expect to harvest about 7.5 acres of wheat. Armed with an automatic binder that cut and tied bundles of grain, the same farmer could harvest 135 acres of wheat profitably. Such technological changes prompted the greatest migration in American history as millions of new farmers moved to the Great Plains. Between 1870 and 1900, more farm acreage was put under the plow than had been in the previous two centuries. With mass-produced tools, increased cultivation areas, and a massive output of foodstuffs, the old American yeoman farmer was beginning to resemble an industrial worker; farms were becoming factories in the field.

The increase in agricultural production—while it might seem advantageous to the average farmer—quickly created a glut in American food markets and prices began to tumble. In the twenty five years after 1870, wheat prices fell from $1.06 to 63.3 cents a bushel; corn dropped from 43.1 to 29.7 cents a bushel; and cotton dropped from 15.1 to 5.8 cents per pound. After paying to warehouse and transport their products to markets, farmers typically took home even less than these market prices indicate. In Kansas, where corn sold for just 10 cents a bushel, farmers burned corn instead of coal for fuel. One Nebraska farmer shot his hogs because he could neither sell them nor give them away. Though agricultural production was easier than ever, this was not the bucolic rural life that Jefferson had imagined. Something was amiss in the countryside. While other industries reached new heights of production and profit, the fortunes of American farmers did not keep pace. As North Carolina farm editor Leonidas L. Polk wrote in 1887, "There is something radically wrong in our industrial system. There is a screw loose. The wheels have dropped out of balance. The railroads have never been so prosperous, and yet agriculture languishes. The banks have never done a better or more profitable business, and yet agriculture languishes. Manufacturing enterprises have never made more money or were in a more flourishing condition, and yet agricultural languishes. Towns and cities flourish and 'boom,' . . . and yet agriculture languishes. Salaries and fees were never so temptingly high and desirable, and yet agriculture languishes."[1]

More than any other factor, the agricultural economy had been waylaid by overproduction. The low prices that stemmed from too many farm goods flooding the market simply meant that farmers could not make enough money to provide for their needs, improve their operations, and pay their bills. Because the central problem of overproduction was nearly impossible to combat, farmers turned their sights onto more accessible enemies—railroads, banks, and the federal government.

The railroads received the largest share of the farmer's animosity. Relying on railroads to transport their goods to urban markets, farmers felt that they were victims of a railroad monopoly. Rates were often higher for farm products than for other goods because many large corporations dominated state legislatures and had negotiated sweetheart deals with railroad companies. Farmers, struggling to eke out a meager existence, could not compete with the deep pockets of large industrialists like Rockefeller and Carnegie. As unorganized agriculturists, they only had one option—to pay the asking price. On long hauls, the farmers enjoyed comparatively low transportation costs because there was competition for their freight (i.e., they could choose from several different railroad companies). On local and short hauls, however, where competition was not so keen, the rates were disproportionately high. In one famous example, it cost farmers in Minnesota more to ship their grain to St. Paul or Minneapolis than to New York. As far as the farmer was concerned, the free market system had failed to bring competition to the Great Plains—the hidden hand of laissez-faire economics actually carried a stick that beat farmers into economic submission.

The banking system provided another terror to residents of America's heartland. Requiring loans to pay for annual start-up costs like seed and machinery, farmers found that banks did not cater to their financial needs. Banks would not allow farmers to use real estate or farm property—a farmer's primary asset—as collateral for loans. Additionally, the fiscal banking year was often at odds with the seasonal rhythm of farm life. Banks seemed to be large, impersonal organizations located in distant cities that cared little for the farmer's personal or professional needs. Moreover, since there were few sources of credit available to southern and western farmers, they were forced to take money wherever they could get it—often at interest rates as high as twenty-five percent. To compound the problems facing farmers, they were often required to repay loans in years when crop prices were falling. Besieged by decreasing income and increasing interest rates, farmers' prospects spiraled downward.

Adding to agricultural misfortune, the monetary policy of the federal government made it difficult for farmers to pay their creditors. Remaining strictly tied to the gold standard, money was tight for all Americans. More than other groups, however, farmers with their high debt loads were particularly affected by the monometallic standard. Farmer politicians likewise derided the high tariffs enacted by the Congress. Designed to protect machinery companies and other large industrial concerns from foreign competition, U.S. tariff policy hit farmers on both sides of the business ledger. Not only were they required to pay higher prices for manufactured goods like combines, their foodstuffs did not receive tariff protections and were thus open to the vagaries of the world agricultural markets. Buying protected goods and selling unprotected products just pushed the farming community further into decline—and farmers placed the blame squarely on the shoulders of the federal government.

Railroad rate discrimination, insensitive banks, and government policies that unfairly burdened agricultural workers combined to push farmers toward organization. They realized that to compete with their well-organized (and well-heeled) opponents, they needed to band together. One lone farmer could have little impact on the economic system, but collectively American farmers could hope to create institutions responsive to their needs as well as elect representatives who would create state policies favorable to American agriculture. Keenly aware of the problems of the modern economy and particularly eager for government assistance in ameliorating them, farmers created a series of organizations designed to assuage the problems of rural life. The result of these organizations would be the emergence of one of the most powerful movements of political protest in American history—Populism.

Though occasional cooperative farm movements had flowered early in the nineteenth century, the first major farm organization was created by Oliver H. Kelley in 1867. Appalled by what he considered the isolation and drabness of rural life, Kelley established the National Grange of the Patrons of Husbandry, often called the Grange. Initially, the Grange was less a movement of protest than a social and self-help association. Their modest purposes included teaching new agricultural techniques to increase farm efficiency and providing a forum where farm families could meet together to relieve the loneliness of farm life. After the Panic of 1873 depressed farm prices, the Grange received an infusion of new members. Within two years, more than 800,000 farmers belonged to 20,000 local lodges. Buoyed by this newfound strength, the Grange shifted away from social issues and contemplated the economic possibilities of cooperation. To eliminate the hated "middle men" that subtracted from their profits, farmers set up cooperative stores, creameries, grain elevators, and warehouses. Ensuring that rural money remained in the countryside (rather than flowing to urban areas), the Grange established insurance companies and factories that built furniture, stoves and other items. These farmers were not turning their backs on capitalism; rather, they were trying to mold the capitalist system to suit their needs. Having been the victim of industrial titans for too long, farmers substituted a more humane version of cooperative capitalism that kept profits close to home. As one leading historian of the agrarian movement describes, "Populists sought what they called a 'cooperative commonwealth' in order that individual human striving might be fairly respected. The cooperative ethos was the animating spirit of the popular movement they created."[2] Firmly ensconced in the tradition of republican individualism, nineteenth-century farmers sought new methods to re-enthrone the fundamental political principles of the nation's founding.

Politically, the Grange worked to elect state legislators who were committed to their programs. Rather than create their own separate political party, however, the Grange worked within the existing parties, supporting sympathetic candidates. The primary objective of the Grange's political ambitions was to subject railroads to government control. At the peak of their power, when several midwestern legislatures fell under Granger domination, the legislatures enacted "Granger laws" imposing reasonable rates on railroads. Though railroads typically refused to abide by the legislative mandates, the Grange's belief in state control over the railroads was validated by the Supreme Court in 1877. In *Munn v. Illinois*, the Supreme Court found that an Illinois law fixing maximum rates for grain storage fell within the state's police power to regulate businesses affected with "a public interest." Granger policies and tactics might have received the Court's seal of approval, but the Granger laws failed to change the economic landscape significantly. Corporations eventually convinced the state legislatures to repeal the laws or won victories in state courts. Corporate power, and a resurgence in agricultural prosperity in the late 1870s, spelled doom for Granger organizations. By 1880, membership had decreased to 100,000 and their political power likewise dwindled.

Grangers were not the only powerful farm organization established in the late nineteenth century. As early as 1875, farmers in parts of the South (most notably in Texas) began uniting in "Farmer's Alliances." The Alliances struggled for the next decade to gain new members. It was not until the mid-1880s, when organizational leadership fell to C.W. McCune, that the Southern Alliance experienced much growth. In 1880, a Northwestern Alliance was organized in Chicago; a similar organization for African-American farmers was created as the National Colored Farmers' Alliance and Cooperative Union. Like Granger programs, Alliance members formed cooperatives and other marketing mechanisms including stores, banks, processing plants, and other facilities that freed them from the hated "furnishing merchants" who kept many farmers in debt. By fostering a sense of mutual, neighborly responsibility, Alliance groups hoped to create a community where economic cooperation replaced the cut-throat competition of unbridled capitalism.

At points in the Alliance experience, the concept of cooperation broadened to include a component of interracial solidarity. Beginning in Texas in 1886, African-American farmers, often helped by white organizers, created what would become the Colored Farmers' National Alliance and Cooperative Union, which contained both black and white members. This new organization represented "a fragile opening in the cloistered world of white supremacy" and articulated a radical alternative to the segregated world of Gilded Age America.[3] Farmers of all races understood that their common grievances did much more to unify them than racial dividing lines drove them apart. Bound by racism, the Colored Farmers' National Alliance never sponsored large cooperative efforts like other Alliance groups; rather, they focused their energies on creating equality within the political arm of the Populist movement. Though ultimately African Americans gained little power within the farmer movement, the black Alliances paved the way for future black organizations concerned with civil rights in the twentieth century.

Within the Alliance organizations, women played a key role. From the beginning, female members possessed full voting privileges and many women served as officers and lectured throughout the country. One Alliance lecturer, Mary Elizabeth Lease, became famous for advising farmers "to raise less corn, and more hell." Lease's belligerent example to the contrary, most Alliance women emphasized issues like temperance which particularly concerned many women. Similar to their urban counterparts, female reformers saw sobriety as the answer to many social problems in rural areas. From their perspective, farmers should have raised more corn, and consumed less corn mash.

Building on the example of the Granger laws, Alliance organizations also turned toward the political arena to redress their grievances. Combining their efforts in 1889, the Southern and Northwestern Alliances agreed to a loose merger when the state organizations of Kansas and South and North Dakota agreed to enter the Southern Alliance (renamed the National Farmer's Alliance and Industrial Union). With a renewed national organization, farmer politicians set their sights on influencing national politics. Unlike the Grangers, Alliance-inspired politics extended beyond the traditional political parties to create their own viable reform party.

Early attempts to organize farmers around a political platform enjoyed modest success. At a national convention meeting in Ocala, Florida in 1890, the Alliance groups issued the first version of their political demands. Political success quickly followed on the heels of the Ocala convention. In the off-year elections of 1890, Alliance-supported candidates (a separate farmer's party would not emerge until 1892) won some measure of control in twelve state legislatures and captured six governorships, three seats in the U.S. Senate, and approximately fifty representatives in the U.S. House. The voices of American farmers now had some say in Washington, but the 1890 victories were just a glimmer of what was to come.

Buoyed by their success in 1890, farmer politicians looked to consolidate their forces and make a meaningful impact in the presidential election year of 1892. They believed that to accomplish their goals, they could no longer work within the Democratic or Republican party structures. A new political party was needed that focused specifically on the problems affecting American agriculture. Officially organized in Cincinnati in May 1891, the farmer-led People's Party of the U.S.A. anxiously awaited its coming-out party to be held the next summer. On July 2, 1892, in the middle of the American heartland at Omaha, Nebraska, the farmer's party made its grand entrance onto the national political stage. Known widely as the Populist party—because its political philosophy catered to common people—the People's Party wasted little time in advertising its message to the American public. Unlike the existing parties—which seemed bent on maintaining power through political patronage and pandering to the lowest political denominators—the Populists presented a platform calling for radical change in American economic and social life. As the primary document of American populism, the Omaha platform captured the Populist vision of a reconstructed society that was more equitable for farmers and working people. In attacking the existing political system, Populist leaders turned to the language of republicanism that the founders had directed toward the British monarchy more than a century before. The preamble to the Omaha platform set the scene: "We meet in the midst of a nation brought to the very verge of moral, political and material ruin. Corruption dominates the ballot-box, the legislature, the Congress, and touches even the ermine of the bench. . . . Business prostrated, homes are covered with mortgages, labor is impoverished, and the land is concentrating in the hands of capitalists. . . . The fruits of the toil of millions are boldly stolen to build up colossal fortunes for a few. . . . We have witnessed for more than a quarter of a century the struggles of the two great parties for power and plunder. . . . Neither do they now promise us any substantial reform. . . . They propose to sacrifice our homes, lives and children on the altar of mammon." The republican spirit was far from dead. In fact, it had spawned a second revolution, centered in the heartland and focused on reforming American politics.

The changes demanded by the People's Party platform addressed the grievances of American farmers. Monopoly, the banking system, and increasing debt had long afflicted the agricultural sector, and Populists proposed creative (if ultimately unworkable) solutions. To create a more elastic money supply, they called for the free coinage of silver at the ratio of 16 to 1. National bank notes were to be abolished in favor of a national currency issued by the federal government only. The amount of money in circulation was pegged at not less than $50 per capita. A sub-treasury system that held farmer's crops in government-sponsored silos until they could fetch an adequate market price sought to alleviate a farmer's dependence on the fluctuations of the market economy. Further changes included the radical call for government ownership and operation of all transportation and communication lines including railroads, telegraphs, and telephones. Additionally, the government would return all unused land that had been granted to railroad companies and alien ownership of land would be outlawed. A graduated income tax, creation of postal savings banks, immigration restrictions, and an eight-hour day for industrial laborers promised massive changes in the relationship between the people and the government. Proposed changes in the political process included the direct election of U.S. Senators (they had previously been appointed by state legislatures), the adoption of the secret ballot, and the creation of referendum and initiative reforms which would give voters greater control over the legislative process. This represented a revolutionary call to political arms.

Though populists intended to reform American capitalism, they were not socialists. They held an abiding belief in cooperation but understood that human nature was also competitive. Populists did not seek to destroy capitalism but they did design a major overhaul of the economic and industrial system. Neither socialist nor capitalist completely, farmer-politicians were democrats who wanted to see political power returned to average Americans in local areas. This was the core of their vision. In the 1892 election, Americans were presented with a new alternative to politics as they knew it. It was up to voters to decide if the Populist vision would become a reality.

Results from the 1892 election proved that Populism had a future: presidential candidate James B. Weaver garnered more than a million popular votes and won several western states; three Senators and eleven representatives were also elected from the People's Party. Though successful on one level, the election likewise demonstrated that Populist ideas had not penetrated the major population centers of the Northeast. Weaver failed to gain more than five percent of the vote in any of the states east of the Mississippi River and north of the Ohio River. If they were ever to win a national presidential election, the Populists would have to find a candidate and a platform that could appeal to voters throughout the nation. Though Populism had a strong lock on rural voters, it would fail without support from the urban working class.

Four years later, Populists still faced the difficult task of attracting urban voters. When the Democratic party nominated thirty-six year old William Jennings Bryan—a Nebraskan sympathetic to Populist issues—and called for the free and unlimited coinage of silver, the People's Party faced a dilemma. If they chose a candidate to oppose Bryan, they ran the risk of fracturing support for their monetary policies. If they chose to back Bryan, they increased their chances at national election but would lose their party identity in the process. After great debate, Populists chose to support Bryan and "fusion" with the Democratic party. Though Bryan campaigned vigorously (the "Boy Orator of the Platte" delivered over 600 speeches during a 14-week campaign trip), he was unable to overcome the deep pockets and business connections of the Republican candidate William McKinley. When Bryan came up short on election day (he, too, failed to carry any northeastern states), the People's Party was effectively dead. Their gamble with democratic fusion had fizzled. Though the party limped on for several more elections, no Populist candidate ever posed a threat to the established parties.

While the Populist party might have been in tatters at the end of the nineteenth century, Populist ideas continued to influence political thought well into the twentieth century. Many of the reforms passed during the Progressive era—including graduated income tax, direct election of Senators, initiative, referendum, and recall, the creation of the Federal Reserve System, and railroad regulation, among others—had their genesis in Populist thought. Recognizing that the American political system drastically needed reform, the Populists offered a humane, rational alternative to competitive capitalism. Though their cooperative techniques never fully caught on, their ideas for political reform continue to impact American politics today.

Farmers were not the only American workers facing difficulties in the last decades of the nineteenth century. The mechanization of industry and the movement toward mass production changed industrial worker's lives just as they had transformed farming. The skilled workers who had once formed the backbone of American industry found themselves replaced by unskilled workers (often immigrants) operating machines. The culture surrounding skilled work—a generally convivial atmosphere where workers maintained some control over production because they were difficult to replace—eroded as machines replaced skilled men (there were few skilled women workers) in the production process. Coupled with a large labor surplus caused by increasing immigration, the mechanization of industry meant fewer positions for skilled laborers and lower wages.

American factories were often brutal, dirty, and dangerous. Most factory laborers worked ten hours a day, six days a week; in the steelmaking industry, 84-hour work weeks were not unusual. Each year, industrial accidents maimed or killed hundreds of thousands of workers. Without insurance or a government-sponsored safety net, injured workers had to rely on their families for support. Seasonal unemployment also posed a problem as many industries remained open only part of the year; the unemployed, like the injured, had no unemployment benefits to fall back on and were often left destitute. If lucky enough to have a steady job that did not destroy his or her body, working conditions often numbed a worker's mind. Performing repetitive tasks for a long period of time (one worker in a shoe factory nailed on nearly 5000 heels per day) required little skill and even less imagination. For all of this, the average worker in an industrial factory received $400 to $500 a year, below the $600 that was necessary to provide a reasonable level of comfort.

The prospects for industrial workers during the Gilded Age were not altogether gloomy, however. Between 1870 and 1890, workers wages rose 10% while the consumer price index actually fell. Workers, therefore, could buy more with their incomes. This economic reality, however, offered cold comfort to workers who looked at the lavish lifestyles of industrial titans and wondered why their back-breaking work had earned a fortune for someone else. If we are the ones creating the wealth, workers asked, why shouldn't we get to keep more of it?

In addressing their grievances, workers—like farmers—shifted away from competitive capitalism and promoted cooperation among themselves. One laborer, like one farmer, could do little to change the economic system that was exacting such a heavy toll; together, however, a combination of workers might gain some control over the production process. To acquire the volume of a collective voice, American workers turned to labor unions and collective bargaining to remedy economic and social problems. Along the way, however, workers articulated an alternate vision of American society that was largely based in the vision of the republic's founders. A quest for democracy, freedom, and equality composed labor's battle cry.

In the decades after mid-century, with industrialization proceeding apace throughout urban areas, labor unions coalesced around two diverging methods of organization. "Industrial" unions invited all laborers to join, regardless of skill status. Because workers in an integrated economy were intrinsically connected (for example, railroad workers transported industrial goods made by factory workers), organizers believed that they could increase their bargaining leverage by involving all workers in their cause. The Knights of Labor typified nineteenth-century industrial unions; the Industrial Workers of the World was a twentieth-century counterpart. Other unions, most notably the American Federation of Labor, organized "craft" unions. Membership in craft unions was limited to skilled workers like carpenters, cigar makers, and iron workers. Because skilled workers could not be easily replaced, they held a particular advantage in negotiating with business owners. Unionists of both types were seeking to redefine the employer-employee relationship by giving workers the power of collective action.

The first inklings of a cooperative labor organization emerged just after the Civil War. In 1866, William H. Sylvis organized the National Labor Union as a reform organization which demanded an eight-hour day, the abolition of slums, and the establishment of producers' cooperatives. According to the preamble to the constitution of the National Union of Iron Molders, workers sought to realize the republican dream of economic independence and freedom from servile masters: "What position are we, the Mechanics of America to hold in Society? Are we to receive an equivalent for our labor sufficient to maintain us in comparative independence and respectability, to procure the means with which to educate our children . . . or must we be forced to bow the suppliant knee to wealth, and earn by unprofitable toil a life too void of solace to confirm the very chains that bind us to our doom?"[4] Though suffused with republican rhetoric, Sylvis's labor union did not preach equality. Excluding women workers—union leaders contended that women drove labor prices down by competing with men for jobs—the NLU was designed as a loose federation of autonomous societies, many of which were scarcely connected to labor issues. Relying heavily on Sylvis for leadership, the group, which numbered 640,000 members at its apex, could not survive his death in 1869. Though short-lived, the NLU played an important role in preparing the way for future labor organizations which would learn from Sylvis's mistakes.

Building on the limited success of the NLU, the next labor group to organize—the Knights of Labor in 1869—admitted virtually any worker to their society. Adhering to industrial unionism, only lawyers, bankers, stock brokers, liquor dealers, and professional gamblers were barred from admittance. Even members of management were invited—though few felt welcome enough to join. Skilled and unskilled, black and white, members of this inclusive labor union were, as they wrote, combining "to secure to the toilers a proper share of the wealth they create." To obtain a fair portion for American workers, the Knights worked for the eight-hour day, abolition of child labor, and the settlement of industrial disputes through arbitration rather than strikes. In addition, cooperative stores and factories gave workers a share in the profits of mass production. The strength of the Knights increased dramatically in the 1880s after several labor disputes were resolved in their favor. Victories in an 1884 uprising against the Union Pacific Railroad and a strike against Jay Gould's Wabash Railroad the next year proved a boon to the organization. Membership peaked in 1886 at approximately 700,000. But just as quickly as they ascended, the Knights fell on hard times. When the colorful union leader Terrence V. Powderly refused to support new strikes against railroads and Chicago meatpackers, the union's membership deserted. By 1890, only 100,000 Knights remained.

Despite the union's meteoric rise and fall, the union offered American workers a vision of cooperative capitalism that portrayed Knights as the heirs of the nation's founders. George McNeill, a Knights' leader in Boston, wondered "whether this grand republic, born and baptized in blood, should go down at last in red and fiery flame, or whether, when it had served its purpose to humanity, it should simply go down like the golden glory of the setting sun, full of hope and promise of a brighter and grander day." Ultimately, according to this union leader, "the success or failure of the republican experiment rests with us."[5] The Knights' ideology promised an alternative to the economic domination of industrial leaders. Knights celebrated the contributions of working men and women and helped forge a working-class culture through dances, balls, newspapers, and other public displays of solidarity. Membership in the Knights of Labor provided workers with cultural and economic choices. Knights learned that through cooperation and collective bargaining, all industrial workers could improve their positions in society.

The American Federation of Labor, organized as a coalition of autonomous craft unions in 1881, brought entirely new methods to the struggle between labor and capital. Renouncing the Knights' approach of a single labor organization that represented every worker, AFL members were mainly skilled workers. As a rule, the union generally refused to organize unskilled workers who did not fit into the craft-based structure of the organization. Under the leadership of former cigar maker Samuel Gompers, the AFL rejected most cooperative economic schemes and focused on the instrumentality of collective bargaining. Accepting the basic premises of capitalism, AFL leadership simply tried to insure that working people received their share of industrial profits. In the main, the AFL followed the tenets of "bread and butter" unionism in demanding better wages, better hours, better working conditions, and the right to organize. Theirs was no cooperative scheme to create a more equitable economy; rather, through collective bargaining or strikes when necessary, the AFL would secure a fair share for skilled workers. Unskilled workers were left to fend for themselves. Though less expansive than the Knights in their labor ideology, the AFL offered skilled workers the opportunity to level the playing field in relation to company owners.

The growing antagonism between industrial leaders and labor unions regularly erupted into violent clashes that pitted workers against the combined power of capitalists and the state. Two major incidents in the 1890s—strikes in Homestead, Pennsylvania and Pullman, Illinois—exemplified the rift between labor and capital that threatened to rend the social fabric of the nation.

At the Carnegie Steel Co. plant in Homestead, skilled laborers belonging to the Amalgamated Association of Iron and Steel Workers walked off the plant floor in July 1892 to protest a series of wages cuts proposed by company management. When Carnegie's second-in-command, Henry Clay Frick, chose not to negotiate with the union any further, the animosity between the two sides was tempered like the rock-hard steel that was once the pride of Homestead. Frick fanned the flames of dispute by arranging for 300 Pinkerton detectives to protect the non-union workers hired by the Carnegie company. When, on July 6, the Pinkertons attempted to float into the plant by way of the Monongahela River, strikers poured oil on the water and set it ablaze. Armed with guns and dynamite, the strikers and detectives waged a day-long battle which resulted in seven deaths. Eventually, the detectives fled. For a time, it looked as though the strikers' tactics might have worked; one week later, however, Governor Robert Pattison of Pennsylvania, under pressure from the company and many of his constituents, ordered 8000 state militia members to impose order in Homestead. Faced with such an overwhelming show of state power, the strikers offered little resistance. Quickly, order was restored as the militia protected the non-union workers manning the plant. In the long run, organized labor lost more than a strike at Homestead. When Russian-born anarchist Alexander Berkman nearly killed Frick in a botched assassination attempt, public opinion turned sharply against the strikers. Labor unions were hard enough for most Americans to accept. When labor appeared to be allied with anarchism, the public agreed with Frick in calling for the end of the union. In a letter to Carnegie (who had been on a Scottish holiday during the uprising), Frick wrote, "We had to teach our employees a lesson, and we have taught them one that they will never forget." Indeed, both steelworkers and the American public remembered the lessons of Homestead for many years—if not forever, as Frick speculated. Tainted with a reputation for anarchy, steel workers would not form an effective labor union until the 1930s.

The combination of industrial power and state authority played a key role in another strike during the decade, this one at Pullman in 1894. The town of Pullman, Illinois had been designed as a model industrial town that would house workers who manufactured railroad sleeping and parlor cars for the Pullman Palace Car Company. In literature distributed by the company, the town was decorated with "bright beds of flowers and green velvety stretches of lawn" and "shaded with trees and dotted with parks and pretty water vistas and . . . artistic sweeps of landscape gardening." Moreover, the city's surroundings were thought to bring workers and owners closer because the city contained "the helpful combination of Capital and Labor without strife or stratification, upon the lines of mutual recognition."[6] Under the surface beauty of Pullman, however, things were not so placid. When, from September 1893 to May 1894, Pullman Company officials slashed wages between 25 and 40 percent, workers grew restless. Agitation increased when the company was unwilling to lower rent prices in its company housing, which were already higher than comparable accommodations in surrounding areas. In June 1894, the workers left their jobs and persuaded Eugene V. Debs, leader of the American Railway Union, to support their cause by refusing to handle any Pullman car or equipment along the railways. Within days, transportation between Chicago and the West Coast was paralyzed as thousands of railroad workers in twenty-seven states joined a sympathy boycott to support the Pullman workers. The familiar lines had been drawn once again. "The struggle with the Pullman Company," Debs wrote, "has developed into a contest between the producing classes and the money power of the country. We stand upon the ground that the workingmen are entitled to a just proportion of the proceeds of their labor."

When Pullman officials appealed to Illinois Governor John Peter Altgeld, a politician sympathetic to workers, he refused to dispatch the state militia to protect the company's assets. Stymied on the state level, railroad executives approached the federal government where they found politicians more amenable to their solution. Arguing that the stoppage of the U.S. mail aboard the railroad cars violated federal law, U.S. Attorney General Richard Olney, a former railroad lawyer, ordered 2,000 federal troops to Chicago and a federal court issued an injunction forbidding the strike to continue. Backed by the protection of federal troops—and with union leaders like Debs in jail—new workers were hired and the strike collapsed. Once again, the powers of business leaders and the state had combined to crush labor's rising fortunes.

A variety of factors limited both American farmers and laborers in their quest for a more equal society. First, the increasing economic and political power of industry meant that organizations of farmers and workers would face nearly insurmountable odds in attempting to reform the system. Second, the close relationship between business and government allowed business leaders to direct the legislative and military policies of both state and federal governments. Opposing an industry-government alliance required more firepower than Populists and labor unions could muster. Third, the entrenched two-party system foreclosed almost any opportunity for a successful third party to emerge on the national level. If Populists could have attracted more workers to their political cause, the story might have a different ending. Unable to gain urban support, however, the Populists were doomed. Finally, the veneration of laissez-faire capitalism by most Americans made any attempt to revise industrial capitalism extremely suspect. A drastic change in the system would have destroyed an ideological belief held very closely by Americans of all economic stations. That, in the end, would prove the most difficult obstacle.

Populism and unionism were stark examples of the power of common people to raise their collective voice and change American society. Social and economic modifications might have been slow in coming—

Populist ideas would not be implemented until the progressive era while labor unions remained weak until the 1930s—but they eventually made a major impact on American life. In the end, both of the popular movements offered alternate visions to the culture of laissez-faire embraced by industrial and political leaders in the years after the Civil War. In revising the republican vision that was the bedrock of American society, agrarian and labor reformers hoped to create a new "city on a hill," a haven of economic and political equality that would survive the storms of an industrial age. Though they came up short, future reformers would pick up and implement many of their ideas in the twentieth century.

Suggestions for Further Reading:

Brands, H.W. *The Reckless Decade: America in the 1890s.* (St. Martin's Press, 1995).

Clanton, Gene. *Populism: The Humane Preference in America.* (Twayne, 1991).

Goodwyn, Lawrence. *Democratic Promise: The Populist Moment in America.* (Oxford University Press, 1976.)

Hofstadter, Richard. *The Age of Reform.* (Random House, 1955).

McMath, Robert. *American Populism: A Social History.* (Farrar, Straus, & Giroux, 1993).

Montgomery, David. *The Fall of the House of Labor: The Workplace, the State, and American Labor Activism, 1865–1925.* (Cambridge University Press, 1987).

Painter, Nell Irwin. *Standing at Armageddon: The United States, 1877–1919.* (W.W. Norton, 1987).

Notes

[1] Vincent P. DeSantis, *The Shaping of Modern America: 1877–1916* (Arlington Heights, Illinois: The Forum Press, Inc., 1973), 57–58.

[2] Lawrence Goodwyn, *Democratic Promise: The Populist Moment in America* (New York: Oxford University Press, 1976), xv.

[3] Ibid., 301.

[4] Quoted in David Montgomery, "William H. Sylvis and the Search for Working-Class Citizenship," 9, in Melvyn Dubofsky and Warren Van Tine, eds., *Labor Leaders in America* (Urbana: University of Illinois Press, 1987).

[5] Quoted in Jama Lazerow, "Power and Respectability: The Knights of Labor," 244–245, in Eileen Boris and Nelson Lichtenstein, eds., *Major Problems in the History of American Workers* (Lexington, MA: D.C. Heath and Company, 1991). Lazerow's article originally appeared as "The Workingman's Hour:

The Knights of Labor in 1886," *Labor History* 21 (Spring 1980): 200–215, 217–220.

[6] H.W. Brands, *The Reckless Decade: America in the 1890s* (New York: St. Martin's Press, 1995), 147.

THE PROGRESSIVE STRUGGLE TO REFORM THE AMERICAN DEMOCRATIC REPUBLIC

Thomas G. Alexander
Department of History

In founding the American Republic, the revolutionaries had rejected the British Constitution in part because they disagreed with Parliament's interpretation of civil rights and rule of law. By the time of the American Revolution, Britain had become a constitutional monarchy governed by a decidedly undemocratic Parliament. The aristocrats selected for Parliament did not have to reside in the district they represented, and in the British view, members represented the people in the American colonies as well. Moreover, the British assumed the constitutionality of any law Parliament passed.

Americans regarded this British view called "virtual representation" as errant nonsense. Americans believed that members of Congress and of state legislatures had to live in the districts they represented, and they had to run for office frequently. Unlike Britain where only a few of the elite enjoyed the franchise, in the more democratic American system, most men could vote, and frequent elections allowed the voters to reelect those representatives who shared their convictions and to remove those who did not.

Just as the Americans believed that the British system with a limited franchise and minority rule offered insufficient protection for individual liberty, they also understood that willful majorities could abuse powerless minorities. Recognizing both tendencies, Thomas Jefferson wrote in the Declaration of Independence of self-evident natural rights. By implication, legislatures, whether aristocratic or democratic, committed a crime against nature and reason when they abridged such rights.

Later, James Madison and his colleagues embodied in the Constitution and Bill of Rights certain liberties to protect citizens against abusive governments. Moreover, Madison believed that the size and diversity of the republic itself offered an additional protection against potentially abusive factions. In the Tenth Federalist Paper Madison argued that by spreading the republic over a large area, factions would diffuse themselves so that none could form a bloc powerful enough to restrict the liberties of the people.

By the late nineteenth century, however, many Americans had become convinced that powerful minority factions had indeed ravished the rights of the majority. In their view, such basic constitutional rights as majority representation and the protection of liberty had become meaningless because well-financed minorities, especially business monopolies and political bosses, had so captured the reigns of power that the lives, liberties, and property of middle and working class people hung in jeopardy.

Various people saw the causes of these abuses and their solution from different vantage points. Some observers like Herbert Croly believed that the problem had resulted from the perversion of the system envisioned by the founders and they wanted to use governmental power to restore democracy.[1] Others like Charles Beard believed that the founders had purposely drafted the Constitution to protect wealthy minorities.[2] Whatever the reason for the imbalance, many observers believed that the remedy for the existing problems lay in passing and enforcing corrective legislation and amending the state and federal constitution to restore the reigns of government to the hands of the majority.

In the late 19th century people who called themselves Populists sought to counteract minority abuse and majority impotence. A social, economic, and political movement of farmers and miners, Populism reached its greatest influence between 1892 and 1896. Encapsulating Populist outrage, Mary E. Lease charged that "Wall Street owns the country. . . . The great common people of the country are slaves, and monopoly is the master."[3]

Most Populists believed that railroads, banks, industrialists—in short large business corporations—had sucked the lifeblood out of American communities. In their view, railroads charged farmers and small businesses exorbitant freight rates. Monopolies controlled the supply and price of beef, sugar, and kerosene, which people used for lighting. Organizing to counteract these forces, the Populists lobbied with state legislatures and Congress for laws to restrict monopoly power.

As the Populist movement gained support in rural and mining areas, working class and middle class people in cities and towns, who began to call themselves Progressives, shared similar outrage over the political and economic power of abusive individuals and organizations. Some historians see Populism and Progressivism as closely related to one another. Others see Progressivism as a different—ordinarily urban—phenomenon.[4]

Whatever its source, we generally call those who worked for the return of power to the majority "Progressives," and we generally date the Progressive Era from the 1890s to about 1920. *In general, we can define the Progressives as those citizens who tried to restore democracy as envisioned by the founders by using governmental power to protect the majority from abuse by powerful and well-financed minorities.*

One of the most articulate Progressives, Herbert Croly, published his views in *The Promise of American Life* (1909). Croly argued that the enemies of effective democracy "the [political] 'Boss' and the 'tainted' millionaire" had managed to corrupt the American democratic republic by perverting the philosophies of *laissez faire* and individualism.[5]

As a corrective, Croly called on the nation to restore the balance by using vigorous governmental action. "In reviving the practice of vigorous national action for the achievement of a national purpose," Croly wrote, "the better reformers have . . . been looking in the direction of a much more trustworthy and serviceable political principal [than individualism and governmental non-interference]. . . . [This view] implies the rejection of a large part of the Jeffersonian creed, and a renewed attempt to establish in its place the popularity of its Hamiltonian rival. On the other hand, it involves no less surely the transformation of [elitist] Hamiltonianism into a thoroughly democratic political principle."[6]

How, in the view of the Progressives, had these powerful minorities managed to gain so much power? In large part, the privileged status against which Lease preached and Croly wrote resulted from the protection provided to wealthy and well-connected minorities by state and federal courts, American presidents, city officials, and state governors. In the case of the courts, protection for the privileged relied, in part, on the insinuation into the American legal and political system of two philosophies.

The first of these, *laissez faire,* both Lease and Croly thought outmoded. Advocates understood *laissez faire* to mean that government could provide subsidies and protection to business, but that it must leave property owners and company managers free to treat the public and their employees as they thought appropriate.

The second philosophy was the brand of Social Darwinism espoused by English philosopher Herbert Spencer and Yale sociologist William

Graham Sumner. Social Darwinism relied on the concept of "survival of the fittest." The phrase originated with Spencer, not with Charles Darwin as is often supposed. Spencer and Sumner argued that the most able people claw their way to the top.[7] By doing so, they improved society. Moreover, they said, society could only damage itself by assisting the poor or abused. As tobacco entrepreneur James Buchanan Duke put it, let buffalo gore buffalo, and the pasture belong to the stronger.

Taking the lead from Spencer and Sumner, in the late nineteenth century, the United States Supreme Court grafted these two notions into the due process clauses of the Fifth and Fourteenth Amendments to the U S Constitution. By accomplishing this feat, activist judges thwarted many of the efforts of the Congress and state legislatures to pass laws to protect firms, consumers, and employees from the exploitive actions of powerful businesses.

Judicial activism had played a part in the American court system at least since the Chief Justiceship of John Marshall. Nevertheless, in the early republic, the courts had generally held that the due process clause protected those accused of crimes from arbitrary punishment and those with vested rights from the confiscation of property without equitable compensation. With these exceptions, as long as legislatures passed laws with general applicability, the state could regulate business.

In the late nineteenth century the courts began to offer greater protection from legislative action to powerful businesses. As the courts engrafted *laissez faire* and Social Darwinism into the Fifth and Fourteenth Amendments, the judges began to limit severely the authority of state legislatures and Congress to establish rules to prevent the ravishing of one business by another or of employees by their employers.[8]

We see examples of the engrafting of Spencerian views into the due process clauses in a number of cases. For instance, the New York state legislature passed a law designed to protect the health of bakers. Bakers labored in the heat, damp, and dust, and the members of the legislature hoped to mitigate the injury from such unhealthy surroundings by limiting their hours of work to ten per day or sixty per week.

The U S Supreme Court disagreed. In a 5 to 4 decision, written by Justice Rufus Wheeler Packham, in the case of *Lochner v. New York* (1905), the court struck down the law as a deprivation of life, liberty, and property without due process.

Recognizing that the majority decision owed more to Social Darwinism and *laissez faire* than to the founders, Associate Justice Oliver

Wendell Holmes wrote a ringing dissent. In patent outrage, Holmes wrote that "This case, is decided upon an economic theory which a large part of the country does not entertain. . . . The 14th Amendment does not enact Mr. Herbert Spencer's Social Statics. . . ." Moreover, he wrote, "a Constitution is not intended to embody a particular economic theory, whether of paternalism . . . or of *laissez faire.* It is made for people of fundamentally differing views, and the accident of finding certain opinions natural and familiar, or novel and even shocking, ought not to conclude our judgment on the question whether statutes embodying them conflict with the Constitution of the United States."[9]

In some cases, state governors or the president of the United States, imbued with Social Darwinist or *laissez faire* notions, combined with the courts to prevent workers from taking the initiative to bargain with their employers over wages and working conditions. The Homestead lockout offers an example.[10]

In the late 1880s, a number of steel manufacturers began to install open-hearth furnaces in their plants. Efficient and easier to operate than previous systems, these furnaces allowed some firms like the Carnegie Steel Company at Homestead, Pennsylvania to reduce their reliance on skilled workers such as those belonging to the Amalgamated Iron and Steel Workers Union. With the new furnaces in place, in 1892 Andrew Carnegie and his plant manager, Henry Clay Frick, used governmental assistance to help break the union, increase hours, and decrease wages.

As an opening step, Frick announced a wage cut, at the same time ordering the plant employees to increase production. When the steel workers balked, he began locking them out of the plant, and on July 2, 1892 he fired all 3,800 Homestead plant workers.

The discharged employees took over the town of Homestead and organized an advisory committee which directed the labor action, and they tried to negotiate with Frick. Refusing to talk with the workers, Frick responded by hiring 300 armed Pinkerton detectives to force the former employees to leave the plant and town and to escort in strikebreakers to take their jobs. Arriving at Homestead by barge on July 6, 1892, the Pinkertons attacked 10,000 angry workers, many of them carrying weapons. In the battle that followed, nine workers and seven Pinkertons died. The local sheriff, who sided with Frick and Carnegie, could not find enough sympathetic local citizens to deputize in order to put down the workers, so he appealed to Pennsylvania Governor William Stone for help.

Stone ordered 8,000 state militiamen to Homestead. The armed militiamen drove out the former employees and protected the incoming strikebreakers, who reopened the plant on Frick's terms. A triumphant Carnegie lengthened hours and reduced wages. These actions increased production, the company's profits, and Carnegie's wealth. In sentencing the leading workers to jail, Pennsylvania Judge Edward Paxson denied that they had any stake in their jobs except those granted by their employer. By their attempts to negotiate with Frick, he insisted, they were interfering with the rights of others.

Similarly, in the Pullman strike of 1894 President Grover Cleveland used both the U S Army and the courts to prevent workers from negotiating with their employers. George Pullman, president of the Pullman Palace Car Company, owned a company town outside Chicago in which he rented houses to many of the employees. In 1893, the United States began to sink into a severe depression. Unemployment reached 20 percent of the nation's labor force. Since the company's income declined, Pullman prudently laid off a third of his workers and cut the wages of the rest by 30 percent. In spite of the wage cuts and the decline in prices, he refused to reduce the price of food in the company store or to lower the rent that his workers paid for houses in the company town.

Protesting Pullman's actions, the employees tried to negotiate with the company. When the company refused, they went out on strike. In support of the Pullman strike, the American Railway Union began to detach Pullman sleeping cars from the trains they operated. Recognizing this as a dispute between Pullman and the workers, ARU officials said that they had no quarrel with the federal government, and that they would not interfere with the mails. Moreover, Illinois Governor John Peter Altgeld, who thought Pullman should negotiate with his workers, said that the strikers were quite orderly and that state did not need federal assistance to protect property or prevent loss of life.

Ignoring the union statements, Altgeld's protest, and the provision in Article 4, Section 4 of the constitution which required an application of a state governor to protect a state "against domestic Violence," President Grover Cleveland intervened. On the pretext of protecting mail shipments and interstate commerce (which were legitimate federal responsibilities), Cleveland ordered Attorney General Richard Olney, a former railroad attorney, to secure an injunction against the ARU and its president Eugene V. Debs. When the union defied the injunction by continuing to disconnect Pullman cars, Cleveland sent federal troops to operate the railroads.

Calling out the army led to violence and death. In place of an orderly work stoppage, rioting and clashes between the strikers and the troops led to the killing of thirty-four people. After a period of conflict, the army broke the strike and a federal judge sentenced Debs to six months in jail for defying the injunction.

Conflicts such as those at Homestead and Pullman and the conditions of work in a number of businesses led Progressives to lobby with Congress and the state legislatures to protect the workers. The laws did not go as far as to require employers to bargain with their employees, but they did change the bargaining rules. During the nineteenth century, some employers fought union organization by circulating blacklists of employees who favored unions, some required employees to sign yellow dog contracts in which the workers promised not to join a labor union as a condition of employment.

Under the constitution, Congress could not legislate on purely intrastate matters, but it could pass laws regulating interstate commerce. In an attempt to prevent blacklisting and yellow dog contracts, Congress outlawed such practices in the Erdman Railroad Act of 1898.

Given the antagonism against workers, the prevailing philosophy of *laissez faire,* and the privileged position of corporations, the courts refused to countenance these restrictions. In *Adair v. United States (*1908) the court ruled that the anti-yellow dog provision of the Erdman Act violated the due process clause of the Fifth Amendment by impairing the freedom of contracts.[11]

By viewing the laws through lenses shaped by *laissez faire* and Social Darwinism, the court said that the rules themselves violated due process. In this and other cases, the courts adopted what legal scholars call "substantive due process." Under this theory, legislatures could not simply establish rules for employees and employers to follow in labor negotiations. Rather, the courts said, the legislation itself denied due process by limiting the businesses' and the workers' freedom of contract.[12]

Instead of attacking the theory of substantive due process directly, Progressives mounted a flanking attack by showing that such items as unhealthy working conditions, dangerous goods, and unethical services warranted corrective action. Under Progressive pressure, both state legislatures and Congress set up commissions to investigate such matters and recommend legislation. Using these studies, the legislators passed some laws designed to correct abuses; and progressive lawyers cited the studies to support legal action. Changes took place most rapidly in the states. Following sociological and economic studies, a number of states required the inspection of underground mines, ordered employers to correct conditions dangerous to the lives and health of employees, and limited the hours of work in dangerous occupations. Some states passed minimum wage laws for women. Some required employers to carry insurance against industrial accidents.

In spite of decisions like *Lochner,* the Progressives gathered sufficient evidence of unsafe and unhealthy working conditions that the courts ignored *laissez faire a*nd Social Darwinism in some cases. In most of these cases, the courts found the conditions dangerous enough that they approved the restrictions as reasonable limitations on freedom of contract.

The state of Utah, for instance, tried to protect the lives of miners from accidents caused by fatigue by prohibiting them from working more than eight hours per day. The law had the support of workers' organizations and also of prominent mine owners like Thomas Kearns. Recognizing mining as an extremely dangerous occupation, courts upheld the statute in *Holden v. Hardy* (1898) as a reasonable restriction on freedom of contract.[12]

Many business leaders and workers supported the changes that led to state workers' accident insurance laws, generally called workers' compensation. In an age in which most companies carried no health insurance, injured workers often needed money immediately to pay for treating serious injuries. The common law assumed that workers recognized and accepted the dangers of high-risk occupations like underground mining or heavy manufacturing, and only under the most extreme employer negligence could they or their families collect damages for an accident which crippled or killed them. Nevertheless, some employers feared for their own liability in such cases; others sympathized with injured workers. In general, workers' compensation laws severely limited the workers' right to sue in return for guaranteed compensation following work-related injuries. By 1915 some 30 states had enacted such legislation.

In 1917, the Supreme Court upheld these workers' compensation laws. Justice Mahlon Pitney, writing for the court, said that such laws were "evidently . . . intended as a just settlement of a difficult problem, affecting one of the most important of social relations." Thus, he and the court's majority considered worker's compensation laws reasonable restrictions on freedom of contract.[13]

Just as some Progressives worried about workers' health, many agitated for laws to help women. Many Progressives demanded laws to shield mothers and the pregnant, to shelter those employed in dangerous occupations, and to grant political rights to women.

Much of this pressure for reform came from women organized in clubs. In the late nineteenth century, a large number of middle class women formed clubs to study literature, the theatre, and the arts.[14] In order to coordinate the activities of these clubs, in 1890 a group of national women's leaders organized the General Federation of Womens Clubs. In many states, women followed suit by organizing state federations of womens clubs. As Progressive sentiment gained popularity, many of these club women broadened their interests from literature and the arts to civics, health, and education.

In addition to organizing clubs, some middle class women established settlement houses to try to meet the needs of urban working classes and immigrants. In 1889, Vida Scudder and her associates organized the College Settlement in New York and Jane Addams and Ellen Gates Starr set up Hull House in Chicago. The opportunity to work in settlement houses attracted women like Florence Kelley, Lillian Wald, and Mary Brewster. The settlement houses sponsored nurseries, milk stations, and other services; and they offered classes on household management, the arts, political science, and other topics.

In addition, like the women's clubs, the settlement houses served as rallying centers for women who favored various types of Progressive reform. For instance, in an effort to promote the interests of labor and to protect consumers from predatory businesses, in 1899 Florence Kelley led out in the organization of the National Consumers' League. The league campaigned for consumer causes, for laws to require employers to provide a safe and healthy workplace, for minimum wages for women, and for the protection of children.

Beginning with an 1893 Illinois law that limited the hours of work for women in factories to eight per day, various states began passing legislation to protect working women. A 1903 Oregon law limited the employment of women in factories and laundries to ten hours per day. When laundryman Curt Muller challenged the constitutionality of the law, Kelley hired Louis Brandeis, a prominent public interest attorney from Kentucky, to represent the workers. Citing sociological and economic studies to show the reasonableness of such laws, Brandeis filed a path-breaking brief with the Supreme Court. Containing only two pages of legal precedents, Brandeis's brief included more than a hundred pages of citations from investigations of working and health conditions. These studies, Brandeis argued, showed that excessive work endangered the health of mothers—indeed of all women. Convinced by Brandeis's evidence, the court approved the Oregon statute as a reasonable limitation on freedom of contract.[15]

Increasingly, club and settlement house women turned their attention to such concerns as poverty, school systems, child abuse, urban government, water systems, living conditions, air pollution, street paving, and sewer systems. In many cases, the women justified these activities as urban housekeeping—an extension of their role as wives and mothers. How could parents, they asked, raise healthy, educated children if their towns lacked pure water, garbage collection, efficient sewers, good schools, or effective governments? What if copper smelters, coal-burning trains, or badly-tended home furnaces polluted the air and infected people with respiratory diseases?

In addition, many people began to question the inequity of allowing men to vote and hold office while denying the same rights to half the people. In 1869 and 1870, Wyoming and Utah territories gave women the vote. By 1914, Idaho, Colorado, California, Oregon, Kansas, Arizona, Nevada, and Montana joined Wyoming and Utah. Not satisfied with such gains, Susan B. Anthony and Carrie Chapman Catt led a campaign for woman suffrage through a national constitutional amendment. The Progressive Party endorsed the amendment in its 1912 platform, and the Democratic Party supported the proposal in 1916. Not until 1919, however, did Congress approve the amendment. The states ratified it in August 1920, shortly before the presidential election.

As women sought political rights and greater protection in the workplace, various Americans sought similar rights for minorities such as immigrants and African-Americans. In spite of the promises of the 13th, 14th, and 15th amendments, African-Americans found themselves generally discriminated against in voting and educational opportunities throughout the south and in access to white color and management jobs throughout the nation. The Supreme Court had tacitly endorsed such discrimination by approving the principle of separate but equal in its 1896 *Plessy v. Ferguson* decision.[16]

Some black leaders like Booker T. Washington, a former slave and the founder of Alabama's Tuskegee Institute, publicly urged blacks to accept their segregated condition, while working behind the scenes for greater acceptance and equality. Shortly after his inauguration as President, Theodore Roosevelt created a furor throughout the south by inviting Washington to lunch at the White House.

Other black leaders declined to accept second class status. W. E. B. Du Bois, Massachusetts-born and German-educated with a Ph. D. from Harvard, led a group that in 1909 organized the National Association for the Advancement of Colored People (NAACP). During the Progressive Era, blacks organized boycotts in the south against segregated public utilities and banks. During the same period, many African-Americans moved to northern cities in the expectation of better working conditions and higher pay.

Still, African-Americans made few gains during the Progressive Era. In various cities, race riots—attacks on black neighborhoods by armed whites—took place. After his inauguration as president in 1913, Woodrow Wilson actually resegregated a number of previously desegregated executive departments, in an effort to placate southerners.[17]

In spite of the abuse of immigrants and African-Americans, living conditions improved for working class and middle-class Euro-Americans. As men and women became increasingly concerned about the quality of life, they complained successfully about the inadequacy of city services. In a number of cases, Progressives attributed these deficiencies to urban bosses who catered to powerful businesses. Those with power often paid dearly in bribes, thinly described as campaign contributions, for street car, gas, and electric franchises.

In an attempt to prevent such abuses, many of the Progressives lobbied for non-partisan governments that operated on business-like principles. In many cases, they took their pleas to state legislatures which passed laws allowing the cities to set up commission or city manager governments.

Those who favored the commission system saw the city as analogous to a business corporation. The voters elected a full time governing body usually made up of five commissioners. Like business managers, each of the commission members supervised several departments. The Commissioner of Public Safety, for instance, might manage the police and fire departments. The Commissioner of Municipal Services might manage garbage collection and the water and sewage facilities. By 1911 nineteen states had given their cities authority to govern through city commissions, and cities like Galveston and Dallas Texas; Des Moines, Iowa; Memphis, Tennessee; and Salt Lake City, Utah had adopted the commission system.[18]

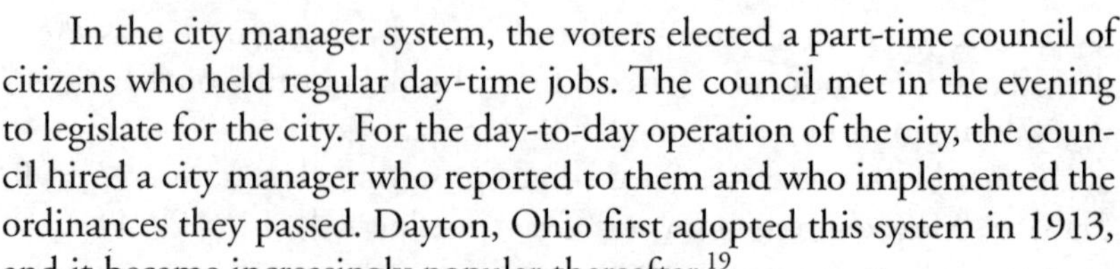

In the city manager system, the voters elected a part-time council of citizens who held regular day-time jobs. The council met in the evening to legislate for the city. For the day-to-day operation of the city, the council hired a city manager who reported to them and who implemented the ordinances they passed. Dayton, Ohio first adopted this system in 1913, and it became increasingly popular thereafter.[19]

Just as some Progressives worked to improve conditions in the cities, others tried to reform the states. Because of their political and economic clout, railroad corporations, which were among the largest firms in the United States, managed to convince legislators to hold their tax rates below those of other taxpayers. In return, the railroads gave free passes and generous campaign contributions. Since property taxes constituted the major sources of revenue in most states, these levies fell most heavily on farmers, business people, and homeowners with little political clout.

As the fastest form of transportation, many of the railroads held virtual monopolies. Before the general availability of trucks, wagons—an extremely expensive and slow form of transportation—offered an unattractive alternative. People could ship on canals and river boats in areas blessed with abundant water. Unfortunately, many areas lacked the water, and boats moved at a relatively slower rate. For some goods, a lengthy but relatively less expensive haul seemed an attractive alternative. Nevertheless, railroads generally delivered perishable goods to market more rapidly than boats.

Scandalized by the favoritism shown railroads and other utility monopolies, Progressives lobbied for property assessments at fair market value and for the regulation of the rates they charged the public. Some governors took up the Progressive cause. These included Robert M. LaFollette in Wisconsin, Charles Evans Hughes in New York, Woodrow Wilson in New Jersey, Albert E. Cummings in Iowa, William U'Ren in Oregon, Hiram Johnson in California, Joseph Folk in Missouri, James K. Vardaman in Mississippi, and Simon Bamberger in Utah. Progressive legislatures began to enact laws to regulate utilities and to assess their property on the same basis as other businesses.[20]

Between 1903 and 1917 most states established public utilities commissions to regulate monopolies such as railroads, electric utilities, natural gas companies, and telephone companies. Most of the laws permitted the commissions to investigate such matters as the actual value of the company's property, the cost of services, pricing practices, and rates of return. With that information, the commissions tried to set equitable utility rates.

States also enacted other Progressive measures as well. Some states passed laws regulating stock sales. Generally called blue sky laws, these laws attempted to protect people from the misrepresentation of the value of securities. Others regulated or prohibited child labor. Some passed laws regulating campaign contributions.

As Progressives in the cities and the states agitated for laws to restore democracy and to regulate monopolies, they also began to lobby for similar legislation on the national level. Congress passed much of the legislation after Theodore Roosevelt, generally acknowledged as the first of the Progressive presidents, took office. Son of a prominent New York family, Roosevelt had served as New York City police commissioner and assistant secretary of the Navy before leading a cavalry unit in the Spanish American War. After returning from the war, he won election as governor of New York. In 1900 Roosevelt won the Republican nomination for the vice presidency. The assassination of William McKinley propelled him into the White House in September 1901.

Fundamentally conservative, Roosevelt did not oppose large business organizations. Nevertheless, finding it difficult to stomach the abuses of wealth he distinguished those he considered evil from those he thought angelic. He earned the reputation as a "trust buster" largely because of his vigorous prosecution of a few monopolies such as the Northern Securities Company.

A holding company organized by J. P. Morgan, the Northern Securities Co. controlled virtually all railroad traffic west of Chicago. McKinley had contemplated a suit to break up the monopoly before his assassination, and in 1902, Roosevelt ordered Attorney General Philander C. Knox to do so. Entering a suit under the Sherman Anti-trust Act of 1890, Knox forced the dissolution of the monopoly. Between 1902 and the end of his second term in 1909, Roosevelt instituted 44 antitrust suits.

In contrast with the attitude of despotic employers like Carnegie, Pullman, and Frick, and with their political supporters like Cleveland, Olney, and Stone, Roosevelt believed that enlightened businessmen should negotiate with reasonable employees.[21] Early in his administration he used the presidency to support that view. In May 1902, more than 50,000 anthracite coal miners led by John F. Mitchell struck for higher wages, an eight hour day, and union recognition. Resisting negotiation, the coal mine owners led by George F. Baer of the Reading Railroad, issued a statement in which they claimed that God had given them the right to control of the property of the nation.

Unwilling to negotiate, the owners closed down the mines, and they called on the state and federal authorities to drive out the strikers as Cleveland had done in the Pullman Strike. After investigating conditions and waiting for a possible compromise, Roosevelt called a meeting of the owners and workers at the White House on October 3, 1902. At the meeting Mitchell emphasized his willingness to negotiate or to accept arbitration of the dispute. Baer and the owners, by contrast, called the workers "outlaws," and they renewed their demand that Roosevelt call out the troops to break the strike. They also demanded that he apply to the courts for an injunction to stop the workers' interference with interstate commerce.

Affronted by the intransigence of the owners, Roosevelt took matters into his own hands. He first considered calling out the army, not to break the strike as Baer had hoped, but to operate the mines. After consulting with advisors like Knox and Secretary of War Elihu Root, Roosevelt tried to settle the conflict with the help of Pennsylvania Senators Matthew Quay and Boies Penrose and New York Senators Benjamin B. Odell and Orville H. Platt.

When that failed, he turned to America's top financier, J. P. Morgan. Morgan interceded with the mine owners, and a second conference at the White House on October 13 led to an agreement that the miners would go back to work. The owners reluctantly agreed to accept the miners' request to appoint an arbitration commission to negotiate a resolution of the dispute. The commission's report of March 1903 led to a 10 percent wage increase and some reduction of hours, but not to union recognition.

Through the power of the presidency, Roosevelt had helped settle the dispute while establishing a precedent for making the industrial system more democratic. Instead of calling out the troops to break the strike like Stone or Cleveland, Roosevelt offered both the owners and the workers what he called a "square deal." Far from accepting the divine right of property as asserted by George Baer, Roosevelt believed that both workers and owners had an interest in the outcome of the negotiations. Moreover, although no laws governed the situation, Roosevelt recognized that the public had an interest as well in promoting industrial peace by recognizing the concerns of all parties to the dispute.

In addition to instituting suits against abusive monopolies and promoting negotiations between employees and employers, Roosevelt worked with Congress to pass legislation to regulate business practices. The Elkins Act (1903) prohibited rebates to privileged shippers. The Hepburn Act (1906) authorized the Interstate Commerce Commission to set reasonable railroad rates. The Pure Food and Drug Act (1906) prohibited the manufacture and sale of adulterated food and drugs; and the Meat Inspection Act (1906) provided for the federal inspection of packing plants and the enforcement of sanitary conditions.

Advocate of a strenuous life and owner of a ranch in South Dakota, Roosevelt became increasingly alarmed over the destruction of natural resources. Responding to his initiative, in 1905, Congress established the Forest Service to manage public timber set aside in national forests. Roosevelt also organized the 1908 White House Conference on Conservation which called attention to the need for the prudent use of natural resources, and he set up the National Conservation Commission which began an inventory of these resources.

An astute politician, Roosevelt seems to have intuited how far the public supported him and how far he could push Congress. By contrast, Roosevelt's hand-picked successor, William Howard Taft, lacked his political astuteness. Though Taft instituted twice as many anti-trust suits during his four year term as Roosevelt did in the seven years from 1902 to 1908, and he secured the passage of the Mann-Elkins and Physical Valuation Acts which provided further regulation of railroads and other public utilities, he offended the Progressives by failing to support even lower taxes on imported goods than those of the Payne-Aldrich Tariff Act of 1909. Taft also outraged Progressives by firing Chief Forester Gifford Pinchot after Pinchot became entangled in a dispute over conservation with Secretary of the Interior Richard A. Ballinger.

Enraged over Taft's actions, Progressive Republicans under the leadership of Senators Robert M. LaFollette of Wisconsin and Jonathan Bourne of Oregon organized the National Progressive Republican League in 1911. LaFollette hoped to run for president in 1912, but Roosevelt undermined his candidacy by entering the campaign himself.

With Roosevelt on the stump, the 1912 Presidential campaign became a national referendum on Progressive principles. By controlling the June 1912 Republican National Convention, Taft's supporters excluded virtually all pro-Roosevelt delegates. After the convention nominated Taft, Roosevelt's partisans met to organize the Progressive Party and to nominate him for the presidency. After considerable infighting, the Democratic Party nominated New Jersey Governor and former Princeton University president, Woodrow Wilson, for the presidency.

Most observers wrote off Taft's candidacy as the forlorn hope of a defeated man, and for the first time in American history one of the principal candidates for the presidency represented a third party. Wilson won the election, Roosevelt came in second, and Taft pulled in a distant third.

As Progressives, Roosevelt and Wilson agreed on a great deal, but they differed in their views about large corporations. Promoting the Jeffersonian ideal of a nation of independent producers, Wilson believed that human liberty stood in jeopardy as long as "industrial masters" anointed themselves as "Guardians" of the interests of the American people.[22] To promote democracy, he favored the breakup of all large monopolies. Roosevelt, on the other hand, recognized the value of large industrial combinations. Instead of simply breaking them up, he favored the regulation of "good" monopolies in the public interest.[23]

After his inauguration, Wilson worked with Congress to enact a program that seemed like a compromise between the Democratic and Progressive platforms. With Wilson's support, Congress reduced the tariff and enacted a graduated income tax. Taking a tough stand against monopoly, Wilson supported the Clayton Antitrust Act which defined practices such as interlocking directorates and exclusive tie-in contracts as sufficient evidence of restraint of trade. At the same time he supported the Federal Trade Commission Act which established an independent commission to investigate the activities of large businesses, and to determine whether they had engaged in conspiracies in restraint of trade. The FTC seemed much more like a Rooseveltian effort to determine the reasonableness of corporate activities than a Jeffersonian measure designed to break up all gigantic firms.

Wilson also supported a number of other Progressive measures, many of which found extensive support in the business community. In an attempt to provide more effective regulation of the nation's money supply, the administration supported the organization of the Federal Reserve System in 1913. Wilson also supported the Adamson law limiting hours of work on railroads and the Keating-Owens Child Labor Act of 1916 which barred from interstate commerce the products of the labor of children.

Using *laissez faire* and Social Darwinist principles, the Supreme Court declared the child labor act unconstitutional in 1918. In a 5 to 4 ruling written by Justice William R. Day, the court struck down the law because it prohibited rather than regulated the interstate transportation of the fruits of child labor. Day crafted this argument, although the court had allowed Congress to outlaw the interstate transportation of lottery tickets, adulterated food, and prostitutes. The court majority seems to have considered the lives and health of children less precious than the peoples' stomachs and personal morality.

Beyond such pieces of business regulation, Progressives also tried to refashion political institutions to make them more democratic. In some cases, such efforts led to the amendment of the state and federal constitutions. Many states adopted the initiative, which allowed people to petition for laws and to adopt them by direct vote; the referendum, which allowed a legislature to direct the people vote on a piece of legislation; and the recall, which authorized the public to vote on the retention of an official previously elected to office.

Congress also adopted amendments to expand democratic rule. As previously noted, the nation adopted the woman suffrage amendment in 1920. Progressives hoped to lessen the clout of powerful interests by approving the 17th Amendment which provided for direct election of senators instead of their election by members of the state legislatures. Progressives also tried to shift a greater burden of taxation to those most able to afford to pay by adopting the 16th amendment which authorized taxes on incomes and inheritances. The 18th amendment inaugurated prohibition, which was designed to improve society by eliminating the consumption of alcohol.

With these surveys of the motivation and the changes authorized by Progressives, we can ask how the principles and actions of the Progressive Era relate to America's founding? Some Progressives like Croly and Roosevelt intended to use Hamiltonian means to achieve Jeffersonian ends. Others like Wilson and William Jennings Bryan hoped to restore the Jeffersonian republic. Whatever their persuasion, virtually all Progressives, believed that the American democratic republic had evolved into something quite foreign to that envisioned by the founders. Instead of guaranteeing majority rule while protecting minority rights, it had vested inordinate power in well-financed minorities. Thus, we should understand that some of the most significant amendments to the constitutions of the states and the federal government and the laws passed by Congress and the state legislatures were crafted—however inexpertly—to extend the power of working class and middle class people and to restrict the power of the wealthy and privileged.

Some efforts succeeded, others did not. Women gained political power, but they tended to vote the same way men did, and the senators elected directly tended to come from the same social classes and to represent views similar to those elected by legislatures. Direct legislation like the initiative, referendum, and recall helped powerful interests who could mount effective campaigns as often as it did those who sought change to improve the condition of the abused. Although the income tax changed the source of revenue from the tariff on the federal level and property on the state level, the middle class still tended to pay a larger share of their income in taxes than did the very wealthy. Changes in urban governmental systems helped promote effective government in many cities, but we would have a difficult time proving the superiority of the commission or city manager systems over the mayor-council systems that they replaced. Anti-trust suits against a few monopolies did not reduce the movement toward combination, which still continues today. The Progressives did very little for minorities such as immigrants and African-Americans, and their condition may have actually deteriorated during the Wilson administration. The courts effectively thwarted a number of attempts to prohibit child labor. Herbert Hoover called Prohibition a "noble experiment," and it did curb the use of alcohol, but it also helped to promote criminal organizations, and it led many people to hold the law in contempt.

On the other hand, some of the Progressive measures did improve society. The Progressives generally improved city streets, water and sewer systems, garbage collection, and educational systems. They extended the vote to the half of the population that had been disfranchised since the founding. Regulation of the workplace tended to improve conditions for many workers, and workers' compensation helped employees to get more adequate treatment for injuries on the job. Federal and state pure food and meat inspection acts generally guaranteed safer and better quality foods. Regulation of public utilities tended to reduce the inequities for ratepayers, though in practice the utilities themselves often tended to take a greater interest in the activities of regulatory commissions than the general public did. The Federal Reserve System helped somewhat to stabilize the money supply, but did not allow the United States to avoid the Great Depression. Rather, changes in the system made during the 1930s have helped us to avoid another massive economic collapse. The regulation of lands by the Forest Service tended to facilitate the more careful use of public resources.

Overall, while the Progressives did make the American system more democratic, they failed in their efforts to improve society roughly as often as they succeeded. With all their successes, they failed to curb the power of abusive interests and to restore the sort of democratic republic envisioned by the founders.

Notes

1 Herbert Croly, *The Promise of American Life* ed. Arthur M. Schlesinger, Jr. (Cambridge: Belknap Press of Harvard University Press, 1965).

2 See Charles A. Beard, *An Economic Interpretation of the Constitution of the United States* (New York: Macmillan, 1961 [orig. ed. 1913), 152–188.

3 Cited in Steven J. Diner, *A Very Different Age: Americans of the Progressive Era* (New York: Hill and Wang, 1998), 14.

4 The earliest studies offering these contrasting views include: John D. Hicks, *The Populist Revolt* (Minneapolis, 1931) who sees Progressivism as a continuation of Populism, and Richard Hofstadter, *The Age of Reform: From Bryan to F. D. R.* (new York, 1955) who views it as an urban movement only slightly related to the Populists. For two more recent statements of the urban and rural views see: David Sarasohn, *The Party of Reform: Democrats in the Progressive Era* (Jackson: University Press of Mississippi, 1989) and Kevin Mattson, *Creating a Democratic Public: The Struggle for Urban Participatory Democracy During the Progressive Era* (University Park, PA: Pennsylvania State University Press, 1998).

5 Croly, *The Promise of American Life,* 148–49.

6 Croly, *The Promise of American Life,* 152–53.

7 See Herbert Spencer, *Social Statics, Together with Man Versus the State* (New York: D. Appleton, 1910) and William Graham Sumner, *What the Social Classes Owe to Each Other* (Caldwell, ID: Caxton, 1952. Sumner opposed protective tariffs, but many businessmen ignored his advice on that subject.

8 On these matters see *Smythe v. Ames* (196 U. S. 466 (1898), *Allgeyer v. Louisiana* 165 U.S. 578 (1897), and *Lochner v. New York* 198 U.S. 45 (1905).

9 Cited in Alfred H. Kelly & Winfred A. Harbison, *The American Constitution Its Origins and Development* (Third Edition; New York: W. W. Norton, 1963), 525.

10 The following discussion is based on Leon Wolff, *Lockout: The Story of the Homestead Strike of 1892* (New York, 1965) and shorter accounts in *The Reader's Companion to American History,* eds. Eric Foner and John A. Garraty (Boston: Houghton Mifflin, 1991), sv. Homestead Strike; and Steven J.

Diner, *A Very Different Age: Americans of the Progressive Era* (New York: Hill and Wang, 1998), 52-53 (which misdated the lockout as 1893).

[11] *Adair v. United States,* 208 U.S. 161 (1908).

[12] *Holden v. Hardy,* 169 U.S. 366 (1898).

[13] *New York Central Rail Road Company v. White* 238 U. S. 188 (1917).

[14] On the development of clubs see Karen J. Blair, *The Clubwoman as Feminist: True Womanhood Redefined,* 1868-1914 (New York: Holmes & Meier, 1980).

[15] *Muller v. Oregon* 208 U. S. 412 (1908).

[16] *Plessy v. Ferguson,* 163 U.S. 537 (1896).

[17] Arthur S. Link, *Woodrow Wilson and the Progressive Era, 1910–1917* (New York: Harper and Row, 1963 [orig. ed. 1954]), 63–65.

[18] Diner, *A Very Different Age,* 205–06.

[19] Diner, *A Very Different Age,* 206.

[20] This list of governors and states is based in part on Diner, *A Very Different Age,* 211–212.

[21] This discussion of the anthracite coal strike is based on George E. Mowry, *The Era of Theodore Roosevelt and the Birth of Modern America, 1900–1912* (New York: Harper and Row, 1962 [Orig. ed. 1958]), 134-138.

[22] Woodrow Wilson, *The New Freedom: A Call for the Emancipation of the Generous Energies of a People* ed. William E. Leuchtenburg (Englewood Cliffs, NJ: Prentice-Hall, 1961), 165.

[23] Theodore Roosevelt, *The New Nationalism* ed. William E. Leuchtenburg (Englewood Cliffs, NJ: Prentice Hall, 1961), 24–27, 34–37, 106–07.

[24] *Hammer v. Dagenhart,* 247 U.S. 251 (1918).

THE GREAT DEPRESSION AND THE NEW DEAL

Gary Daynes

The stock market crash in October of 1929 marked the beginning of the greatest economic breakdown in our nation's history. At the Depression's worst, unemployment reached as high as 25 percent, while one hundred eighty-five thousand businesses went bankrupt. Nearly four thousand banks had collapsed by 1932, and American farmers all over the country suffered the effects of overproduction and then of drought. Furthermore, city streets were flooded as thousands waited in bread lines or stood outside the local employment bureau. It was a sight never before seen in America, and one that caused many to doubt the reliability of democratic capitalism.

In their desperation, the American people demanded a change. Their demands were met with the 1932 presidential election of the Democrat Franklin Delano Roosevelt. Roosevelt was more than willing to implement change and promised to do so by way of "bold, persistent experimentation." Such experimentation came in the form of a number of federal government programs that, collectively, were known as the New Deal.

The New Deal was a legislative program more comprehensive than any in our history. It sought to bring the economy under control with the introduction of the National Recovery Administration (NRA). It attempted to improve the situation of the American farmer through the Agricultural Adjustment Administration (AAA). It offered hope to the unemployed by providing many with jobs and a modest salary by way of the Works Progress Administration (WPA). It established welfare programs such as social security so as to redistribute wealth more equally. And finally, it subscribed to Keynesian economics by resorting to deficit spending in order to prime the economic pump. In short, the New Deal embodied the progressive idea that strong government and strong governmental leadership were keys to solving the nation's ills.

The following selections are primary sources that help tell the story of the Depression and evaluate the strengths and weaknesses of the New Deal. The first, "Women on The Breadlines" by Meridel Le Seuer (1932), is an article in which Le Seuer, a journalist, described in detail the despair she encountered among unemployed women in Minneapolis in the early 1930s. As you read her report, notice the conditions in which women, and families in general, were forced to live. Also, consider the tone of the article as the author analyzed women's attitudes in dealing with contemporary struggles. What were some of their main concerns? What role do you think individuals, governments, and the market should play under such circumstances?

The next two selections are speeches given by Franklin D. Roosevelt. Using radio as a new medium of communication, Roosevelt proved a very effective speaker and was able to reach the common man directly in his own home. The first selection, "First Inaugural Address (1933)," was given when Roosevelt took office at the lowest point of the Depression. Here he set forth his general strategy for dealing with the crash of 1929. The second selection, another speech delivered over the radio, is referred to as "The Second Fireside Chat of 1934." In this selection FDR positively evaluated the first years' performance of certain New Deal programs, particularly those concerning industry and labor.

As you analyze both speeches, work to understand Roosevelt's views of the Federal Government. Also, pay attention to the references made in both speeches concerning fundamental principles of the founding and of the Constitution. Why, and in what ways does he reference such principles? How do you think the Founders would react to those references?

The fourth selection, "The New Deal and the Common Man (1934, 1936)," includes letters from middle and lower income Americans to either FDR or his wife Eleanor. Roosevelt and the New Deal proved especially popular among these classes, and the following letters help to explain why. What were the sources of this support and which New Deal programs in particular prompted letters such as these?

The remaining selections illustrate opposition to New Deal legislation. The first includes the eight principal aims of a movement known as "Share Our Wealth" in 1935. Huey Long, a member of the Senate, led the movement. At first, Long was a supporter of Roosevelt and the New Deal, but he soon broke with the President and began advocating a much more extreme position. For Senator Long, the solution to the Depression was to be found in granting the state virtually unlimited power to be used in guaranteeing a more equal distribution of wealth.

The next two articles, attacks from the right, illustrate a more conservative point of view. In the first, "The New Deal Is A Danger To Freedom (1936)," Hoover shows his support for the 1936 Republican presidential candidate by attempting to explain how the New Deal contradicts American principles of liberty and freedom. The final selection includes excerpts from "The Republican Party Platform" of 1936 wherein party members offer, as an alternative to New Deal legislation, a specific set of ideas "in defense of American institutions."

In analyzing these opposing views, consider the following: Why did Americans, unlike Europeans who faced similar circumstances in the early 1930's, reject extreme measures such as those presented by Huey Long? Why, and in what ways, do conservative republicans make reference to the principles of the American Founding? How do such references compare to those made by FDR? With whom do you think the Founders would agree and why? Why, in your opinion, did the Democratic Party win by such an overwhelming landslide in both the presidential race and in the Congress in 1936?

Meridel Le Sueur, Women on the Breadlines, 1932

I am sitting in the city free employment bureau. It's the woman's section. We have been sitting here now for four hours. We sit here every day, waiting for a job. There are no jobs. Most of us have had no breakfast. Some have had scant rations for over a year. Hunger makes a human being lapse into a state of lethargy, especially city hunger. Is there any place else in the world where a human being is supposed to go hungry amidst plenty without an outcry, without protest, where only the boldest steal or kill for bread, and the timid crawl the streets, hunger like the beak of a terrible bird at the vitals?

We sit looking at the floor. No one dares think of the coming winter. There are only a few more days of summer. Everyone is anxious to get work to lay up something for that long siege of bitter cold. But there is no work. Sitting in the room we all know it. That is why we don't talk much. We look at the floor dreading to see that knowledge in each other's eyes. There is a kind of humiliation in it. We look away from each other. We look at the floor. Its too terrible to see this animal terror in each other's eyes.

So we sit hour after hour, day after day, waiting for a job to come in. There are many women for a single job. A thin sharp woman sits inside the wire cage looking at the book. For four hours we have watched her looking at that book. She has a hard little eye. In the small bare room there are half a dozen women sitting on the benches waiting. Many come and go. Our faces are all familiar to each other, for we wait here everyday.

This is a domestic employment bureau. Most of the women who come here are middle aged, some have families, some raised their families and are now alone, some have men who are out of work. Hard times and the man leaves to hunt for work. He doesn't find it. He drifts on. The woman probably doesn't hear from him for a long time. She expects it. She isn't surprised. She struggles alone to feed the many mouths. Sometimes she gets help from the charities. If she's clever she can get herself a good living from the charities, if she's naturally a lick spittle, naturally a little docile and cunning. If she's proud then she starves silently, leaving her children to find work, coming home after a day's searching to wrestle with her house, her children.

Some such story is written on the faces of all these women. There are young girls too, fresh from the country. Some are made brazen too soon by the city. There is a great exodus of girls from the farms into the city now. Thousands of farms have been vacated completely in Minnesota. The girls are trying to get work. The prettier ones can get jobs in the stores when there are any, or waiting on tables but these jobs are only for the attractive and the adroit, the others, the real peasants have a more difficult time. . . .

Its one of the great mysteries of the city where women go when they are out of work and hungry. There are not many women in the bread line. There are no flop houses for women as there are for men, where a bed can be had for a quarter or less. You don't see women lying on the floor at the mission in the free flops. They obviously don't sleep in the jungle or under newspapers in the park. There is no law I suppose against their being in these places but the fact is they rarely are.

Yet there must be as many women out of jobs in cities and suffering extreme poverty as there are men. What happens to them? Where do they go? Try to get into the Y.W. without any money or looking down at heel. Charities take care of very few and only those that are called "deserving." The lone girl is under suspicion by the virgin women who dispense charity.

I've lived in cities for many months broke, without help, too timid to get in bread lines. I've known many women to live like this until they simply faint on the street from privations, without saying a word to anyone. A woman will shut herself up in a room until it is taken away from her, and eat a cracker a day and be as quiet as a mouse so there are no social statistics concerning her.

I don't know why it is, but a woman will do this unless she has dependents, will go for weeks, verging on starvation, crawling in some hole, going through the streets ashamed, sitting in libraries, parks, going for days without speaking to a living soul like some exiled beast, keeping the runs mended in her stockings, shut up in terror in her own misery, until she becomes too super sensitive and timid to even ask for a job.

Bernice says even strange men she has met in the park have sometimes, that is in better days, given her a loan to pay her room rent. She has always paid them back.

In the afternoon the young girls, to forget the hunger and the deathly torture and fear of being jobless, try and pick up a man to take them to a ten cent show. They never go to more expensive ones, but they can always find a man willing to spend a dime to have the company of a girl for the afternoon.

Sometimes a girl facing the night without shelter will approach a man for lodging. A woman always asks a man for help. Rarely another woman. I have known girls to sleep in men's rooms for the night, on a pallet without molestation, and given breakfast in the morning.

Its no wonder these young girls refuse to marry, refuse to rear children. They are like certain savage tribes, who, when they have been conquered refuse to breed.

Not one of them but looks forward to starvation, for the coming winter. We are in a jungle and know it. We are beaten, entrapped. There is no way out. Even if there were a job, even if that thin acrid woman came and gave everyone in the room a job for a few days, a few hours, at thirty cents an hour, this would all be repeated tomorrow, the next day and the next.

Not one of these women but knows, that despite years of labour there is only starvation, humiliation in front of them. . . .

So we sit in this room like cattle, waiting for a non-existent job, willing to work to the farthest atom of energy, unable to work, unable to get food and lodging, unable to bear children; here we must sit in this shame looking at the floor, worse than beasts at a slaughter.

It is appalling to think that these women sitting so listless in the room may work as hard as it is possible for a human being to work, may labour night and day, like Mrs. Gray wash street cars from midnight to dawn and offices in the early evening, scrubbing for fourteen and fifteen hours a day, sleeping only five hours or so, doing this their whole lives, and never earn one day of security, having always before them the pit of the future. The endless labour, the bending back, the water soaked hands, earning never more than a weeks wages, never having in their hands more life than that.

Its not the suffering, not birth, death, love that the young reject, but the suffering of endless labour without dream, eating the spare bread in bitterness, a slave without the security of a slave.

Franklin D. Roosevelt, First Inaugural Address, 1933

I am certain that my fellow Americans expect that on my induction into the Presidency I will address them with a candor and a decision which the present situation of our Nation impels. This is preeminently the time to speak the truth, the whole truth, frankly and boldly. Nor need we shrink from honestly facing conditions in our country to-day. This great Nation will endure as it has endured, will revive and will prosper. So, first of all, let me assert my firm belief that the only thing we have to fear is fear itself—nameless, unreasoning, unjustified terror which paralyzes needed efforts to convert retreat into advance. In every dark hour of our national life a leadership of frankness and vigor has met with that understanding and support of the people themselves which is essential to victory. I am convinced that you will again give the support to leadership in these critical days.

In such a spirit on my part and on yours we face our common difficulties. They concern, thank God, only material things. Values have shrunken to fantastic levels; taxes have risen; our ability to pay has fallen; government of all kinds is faced by serious curtailment of income; the means of exchange are frozen in the currents of trade, the withered leaves of industrial enterprise lie on every side; farmers find no markets for their produce; the savings of many years in thousands of families are gone.

More important, a host of unemployed citizens face the grim problem of existence, and an equally great number toil with little return. Only a foolish optimist can deny the dark realities of the moment.

Yet our distress comes from no failure of substance. We are stricken by no plague of locusts. Compared with the perils which our forefathers conquered because they believed and were not afraid, we have still much to be thankful for. Nature still offers her bounty and human efforts have multiplied it. Plenty is at our doorsteps, but a generous use of it languishes in the very sight of the supply. Primarily this is because the rulers of the exchange of mankind's goods have failed, through their own stubbornness and their own incompetence, have admitted their failure, and abdicated. Practices of the unscrupulous money changers stand indicted in the court of public opinion, rejected by the hearts and minds of men. . . .

Happiness lies not in the mere possession of money; it lies in the joy of achievement, in the thrill of creative effort. The joy and moral stimulation of work no longer must be forgotten in the mad chase of evanescent profits. These dark days will be worth all they cost us if they teach us that our true destiny is not to be ministered unto but to minister to ourselves and to our fellow men. . . .

Our greatest primary task is to put people to work. This is no unsolvable problem if we face it wisely and courageously. It can be accomplished in part by direct recruiting by the Government itself, treating the task as we would treat the emergency of a war, but at the same time, through this employment, accomplishing greatly needed projects to stimulate and reorganize the use of our natural resources.

Hand in hand with this we must frankly recognize the overbalance of population in our industrial centers and, by engaging on a national scale in a redistribution, endeavor to provide a better use of the land for those best fitted for the land. The task can be helped by definite efforts to raise the values of agricultural products and with this the power to purchase the output of our cities. It can be helped by preventing realistically the tragedy of the growing loss through foreclosure of our small homes and our farms. It can be helped by insistence that the Federal, State, and local governments act forthwith on the demand that their cost be drastically reduced. It can be helped by the unifying of relief activities which to-day are often scattered, uneconomical, and unequal. It can be helped by national planning for and supervision of all forms of transportation and of communications and other utilities which have a definitely public character. There are many ways in which it can be helped, but it can never be helped merely by talking about it. We must act and act quickly.

Finally, in our progress toward a resumption of work we require two safeguards against a return of the evils of the old order; there must be a strict supervision of all banking and credits and investments; there must be an end to speculation with other people's money, and there must be provision for an adequate but sound currency.

There are the lines of attack. I shall presently urge upon a new Congress in special session detailed measures for their fulfillment, and I shall seek the immediate assistance of the several States. Through this program of action we address ourselves to putting our own national house in order and making income balance outgo. . . .

In the field of world policy I would dedicate this Nation to the policy of the good neighbor—the neighbor who resolutely respects himself and, because he does so, respects the rights of others—the neighbor who respects his obligations and respects the sanctity of his agreements in and with a world of neighbors.

If I read the temper of our people correctly, we now realize as we have never realized before our interdependence on each other; that we can not merely take but we must give as well; that if we are to go forward, we must move as a trained and loyal army willing to sacrifice for the good of a common discipline, because without such discipline no progress is made, no leadership becomes effective. We are, I know, ready and willing to submit our lives and property to such discipline, because it makes possible a leadership which aims at a larger good. This I propose to offer, pledging that the larger purposes will bind upon us all as a sacred obligation with a unity of duty hitherto evoked only in time of armed strife.

With this pledge taken, I assume unhesitatingly the leadership of this great army of our people dedicated to a disciplined attack upon our common problems.

Action in this image and to this end is feasible under the form of government which we have inherited from our ancestors. Our Constitution is so simple and practical that it is possible always to meet extraordinary needs by changes in emphasis and arrangement without loss of essential form. That is why our constitutional system has proved itself the most superbly enduring political mechanism the modern world has produced. It has met every stress of vast expansion of territory, of foreign wars, of bitter internal strife, of world relations.

It is to be hoped that the normal balance of executive and legislative authority may be wholly adequate to meet the unprecedented task before us. But it may be that an unprecedented demand and need for undelayed action may call for temporary departure from that normal balance of public procedure.

I am prepared under my constitutional duty to recommend the measures that a stricken nation in the midst of a stricken world may require. These measures, or such other measures as the Congress may build out of its experience and wisdom, I shall seek, within my constitutional authority, to bring to speedy adoption.

But in the event that the Congress shall fail to take one of these two courses, and in the event that the national emergency is still critical, I shall not evade the clear course of duty that will then confront me. I shall ask the Congress for the one remaining instrument to meet the crisis—broad Executive power to wage a war against the emergency, as great as the power that would be given to me if we were in fact invaded by a foreign foe.

The Second Fireside Chat of 1934

Franklin Delano Roosevelt

Three months have passed since I talked with you shortly after the adjournment of the Congress. Tonight I continue that report, though, because of the shortness of time, I must defer a number of subjects to a later date.

Recently the most notable public questions that have concerned us all have had to do with industry and labor and with respect to these, certain developments have taken place which I consider of importance. I am happy to report that after years of uncertainty, culminating in the collapse of the spring of 1933, we are bringing order out of the old chaos with a greater certainty of the employment of labor at a reasonable wage and of more business at a fair profit. These governmental and industrial developments hold promise of new achievements for the Nation.

Men may differ as to the particular form of governmental activity with respect to industry and business, but nearly all are agreed that private enterprise in times such as these cannot be left without assistance and without reasonable safeguards lest it destroy not only itself but also our processes of civilization. The underlying necessity for such activity is indeed as strong now as it was years ago when Elihu Root said the following very significant words:

> Instead of the give and take of free individual contract, the tremendous power of organization has combined great aggregations of capital in enormous industrial establishments working through vast agencies of commerce and employing great masses of men in movements of production and transportation and trade, so great in the mass that each individual concerned in them is quite helpless by himself. The relations between the employer and the employed, between the owners of aggregated capital and the units of organized labor, between the small producer, the small trader, the consumer, and the great transporting and manufacturing and distributing agencies, all present new questions for the

> solution of which the old reliance upon the free action of individual wills appears quite inadequate. And in many directions, the intervention of that organized control which we call government seems necessary to produce the same result of justice and fight conduct which obtained through the attrition of individuals before the new conditions arose.

It was in this spirit thus described by Secretary Root that we approached our task of reviving private enterprise in March, 1933. Our first problem was, of course, the banking situation because, as you know, the banks had collapsed. Some banks could not be saved but the great majority of them, either through their own resources or with Government aid, have been restored to complete public confidence. This has given safety to millions of depositors in these banks. Closely following this great constructive effort we have, through various Federal agencies, saved debtors and creditors alike in many other fields of enterprise, such as loans on farm mortgages; loans to the railroads and insurance companies and, finally, help for home owners and industry itself.

In all of these efforts the Government has come to the assistance of business and with the full expectation that the money used to assist these enterprises will eventually be repaid. I believe it will be.

The second step we have taken in the restoration of normal business enterprise has been to clean up thoroughly unwholesome conditions in the field of investment. In this we have had assistance from many bankers and business men, most of whom recognize the past evils in the banking system, in the sale of securities, in the deliberate encouragement of stock gambling, in the sale of unsound mortgages and in many other ways in which the public lost billions of dollars. They saw that without changes in the policies and methods of investment there could be no recovery of public confidence in the security of savings. The country now enjoys the safety of bank savings under the new banking laws, the careful checking of new securities under the Securities Act and the curtailment of rank stock speculation through the Securities Exchange Act. I sincerely hope that as a result people will be discouraged in unhappy efforts to get rich quick by speculating in securities. The average person almost always loses. Only a very small minority of the people of this country believe in gambling as a substitute for the old philosophy of Benjamin Franklin that the way to wealth is through work.

In meeting the problems of industrial recovery the chief agency of the Government has been the National Recovery Administration [N.R.A.].

Under its Guidance, trades and industries covering over 90 percent of all industrial employees have adopted codes of fair competition, which have been approved by the President. Under these codes, in the industries covered, child labor has been eliminated. The work day and the work week have been shortened. Minimum wages have been established and other wages adjusted toward a rising standard of living. The emergency purpose of the N.R.A. was to put men to work and since its creation more than four million persons have been reemployed, in great part through the cooperation of American business brought about under the codes.

Benefits of the Industrial Recovery Program have come, not only to labor in the form of new jobs, in relief from overwork and in relief from underpay, but also to the owners and managers of industry because, together with a great increase in the payrolls, there has come a substantial rise in the total of industrial profits—a rise from a deficit figure in the first quarter of 1933 to a level of sustained profits within one year from the inauguration of N.R.A.

Now it should not be expected that even employed labor and capital would be completely satisfied with present conditions. Employed workers have not by any means all enjoyed a return to the earnings of prosperous times, although millions of hitherto underprivileged workers are today far better paid than ever before. Also, billions of dollars of invested capital have today a greater security of present and future earning power than before. This is because of the establishment of fair, competitive standards and because of relief from unfair competition in wage cutting which depresses markets and destroys purchasing power. But it is an undeniable fact that the restoration of other billions of sound investments to a reasonable earning power could not be brought about in one year. There is no magic formula, no economic panacea, which could simply revive overnight the heavy industries and the trades dependent upon them.

Nevertheless the gains of trade and industry, as a whole, have been substantial. In these gains and in the policies of the Administration there are assurances that hearten all forward-looking men and women with the confidence that we are definitely rebuilding our political and economic system on the lines laid down by the New Deal—lines which as I have so often made clear, are in complete accord with the underlying principles of orderly popular government which Americans have demanded since the white man first came to these shores. We count, in the future as in the past, on the driving power of individual initiative and the incentive of fair profit, strengthened with the acceptance of those obligations to the public interest which rest upon us all. We have the right to expect that this driving power will be given patriotically and whole-heartedly to our Nation. . . .

Closely allied to the N.R.A. is the program of public works provided for in the same Act and designed to put more men back to work, both directly on the public works themselves, and indirectly in the industries supplying the materials for these public works. To those who say that our expenditures for public works and other means for recovery are a waste that we cannot afford, I answer that no country, however rich, can afford the waste of its human resources. Demoralization caused by vast unemployment is our greatest extravagance. Morally, it is the greatest menace to our social order. Some people try to tell me that we must make up our minds that for the future we shall permanently have millions of unemployed just as other countries have had them for over a decade. What may be necessary for those countries is not my responsibility to determine. But as for this country, I stand or fall by my refusal to accept as a necessary condition of our future a permanent army of unemployed. On the contrary, we must make it a national principle that we will not tolerate a large army of unemployed and that we will arrange our national economy to end our present unemployment as soon as we can and then to take wise measures against its return. I do not want to think that it is the destiny of any American to remain permanently on relief rolls. . . .

In our efforts for recovery we have avoided, on the one hand, the theory that business should and must be taken over into an all-embracing Government. We have avoided, on the other hand, the equally untenable theory that it is an interference with liberty to offer reasonable help when private enterprise is in need of help. The course we have followed fits the American practice of Government, a practice of taking action step by step, or regulating only to meet concrete needs, a practice of courageous recognition of change. I believe with Abraham Lincoln, that "The legitimate object of Government is to do for a community of people whatever they need to have done but cannot do at all or cannot do so well for themselves in their separate and individual capacities."

I am not for a return to that definition of liberty under which for many years a free people were being gradually regimented into the service of the privileged few. I prefer and I am sure you prefer that broader definition of liberty under which we are moving forward to greater freedom, to greater security for the average man than he has ever known before in the history of America.

Letters Received by the First Lady and the President

Cedarburg, Wis.
10:45 a.m. Mar. 5,1934

Mrs. F. D. Roosevelt
Washington, D.C.

My dear Friend:

Just listened to the address given by your dear husband, our wonderful President. During the presidential campaign of 1932 we had in our home a darling little girl, three years old. My husband & I were great admirers of the Dem. candidate and so Dolores had to listen to much talk about the great man who we hoped and prayed would be our next Pres. We are Lutherans and she is Catholic so you'll get quite a thrill out of what I'm to tell you now. That fall Judge Karel of Mil. sent me a fine picture of our beloved President, which I placed in our Public Library. When I received this fine picture my dear mother (who has since been called Home) said to Dolores "Who is this man?" and Dolores answered without any hesitation "Why who else, but Saint Roosevelt!" The old saying goes fools and children often tell the truth and indeed we all feel if there ever was a Saint. He is one. As long as Pres. Roosevelt will be our leader under Jesus Christ we feel no fear. His speech this morning showed he feels for the "least of these" I am enclosing a snap shot of the dear little girl who acclaimed our President a Saint and rightly so.

I'm sure Pres. Roosevelt had a great day on Feb. 16, the world day of prayer, when many hearts were lifted in prayer for him all over this great land of ours.

We shall continue to ask our heavenly Father to guide and guard him in his great task as leader of the great American people.

With all good wishes for you and your fine family I am your most sincerely

Mrs. L.K.S.

Nov 25, 1934
Arkansas City, Kansas

Mrs. Eleanor Roosevelt
White House
Washington, D.C.

Dear Madam:

I beg to inform you that I have been reading your writings in the Wichita Beacon and I must say that the whole nation should be enthused over them. I especially was carried away with the one on Old Age Pensions. It brought my mind back to the day of the Chicago Convention, when Mr. Roosevelt was nominated for the presidency.

In our little home in Arkansas City, my family and I were sitting around the radio, to hear and we heard you when you flew over from N.Y. and entered the great hall and when he spoke it seems as though some Moses had come to alleviated us of our sufferings. Strange to say when he was speaking to see the moisten eyes and the deep feeling of emotions that gave vent to his every word and when you spoke then we knew that the white house would be filled with a real mother to the nation.

I am . . . glad to say . . . you have not failed us, you have visited the slums, the farms and homes of your people, and formed first handed ideas for their benefits. Oh what a blessing while you have always had a silver spoon in your own mouth you have not failed to try and place one in every mouth in the land and when I read in the Beacon your brilliant ideas of the Old Age Pensions. You said the only thing laking [sic] was the way to do it. So I said the first lady is seeking a way to help us and so let us help her to find it. . . .

Dear Madam, I am afraid to write more to you at this time as this is my first letter to the lady of the land as the others did not seem to be interested in the welfare of the people. Wife and I pray continually to God for your success. Every time the news boy hollers Extra our hearts are filled with fear that something has happened to the president, but as we go marching on to higher hills of prosperity through the new deal we are hoping and working to that point that all will be well. But one thing I was just about to forget I think that the home building program should be furnished means for back taxes included for repairs and etc. As many places are handicapped to get loans from government on account of being back taxes. Our heart in hand is ever with you and the Pres. to carry on.

Respectfuly Yours,
P.F.A. [male]

[Columbus, Ga.
October 24, 1934]

[Dear President Roosevelt:]

I hope you can spare the time for a few words from a cotton mill family, *out of work* and almost out of heart and in just a short while out of a house in which to live. you know of course that the realators are putting the people out when they cannot pay the rent promptly. and how are we to pay the rent so long as the mills refuse us work, merely because we had the nerve to ask or "demand," better working conditions.[1]

I realize *and* appreciate the aid and food which the government is giving to the poor people out of work *Thanks to you.*

but is it even partly right for us to be thrown out of our homes, when we have no chance whatever of paying, so long as the big corporations refuse of work. I for one am very disheartened *and* disappointed guess my notice to move will come next.

what are we to do. wont you try to help us wont you appeal, "for *us* all," to the real estate people and the factories

hoping you'll excuse this, but I've always thought of F.D.R. as my personal friend.

C.L.F. [male]

[Akron, Ohio
February 1936]

My Dear Mrs Roosevelt.[2]

I thought I would write a letter hoping you would find time to read it, and if you thought it was worth while answering it, I would be glad of any advise you would care to give me. A few weeks ago, I heard your talk over the air, on the subject of the Old age pension, and I got to thinking what a blessing it would be to my mother, if it was possible for her to receive that pension, if the bill should pass. My mother has been in this country since April 1914 but she has never made herself a American Citizen, as she was sixty years old when she came here, and now she is eighty. Mother come out to this country nineteen years ago [from Scotland][3]. . . .

I thought as long as I lived there was no need to worry about her being taken care of, but I never dreamed of a depression like we have had well it has changed the whole course of our lives we have suffered, and no one knowes but our own family, I have two children one nineteen, graduated from high school last June, and the girl graduates this coming June, and we have had the awfullest time trying to get the bare necessary things in life.

I am in no position to do the right thing for mother, I cant give her anything but her living but I thought if it was possible for her to get that pension it would be like a gift from heaven, as in all the years she has been in this country she has never had a dollar of her own.

I wish she could get it her days may not be long on this earth, and if she just had a little money coming once in a while, to make her feel independent of her family, I at least would know that if anything happened to me she could get a living, and not have to go back to the rest of her family, because she says she would rather go to a poor house, than live with any of the others.

Mrs Roosevelt you might think I have lots of nerve writing to you when you have so much to attend to but I could not help admiring you for the splended way you talked about the old people of this nation I feel sorry for all of them, they seem to be forgotten, and most young people think they have had there day and should be glad to die. but this is not my idea, I think that their last few years should be made as plesent for them as it is possible, I know that if it was in my power to make my mother happy by giving her what she justly deservs, I would gladly do so. Well whither my mother ever gets anything or not, I hope all the other old people that is intilted to it gets it soon, because there is nothing sadder than old people who have struggled hard all there lives to give there family a start in life, then to be forgotten, when they them self need it most.

I will finish now but befor I do I want to thank you Mrs Roosevelt and also Mr Roosevelt for the good both of you are doing for this country you have gave people new hope and every real American has faith in you and may you both be spared to carry on the good work and lead this nation on to victory.

Yours Respectfully,
Mrs J. S.
Akron, Ohio.

Notes

[1] This is a reference to the unsucessful 1934 textile workers' strike—Ed.

[2] Misspellings are part of the original letter—Ed.

[3] Eighteen years ago—Ed.

Huey Long, Share Our Wealth, 1935

Here is the whole sum and substance of the Share Our Wealth movement:

1. Every family to be furnished by the government a homestead allowance, free of debt, of not less than one-third the average family wealth of the country, which means, at the lowest, that every family shall have the reasonable comforts of life up to a value of from $5,000 to $6,000: No person to have a fortune of more than 100 to 300 times the average family fortune, which means that the limit to fortune is between $1,500,000 and 5,000,000, with annual capital levy taxes imposed on all above 1,000,000.
2. The yearly income of every family shall be not less than one-third of the average family income, which means that, according to the estimates of the statisticians of the U. S. Government and Wall Street, no family's annual income would be less than from $2,000 to $2,500: No yearly income shall be allowed to any person larger than from 100 to 300 times the size of the average family income, which means that no person would be allowed to earn in any year more than $600,000 to $1,800,000, all to be subject to present income tax laws.
3. To limit or regulate the hours of work to such an extent as to prevent over-production; the most modern and efficient machinery would be encouraged so that as much would be produced as possible so as to satisfy all demands of the people, but also to allow the maximum time to the workers for recreation, convenience, education, and luxuries of life.
4. An old age pension to the persons over 60.
5. To balance agricultural production with what can be consumed according to the laws of God, which includes the preserving and storing of surplus commodities to be paid for and held by the Government for emergencies when such are needed. Please bear in mind, however, that when the people of America have had money to buy things they needed, we have never had a surplus of

any commodity. This plan of God does not call for destroying any of the things raised to eat or wear, nor does it countenance whole destruction of hogs, cattle or milk.

6. To pay the veterans of our wars what we owe them and to care for their disabled.
7. Education and training for all children to be equal in opportunity in all schools, colleges, universities and other institutions for training in the professions and vocations of life; to be regulated on the capacity of children to learn, and not on the ability of parents to pay the costs. Training for life's work to be as much universal and thorough for all walks in life as has been the training in the arts of killing.
8. The raising of revenues and taxes for the support of this program to come from the reduction of swollen fortunes from the top, as well as for the support of public works to give employment whenever there may be any slackening necessary in private enterprise.

The New Deal Is a Danger to Freedom

Herbert Hoover

Through four years of experience this New Deal attack upon free institutions has emerged as the transcendent issue in America.

All the men who are seeking for mastery in the world today are using the same weapons. They sing the same songs. They all promise the joys of Elysium without effort.

But their philosophy is founded on the coercion and compulsory organization of men. True liberal government is founded on the emancipation of men. This is the issue upon which men are imprisoned and dying in Europe right now. . . .

Freedom does not die from frontal attack. It dies because men in power no longer believe in a system based upon liberty. . . .

I gave the warning against this philosophy of government four years ago from a heart heavy with anxiety for the future of our country. It was born from many years' experience of the forces moving in the world which would weaken the vitality of American freedom. It grew in four years of battle as President to uphold the banner of free men.

And that warning was based on sure ground from my knowledge of the ideas that Mr. Roosevelt and his bosom colleagues had covertly embraced despite the Democratic platform.

Those ideas were not new. Most of them had been urged upon me.

During my four years powerful groups thundered at the White House with these same ideas. Some were honest, some promising votes, most of them threatening reprisals, and all of them yelling "reactionary" at us.

I rejected the notion of great trade monopolies and price-fixing through codes. That could only stifle the little business man by regimenting him under the big brother. That idea was born of certain American Big Business and grew up to be the NRA.

I rejected the schemes of "economic planning" to regiment and coerce the farmer. That was born of a Roman despot 1,400 years ago and grew up into the AAA.

I refused national plans to put the government into business in competition with its citizens. That was born of Karl Marx.

I vetoed the idea of recovery through stupendous spending to prime the pump. That was born of a British professor.

I threw out attempts to centralize relief in Washington for politics and social experimentation. I defeated other plans to invade States' rights, to centralize power in Washington. Those ideas were born of American radicals.

I stopped attempts at currency inflation and repudiation of government obligation. That was robbery of insurance policy holders, savings bank depositors and wage-earners. That was born of the early Brain Trusters.

I rejected all these things because they would not only delay recovery but because I knew that in the end they would shackle free men.

Rejecting these ideas we Republicans had erected agencies of government which did start our country to prosperity without the loss of a single atom of American freedom. . . .

Our people did not recognize the gravity of the issue when I stated it four years ago. That is no wonder, for the day Mr. Roosevelt was elected recovery was in progress, the Constitution was untrampled, the integrity of the government and the institutions of freedom were intact.

It was not until after the election that the people began to awake. Then the realization of intended tinkering with the currency drove bank depositors into the panic that greeted Mr. Roosevelt's inauguration.

Recovery was set back for two years, and hysteria was used as the bridge to reach the goal of personal government.

I am proud to have carried the banner of free men to the last hour of the term my countrymen entrusted it to me. It matters nothing in the history of a race what happens to those who in their time have carried the banner of free men. What matters is that the battle shall go on.

The people know now the aims of this New Deal philosophy of government.

We propose instead leadership and authority in government within the moral and economic framework of the American System.

We propose to hold to the Constitutional safeguards of free men.

We propose to relieve men from fear, coercion and spite that are inevitable in personal government.

We propose to demobilize and decentralize all this spending upon which vast personal power is being built. We propose to amend the tax laws so as not to defeat free men and free enterprise.

We propose to turn the whole direction of this country toward liberty, not away from it.

The New Dealers say that all this that we propose is a worn-out system; that this machine age requires new measures for which we must sacrifice some part of the freedom of men. Men have lost their way with a confused idea that governments should run machines.

Man-made machines cannot be of more worth than men themselves. Free men made these machines. Only free spirits can master them to their proper use.

The relation of our government with all these questions is complicated and difficult. They rise into the very highest ranges of economics, statesmanship and morals.

And do not mistake. Free government is the most difficult of all government. But it is everlastingly true that the plain people will make fewer mistakes than any group of men no matter how powerful. But free government implies vigilant thinking and courageous living and self-reliance in a people.

Let me say to you that any measure which breaks our dikes of freedom will flood the land with misery.

Republican Party Platform, 1936

America is in peril. The welfare of American men and women and the future of our youth are at stake. We dedicate ourselves to the preservation of their political liberty, their individual opportunity and their character as free citizens, which today for the first time are threatened by Government itself.

For three long years the New Deal Administration has dishonored American traditions and flagrantly betrayed the pledges upon which the Democratic Party sought and received public support.

> The powers of Congress have been usurped by the President.
>
> The integrity and authority of the Supreme Court have been flouted.
>
> The rights and liberties of American citizens have been violated.
>
> Regulated monopoly has displaced free enterprise.
>
> The New Deal Administration constantly seeks to usurp the rights reserved to the States and to the people.
>
> It has insisted on the passage of laws contrary to the Constitution.
>
> It has intimidated witnesses and interfered with the right of petition.
>
> It has dishonored our country by repudiating its most sacred obligations.
>
> It has been guilty of frightful waste and extravagance, using public funds for partisan political purposes.
>
> It has promoted investigations to harass and intimidate American citizens, at the same time denying investigations into its own improper expenditures.

It has created a vast multitude of new offices, filled them with its favorites, set up a centralized bureaucracy, and sent out swarms of inspectors to harass our people.

It had bred fear and hesitation in commerce and industry, thus discouraging new enterprises, preventing employment and prolonging the depression.

It secretly has made tariff agreements with our foreign competitors, flooding our markets with foreign commodities.

It has coerced and intimidated voters by withholding relief from those opposing its tyrannical policies.

It has destroyed the morale of many of our people and made them dependent upon Government.

Appeals to passion and class prejudice have replaced reason and tolerance.

To a free people these actions are insufferable. This campaign cannot be waged on the traditional differences between the Republican and Democratic parties. The responsibility of this election transcends all previous political divisions. We invite all Americans, irrespective of party, to join us in defense of American institutions.

Constitutional Government and Free Enterprise

We Pledge Ourselves:

1. To maintain the American system of constitutional and local self government, and to resist all attempts to impair the authority of the Supreme Court of the United States, the final protector of the rights of our citizens against the arbitrary encroachments of the legislative and executive branches of Government. There can be no individual liberty without an independent judiciary.
2. To preserve the American system of free enterprise, private competition, and equality of opportunity, and to seek its constant betterment in the interests of all.

Reemployment

The only permanent solution of the unemployment problem is the absorption of the unemployed by industry and agriculture. To that end, we advocate:

Removal of restrictions on production.

Abandonment of all New Deal policies that raise production costs, increase the cost of living, and thereby restrict buying, reduce volume and prevent reemployment.

Encouragement instead of hindrance to legitimate business.

Withdrawal of Government from competition with private payrolls.

Elimination of unnecessary and hampering regulations.

Adoption of such policies as will furnish a chance for individual enterprise, industrial expansion, and the restoration of jobs.

Relief

The necessities of life must be provided for the needy, and hope must be restored pending recovery. The administration of relief is a major failure of the New Deal. It has been faithless to those who most deserve our sympathy. To end confusion, partisanship, waste and incompetence,

We Pledge

1. The return of responsibility for relief administration to non-political local agencies familiar with community problems.
2. Federal grants-in-aid to the States and Territories while the need exists, upon compliance with these conditions: (a) a fair proportion of the total relief burden to be provided from the revenues of States and local governments; (b) all engaged in relief administration to be selected on the basis of merit and fitness; (c) adequate provision to be made for the encouragement of those persons who are trying to become self-supporting.
3. Undertaking of Federal public works only on their merits and separate from the administration of relief.
4. A prompt determination of the facts concerning relief and unemployment.

Security

Real security will be possible only when our productive capacity is sufficient to furnish a decent standard of living for all American families and to provide a surplus for future needs and contingencies. For the attainment of that ultimate objective, we look to the energy, self-reliance and character of our people, and to our system of free enterprise.

Society has an obligation to promote the security of the people, by affording some measure of protection against involuntary unemployment and dependency in old age. The New Deal policies, while purporting to provide social security, have, in fact, endangered it.

We propose a system of old age security. . . .

We propose to encourage adoption by the States and Territories of honest and practical measures for meeting the problems of unemployment insurance.

The unemployment insurance and old age annuity sections of the present Social Security Act are unworkable and deny benefits to about two-thirds of our adult population, including professional men and women and all those engaged in agriculture and domestic service, and the self employed, while imposing heavy tax burdens upon all. The so-called reserve fund estimated at forty-seven billion dollars for old age insurance is no reserve at all, because the fund will contain nothing but the Government's promise to pay, while the taxes collected in the guise of premiums will be wasted by the Government in reckless and extravagant political schemes.

Labor

The welfare of labor rests upon increased production and the prevention of exploitation. We pledge ourselves to:

Protect the right of labor to organize and to bargain collectively through representatives of its own choosing without interference from any source.

Prevent governmental job holders from exercising autocratic powers over labor.

Support the adoption of State laws and interstate compacts to abolish sweatshops and child labor, and to protect women and children with respect to maximum hours, minimum wages and working conditions. We believe that this can be done within the Constitution as it now stands.

Agriculture

The farm problem is an economic and social, not a partisan problem, and we propose to treat it accordingly. . . .

Our paramount object is to protect and foster the family type of farm, traditional in American life, and to promote policies which will bring about an adjustment of agriculture to meet the needs of domestic and foreign markets. As an emergency measure, during the agricultural depression, Federal benefit payments or grants-in-aid when administered within the means of the Federal Government are consistent with a balanced budget.

We Propose

1. To facilitate economical production and increased consumption on a basis of abundance instead of scarcity.
2. A national land-use program, including the acquisition of abandoned and non-productive farm lands by voluntary sale or lease, subject to approval of the legislative and executive branches of the States concerned, and the devotion of such land to appropriate public use, such as watershed protection and flood prevention, reforestation, recreation, and conservation of wild life.
3. That an agricultural policy be pursued for the protection and restoration of the land resources, designed to bring about such a balance between soil-building and soil-depleting crops as will permanently insure productivity, with reasonable benefits to cooperating farmers on family-type farms, but so regulated as to eliminate the New Deal's destructive policy towards the dairy and live-stock industries.
4. To extend experimental aid to farmers developing new crops suited to our soil and climate. . . .

Regulation of Business

We recognize the existence of a field within which governmental regulation is desirable and salutary. The authority to regulate should be vested in an independent tribunal acting under clear and specific laws establishing definite standards. Their determinations on law and facts should be subject to review by the Courts. We favor Federal regulation, within the Constitution, of the marketing of securities to protect investors. We favor also Federal regulation of the interstate activities of public utilities. . . .

Government Finance

The New Deal Administration has been characterized by shameful waste and general financial irresponsibility. It has piled deficit upon deficit. It threatens national bankruptcy and the destruction through inflation of insurance policies and savings bank deposits.

We Pledge Ourselves to:

Stop the folly of uncontrolled spending.

Balance the budget—not by increasing taxes but by cutting expenditures, drastically and immediately.

Revise the Federal tax system and coordinate it with State and local tax systems.

Use the taxing power for raising revenue and not for punitive or political purposes.

Money and Banking

We advocate a sound currency to be preserved at all hazards.

The first requisite to a sound and stable currency is a balanced budget.

We oppose further devaluation of the dollar.

We will restore to the Congress the authority lodged with it by the Constitution to coin money and regulate the value thereof by repealing all the laws delegating this authority to the Executive.

We will cooperate with other countries toward stabilization of currencies as soon as we can do so with due regard for our national interests and as soon as other nations have sufficient stability to justify such action.

Conclusion

We assume the obligations and duties imposed upon Government by modern conditions. We affirm our unalterable conviction that, in the future as in the past, the fate of the nation will depend, not so much on the wisdom and power of Government, as on the character and virtue, self-reliance, industry and thrift of the people and on their willingness to meet the responsibilities essential to the preservation of a free society.

Finally, as our party affirmed in its first Platform in 1856: "Believing that the spirit of our institutions as well as the Constitution of our country guarantees liberty of conscience and equality of rights among our citizens, we oppose all legislation tending to impair them," and "we invite the affiliation and cooperation of the men of all parties, however differing from us in other respects, in support of the principles herein declared."

The acceptance of the nomination tendered by this Convention carries with it, as a matter of private honor and public faith, an undertaking by each candidate to be true to the principles and program herein set forth.

AMERICAN FOREIGN POLICY

Gary Daynes

At the core of American foreign policy is an idealistic assumption of American virtue. Each step in the ever-changing approach to outsiders stems from the basic belief that America has an ideal model of government and economic system and that the American system should be a model for the rest of the world.

In the early years of the nation, foreign policy was approached with the caution befitting a new, weak, and geographically isolated nation. President George Washington dedicated his 1796 Farewell Address to the topic. Washington asserted that "The nation which indulges toward another an habitual hatred or an habitual fondness is in some degree a slave." He declared it the policy of the United States to "steer clear of permanent alliances with any portion of the foreign world." Washington's declaration determined foreign policy for the better part of the 19th Century and remains a strong argument for caution in our government today.

The next significant step came on December 2, 1823 when President James Monroe addressed Congress. In what came to be called "The Monroe Doctrine"; the President defined the Western Hemisphere as an American sphere of influence. Monroe warned European powers "we should consider any attempt on their part to extend their system to any portion of this hemisphere as dangerous to our peace and safety." The Monroe Doctrine has created a love-hate relationship between the U.S. and its Latin American neighbors. At times the U. S. and Latin America have worked together to the benefit of the hemisphere. But the Mexican-American War of 1848, the Spanish-American War in 1898, and the dozens of U. S. incursions into Latin America in the 20th century, have at times made the Monroe Doctrine seem like a recipe for U. S. imperialism.

During most of the 19th century, the United States played a minimal role on the world stage. That role began to grow at the end of the century as the American economy sought raw materials and markets around the globe. One of the first drastic departures from strict isolationism came in the person of Teddy Roosevelt. It was Roosevelt, however, who turned the expansion into an imperialistic attempt to gain footing in the Philippines, Cuba, and other countries. In what has been called the Roosevelt Corollary to the Monroe Doctrine, the President articulated what was becoming practice: the U. S. would work to see that the entire Western Hemisphere adopted American-style democracy. It was the responsibility of a virtuous and free nation to defend and extend the rights that made America free. Roosevelt set America up as a guardian of freedom in the Western Hemisphere.

President Woodrow Wilson took Roosevelt's notion one step further by extending it to the entire world. At the end of the First World War, Wilson called on the world to accept the "Fourteen Points". To Wilson, the ultimate goal of American foreign policy was a "society of free nations," or what would come to be the League of Nations. In fact, his Fourteenth Point called for the formation of "a general association of nations." In a sharp departure from George Washington's views, he declared that "we feel ourselves to be intimate partners of all governments and peoples associated together against the imperialists." Again, the motivating factor for American action was the virtuous desire to maintain freedom and fight imperialists.

In the years following World War I, America became more aware of its place in the international scene and focus turned to the "other" hemisphere. Foreign relations began to effect the lives of citizens as awareness of America as an international player was heightened. World War II deepened America's involvement in world politics as the Pearl Harbor bombing hurled the nation into war. With the victory over Japan, America rose to the status of leader of the free world. The deployment of nuclear weapons, the extensive military involvement, and the rise of Hitler caused Americans to take foreign policy more seriously. The Soviet Union, in particular, became a focus of international diplomacy for the United States.

One of the most influential U.S. diplomats of the time, George Kennan, sent a "Long Telegram" from Moscow in February of 1946 in which he declared that no "peaceful coexistence" could be maintained with the Soviet Union. The picture he painted made Russians shady and cunning. Kennan asserted that Russians had established an underground world called the "Comintern" and intended to undermine the "Western Powers." The tone of the telegram reveals the fear that Americans held for the Russians and was typical of the Cold War mentality that followed the war.

According to Kennan, "world communism is like a malignant parasite which feeds only on diseased tissue." It was this parasite that needed to be contained before it spread. The term "containment" became the watchword for American foreign policy during the Cold War. American presidents from Truman to Nixon sought to contain the spread of communism around the world. The desire for containment led to U. S. involvement in wars in Korea and Vietnam, as well as many other smaller conflicts.

The 1980s marked a transition in foreign policy. Following the conflict, paranoia, and fears that accompanied the Cold War, a weary nation was ready for change. The words of Ronald Reagan in 1982 describe it best. He said, "I believe we live now at a turning point . . . the ultimate determinant in the struggle that's now going on in the world will not be bombs and rockets but a test of wills and ideas, a trial of spiritual resolve, the values we hold, the beliefs we cherish, the ideals to which we are dedicated." After 35 years of containment, Reagan called for a more activist foreign policy, one determined to destroy communism. The U. S. attempted to push communism out of Nicaragua and El Salvador, and to spend communism to death in the Soviet Union. Both efforts were successful (though not always neat and clean). Reagan's definition of foreign policy as an effort to defend American values around the world continues to drive American foreign policy. It stood behind the Persian Gulf War and it stands behind America's current involvement in Kosova.

The new policy of post-Cold war America is a synthesis of previous mistakes and successes. It is not the Washingtonian isolationism nor the containment of the Cold War. It seeks to spread American ideals, but with caution. While caution often seems to be the best course, it attracts critics from all sides—isolationists who say that the U. S. has no business getting involved in the internal affairs of Yugoslavia, and activists who urge Americans to defend human rights and democracy all over the world.

As you read the following documents be sure you understand how American foreign policy has changed over time. What events have caused the United States to become more active around the globe? Should the U.S. defend democracy? Even if it requires the use of un-democratic means?

George Washington's Farewell Address
17 September 1796

Friends, and fellow citizens:

Observe good faith and justice toward all nations. Cultivate peace and harmony with all. Religion and morality enjoin this conduct. And can it be that good policy does not equally enjoin it? It will be worthy of a free, enlightened, and at no distant period a great nation to give to mankind the magnanimous and too novel example of a people always guided by an exalted justice and benevolence. Who can doubt that in the course of time and things the fruits of such a plan would richly repay any temporary advantages which might be lost by a steady adherence to it? Can it be, that Providence has not connected the permanent felicity of a nation with its Virtue? The experiment, at least, is recommended by every sentiment which ennobles human nature. Alas! is it rendered impossible by its vices?

In the execution of such a plan nothing is more essential than that permanent, inveterate antipathies against particular nations and passionate attachments for others should be excluded, and that in place of them just and amicable feelings toward all should be cultivated. The nation which indulges toward another an habitual hatred or an habitual fondness is in some degree a slave. It is a slave to its animosity or to its affection, either of which is sufficient to lead it astray from its duty and its interest. Antipathy in one nation against another disposes each more readily to offer insult and injury, to lay hold of slight causes of umbrage, and to be haughty and intractable when accidental or trifling occasions of dispute occur. Hence frequent collisions, obstinate, envenomed, and bloody contests. The nation prompted by ill will and resentment sometimes impels to war the government contrary to the best calculations of policy. The government sometimes participates in the national propensity, and adopts through passion what reason would reject. At other times it makes the animosity of the nation subservient to projects of hostility, instigated by pride, ambition, and other sinister and pernicious motives.

The peace often, sometimes perhaps the liberty, of nations has been the victim.

So likewise, a passionate attachment of one nation for another produces a variety of evils. Sympathy for the favorite nation, facilitating the illusion of an imaginary common interest in cases where no real common interest exists, and infusing into one the enmities of the other, betrays the former into a participation in the quarrels and wars of the latter without adequate inducements or justification. It leads also to concessions to the favorite nation of privileges denied to others, which is apt doubly to injure the nation making the concessions by unnecessarily parting with what ought to have been retained, and by exciting jealousy, ill will, and a disposition to retaliate in the parties from whom equal privileges are withheld; and it gives to ambitious, corrupted, or deluded citizens (who devote themselves to the favorite nation) facility to betray or sacrifice the interests of their own country without odium, sometimes even with popularity, gilding with the appearances of a virtuous sense of obligation, a commendable deference for public opinion, or a laudable zeal for public good the base or foolish compliances of ambition, corruption, or infatuation.

As avenues to foreign influence in innumerable ways, such attachments are particularly alarming to the truly enlightened and independent patriot. How many opportunities do they afford to tamper with domestic factions, to practice the arts of seduction, to mislead public opinion, to influence or awe the public councils! Such an attachment of a small or weak toward a great and powerful nation dooms the former to be the satellite of the latter. Against the insidious wiles of foreign influence (I conjure you to believe me, fellow-citizens) the jealousy of a free people ought to be *constantly* awake, since history and experience prove that foreign influence is one of the most baneful foes of republican government. But that jealousy, to be useful, must be impartial, else it becomes the instrument of the very influence to be avoided, instead of a defense against it. Excessive partiality for one foreign nation and excessive dislike of another cause those whom they actuate to see danger only on one side, and serve to veil and even second the arts of influence on the other. Real patriots who may resist the intrigues of the favorite are liable to become suspected and odious, while its tools and dupes usurp the applause and confidence of the people to surrender their interests.

The great rule of conduct for us in regard to foreign nation is, in extending our commercial relations to have with them as little *political* connection as possible. So far as we have already formed engagements let them be fulfilled with perfect good faith. Here let us stop.

Europe has a set of primary interests which to us have none or a very remote relation. Hence she must be engaged in frequent controversies, the causes of which are essentially foreign to our concerns. Hence, therefore, it must be unwise in us to implicate ourselves by artificial ties in the ordinary vicissitudes of her politics or the ordinary combinations and collisions of her friendships or enmities.

Our detached and distant situation invites and enables us to pursue a different course. If we remain one people, under an efficient government, the period is not far off when we may defy material injury from external annoyance; when we may take such an attitude as will cause the neutrality we may at any time resolve upon to be scrupulously respected; when belligerent nations, under the impossibility of making acquisitions upon us, will not lightly hazard the giving us provocation; when we may choose peace or war, as our interest, by justice, shall counsel.

The Monroe Doctrine
Message of President James Monroe to Congress
2 December 1823

Fellow-Citizens of the Senate and House of Representatives:

Many important subjects will claim your attention during the present session, of which I shall endeavor to give, in aid of your deliberations, a just idea in this communication. I undertake this duty with diffidence, from the vast extent of the interests on which I have to treat and of their great importance to every portion of our Union. I enter on it with zeal from a thorough conviction that there never was a period since the establishment of our Revolution when, regarding the condition of the civilized world and its bearing upon us, there was greater necessity for devotion in public servants to their respective duties, or for virtue, patriotism, and union in our constituents.

At the proposal of the Russian Imperial Government, made through the minister of the Emperor residing here, a full power and instructions have been transmitted to the minister of the United States at St. Petersburg to arrange by amicable negotiation the respective rights and interests of the two nations on the northwest coast of this continent. A similar proposal has been made by his Imperial Majesty to the Government of Great Britain, which has likewise been acceded to. The Government of the United States has been desirous by this friendly proceeding of manifesting the great value which they have inevitably attached to the friendship of the Emperor and their solicitude to cultivate the best understanding with his Government. In the discussions to which this interest has given rise and in the arrangements by which they may terminate the occasion has been judged proper for asserting, as a principle in which the rights and interests of the United States are involved that the American continents, by the free and independent condition which they have assumed and maintain, are henceforth not to be considered as subjects for future colonization by any European powers.

It was stated at the commencement of the last session that a great effort was then making in Spain and Portugal to improve the condition of the people of those countries, and that it appeared to be conducted with extraordinary moderation. It need scarcely be remarked that the result has been so far very different from what was then anticipated. Of events in that quarter of the globe, with which we have so much intercourse and from which we derive our origin, we have always been anxious and interested spectators. The citizens of the United States cherish sentiments the most friendly in favor of the liberty and happiness of their fellow-men on that side of the Atlantic. In the wars of the European powers in matters relating to themselves we have never taken any part, nor does it comport with our policy so to do. It is only when our rights are invaded or seriously menaced that we resent injuries or make preparation for our defense. With the movements in this hemisphere we are of necessity more immediately connected, and by causes which must be obvious to all enlightened and impartial observers. The political system of the allied powers is essentially different in this respect from that of America. This difference proceeds from that which exists in their respective Governments; and to the defense of our own, which has been achieved by the loss of so much blood and treasure, and matured by the wisdom of their most enlightened citizens, and under which we have enjoyed unexampled felicity, this whole nation is devoted. We owe it, therefore, to candor and to the amicable relations existing between the United States and those powers to declare that we should consider any attempt on their part to extend their system to any portion of this hemisphere as dangerous to our peace and safety. With the existing colonies or dependencies of any European power we have not interfered and shall not interfere. But with the Governments who have declared their independence and maintained it, and whose independence we have, on great consideration and on just principles, acknowledged, we could not view any interposition for the purpose of oppressing them, or controlling in any other manner their destiny, by any European power in any other light than as the manifestation of an unfriendly disposition toward the United States. In the war between those new Governments and Spain we declared our neutrality at the time of their recognition, and to this we have adhered, and shall continue to adhere, provided no change shall occur which, in the judgment of the competent authorities of this Government, shall make a corresponding change on the part of the United States indispensable to their security.

The late events in Spain and Portugal shew that Europe is still unsettled. Of this important fact no stronger proof can be adduced than that the allied powers should have thought it proper, on any principle satisfactory to themselves, to have interposed by force in the internal concerns of Spain. To what extent such interposition may be carried, on the same principle, is a question in which all independent powers whose governments differ from theirs are interested, even those most remote, and surely none more so than the United States. Our policy in regard to Europe, which was adopted at an early stage of the wars which have so long agitated that quarter of the globe, nevertheless remains the same, which is, not to interfere in the internal concerns of any of its powers; to consider the government *de facto* as the legitimate government for us; to cultivate friendly relations with it, and to preserve those relations by a frank, firm, and manly policy, meeting in all instances the just claims of every power, submitting to injuries from none. But in regard to those continents circumstances are eminently and conspicuously different. It is impossible that the allied powers should extend their political system to any portion of either continent without endangering our peace and happiness; nor can anyone believe that our southern brethren, if [left] to themselves, would adopt it of their own accord. It equally impossible, therefore, that we should behold such interposition in any form with indifference. If we look to the comparative strength and resources of Spain and those new Governments, and their distance from each other, it must be obvious that she can never subdue them. It is still the true policy of the United States to leave the parties to themselves, in the hope that other powers will pursue the same course.

The Roosevelt Corollary to the Monroe Doctrine

Theodore Roosevelt's Annual Message to Congress 6 December 1904

To the Senate and House of Representatives:

The Nation continues to enjoy noteworthy prosperity. Such prosperity is of course primarily due to the high individual average of our citizenship, taken together with our great natural resources; but an important factor therein is the working of our long-continued governmental policies. The people have emphatically expressed their approval of the principles underlying these policies, and their desire that these principles be kept substantially unchanged, although of course applied in a progressive spirit to meet changing conditions.

Foreign Policy

In treating of our foreign policy and of the attitude that this great Nation should assume in the world at large, it is absolutely necessary to consider the Army and the Navy, and the Congress, through which the thought of the Nation finds its expression, should keep ever vividly in mind the fundamental fact that it is impossible to treat our foreign policy, whether this policy takes shape in the effort to secure justice for others or justice for ourselves, save as conditioned upon the attitude we are willing to take toward our Army, and especially toward our Navy. It is not merely unwise, it is contemptible, for a nation, as for an individual, to use high-sounding language to proclaim its purposes, or to take positions which are ridiculous if unsupported by potential force, and then to refuse to provide this force. If there is no intention of providing and keeping the force necessary to back up a strong attitude, then it is far better not to assume such an attitude.

The steady aim of this Nation, as of all enlightened nations, should be to strive to bring ever nearer the day when there shall prevail throughout the world the peace of justice. There are kinds of peace which are highly undesirable, which are in the long run as destructive as any war. Tyrants and oppressors have many times made a wilderness and called it peace. Many times peoples who were slothful or timid or shortsighted, who had been enervated by ease or by luxury, or misled by false teachings, have shrunk in unmanly fashion from doing duty that was stern and that needed self-sacrifice, and have sought to hide from their own minds their shortcomings, their ignoble motives, by calling them love of peace. The peace of tyrannous terror, the peace of craven weakness, the peace of injustice, all these should be shunned as we shun unrighteous war. The goal to set before us as a nation, the goal which should be set before all mankind, is the attainment of the peace of justice, of the peace which comes when each nation is not merely safe-guarded in its own rights, but scrupulously recognizes and performs its duty toward others. Generally peace tells for righteousness; but if there is conflict between the two, then our fealty is due first to the cause of righteousness. Unrighteous wars are common, and unrighteous peace is rare; but both should be shunned. The right of freedom and the responsibility for the exercise of that right can not be divorced. One of our great poets has well and finely said that freedom is not a gift that tarries long in the hands of cowards. Neither does it tarry long in the hands of those too slothful, too dishonest, or too unintelligent to exercise it. The eternal vigilance which is the price of liberty must be exercised, sometimes to guard against outside foes; although of course far more often to guard against our own selfish or thoughtless shortcomings.

If these self-evident truths are kept before us, and only if they are so kept before us, we shall have a clear idea of what our foreign policy in its larger aspects should be. It is our duty to remember that a nation has no more right to do injustice to another nation, strong or weak, than an individual has to do injustice to another individual; that the same moral law applies in one case as in the other. But we must also remember that it is as much the duty of the Nation to guard its own rights and its own interests as it is the duty of the individual so to do. Within the Nation the individual has now delegated this right to the State, that is, to the representative of all the individuals, and it is a maxim of the law that for every wrong there is a remedy. But in international law we have not advanced by any means as far as we have advanced in municipal law. There is as yet no judicial way of enforcing a right in international law. When one nation wrongs another or wrongs many others, there is no tribunal before which the wrongdoer can be brought. Either it is necessary supinely to acquiesce in the wrong, and thus put a premium upon brutality and aggression, or else it is necessary for the aggrieved nation valiantly to stand up for its rights. Until some method is devised by which there shall be a degree of international control over offending nations, it would be a wicked thing for the most civilized powers, for those with most sense of international obligations and with keenest and most generous appreciation of the difference between right and wrong, to disarm. If the great civilized nations of the present day should completely disarm, the result would mean an immediate recrudescence of barbarism in one form or another. Under any circumstances a sufficient armament would have to be kept up to serve the purposes of international police; and until international cohesion and the sense of international duties and rights are far more advanced than at present, a nation desirous both of securing respect for itself and of doing good to others must have a force adequate for the work which it feels is allotted to it as its part of the general world duty. Therefore it follows that a self-respecting, just, and far-seeing nation should on the one hand endeavor by every means to aid in the development of the various movements which tend to provide substitutes for war, which tend to render nations in their actions toward one another, and indeed toward their own peoples, more responsive to the general sentiment of humane and civilized mankind; and on the other hand that it should keep prepared, while scrupulously avoiding wrongdoing itself, to repel any wrong, and in exceptional cases to take action which in a more advanced stage of international relations would come under the head of the exercise of the international police. A great free people owes it to itself and to all mankind not to sink into helplessness before the powers of evil.

Policy Toward Other Nations of the Western Hemisphere

It is not true that the United States feels any land hunger or entertains any projects as regards the other nations of the Western Hemisphere save such as are for their welfare. All that this country desires is to see the neighboring countries stable, orderly, and prosperous. Any country whose people conduct themselves well can count upon our hearty friendship. If a nation shows that it knows how to act with reasonable efficiency and decency in social and political matters, if it keeps order and pays its obligations, it need fear no interference from the United States. Chronic wrongdoing, or an impotence which results in a general loosening of the ties of civilized society, may in America, as elsewhere, ultimately require intervention by some civilized nation, and in the Western Hemisphere the adherence of the United States to the Monroe Doctrine may force the United States, however reluctantly, in flagrant cases of such wrongdoing or impotence, to the exercise of an international police power. If every country washed by the Caribbean Sea would show the progress in stable and just civilization which with the aid of the Platt Amendment Cuba has shown since our troops left the island, and which so many of the republics in both Americas are constantly and brilliantly showing, all question of interference by this Nation with their affairs would be at an end. Our interests and those of our southern neighbors are in reality identical. They have great natural riches, and if within their borders the reign of law and justice obtains, prosperity is sure to come to them. While they thus obey the primary laws of civilized society they may rest assured that they will be treated by us in a spirit of cordial and helpful sympathy. We would interfere with them only in the last resort, and then only if it became evident that their inability or unwillingness to do justice at home and abroad had violated the rights of the United States or had invited foreign aggression to the detriment of the entire body of American nations. It is a mere truism to say that every nation, whether in America or anywhere else, which desires to maintain its freedom, its independence, must ultimately realize that the right of such independence can not be separated from the responsibility of making good use of it.

In asserting the Monroe Doctrine, in taking such steps as we have taken in regard to Cuba, Venezuela, and Panama, and in endeavoring to circumscribe the theater of war in the Far East, and to secure the open door in China, we have acted in our own interest as well as in the interest of humanity at large. There are, however, cases in which, while our own interests are not greatly involved, strong appeal is made to our sympathies. Ordinarily it is very much wiser and more useful for us to concern ourselves with striving for our own moral and material betterment here at home than to concern ourselves with trying to better the condition of things in other nations. We have plenty of sins of our own to war against, and under ordinary circumstances we can do more for the general uplifting of humanity by striving with heart and soul to put a stop to civic corruption, to brutal lawlessness and violent race prejudices here at home than by passing resolutions and wrongdoing elsewhere. Nevertheless there are occasional crimes committed on so vast a scale and of such peculiar horror as to make us doubt whether it is not our manifest duty to endeavor at least to show our disapproval of the deed and our sympathy with those who have suffered by it. The cases must be extreme In which such a course is justifiable. There must be no effort made to remove the mote from our brother's eye if we refuse to remove the beam from our own. But in extreme cases action may be justifiable and proper. What form the action shall take must depend upon the circumstances of the case; that is, upon the degree of the atrocity and upon our power to remedy it. The cases in which we could interfere by force of arms as we interfered to put a stop to intolerable conditions in Cuba are necessarily very few. Yet it is not to be expected that a people like ours, which in spite of certain very obvious shortcomings, nevertheless as a whole shows by its consistent practice its belief in the principles of civil and religious liberty and of orderly freedom, a people among whom even the worst crime, like the crime of lynching, is never more than sporadic, so that individuals and not classes are molested in their fundamental rights—it is inevitable that such a nation should desire eagerly to give expression to its horror on an occasion like that of the massacre of the Jews in Kishenef, or when it witnesses such systematic and long-extended cruelty and oppression as the cruelty and oppression of which the Armenians have been the victims, and which have won for them the indignant pity of the civilized world.

Theodore Roosevelt

Woodrow Wilson, The Fourteen Points (1918)

It will be our wish and purpose that the processes of peace, when they are begun, shall be absolutely open and that they shall involve and permit henceforth no secret understandings of any kind. The day of conquest and aggrandizement is gone by; so is also the day of secret covenants entered into in the interest of particular governments and likely at some unlooked-for moment to upset the peace of the world. . . .

We entered this war because violations of right had occurred which touched us to the quick and made the life of our own people impossible unless they were corrected and the world secure once for all against their recurrence.

What we demand in this war, therefore, is nothing peculiar to ourselves. It is that the world be made fit and safe to live in; and particularly that it be made safe for every peace-loving nation which, like our own, wishes to live its own life, determine its own institutions, be assured of justice and fair dealing by the other peoples of the world as against force and selfish aggressions.

All the peoples of the world are in effect partners in this interest, and for our own part we see very clearly that unless justice be done to others it will not be done to us. The program of the world's peace, therefore, is our program; and that program, the only possible program, as we see it, is this:

1. Open covenants of peace, openly arrived at, after which there shall be no private international understandings of any kind but diplomacy shall proceed always frankly and in the public view.
2. Absolute freedom of navigation upon the seas, outside territorial waters, alike in peace and in war, except as the seas may be closed in whole or in part by international action for the enforcement of international covenants.
3. The removal, so far as possible, of all economic barriers and the establishment of an equality of trade conditions among all the na-

tions consenting to the peace and associating themselves for its maintenance.

4. Adequate guarantees given and taken that national armaments will be reduced to the lowest points consistent with domestic safety.
5. A free, open-minded, and absolutely impartial adjustment of all colonial claims, based upon a strict observance of the principle that in determining all such questions of sovereignty the interests of the populations concerned must have equal weight with the equitable claims of the government whose title is to be determined.
6. The evacuation of all Russian territory and such a settlement of all questions affecting Russia as will secure the best and freest cooperation of the other nations of the world in obtaining for her an unhampered and unembarrassed opportunity for the independent determination of her own political development and national policy and assure her of a sincere welcome into the society of free nations under institutions of her own choosing; and, more than a welcome, assistance also of every kind that she may need and may herself desire. The treatment accorded Russian by her sister nations in the months to come will be the acid test of their good will, of their comprehension of her needs as distinguished from their own interests, and of their intelligent and unselfish sympathy.
7. Belgium, the whole world will agree, must be evacuated and restored, without any attempt to limit the sovereignty which she enjoys in common with all other free nations. No other single act will serve as this will serve to restore confidence among the nations in the laws which they have themselves set and determined for the government of their relations with one another. Without this healing act the whole structure and validity of international law is forever impaired.
8. All French territory should be freed and the invaded portions restored, and the wrong done to France by Prussia in 1871 in the matter of Alsace-Lorraine, which has unsettled the peace of the world for nearly fifty years, should be righted, in order that peace may once more be made secure in the interest of all.
9. A readjustment of the frontiers of Italy should be affected along clearly recognizable lines of nationality.

10. The peoples of Austria-Hungary, whose place among the nations we wish to see safeguarded and assured, should be accorded the freest opportunity of autonomous development.
11. Rumania, Serbia, and Montenegro should be evacuated; occupied territories restored; Serbia accorded free and secure access to the sea; and the relations of the several Balkan states to one another determined by friendly counsel along historically established lines of allegiance and nationality; and international guarantees of the political and economic independence and territorial integrity of the several Balkan states should be entered into.
12. The Turkish portions of the present Ottoman Empire should be assured a secure sovereignty, but the other nationalities which are now under Turkish rule should be assured an undoubted security of life and an absolutely unmolested opportunity of autonomous development, and the Dardanelles should be permanently opened as a free passage to the ships and commerce of all nations under international guarantees.
13. An independent Polish state should be erected which should include the territories inhabited by indisputably Polish populations, which should be assured a free and secure access to the sea, and whose political and economic independence and territorial integrity should be guaranteed by international covenant.
14. A general association of nations must be formed under specific covenants for the purpose of affording mutual guarantees of political independence and territorial integrity to great and small states alike.

In regard to these essential rectifications of wrong and assertions of right we feel ourselves to be intimate partners of all the governments and peoples associated together against the imperialists. We cannot be separated in interest or divided in purpose. We stand together until the end. . . .

An evident principle runs through the whole program I have outlined. It is the principle of justice to all peoples and nationalities, and their right to live on equal terms of liberty and safety with one another, whether they be strong or weak.

Unless this principle be made its foundation no part of the structure of international justice can stand. The people of the United States could act upon no other principle; and to the vindication of this principle they are ready to devote their lives, their honor, and everything that they possess. The moral climax of this the culminating and final war for human liberty has come, and they are ready to put their own strength, their own highest purpose, their own integrity and devotion to the test.

Woodrow Wilson, *Message to Congress,* January 8, 1918.

The Long Telegram
George Kennan, Moscow
22 February 1946

I apologize in advance for this burdening of telegraphic channel; but questions involved are of such urgent importance, particularly in view of recent events, that our answers to them, if they deserve attention at all, seem to me to deserve it at once. There follows:

Part 1: Basic Features of Postwar Soviet Outlook as Put Forward by Official Propaganda Machine, Are as Follows

(a) USSR still lives in antagonistic "capitalist encirclement" with which in the long run there can be no permanent peaceful coexistence. As stated by Stalin in 1927 to a delegation of American workers: "in course of further development of international revolution there will emerge two centers of world significance: a socialist center, drawing to itself the countries which tend toward socialism, and a capitalist center, drawing to itself the countries that incline toward capitalism. Battle between these two centers for command of world economy will decide fate of capitalism and of communism in entire world.

(b) Capitalist world is beset with internal conflicts, inherent in nature of capitalist society. These conflicts are insoluble by means of peaceful compromise. Greatest of them is that between England and US.

(c) Internal conflicts of capitalism inevitably generate wars. Wars thus generated may be of two kinds: intra-capitalist wars between two capitalist states and wars of intervention against socialist world. Smart capitalists, vainly seeking escape from inner conflicts of capitalism, incline toward latter.

(d) Intervention against USSR, while it would be disastrous to those who undertook it, would cause renewed delay in progress of Soviet socialism and must therefore be forestalled at all costs.

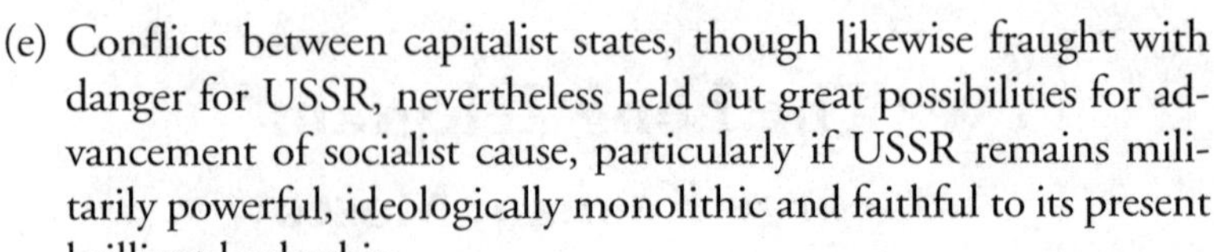

(e) Conflicts between capitalist states, though likewise fraught with danger for USSR, nevertheless held out great possibilities for advancement of socialist cause, particularly if USSR remains militarily powerful, ideologically monolithic and faithful to its present brilliant leadership.

(f) It must be borne in mind that capitalist world is not all bad. In addition to hopelessly reactionary and bourgeois elements, it includes (1) certain wholly enlightened and positive elements united in acceptable communist padres and (2) certain other elements (now described for tactical reasons as progressive or democratic) whose reactions, aspirations and activities happen to be "objectively" favorable to interests of USSR. These last must be encouraged and utilized for Soviet purposes.

(g) Among negative elements of bourgeois-capitalist society, most dangerous of all are those whom Lenin called false friends of the people, namely moderate-socialist or social-democratic leaders (in other words, non-Communist left-wing). These are more dangerous than out-and-out reactionaries, for latter at least march under their true colors, whereas moderate left-wing leaders confuse people by employing devices of socialism to serve interests of reactionary capital.

So much for premises. To what deductions do they lead from standpoint of Soviet policy? To following:

(a) Everything must be done to advance relative strength of USSR as factor in international society. Conversely, no opportunity must be missed to reduce strength and influence, collectively as well as individually, of capitalist powers.

(b) Soviet efforts, and those of Russia's friends abroad, must be directed toward deepening and exploiting of differences and conflicts between capitalist powers. If these eventually deepen into an "imperialist" war, this war must be turned into revolutionary upheavals within the various capitalist countries.

(c) "Democratic-progressive" elements abroad are to be utilized to maximum to bring pressure to bear on capitalist governments along lines agreeable to Soviet interests.

(d) Relentless battle must be waged against socialist and social-democratic leaders abroad.

At bottom of Kremlin's neurotic view of world affairs is traditional and instinctive Russian sense of insecurity. Originally, this was insecurity of a peaceful agricultural people trying to live on vast exposed plain in neighborhood of fierce nomadic peoples. To this was added, as Russia came into contact with economically advanced West, fear of more competent, more powerful, more highly organized societies in that area. But this latter type of insecurity was one which afflicted Russian rulers rather than Russian people; for Russian rulers have invariably sensed that their rule was relatively archaic in form, fragile and artificial in its psychological foundations, unable to stand comparison or contact with political systems of Western countries. For this reason they have always feared foreign penetration, feared direct contact between Western world and their own, feared what would happen if Russians learned truth about world without or if foreigners learned truth about world within. And they have learned to seek security only in patent but deadly struggle for total destruction of rival power, never in compacts and compromises with it.

It was no coincidence that Marxism, which had smouldered ineffectively for half a century in Western Europe, caught hold and blazed for the first time in Russia. Only in this land which had never known a friendly neighbor or indeed any tolerant equilibrium of separate powers, either internal or international, could a doctrine thrive which viewed economic conflicts of society as insoluble by peaceful means. After establishment of Bolshevist regime, Marxist dogma, rendered even more truculent and intolerant by Lenin's interpretation, become a perfect vehicle for sense of insecurity with which Bolsheviks, even more than previous Russian rulers, were afflicted. In this dogma, with its basic altruism of purpose, they found justification for their instinctive fear of outside world, for the dictatorship without which they did not know how to rule, for cruelties they did not dare not to inflict, for sacrifices they felt bound to demand. In the name of Marxism they sacrificed every single ethical value in their methods and tactics. Today they cannot dispense with it. It is fig leaf of their moral and intellectual respectability. Without it they would stand before history, at best, as only the last of that long succession of cruel and wasteful Russian rulers who have relentlessly forced country on to ever new heights of military power in order to guarantee external security of their internally weak regimes. This is why Soviet purposes must always be solemnly clothed in trappings of Marxism, and why no one should underrate importance of dogma in Soviet affairs. Thus Soviet leaders are driven [by] necessities of their own past and present position to put forward a dogma which [apparent omission] outside world as evil, hostile and menacing, but as bearing within itself germs of creeping disease and destined to be wracked with growing internal convulsions until it is given final coup de grace by rising power of socialism and yields to new and better world. This thesis provides justification for that increase of military and police power of Russian state, for that isolation of Russian population from outside world, and for that fluid and constant pressure to extend limits of Russian police power which are together the natural and instinctive urges of Russian rulers. Basically this is only the steady advance of uneasy Russian nationalism, a centuries old movement in which conceptions of offense and defense are inextricably confused. But in new guise of international Marxism, with its honeyed promises to a desperate and war-torn outside world, it is more dangerous and insidious than ever before.

There is good reason to suspect that this Government is actually a conspiracy within a conspiracy; and I for one am reluctant to believe that Stalin himself receives anything like an objective picture of outside world. Here there is ample scope for the type of subtle intrigue at which Russians are past masters. Inability of foreign governments to place their case squarely before Russian policy makers—extent to which they are delivered up in their relations with Russia to good graces of obscure and unknown advisers whom they never see and cannot influence—this to my mind is most disquieting feature of diplomacy in Moscow, and one which Western statesmen would do well to keep in mind if they would understand nature of difficulties encountered here.

Part 5. [Practical Deductions from Standpoint of US Policy]

In summary, we have here a political force committed fanatically to the belief that with US there can be no permanent modus vivendi, that it is desirable and necessary that the internal harmony of our society be disrupted, our traditional way of life be destroyed, the international authority of our state be broken, if Soviet power is to be secure. This political force has complete power of disposition over energies of one of world's greatest peoples and resources of world's richest national territory, and is borne along by deep and powerful currents of Russian nationalism. In addition, it has an elaborate and far-flung apparatus for exertion of its influence in other countries, an apparatus of amazing flexibility and versatility, managed by people whose experience and skill in underground methods are presumably without parallel in history. Finally, it is seemingly inaccessible to considerations of reality in its basic reactions. For it, the vast fund of objective fact about human society is not, as with us, the measure against which outlook is constantly being tested and re-formed, but a grab bag from which individual items are selected arbitrarily and tendenciously to bolster an outlook already preconceived. This is admittedly not a pleasant picture. Problem of how to cope with this force [is] undoubtedly greatest task our diplomacy has ever faced and probably greatest it will ever have to face. It should be point of departure from which our political general staff work at present juncture should proceed. It should be approached with same thoroughness and care as solution of major strategic problem in war and, if necessary, with no smaller outlay in planning effort. I cannot attempt to suggest all answers here. But I would like to record my conviction that problem is within our power to solve—and that without recourse to any general military conflict. And in support of this conviction there are certain observations for a more encouraging nature I should like to make.

(1) Soviet power, unlike that of Hitlerite Germany, is neither schematic nor adventuristic. It does not work by fixed plans. It does not take unnecessary risks. Impervious to logic of reason, and it is highly sensitive to logic of force. For this reason it can easily withdraw—and usually does—when strong resistance is encountered at any point. Thus, if the adversary has sufficient force and makes clear his readiness to use it, he rarely has to do so. If situations are properly handled there need be no prestige-engaging showdowns.

(2) Gauged against Western world as a whole, Soviets are still by far the weaker force. Thus, their success will really depend on degree of cohesion, firmness and vigor which Western world can muster. And this is factor which it is within our power to influence.

(3) Success of Soviet system, as form of internal power, is not yet finally proven. It has yet to be demonstrated that it can survive supreme test of successive transfer of power from one individual or group to another. Lenin's death was first such transfer, and its effects wracked Soviet state for 15 years. After Stalin's death or retirement will be second. But even this will not be final test. Soviet internal system will now be subjected, by virtue of recent territo-

rial expansions, to series of additional strains which once proved severe tax on Tsardom. We here are convinced that never since termination of civil war have mass of Russian people been emotionally farther removed from doctrines of Communist Party than they are today. In Russia, party has now become a great and—for the moment—highly successful apparatus of dictatorial administration, but it has ceased to be a source of emotional inspiration. Thus, internal soundness and permanence of movement need not yet be regarded as assured.

(4) All Soviet propaganda beyond Soviet security sphere is basically negative and destructive. It should therefore be relatively easy to combat it by any intelligent and really constructive program.

For these reasons I think we may approach calmly and with good heart problem of how to deal with Russia. As to how this approach should be made, I only wish to advance, by way of conclusion, following comments:

(1) Our first step must be to apprehend, and recognize for what it is, the nature of the movement with which we are dealing. We must study it with same courage, detachment, objectivity, and same determination not to be emotionally provoked or unseated by it, with which doctor studies unruly and unreasonable individual.

(2) We must see that our public is educated to realities of Russian situation. I cannot overemphasize importance of this. Press cannot do this alone. It must be done mainly by Government, which is necessarily more experienced and better informed on practical problems involved. In this we need not be deterred by [ugliness?] of picture. I am convinced that there would be far less hysterical anti-Sovietism in our country today if realities of this situation were better understood by our people. There is nothing as dangerous or as terrifying as the unknown. It may also be argued that to reveal more information on our difficulties with Russia would reflect unfavorably on Russian- American relations. I feel that if there is any real risk here involved, it is one which we should have courage to face, and sooner the better. But I cannot see what we would be risking. Our stake in this country, even coming on heels of tremendous demonstrations of our friendship for Russian people, is remarkably small. We have here no investments to guard, no actual trade to lose, virtually no citizens to protect, few cultural

contacts to preserve. Our only stake likes in what we hope rather than what we have; and I am convinced we have better chance of realizing those hopes if our public is enlightened and if our dealings with Russians are placed entirely on realistic and matter-of-fact basis.

(3) Much depends on health and vigor of our own society. World communism is like malignant parasite which feeds only on diseased tissue. This is point at which domestic and foreign policies meet. Every courageous and incisive measure to solve internal problems of our own society, to improve self-confidence, discipline, morale and community spirit of our own people, is a diplomatic victory over Moscow worth a thousand diplomatic notes and joint communiqués. If we cannot abandon fatalism and indifference in face of deficiencies of our own society, Moscow will profit—Moscow cannot help profiting by them in its foreign policies.

(4) We must formulate and put forward for other nations a much more positive and constructive picture of sort of world we would like to see than we have put forward in past. It is not enough to urge people to develop political processes similar to our own. Many foreign peoples, in Europe at least, are tired and frightened by experiences of past, and are less interested in abstract freedom than in security. They are seeking guidance rather than responsibilities. We should be better able than Russians to give them this. And, unless we do, Russians certainly will.

(5) Finally we must have courage and self-confidence to cling to our own methods and conceptions of human society. After all, the greatest danger that can befall us in coping with this problem of Soviet communism is that we shall allow ourselves to become like those with whom we are coping.

Ronald Reagan, Speech to the House of Commons (1982)

We're approaching the end of a bloody century plagued by a terrible political invention-totalitarianism. Optimism comes less easily today, not because democracy is less vigorous, but because democracy's enemies have refined their instruments of repression. Yet optimism is in order because day by day democracy is proving itself to be a not at all fragile flower. From Stettin on the Baltic to Varna on the Black Sea, the regimes planted by totalitarianism have had more than thirty years to establish their legitimacy. But none—not one regime—has yet been able to risk free elections. Regimes planted by bayonets do not take root.

The strength of the Solidarity movement in Poland demonstrates the truth told in an underground joke in the Soviet Union. It is that the Soviet Union would remain a one-party nation even if an opposition party were permitted because everyone would join the opposition party. . . .

If history teaches us anything, it teaches self-delusion in the face of unpleasant facts is folly. We see around us the marks of our terrible dilemma-predictions of doomsday, antinuclear demonstrations, an arms race in which the West must, for its own protection, be an unwilling participant. At the same time we see totalitarian forces in the world who seek subversion and conflict around the globe to further their barbarous assault on the human spirit. What, then, is our course? Must civilization perish in a hail of fiery atoms? Must freedom wither in a quiet, deadening accommodation with totalitarian evil? . . .

It may not be easy to see; but I believe we live now at a turning point.

In an ironic sense Karl Marx was right. We are witnessing today a great revolutionary crisis, a crisis where the demands of the economic order are conflicting directly with those of the political order. But the crisis is happening not in the free, non-Marxist West, but in the home of Marxism-Leninism, the Soviet Union. It is the Soviet Union that runs against the tide of history by denying human freedom and human dignity to its citizens. It is also deep in economic difficulty. The rate of growth in the national product has been steadily declining since the fifties and is less than half of what it was then.

The dimensions of this failure are astounding: a country which employs one-fifth of its population in agriculture is unable to feed its own people. . . . The decay of the Soviet experiment should come as no surprise to us. Wherever the comparisons have been made between free and closed societies—West Germany and East Germany, Austria and Czechoslovakia, Malaysia and Vietnam—it is the democratic countries that are prosperous and responsive to the needs of their people. . . .

Our military strength is a prerequisite to peace, but let it be clear we maintain this strength in the hope it will never be used, for the ultimate determinant in the struggle that's now going on in the world will not be bombs and rockets but a test of wills and ideas, a trial of spiritual resolve, the values we hold, the beliefs we cherish, the ideals to which we are dedicated.

I've often wondered about the shyness of some of us in the West about standing for these ideals that have done so much to ease the plight of man and the hardships of our imperfect world. This reluctance to use those vast resources at our command reminds me of the elderly lady whose home was bombed in the Blitz. As the rescuers moved about, they found a bottle of brandy she'd stored behind the staircase, which was all that was left standing. And since she was barely conscious, one of the workers pulled the cork to give her a taste of it. She came around immediately and said, "Here now-there now, put it back. That's for emergencies."

Well, the emergency is upon us. Let us be shy no longer. Let us go to our strength. Let us offer hope. Let us tell the world that a new age is not only possible but probable.

THE REAGAN REVOLUTION

Gary Daynes

Ronald Reagan was a model American. A product of a small town, he had worked his way through the Depression as a life guard. High school kept him busy with football games, swim meets, and his responsibilities as student body president. A scholarship and his own savings got him through his college years, where he continued to play football. In 1937, a stroke of luck landed him a job in Hollywood. It was there that the nation became familiar with his boyish features and dazzling smile. When poor vision disqualified him from World War II combat, he made war movies to serve his country. From Hollywood star to war veteran, Reagan was American through and through. Perhaps more importantly, he seemed the ideal of what every American hoped they could become.

Once the war ended, Reagan turned his attention to politics. In 1966, he began the first of two terms as governor of California. There, he cemented the conservative reputation that would carry him to the White House. In 1980, with the nation weary of the social and political unrest that had marked the two previous decades, Ronald Reagan was elected President of the United States. His promises of a 30% tax reduction, limited government, and a strong hand against communism appealed to Americans. He spoke with confidence and hope about a better America and that translated into a landslide victory over President Carter.

Reagan's views of the ideal America shine through in his tribute to Hollywood legend John Wayne. Wayne was much like Reagan in his achievements and background. He was the boy next door, delivering the paper and groceries, making straight A's, and playing football in high school and college. As fortune would have it, he went from stagehand to star in the Hollywood scene. His tough-guy roles represented the American image of cowboy and soldier.

Reagan applauded Wayne's forceful opposition to communism in Hollywood in the 1940s, thus reflecting his own determination to thwart the spread of communism in the international community. Even more significantly, Reagan believed that individual integrity, such as demonstrated by John Wayne, was the only solution to monumental problems at home and abroad. Reagan said, "Duke Wayne symbolized . . . the force of the American will to do what is right in the world. He could have left no greater legacy."

Reagan's ability to articulate concepts made the American public believe in the picture he painted. Beyond the glamour of John Wayne, however, is the reality of his life. He was, like many Americans, faced with failed marriages, excessive drinking, and other related problems. Likewise, the John Wayne movie image of war left many soldiers disappointed and disenchanted when World War II taught them that combat was not as glamorous as they had imagined. Many, in fact, resented his visits to the front lines. While Reagan's tribute idealized American values, it also demonstrated his willingness to overlook unpleasant realities.

Reagan's first term in office brought about important changes in American government. Reagan won a major income tax cut which lowered the highest tax bracket from 70% to 38%. His administration supported the interests of business by deregulating the airline industry and refusing to negotiate with striking members of the air traffic controllers' union. Even more important than his legislative record was the way Reagan led a change in American perceptions of government. Reagan spoke constantly of the need for smaller, less-intrusive government and a stronger nation. This brand of conservatism has come to play a dominant role in American politics today.

In 1985, President Reagan delivered his State of the Union Address to Congress. After four years as President, Reagan took an opportunity to reassess and reaffirm his objectives. He started in characteristic form with these words:

> Tonight America is stronger because of the values that we hold dear. We believe faith and freedom must be our guiding stars, for they show us truth, they make us brave, give us hope and leave us wiser than we were. Our progress began not in Washington, D.C., but in the hearts of our families, communities, workplaces, and voluntary groups which, together, are unleashing the invincible spirit of one great nation under God.

Reagan then outlined his aims. The economy, a main thrust of his administration, had experienced a remarkable 25 consecutive months of growth, with lower inflation, and record employment. On top of the 25 percent tax cut already accomplished, Reagan called for tax exemption for impoverished families to discourage dependence on welfare.

Reagan believed that, "Every dollar the Federal Government does not take from us, every decision it does not make for us will make our economy stronger, our lives more abundant, our future more free." Therefore, government agencies and expenditures were cut dramatically. Two programs, however, were to remain untouched. Military expenditures and space exploration were top priority in the building of America's future. National security was the number one responsibility of the government. That responsibility extended to the fight against communism, and terrorism around the world. Indeed, many people have argued that the high military spending in the U. S. led the Soviet Union to collapse as it attempted to keep up. Thus, the Cold War ended on Reagan's watch.

In the same speech, Reagan expressed particular concern for the civil rights of the citizens. A government could not call itself great if low-income families, minorities, and the elderly were not properly taken care of. With few exceptions, however, specific plans for improvement were never developed in his administration. Instead the Reagan administration hoped that economic growth would lead to a better life for all Americans.

Though incomes grew for all Americans, economic growth benefited the rich more than the poor. Many of the newly rich flaunted their wealth. The growth produced the "Me generation" where reputation, social status, and affluence were all-important. BMW, the stock market, vacation homes, and small families were sure signs of the Yuppies (young urban professionals) that frequented the social clubs of the decade. The time of prosperity also gave way to a tendency for ruthless competition and scandal. During the late 1980s a string of successful Wall Street speculators ended up in jail for securities fraud.

Controversy did not escape the office of the President. Although Reagan enjoyed overwhelming public support, one glaring incident threatened that popularity. In 1986, the U.S. government sold weapons to Iran in exchange for the release of the American hostages in Lebanon, in spite of Reagan's avowal that the U. S. would never negotiate with terrorists. The funds from those sales were illegally used to aid the Contras who were fighting the communist backed Sandinista government in Nicaragua. The Iran-Contra scandal caught Reagan off-guard. First, he appeared before the nation and declared the allegations "utterly false." Vowing to cooperate completely with an investigation he "pledged to get to the bottom of this matter." Later, the President asserted that any action taken was "without my authorization, knowledge or concurrence." This statement was not particularly comforting. It left many Americans wondering what the President had been doing while members of his administration had been breaking the law.

While the Iran-Contra scandal tainted Reagan's final years in office, it did not dim his optimism. In his Farewell Address, Reagan pointed to a glorious future for America. "[New patriotism] is good . . . but it won't count for much, and it won't last unless it's grounded in thoughtfulness and knowledge." His familiar call for individual vigilance became his final message. Reagan believed that Americans could make a difference in their government. He said, "'We the People' tell the government what to do; it doesn't tell us. 'We the People' are the driver, the government is the car." Democracy provides the opportunity to participate and requires "informed patriotism." As President Reagan suggested, each citizen was responsible for the preservation of the American way of life. Citizenship was to be an active experience.

As you read the documents that follow ask yourself these questions: How important is it that the President is a masterful speaker? Does the character of the President matter? Is the smaller government that Reagan called for in accordance with the wishes of the Founders? Does it effect all Americans equally?

Reagan Obituary for John Wayne

In 1979 Ronald Reagan was gearing up for his successful 1980 campaign for the presidency. He took the occasion of John Wayne's death to sound some of the patriotic themes that would serve him so well in 1980 and 1984.

We called him Duke, and he was every bit the giant off screen he was on. Everything about him—his stature, his style, his convictions conveyed enduring strength, and no one who observed his struggle in those final days could doubt that strength was real. Yet there was more. To my wife, Nancy, "Duke Wayne was the most gentle, tender person I ever knew."

In 1960, as president of the Screen Actors' Guild, I was deeply embroiled in a bitter labor dispute between the Guild and the motion-picture industry. When we called a strike, the film industry unleashed a series of stinging personal attacks against me—criticism my wife was finding difficult to take.

At 7:30 one morning the phone rang and Nancy heard Duke's booming voice: "I've been readin' what these damn columnists are saying about Ron. He can take care of himself, but I've been worrying about how all this is affecting you." Virtually every morning until the strike was settled several weeks later, he phoned her. When a mass meeting was called to discuss settlement terms, he left a dinner party so that he could escort Nancy and sit at her side. It was, she said, like being next to a force bigger than life.

Countless others were also touched by his strength. Although it would take the critics 40 years to recognize what he was, the moviegoing public knew all along. In this country and around the world, he was the most popular box-office star of all time. For an incredible 25 years he was rated at or around the top in box-office appeal. His films grossed $700 million—a record no performer in Hollywood has come close to matching. Yet John Wayne was more than an actor; he was a force around which films were made. As Elizabeth Taylor Warner stated last May when testifying in favor of the special gold medal Congress struck for him: "He gave the whole world the image of what an American should be."

Stagecoach to Stardom

He was born Marion Michael Morrison in Winterset, Iowa. When Marion was six, the family moved to California. There he picked up the nickname Duke—after his Airedale. He rose at 4 A.M. to deliver newspapers, and after school and football practice he made deliveries for local stores. He was an A student, president of the Latin Society, head of his senior class and an all-state guard on a championship football team.

Duke had hoped to attend the U.S. Naval Academy and was named as an alternate selection to Annapolis, but the first choice took the appointment. Instead, he accepted a full scholarship to play football at the University of Southern California. There coach Howard Jones, who often found summer jobs in the movie industry for his players, got Duke work in the summer of 1926 as an assistant prop man on the set of a movie directed by John Ford.

One day, Ford, a notorious taskmaster with a rough-and-ready sense of humor, spotted the tall U.S.C. guard on his set and asked Duke to bend over and demonstrate his football stance. With a deft kick, Ford knocked Duke's arms from beneath his body and the young athlete fell on his face. Picking himself up, Duke said in that voice which even then commanded attention, "Let's try that once again." This time Duke sent Ford flying. Ford erupted in laughter, and the two began a personal and professional friendship which would last a lifetime.

From his job in props, Duke worked his way into roles on the screen. During the Depression he played in grade-B westerns until John Ford finally convinced United Artists to give him the role of the Ringo Kid in his classic film *Stagecoach*. John Wayne was on the road to stardom. He quickly established his versatility in a variety of major roles: a young seaman in Eugene O'Neill's *The Long Voyage Home,* a tragic captain in *Reap the Wild Wind,* a rodeo rider in the comedy *A Lady Takes a Chance.*

When war broke out, Duke tried to enlist but was rejected because of an old football injury to his shoulder, his age (34), and his status as a married father of four. He flew to Washington to plead that he be allowed to join the Navy but was turned down. So he poured himself into the war effort by making inspirational war films—among them *The Fighting Seabees, Back to Bataan* and *They Were Expendable.* To those back home and others around the world he became a symbol of the determined American fighting man.

Duke could not be kept from the front lines. In 1944 he spent three months touring forward positions in the Pacific theater. Appropriately, it was a wartime film, *Sands of Iwo Jima,* which turned him into a superstar. Years after the war, when Emperor Hirohito of Japan visited the United States, he sought out John Wayne, paying tribute to the one who represented our nation's success in combat.

As one of the true innovators of the film industry, Duke tossed aside the model of the white-suited cowboy/good guy, creating instead a tougher, deeper-dimensioned western hero. He discovered Monument Valley, the film setting in the Arizona-Utah desert where a host of movie classics were filmed. He perfected the choreographic techniques and stuntman tricks which brought realism to screen fighting. At the same time he decried pornography, and blood and gore in films. "That's not sex and violence," he would say. "It's filth and bad taste."

"I SURE AS HELL DID!"

In the 1940s, Duke was one of the few stars with the courage to expose the determined bid by a band of communists to take control of the film industry. Through a series of violent strikes and systematic blacklisting, these people were at times dangerously close to reaching their goal. With theatrical employers' union leader Roy Brewer, playwright Morrie Ry[] and others, he formed the Motion Picture [ance] for the Preservation of American Id[] to challenge this insidious campaign. Subsequent Congressional investigations in 1947 clearly proved both the communist plot and the importance of what Duke and his friends did.

In that period, during my first term as president of the Actors' Guild, I was confronted with an attempt by many of these same leftists to assume leadership of the union. At a mass meeting I watched rather helplessly as they filibustered, waiting for our majority to leave so they could gain control. Somewhere in the crowd I heard a call for adjournment, and I seized on this as a means to end the attempted takeover. But the other side demanded I identify the one who moved for adjournment.

I looked over the audience, realizing that there were few willing to be publicly identified as opponents of the far left. Then I saw Duke and said, "Why I believe John Wayne made the motion." I heard his strong voice reply, "I sure as hell did!" The meeting—and the radicals' campaign—was over.

Later, when such personalities as actor Larry Parks came forward to admit their Communist Party backgrounds, there were those who wanted to see them punished. Not Duke. "It takes courage to admit you're wrong," he said, and he publicly battled attempts to ostracize those who had come clean.

Duke also had the last word over those who warned that his battle against communism in Hollywood would ruin his career. Many times he would proudly boast, "I was 32nd in the box-office polls when I accepted the presidency of the Alliance. When I left office eight years later, somehow the folks who buy tickets had made me number one."

Duke went to Vietnam in the early days of the war. He scorned VIP treatment, insisting that he visit the troops in the field. Once he even had his helicopter land in the midst of a battle. When he returned, he vowed to make a film about the heroism of Special Forces soldiers.

The public jammed theaters to see the resulting film, *The Green Berets.* The critics, however, delivered some of the harshest reviews ever given a motion picture. The *New Yorker* bitterly condemned the man who made the film. *The New York Times* called it "unspeakable . . . rotten . . . stupid." Yet Duke was undaunted. "That little clique back there in the East has taken great personal satisfaction reviewing my politics instead of my pictures," he often said. "But one day those doctrinaire liberals will wake up to find the pendulum has swung the other way."

Foul-Weather Friend

I never once saw Duke display hatred toward those who scorned him. Oh, he could use some pretty salty language, but he would not tolerate pettiness and hate. He was human, all right: he drank enough whiskey to float a PT boat, though he never drank on the job. His work habits were legendary in Hollywood—he was virtually always the first to arrive on the set and the last to leave.

His torturous schedule plus the great personal pleasure he derived from hunting and deep-sea fishing or drinking and card playing with his friends may have cost him a couple of marriages; but you had only to see his seven children and 21 grandchildren to realize that Duke found time to be a good father. He often said, "I have tried to live my life so that my family would love me and my friends respect me. The others can do whatever the hell they please."

To him, a handshake was a binding contract. When he was in the hospital for the last time and sold his yacht, *The Wild Goose,* for an amount far below its market value, he learned the engines needed minor repairs. He ordered those engines overhauled at a cost to him of $40,000 because he had told the new owner the boat was in good shape.

Duke's generosity and loyalty stood out in a city rarely known for either. When a friend needed work, that person went on his payroll. When a friend needed help, Duke's wallet was open. He also was loyal to his fans. One writer tells of the night he and Duke were in Dallas for the première of *Chisum.* Returning late to his hotel, Duke found a message from a woman who said her little girl lay critically ill in a local hospital. The woman wrote, "It would mean so much to her if you could pay her just a brief visit." At 3 o'clock in the morning he took off for the hospital where he visited the astonished child—and every other patient on the hospital floor who happened to be awake.

I saw his loyalty in action many times. I remember that when Duke and Jimmy Stewart were on their way to my second inauguration as governor of California they encountered a crowd of demonstrators under the banner of the Vietcong flag. Jimmy had just lost a son in Vietnam. Duke excused himself for a moment and walked into the crowd. In a moment there was no Vietcong flag.

Final Curtain

Like any good John Wayne film, Duke's career had a gratifying ending. In the 1970s a new era of critics began to recognize the unique quality of his acting. The turning point had been the film *True Grit.* When the Academy gave him an Oscar for best actor of 1969, many said it was based on the accomplishments of his entire career. Others said it was Hollywood's way of admitting that it had been wrong to deny him Academy Awards for a host of previous films. There is truth, I think, to both these views.

Yet who can forget the climax of the film? The grizzled old marshal confronts the four outlaws and calls out: "I mean to kill you or see you hanged at Judge Parker's convenience. Which will it be?"

"Bold talk for a one-eyed fat man," their leader sneers.

Then Duke cries, "Fill your hand, you sonofabitch!" and, reins in his teeth, charges at them firing with both guns. Four villains did not live to menace another day.

"Foolishness?" wrote Chicago *Sun-Times* columnist Mike Royko, describing the thrill this scene gave him. "Maybe. But I hope we never become so programmed that nobody has the damn-the-risk spirit."

Fifteen years ago when Duke lost a lung in his first bout with cancer, studio press agents tried to conceal the nature of his illness. When Duke discovered this, he went before the public and showed us that a man can fight this dread disease. He went on to raise millions of dollars for private cancer research. Typically, he snorted: "We've got too much at stake to give government a monopoly in the fight against cancer."

Earlier this year, when doctors told Duke there was no hope, he urged them to use his body for experimental medical research, to further the search for a cure. He refused painkillers so he could be alert as he spent his last days with his children. When he died on June 11, a Tokyo newspaper ran the headline, "Mr. America passes on."

"There's right and there's wrong , Duke said in *The Alamo*. "You gotta do one or the other. You do the one and you're living. You do the other and you may be walking around but in reality you're dead."

Duke Wayne symbolized just this, the force of the American will to do what is right in the world. He could have left no greater legacy.

State of Union 1985

Ronald Reagan

I come before you to report on the state of our Union, and I'm pleased to report that after 4 years of united effort, the American people have brought forth a nation renewed, stronger, freer, and more secure than before.

Four years ago we began to change, forever I hope, our assumptions about government and its place in our lives. Out of that change has come great and robust growth—in our confidence, our economy, and our role in the world.

Tonight America is stronger because of the values that we hold dear. We believe faith and freedom must be our guiding stars, for they show us truth, they make us brave, give us hope, and leave us wiser than we were. Our progress began not in Washington, D.C., but in the hearts of our families, communities, workplaces, and voluntary groups which, together, are unleashing the invincible spirit of one great nation under God.

Four years ago we said we would invigorate our economy by giving people greater freedom and incentives to take risks and letting them keep more of what they earned. We did what we promised, and a great industrial giant is reborn.

Tonight we can take pride in 25 straight months of economic growth, the strongest in 34 years; a 3-year inflation average of 3.9 percent, the lowest in 17 years; and 7.3 million new jobs in 2 years, with more of our citizens working than ever before.

New freedom in our lives has planted the rich seeds for future success:

- For an America of wisdom that honors the family, knowing that if [as] the family goes, so goes our civilization;
- For an America of vision that sees tomorrow's dreams in the learning and hard work we do today;
- For an America of courage whose service men and women, even as we meet, proudly stand watch on the frontiers of freedom;

- For an America of compassion that opens its heart to those who cry out for help.

We have begun well. But it's only a beginning. We're not here to congratulate ourselves on what we have done but to challenge ourselves to finish what has not yet been done.

We're here to speak for millions in our inner cities who long for real jobs, safe neighborhoods, and schools that truly teach. We're here to speak for the American farmer, the entrepreneur, and every worker in industries fighting to modernize and compete. And, yes, we're here to stand, and proudly so, for all who struggle to break free from totalitarianism, for all who know in their hearts that freedom is the one true path to peace and human happiness.

Proverbs tell us, without a vision the people perish. When asked what great principle holds our Union together, Abraham Lincoln said, *"Something in [the] Declaration giving liberty, not alone to the people of this country, but hope to the world for all future time."*

We honor the giants of our history not by going back but forward to the dreams their vision foresaw. My fellow citizens, this nation is poised for greatness. The time has come to proceed toward a great new challenge—a second American Revolution of hope and opportunity; a revolution carrying us to new heights of progress by pushing back frontiers of knowledge and space; a revolution of spirit that taps the soul of America, enabling us to summon greater strength than we've ever known; and a revolution that carries beyond our shores the golden promise of human freedom in a world of peace.

Let us begin by challenging our conventional wisdom. There are no constraints on the human mind, no walls around the human spirit, no barriers to our progress except those we ourselves erect. Already, pushing down tax rates has freed our economy to vault forward to record growth.

In Europe, they're calling it *"the American Miracle."* Day by day, we're shattering accepted notions of what is possible. When I was growing up, we failed to see how a new thing called radio would transform our marketplace. Well, today, many have not yet seen how advances in technology are transforming our lives.

In the late 1950s workers at the AT&T semiconductor plant in Pennsylvania produced five transistors a day for $7.50 apiece. They now produce over a million for less than a penny apiece.

New laser techniques could revolutionize heart bypass surgery, cut diagnosis time for viruses linked to cancer from weeks to minutes, reduce hospital costs dramatically, and hold out new promise for saving human lives.

Our automobile industry has overhauled assembly lines, increased worker productivity, and is competitive once again.

We stand on the threshold of a great ability to produce more, do more, be more. Our economy is not getting older and weaker; it's getting younger and stronger. It doesn't need rest and supervision; it needs new challenge, greater freedom. And that word *"freedom"* is the key to the second American Revolution that we need to bring about.

Let us move together with an historic *reform of tax* simplification for fairness and growth. Last year I asked Treasury Secretary—then—Regan to develop a plan to simplify the tax code, so all taxpayers would be treated more fairly and personal tax rates could come further down.

We have cut tax rates by almost 25 percent, yet the tax system remains unfair and limits our potential for growth. Exclusions and exemptions cause similar incomes to be taxed at different levels. Low-income families face steep tax barriers that make hard lives even harder. The Treasury Department has produced an excellent reform plan, whose principles will guide the final proposal that we will ask you to enact.

One thing that tax reform will not be is a tax increase in disguise. We will not jeopardize the mortgage interest deduction that families need. We will reduce personal tax rates as low as possible by removing many tax preferences. We will propose a top rate of no more than 35 percent, and possibly lower. And we will propose reducing corporate rates, while maintaining incentives for capital formation.

To encourage opportunity and jobs rather than dependency and welfare, we will propose that individuals living at or near the poverty line be totally exempt from Federal income tax. To restore fairness to families, we will propose increasing significantly the personal exemption.

And tonight, I am instructing Treasury Secretary James Baker—I have to get used to saying that—to begin working with congressional authors and committees for bipartisan legislation conforming to these principles. We will call upon the American people for support and upon every man and woman in this Chamber. Together, we can pass, this year, a tax bill for fairness, simplicity, and growth, making this economy the engine of our dreams and America the investment capital of the world. So let us begin.

Tax simplification will be a giant step toward unleashing the tremendous pent-up power of our economy. But a second American Revolution must carry the promise of opportunity for all. It is time to liberate the spirit of enterprise in the most distressed areas of our country.

This government will meet its responsibility to help those in need. But policies that increase dependency, break up families, and destroy self-respect are not progressive; they're reactionary. Despite our strides in civil rights, blacks, Hispanics, and all minorities will not have full and equal power until they have full economic power.

We have repeatedly sought passage of enterprise zones to help those in the abandoned comers of our land find jobs, learn skills, and build better lives. This legislation is supported by a majority of you.

Mr. Speaker, I know we agree that there must be no forgotten Americans. Let us place new dreams in a million hearts and create a new generation of entrepreneurs by passing enterprise zones this year. And, Tip, you could make that a birthday present.

Nor must we lose the chance to pass our youth employment opportunity wage proposal. We can help teenagers, who have the highest unemployment rate, find summer jobs, so they can know the pride of work and have confidence in their futures.

We'll continue to support the Job Training Partnership Act, which has a nearly two-thirds job placement rate. Credits in education and health care vouchers will help working families shop for services that they need.

Our administration is already encouraging certain low-income public housing residents to own and manage their own dwellings. It's time that all public housing residents have that opportunity of ownership.

The Federal Government can help create a new atmosphere of freedom. But States and localities, many of which enjoy surpluses from the recovery, must not permit their tax and regulatory policies to stand as barriers to growth.

Let us resolve that we will stop spreading dependency and start spreading opportunity; that we will stop spreading bondage and start spreading freedom.

There are some who say that growth initiatives must await final action on deficit reductions. Well, the best way to reduce deficits is through economic growth. More businesses will be started, more investments made, more jobs created, and more people will be on payrolls paying taxes. The best way to reduce government spending is to reduce the need for spending by increasing prosperity. Each added percentage point per year of real GNP growth will lead to cumulative reduction in deficits of nearly $200 billion over 5 years.

To move steadily toward a balanced budget, we must also lighten government's claim on our total economy. We will not do this by raising taxes. We must make sure that our economy grows faster than the growth in spending by the Federal Government. In our fiscal year 1986 budget, overall government program spending will be frozen at the current level. It must not be one dime higher than fiscal year 1985, and three points are key.

First, the social safety net for the elderly, the needy, the disabled, and unemployed will be left intact. Growth of our major health care programs, Medicare and Medicaid, will be slowed, but protections for the elderly and needy will be preserved.

Second, we must not relax our efforts to restore military strength just as we near our goal of a fully equipped, trained, and ready professional corps. National security is government's first responsibility; so in past years defense spending took about half the Federal budget. Today it takes less than a third. We've already reduced our planned defense expenditures by nearly a hundred billion dollars over the past 4 years and reduced projected spending again this year.

You know, we only have a military-industrial complex until a time of danger, and then it becomes the arsenal of democracy. Spending for defense is investing in things that are priceless—peace and freedom.

Third, we must reduce or eliminate costly government subsidies. For example, deregulation of the airline industry has led to cheaper airfares, but on Amtrak taxpayers pay about $35 per passenger every time an Amtrak train leaves the station. It's time we ended this huge Federal subsidy.

Our farm program costs have quadrupled in recent years. Yet I know from visiting farmers, many in great financial distress, that we need an orderly transition to a market-oriented farm economy. We can help farmers best not by expanding Federal payments but by making fundamental reforms, keeping interest rates heading down, and knocking down foreign trade barriers to American farm exports.

We're moving ahead with Grace Commission reforms to eliminate waste and improve government's management practices. In the long run, we must protect the taxpayers from government. And I ask again that you pass, as 32 States have now called for, an amendment mandating the Federal Government spend no more than it takes in. And I ask for the au-

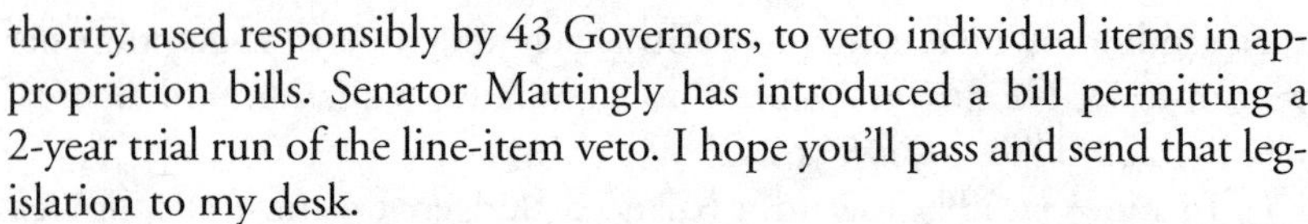

thority, used responsibly by 43 Governors, to veto individual items in appropriation bills. Senator Mattingly has introduced a bill permitting a 2-year trial run of the line-item veto. I hope you'll pass and send that legislation to my desk.

Nearly 50 years of government living beyond its means has brought us to a time of reckoning. Ours is but a moment in history. But one moment of courage, idealism, and bipartisan unity can change American history forever.

Sound monetary policy is key to long-running economic strength and stability. We will continue to cooperate with the Federal Reserve Board, seeking a steady policy that ensures price stability without keeping interest rates artificially high or needlessly holding down growth.

Reducing unneeded redtape and regulations, and deregulating the energy, transportation, and financial industries have unleashed new competition, giving consumers more choices, better services, and lower prices. In just one set of grant programs we have reduced 905 pages of regulations to 31. We seek to fully deregulate natural gas to bring on new supplies and bring us closer to energy independence. Consistent with safety standards, we will continue removing restraints on the bus and railroad industries, we will soon end up legislation—or send up legislation, I should say—to return Conrail to the private sector where it belongs, and we will support further deregulation of the trucking industry.

Every dollar the Federal Government does not take from us, every decision it does not make for us will make our economy stronger, our lives more abundant, our future more free.

Our second American Revolution will push on to new possibilities not only on Earth but in the next frontier of space. Despite budget restraints, we will seek record funding for research and development.

We've seen the success of the space shuttle. Now we're going to develop a permanently manned space station and new opportunities for free enterprise, because in the next decade Americans and our friends around the world will be living and working together in space.

In the zero gravity of space, we could manufacture in 30 days lifesaving medicines it would take 30 years to make on Earth. We can make crystals of exceptional purity to produce super computers, creating jobs, technologies, and medical breakthroughs beyond anything we ever dreamed possible.

As we do all this, we'll continue to protect our natural resources. We will seek reauthorization and expanded funding for the Superfund program to continue cleaning up hazardous waste sites which threaten human health and the environment.

Now, there's another great heritage to speak of this evening. Of all the changes that have swept America the past 4 years, none brings greater promise than our rediscovery of the values of faith, freedom, family, work, and neighborhood.

We see signs of renewal in increased attendance in places of worship; renewed optimism and faith in our future; love of country rediscovered by our young, who are leading the way. We've rediscovered that work is good in and of itself, that it ennobles us to create and contribute no matter how seemingly humble our jobs. We've seen a powerful new current from an old and honorable tradition—American generosity.

From thousands answering Peace Corps appeals to help boost food production in Africa, to millions volunteering time, corporations adopting schools, and communities pulling together to help the neediest among us at home, we have refound our values. Private sector initiatives are crucial to our future.

I thank the Congress for passing equal access legislation giving religious groups the same right to use classrooms after school that other groups enjoy. But no citizen need tremble, nor the world shudder, if a child stands in a classroom and breathes a prayer. We ask you again, give children back a right they had for a century and a half or more in this country.

The question of abortion grips our nation. Abortion is either the taking of a human life or it isn't. And if it is—and medical technology is increasingly showing it is—it must be stopped. It is a terrible irony that while some turn to abortion, so many others who cannot become parents cry out for children to adopt. We have room for these children. We can fill the cradles of those who want a child to love. And tonight I ask you in the Congress to move this year on legislation to protect the unborn.

In the area of education, we're returning to excellence, and again, the heroes are our people, not government. We're stressing basics of discipline, rigorous testing, and homework, while helping children become computer-smart as well. For 20 years Scholastic Aptitude Test scores of our high school students went down, but now they have gone up 2 of the last 3 years. We must go forward in our commitment to the new basics, giving parents greater authority and making sure good teachers are rewarded for hard work and achievement through merit pay.

Of all the changes in the past 20 years, none has more threatened our sense of national well-being than the explosion of violent crime. One does not have to be attacked to be a victim. The woman who must run to her car after shopping at night is a victim. The couple draping their door with locks and chains are victims; as is the tired, decent cleaning woman who can't ride a subway home without being afraid.

We do not seek to violate the rights of defendants. But shouldn't we feel more compassion for the victims of crime than for those who commit crime? For the first time in 20 years, the crime index has fallen 2 years in a row. We've convicted over 7,400 drug offenders and put them, as well as leaders of organized crime, behind bars in record numbers.

But we must do more. I urge the House to follow the Senate and enact proposals permitting use of all reliable evidence that police officers acquire in good faith. These proposals would also reform the habeus corpus laws and allow, in keeping with the will of the overwhelming majority of Americans, the use of the death penalty where necessary.

There can be no economic revival in ghettos when the most violent among us are allowed to roam free. It's time we restored domestic tranquility. And we mean to do just that.

Just as we're positioned as never before to secure justice in our economy, we're poised as never before to create a safer, freer, more peaceful world. Our alliances are stronger than ever. Our economy is stronger than ever. We have resumed our historic role as a leader of the free world. And all of these together are a great force for peace.

Since 1981 we've been committed to seeking fair and verifiable arms agreements that would lower the risk of war and reduce the size of nuclear arsenals. Now our determination to maintain a strong defense has influenced the Soviet Union to return to the bargaining table. Our negotiators must be able to go to that table with the united support of the American people. All of us have no greater dream than to see the day when nuclear weapons are banned from this Earth forever.

Each Member of the Congress has a role to play in modernizing our defenses, thus supporting our chances for a meaningful arms agreement. Your vote this spring on the Peacekeeper missile will be a critical test of our resolve to maintain the strength we need and move toward mutual and verifiable arms reductions.

For the past 20 years we've believed that no war will be launched as long as each side knows it can retaliate with a deadly counterstrike. Well, I believe there's a better way of eliminating the threat of nuclear war. It is a *Strategic Defense Initiative* aimed ultimately at finding a nonnuclear defense against ballistic missiles. It's the most hopeful possibility of the nuclear age. But it's not very well understood.

Some say it will bring war to the heavens, but its purpose is to deter war in the heavens and on Earth. Now, some say the research would be expensive. Perhaps, but it could save millions of lives, indeed humanity itself. And some say if we build such a system, the Soviets will build a defense system of their own. Well, they already have strategic defenses that surpass ours; a civil defense system, where we have almost none; and a research program covering roughly the same areas of technology that we're now exploring. And finally some say the research will take a long time. Well, the answer to that is: *"Let's get started."*

Harry Truman once said that, ultimately, our security and the world's hopes for peace and human progress *"lie not in measures of defense or in the control of weapons, but in the growth and expansion of freedom and self-government."*

And tonight, we declare anew to our fellow citizens of the world: Freedom is not the sole prerogative of a chosen few; it is the universal right of all God's children. Look to where peace and prosperity flourish today. It is in homes that freedom built. Victories against poverty are greatest and peace most secure where people live by laws that ensure free press, free speech, and freedom to worship, vote, and create wealth.

Our mission is to nourish and defend freedom and democracy, and to communicate these ideals everywhere we can. America's economic success is freedom's success; it can be repeated a hundred times in a hundred different nations. Many countries in east Asia and the Pacific have few resources other than the enterprise of their own people. But through low tax rates and free markets they've soared ahead of centralized economies. And now China is opening up its economy to meet its needs.

We need a stronger and simpler approach to the process of making and implementing trade policy, and we'll be studying potential changes in that process in the next few weeks. We've seen the benefits of free trade and lived through the disasters of protectionism. Tonight I ask all our trading partners, developed and developing alike, to join us in a new round of trade negotiations to expand trade and competition and strengthen the global economy—and to begin it in this next year.

There are more than 3 billion human beings living in Third World countries with an average per capita income of $650 a year. Many are victims of dictatorships that impoverished them with taxation and corruption. Let us ask our allies to join us in a practical program of trade and assistance that fosters economic development through personal incentives to help these people climb from poverty on their own.

We cannot play innocents abroad in a world that's not innocent; nor can we be passive when freedom is under siege. Without resources, diplomacy cannot succeed. Our security assistance programs help friendly governments defend themselves and give them confidence to work for peace. And I hope that you in the Congress will understand that, dollar for dollar, security assistance contributes as much to global security as our own defense budget.

We must stand by all our democratic allies. And we must not break faith with those who are risking their lives—on every continent, from Afghanistan to Nicaragua—to defy Soviet-supported aggression and secure rights which have been ours from birth.

The *Sandinista dictatorship of Nicaragua,* with full Cuban-Soviet bloc support, not only persecutes its people, the church, and denies a free press, but arms and provides bases for Communist terrorists attacking neighboring states. Support for freedom fighters is self-defense and totally consistent with the OAS and U.N. Charters. It is essential that the Congress continue all facets of our assistance to Central America. I want to work with you to support the democratic forces whose struggle is tied to our own security.

And tonight, I've spoken of great plans and great dreams. They're dreams we can make come true. Two hundred years of American history should have taught us that nothing is impossible.

Ten years ago a young girl left Vietnam with her family, part of the exodus that followed the fall of Saigon. They came to the United States with no possessions and not knowing a word of English. Ten years ago—the young girl studied hard, learned English, and finished high school in the top of her class. And this May, May 22d to be exact, is a big date on her calendar. Just 10 years from the time she left Vietnam, she will graduate from the United States Military Academy at West Point. I thought you might like to meet an American hero named Jean Nguyen.

Now, there's someone else here tonight, born 79 years ago. She lives in the inner city, where she cares for infants born of mothers who are heroin addicts. The children, born in withdrawal, are sometimes even dropped on her doorstep. She helps them with love. Go to her house some night, and maybe you'll see her silhouette against the window as she walks the floor talking softly, soothing a child in her arms—Mother Hale of Harlem, and she, too, is an American hero.

Jean, Mother Hale, your lives tell us that the oldest American saying is new again: Anything is possible in America if we have the faith, the will, and the heart. History is asking us once again to be a force for good in the world. Let us begin in unity, with justice, and love.

Thank you, and God bless you.

President Reagan's Farewell Speech

The President spoke at 9:02 P.M. from the Oval Office at the White House. The address was broadcast live on nationwide radio and television.

This is the 34th time I'll speak to you from the Oval Office and the last. We've been together 8 years now, and soon it'll be time for me to go. But before I do, I wanted to share some thoughts, some of which I've been saving for a long time.

It's been the honor of my life to be your President. So many of you have written the past few weeks to say thanks, but I could say as much to you. Nancy and I are grateful for the opportunity you gave us to serve.

One of the things about the Presidency is that you're always somewhat apart. You spent a lot of time going by too fast in a car someone else is driving, and seeing the people through tinted glass—the parents holding up a child, and the wave you saw too late and couldn't return. And so many times I wanted to stop and reach out from behind the glass, and connect. Well, maybe I can do a little of that tonight.

People ask how I feel about leaving. And the fact is, 'parting is such sweet sorrow.' The sweet part is California and the ranch and freedom. The sorrow—the goodbyes, of course, and leaving this beautiful place.

You know, down the hall and up the stairs from this office is the part of the White House where the President and his family live. There are a few favorite windows I have up there that I like to stand and look out of early in the morning. The view is over the grounds here to the Washington Monument, and then the Mall and the Jefferson Memorial. But on mornings when the humidity is low, you can see past the Jefferson to the river, the Potomac, and the Virginia shore. Someone said that's the view Lincoln had when he saw the smoke rising from the Battle of Bull Run. I see more prosaic things: the grass on the banks, the morning traffic as people make their way to work, now and then a sailboat on the river.

I've been thinking a bit at that window. I've been reflecting on what the past 8 years have meant and mean. And the image that comes to mind like a refrain is a nautical one—a small story about a big ship, and a refugee, and a sailor. It was back in the early eighties, at the height of the boat people. And the sailor was hard at work on the carrier Midway, which was patrolling the South China Sea. The sailor, like most American servicemen, was young, smart, and fiercely observant. The crew spied on the horizon a leaky little boat. And crammed inside were refugees from Indochina hoping to get to America. The Midway sent a small launch to bring them to the ship and safety. As the refugees made their way through the choppy seas, one spied the sailor on deck, and stood up, and called out to him. He yelled, 'Hello, American sailor. Hello, freedom man.'

A small moment with a big meaning, a moment the sailor, who wrote it in a letter, couldn't get out of his mind. And, when I saw it, neither could I. Because that's what it was to be an American in the 1980's. We stood, again, for freedom. I know we always have, but in the past few years the world again—and in a way, we ourselves—rediscovered it.

It's been quite a journey this decade, and we held together through some stormy seas. And at the end, together, we are reaching our destination.

The fact is, from Grenada to the Washington and Moscow summits, from the recession of '81 to '82, to the expansion that began in late '82 and continues to this day, we've made a difference. The way I see it, there were two great triumphs, two things that I'm proudest of. One is the economic recovery, in which the people of America created—and filled—19 million new jobs. The other is the recovery of our morale. America is respected again in the world and looked to for leadership.

Something that happened to me a few years ago reflects some of this. It was back in 1981, and I was attending my first big economic summit, which was held that year in Canada. The meeting place rotates among the member countries. The opening meeting was a formal dinner of the heads of government of the seven industrialized nations. Now, I sat there like the new kid in school and listened, and it was all Francois this and Helmut that. They dropped titles and spoke to one another on a first-name basis. Well, at one point I sort of leaned in and said, 'My name's Ron.' Well, in that same year, we began the actions we felt would ignite an economic comeback—cut taxes and regulation, started to cut spending. And soon the recovery began.

Two years later, another economic summit with pretty much the same cast. At the big opening meeting we all got together, and all of a sudden, just for a moment, I saw that everyone was just sitting there looking at me. And then one of them broke the silence. 'Tell us about the American miracle,' he said.

Well, back in 1980, when I was running for President, it was all so different. Some pundits said our programs would result in catastrophe. Our views on foreign affairs would cause war. Our plans for the economy would cause inflation to soar and bring about economic collapse. I even remember one highly respected economist saying, back in 1982, that 'The engines of economic growth have shut down here, and they're likely to stay that way for years to come.' Well, he and the other opinion leaders were wrong. The fact is what they call 'radical' was really 'right.' What they called 'dangerous' was just 'desperately needed.'

And in all of that time I won a nickname, 'The Great Communicator.' But I never thought it was my style or the words I used that made a difference: it was the content. I wasn't a great communicator, but I communicated great things, and they didn't spring full bloom from my brow, they came from the heart of a great nation—from our experience, our wisdom, and our belief in the principles that have guided us for two centuries. They called it the Reagan revolution. Well, I'll accept that, but for me it always seemed more like the great rediscovery, a rediscovery of our values and our common sense.

Common sense told us that when you put a big tax on something, the people will produce less of it. So, we cut the people's tax rates, and the people produced more than ever before. The economy bloomed like a plant that had been cut back and could now grow quicker and stronger. Our economic program brought about the longest peacetime expansion in our history: real family income up, the poverty rate down, entrepreneurship booming, and an explosion in research and new technology. We're exporting more than ever because American industry became more competitive and at the same time, we summoned the national will to knock down protectionist walls abroad instead of erecting them at home.

Common sense also told us that to preserve the peace, we'd have to become strong again after years of weakness and confusion. So, we rebuilt our defenses, and this New Year we toasted the new peacefulness around the globe. Not only have the superpowers actually begun to reduce their stockpiles of nuclear weapons—and hope for even more progress is bright—but the regional conflicts that rack the globe are also beginning to cease. The Persian Gulf is no longer a war zone. The Soviets are leaving Afghanistan. The Vietnamese are preparing to pull out of Cambodia, and an American-mediated accord will soon send 50,000 Cuban troops home from Angola.

The lesson of all this was, of course, that because we're a great nation, our challenges seem complex. It will always be this way. But as long as we remember our first principles and believe in ourselves, the future will always be ours. And something else we learned: Once you begin a great movement, there's no telling where it will end. We meant to change a nation, and instead, we changed a world.

Countries across the globe are turning to free markets and free speech and turning away from the ideologies of the past. For them, the great rediscovery of the 1980s has been that, lo and behold, the moral way of government is the practical way of government: Democracy, the profoundly good, is also the profoundly productive.

When you've got to the point when you can celebrate the anniversaries of your 39th birthday you can sit back sometimes, review your life, and see it flowing before you. For me there was a fork in the river, and it was right in the middle of my life. I never meant to go into politics. It wasn't my intention when I was young. But I was raised to believe you had to pay your way for the blessings bestowed on you. I was happy with my career in the entertainment world, but I ultimately went into politics because I wanted to protect something precious.

Ours was the first revolution in the history of mankind that truly reversed the course of government, and with three little words: 'We the People.' 'We the People' tell the government what to do; it doesn't tell us. 'We the People' are the driver; the government is the car. And we decide where it should go, and by what route, and how fast. Almost all the world's constitutions are documents in which governments tell the people what their privileges are. Our Constitution is a document in which 'We the People' tell the government what it is allowed to do. 'We the People' are free. This belief has been the underlying basis for everything I've tried to do these past 8 years.

But back in the 1960s, when I began, it seemed to me that we'd begun reversing the order of things—that through more and more rules and regulations and confiscatory taxes, the government was taking more of our money, more of our options, and more of our freedom. I went into politics in part to put up my hand and say, 'Stop.' I was a citizen politician, and it seemed the right thing for a citizen to do.

I think we have stopped a lot of what needed stopping. And I hope we have once again reminded people that man is not free unless government is limited. There's a clear cause and effect here that is as neat and predictable as a law of physics: As government expands, liberty contracts.

Nothing is less free than pure communism—and yet we have, the past few years, forged a satisfying new closeness with the Soviet Union. I've been asked if this isn't a gamble, and my answer is no because we're basing our actions not on words but deeds. The détente of the 1970s was based not on actions but promises. They'd promise to treat their own people and the people of the world better. But the *gulag* was still the gulag, and the state was still expansionist, and they still waged proxy wars in Africa, Asia, and Latin America.

Well, this time, so far, it's different. President Gorbachev has brought about some internal democratic reforms and begun the withdrawal from Afghanistan. He has also freed prisoners whose names I've given him every time we've met.

But life has a way of reminding you of big things through small incidents. Once, during the heady days of the Moscow summit, Nancy and I decided to break off from the entourage one afternoon to visit the shops on Arbat Street—that's a little street just off Moscow's main shopping area. Even though our visit was a surprise, every Russian there immediately recognized us and called out our names and reached for our hands. We were just about swept away by the warmth. You could almost feel the possibilities in all that joy. But within seconds, a KGB detail pushed their way toward us and began pushing and shoving the people in the crowd. It was an interesting moment. It reminded me that while the man on the street in the Soviet Union yearns for peace, the government is Communist. And those who run it are Communists, and that means we and they view such issues as freedom and human rights very differently.

We must keep up our guard, but we must also continue to work together to lessen and eliminate tension and mistrust. My view is that President Gorbachev is different from previous Soviet leaders. I think he knows some of the things wrong with his society and is trying to fix them. We wish him well. And we'll continue to work to make sure that the Soviet Union that eventually emerges from this process is a less threatening one. What it all boils down to is this: I want the new closeness to continue. And it will, as long as we make it clear that we will continue to act in a certain way as long as they continue to act in a helpful manner. If and when they don't, at first pull your punches. If they persist, pull the plug. It's still trust by verify. It's still play, but cut the cards. It's still watch closely. And don't be afraid to see what you see.

I've been asked if I have any regrets. Well, I do. The deficit is one. I've been talking a great deal about that lately, but tonight isn't for arguments, and I'm going to hold my tongue. But an observation: I've had my share of victories in the Congress, but what few people noticed is that I never won anything you didn't win for me. They never saw my troops, they never saw Reagan's regiments, the American people. You won every battle with every call you made and letter you wrote demanding action. Well, action is still needed. If we're to finish the job. Reagan's regiments will have to become the Bush brigades. Soon he'll be the chief, and he'll need you every bit as much as I did.

Finally, there is a great tradition of warnings in Presidential farewells, and I've got one that's been on my mind for some time. But oddly enough it starts with one of the things I'm proudest of in the past 8 years: the resurgence of national pride that I called the new patriotism. This national feeling is good, but it won't count for much, and it won't last unless it's grounded in thoughtfulness and knowledge.

An informed patriotism is what we want. And are we doing a good enough job teaching our children what America is and what she represents in the long history of the world? Those of us who are over 35 or so years of age grew up in a different America. We were taught, very directly, what it means to be an American. And we absorbed, almost in the air, a love of country and an appreciation of its institutions. If you didn't get these things from your family you got them from the neighborhood, from the father down the street who fought in Korea or the family who lost someone at Anzio. Or you could get a sense of patriotism from school. And if all else failed you could get a sense of patriotism from the popular culture. The movies celebrated democratic values and implicitly reinforced the idea that America was special. TV was like that, too, through the mid-sixties.

But now, we're about to enter the nineties, and some things have changed. Younger parents aren't sure that an unambivalent appreciation of America is the right thing to teach modern children. And as for those who create the popular culture, well-grounded patriotism is no longer the style. Our spirit is back, but we haven't reinstitutionalized it. We've got to do a better job of getting across that America is freedom—freedom of speech, freedom of religion, freedom of enterprise. And freedom is special and rare. It's fragile; it needs production [protection].

So, we've got to teach history based not on what's in fashion but what's important—why the Pilgrims came here, who Jimmy Doolittle was, and what those 30 seconds over Tokyo meant. You know, 4 years ago on the 40th anniversary of D-day, I read a letter from a young woman writing to her late father, who'd fought on Omaha Beach. Her name was Lisa Zanatta Henn, and she said, 'we will always remember, we will never forget what the boys of Normandy did.' Well, let's help her keep her word. If we forget what we did, we won't know who we are. I'm warning of an eradication of the American memory that could result, ultimately, in an erosion of the American spirit. Let's start with some basics: more attention to American history and a greater emphasis on civic ritual.

And let me offer lesson number one about America: All great change in America begins at the dinner table. So, tomorrow night in the kitchen I hope the talking begins. And children, if your parents haven't been teaching you what it means to be an American, let'em know and nail'em on it. That would be a very American thing to do.

And that's about all I have to say tonight, except for one thing. The past few days when I've been at that window upstairs, I've thought a bit of the 'shining city upon a hill.' The phrase comes from John Winthrop, who wrote it to describe the America he imagined. What he imagined was important because he was an early Pilgrim, an early freedom man. He journeyed here on what today we'd call a little wooden boat; and like the other Pilgrims, he was looking for a home that would be free. I've spoken of the shining city all my political life, but I don't know if I ever quite communicated what I saw when I said it. But in my mind it was a tall, proud city built on rocks stronger than oceans, windswept, God-blessed, and teeming with people of all kinds living in harmony and peace; a city with free ports that hummed with commerce and creativity. And if there had to be city walls, the walls had doors and the doors were open to anyone with the will and the heart to get here. That's how I saw it, and see it still.

And how stands the city on this winter night? More prosperous, more secure, and happier than it was 8 years ago. But more than that: After 200 years, two centuries, she still stands strong and true on the granite ridge, and her glow has held steady no matter what storm. And she's still a beacon, still a magnet for all who must have freedom, for all the pilgrims from all the lost places who are hurtling through the darkness, toward home.

We've done our part. And as I walk off into the city streets, a final word to the men and women of the Reagan revolution, the men and women across America who for 8 years did the work that brought America back. My friends: We did it. We weren't just marking time. We made a difference. We made the city stronger, we made the city freer, and we left her in good hands. All in all, not bad, not bad at all.

And so, goodbye, God bless you, and God bless the United States of America.

DIVERSITY AND ADAPTATION: AMERICAN FAMILIES OVER FOUR CENTURIES

Kathryn M. Daynes
Department of History

"Studying about families is easy," one student claimed. "I have lived in a family all of my life." Having grown up in families, everybody feels like an expert. Nevertheless, the nature of families has changed since Jamestown was founded by Europeans almost four centuries ago. The formation of families through courtship and marriage, the division of labor between husbands and wives, attitudes toward children and how they should be raised, and the relationship of the household to the community have all undergone significant modification from colonial times to the present.

Even the popular meaning of the term family has changed. When we think of a family, the image of a father, mother, and children springs to mind. While that fits our most popular modern definition of family, in the past other meanings of family were paramount. When Jamestown was settled, translators of the King James Version of the Bible used family to mean a large kin-group, often consisting of several generations descending from a common father. "Hanoch, of whom cometh the family of the Hanochites: of Pallu, the family of the Palluites" (Numbers 26:5) is a typical example. Later the term family was more likely to include all those living in a household. In 1820 newlywed Chloe Peck wrote her parents from Rochester, New York, "We collected our family together which consists of seven persons"—a surprisingly large family for two people both of whom were marrying for the first time [Quoted in Paul A. Johnson, *A Shopkeeper's Millennium: Society and Revivals in Rochester, New York, 1815–1837* (New York: Hill and Wang, 1978), 43]. Her husband, an established publisher, would have had his workers living in his household along with, perhaps, a relative or two. In the antebellum South, planters also referred to their slaves as part of their families. Only gradually over the nineteenth century, as households increasingly consisted of nuclear families, did the term come to mean mainly a father, mother, and children.

Several factors have helped to shape and modify the American family over the past four centuries. First, the shift from subsistence agriculture to an industrial economy has had a profound impact upon families. Instead of working together on the family farm to sustain themselves as in colonial times, today family members generally leave the household to go to their jobs or to school to prepare for jobs. Second, changes in the patterns of births and deaths—demography—have also altered family life. A typical colonial couple bore seven or more children but could anticipate that several would die before reaching the age to marry. At present American couples typically have two children and expect both to live well beyond maturity. Longer life expectancy also means that couples have the potential for a long married life together, unlike in earlier times when marriages were broken early by the death of one spouse. In addition, families typically have more than three generations alive simultaneously, and young adults are likely to have not only parents but also grandparents living. Third, prevailing ideas about families have varied over time and among groups. Religion has been a fertile source in prescribing ideal family relationships, as has a variety of experts—physicians, sociologists, and philosophers. Added to this were the traditional ideas about families brought by various ethnic groups from other cultures. These three factors—the economy, demography, and ideas—have interacted to change and reshape American families.

Colonial Families

Just how much families have changed can be seen by visiting a typical colonial family. The family included husband, wife, children, servants, and sometimes kin. These households were the most important institutions of colonial society. Families worked together as a unit to grow and produce most of what they consumed and used. What children needed to know to eventually earn their own living they learned within the household. Those who were ill were nursed by the family's females. If family members were disabled, feeble, or insane, they too were cared for within the household. If those unable to care for themselves had no family members to help them, they were taken in by relatives or, failing that, taken into a household paid by the community to care for them. There were no other institutions to serve them. While there were churches for public worship, families were nevertheless a center for Bible study and daily prayer. Under the common law the husband and father of each family was responsible for the orderly conduct of all members of his household, whether related by blood or not. Households were, in short, centers of economic production and exchange, educational and vocational institutes, hospitals, welfare agencies, and houses of religious worship and of correction—little commonwealths that composed the larger community.

Because land for a farm and goods to set up a household were so crucial to newly-formed families, parents, who controlled these resources, had considerable influence over the timing of their children's marriages. They tended to favor first sons, promoting the marriage of oldest sons to the daughters of prosperous families, and they arranged their daughters' marriages by the order in which they were born. Sons whose fathers were living married later than sons who had already received their inheritance because of their fathers' deaths. Since having the means to marry was so crucial, marriage was not so much the result of falling in love, but rather of deciding to marry and then finding a suitable mate.

By law the husband was head of the family. He cast the family's vote, signed any contracts, and owned the family's land, buildings, and personal property. When a woman married, her separate civil identity was lost because it was considered *covered* by her husband's. Under *coverture*, a married woman owned no property because it belonged to her husband. He made contracts even if they concerned only his wife, and he sued in court for money owed to her. If he died without a will, she inherited her dower right, use of one-third of her husband's property during her life time; but after her death the property reverted to her husband's heirs. If the couple had acquired property through the right of the wife and had borne at least one child, however, the husband inherited the use of *all* his wife's property during his lifetime. Children too belonged to the father under the common law. As head of the household, he was responsible for their behavior, and in divorce cases a father retained custody of them.

Just as the law determined the different legal status of husband and wife, tradition clearly prescribed a distinct division of work in the household based on gender. So crucial were the separate tasks performed by both husband and wife to the family's economic well-being that their interdependent roles may be described as *hemispheres*, two distinct halves but dependent on the other to complete the circle of the household.

Growing crops in the fields, often aided by animal power, was men's work. So was taking care of the cattle and sheep, constructing the house and farm buildings, maintaining farm tools, hunting for game and angling for fish, and providing fire wood. A woman's work was done in the house and its immediate environs—or was never quite done because of the multitudinous tasks that fell to a housekeeper's lot. Women not only cooked the meals but also tended the garden and orchards that provided a variety of vegetables and fruits for the table. They also tended the "dunghill fowl," chickens, ducks, and geese; and they were in charge of the dairy, producing milk, butter, and cheese. While women produced some food, they were responsible for preserving all of it. Clothing the family also fell mainly to women. While men sheared the sheep, women were responsible for spinning the thread, weaving the cloth, sewing the clothes, and laundering them when they were soiled.

Many of these tasks were fairly repetitious ones that could be interrupted and easily resumed. This was essential because it was also women's charge to care for infants and young children. This was no short-term responsibility because colonial women bore large families. Women marrying in the seventeenth century had an average of 7.4 children. One-half had six to nine children, while a quarter bore ten or more. Considerable time, then, was spent in caring for children. Just getting children through their first years was an achievement. The proportion of children dying before their first birthdays was extraordinarily high by today's standards: one in ten of those living in healthy rural New England villages, one in four in the Chesapeake, and one in three in New England seaports. Even in the healthiest places seven times more infants died in colonial times than do today. Childhood diseases also took a great toll, and in an unhealthy locale like early eighteenth-century Christ Church Parish, South Carolina, 86 percent of children had died before reaching age twenty.

Tristram and Judith Coffin are examples of one early New England family. Born in England, both immigrated to Massachusetts with their parents by the early 1640s. In 1643 Judith married Henry Somerby and in the next seven years bore four children: Sarah, Elizabeth, John, and Daniel. All four survived the difficult first year of their lives, but John died just ten days before his second birthday. Then, less than nine years after her marriage, Judith was left a widow. The inventory of Henry's estate reveals his life as a farmer. It included fourteen acres of land and eleven acres of marsh and meadow, upon which had grazed two steers, a cow, two calves, and nine swine. Because all the family's household furniture and goods by law belonged to Henry, all these too were listed in his estate inventory, including everything Judith used to prepare the family's meals in the open fireplace: four iron pots, one quart pot, two kettles, a skillet, a frying pan, and a spit.

Because both men's and women's work was necessary to a household's economic well-being, Judith married Tristram Coffin exactly five months after her first husband's death. This second marriage was as fruitful as her first, and within the next seventeen years Judith bore ten children. In healthy New England, these ten children survived infancy, although Enoch died at age eleven. By the time Judith was forty-four, when she bore her thirteenth and last child, she had spent twenty-four years giving birth to a child approximately every two years, caring for the young and growing family, making wheat into bread, turning wool into clothes, and cleaning the household with water from the well. Tristram, as a merchant-tailor and farmer, worked equally as hard to supply the family's needs. He also had to provide dowries for daughters and land for sons so they would have the economic means to establish their own families. When Tristram died at age seventy-two, his youngest son Nathaniel had been married only eleven years. The land provided for Nathaniel was that on which Tristram and Judith lived. Before the land became his at his father's death, Nathaniel and his bride had apparently moved into his parents' house to care for them in their advancing years. The other sons also had been given use of a part of their father's land so they could marry, but they too had to wait until their father's death to receive title to it. The oldest son was forty-five before he became economically independent of his father. Patriarchal authority lasted for the father's lifetime.

When Tristram died, his tombstone commemorated his service as deacon in the first church of Newbury. It also noted his success in another valued gender role for men: "On earth he purchased a good degree" was a tribute to his financial success. The inscription on Judith's tombstone eulogized her as the "virtuous wife of Deac. Tristram Coffin, Esqr. . . . having lived to see 177 of her children and children's children to the 3d generation . . . fruitfull [*sic*] vine was she" [Laurel Thatcher Ulrich, *Good Wives, Image and Reality in the Lives of Women in Northern New England, 1650–1750* (New York: Vintage Books, 1991), 146–48]. She too had succeeded in fulfilling her gender role, although as wife and mother her valued roles were even more closely tied to family than were her husband's.

Spending so many years raising youngsters, Judith and Tristram, like other colonists, knew that children were not miniature adults. But so closely did early Americans associate the ability to speak, reason, and stand erect with humanity's claim to supremacy that they tried to make children appear as adult-like as possible. Infants were wrapped in swaddling bands that kept them stretched to their full length. This was supposed to assure that the baby grew up straight and tall, but it also made infants appear longer because the bands extended beyond the feet. The bands also had the very practical purpose of making infants easier to carry, especially for only slightly older children who were often given the task of tending them. Infants graduated from swaddling bands into standing stools, a short-legged device with a hole in the middle to put the child in. They were designed to keep children upright, an adult-like posture, and to prevent their crawling, definitely too animal-like for colonial tastes. To get their children walking as soon as possible, parents used walking stools, standing stools with wheels, and leading strings, ties sewed to children's clothing that parents could hold to keep toddlers upright as they took their first faltering steps.

When children began to walk, they joined the world of dependency occupied by females and young males, all of whom wore skirts as a symbol of their dependency. Girls would always remain in that world, but as they grew, they acquired the knowledge and skills needed to fulfill a woman's role. Boys, however, left that world of dependency, usually at age six or seven, when they exchanged their skirts for men's attire. While fathers played an important role in raising children, they became the primary parent after their seven-year-old sons made the transition into the men's world. Sometimes children were apprenticed and left home at age seven. Expected to move quickly into helping with the household's multitudinous tasks, children owned few toys; however, they joined in the amusements of adults, including blindman's bluff and hunt-the-bean, games not yet considered only for the young. The boundary between childhood and adulthood was blurred. Age was inconsequential because children were perceived as adults in the making.

Although colonial families broadly shared these traits within the family-based economy, households in different regions played variations on these major themes. The death rate in the seventeenth-century Chesapeake was so high that the eighty thousand who immigrated there between 1635 and 1699 had declined to sixty thousand by 1700. Moreover, about three-quarters of these immigrants were indentured servants, who could not marry until they had served their stipulated time of servitude. For the half of the male servants who lived long enough to become free, chances of marriage were not favorable. In the 1630s six men had immigrated for every woman who arrived. Even by the end of the century, when the greater proportion of native-born people helped to more evenly balance the sex ratio, there were still three men for every two women. For couples who did marry, half of all marriages ended by the death of one spouse within seven years. These short marriages produced only two to three children; and if these children were fortunate enough to survive infancy, two-thirds lost one parent by age eighteen while one-third were orphaned.

Remarriages created complex households: yours, mine, ours, and theirs—children whose widowed parent had remarried and died, leaving children in a household where neither husband nor wife was related to them by blood. For example, Mary and George Keeble had seven children before George died when Mary was about twenty-nine years old. Mary soon married Robert Beverly and had five more children before dying at age forty-one. Her husband Robert almost immediately remarried, taking as his wife Katherine, the widow of Major Hone who already had one child. Robert and Katherine then had four children. Had we visited the household of Robert and Katherine Beverly in 1680, it probably would have included the children of Robert and Katherine, the children of Robert and Mary, Katherine and Major Hone's child, and the youngest of Mary and George Keeble's children, who were not related by blood to either Robert or Katherine. With such instability of nuclear families, kinship bonds took on added importance and were augmented by ties to friends and neighbors. As death rates declined in the eighteenth century, however, families became more stable.

In healthier New England, nuclear families were more stable earlier and hence more central to society than in the Chesapeake. Marriages lasted longer, an average of twenty-four years in one Massachusetts village, before one spouse died, and children were likely to have parents alive when they reached maturity. With a more equal sex ratio, a high proportion of both men and women married, and having longer marriages, couples bore six or seven children. As in the Chesapeake, ties to the larger community were strong. In fact, in the 1670s Massachusetts provided for each town to select discreet persons to be known as tithingmen, each of whom would have the responsibility for keeping order in ten or twelve families in his neighborhood and reporting those who were remiss.

Puritans loved their offspring but as Calvinists they believed children were, as Puritan poet Anne Bradstreet wrote, "Conceiv'd in sin, and born in sorrow" with "A perverse will, a love to what's forbid" [*The Tenth Muse (1650), and, From the Manuscripts* (Gainesville, Fla.: Scholars' Facsimilies & Reprints, 1965), 43, 45]. Because children were inclined toward evil, it was parents' duty to break their children's wills, assuring, wrote one Puritan divine, that the "stubbornness and stoutness of mind arising from natural pride . . . be broken and beaten down" [John Robinson, *The Works of John Robinson* (Boston: Doctrinal Tract and Book Society, 1851), 246]. Quakers, on the other hand, believed children were innocent and should be trained by controlling their environment. To assure that control, parents gave rewards much more than punishments. In contrast to Puritans, who often arranged for apprenticeships in others' households, Quaker parents were much more likely to keep their youth at home. Believing that "in souls there is no sex," Quakers also accorded women a higher status within the household than did Puritans or Virginians. Quaker church epistles spoke of "female heads" of families as well as "male heads," and children referred to their homes as "my father's and mother's house," unlike the phrase "my father's house" in use elsewhere. Thus, the broad, general contours of colonial households accommodated diversity among early American white families.

Families during the Revolutionary Era

By 1750 these general contours were challenged by ideas from the same sources that underlay the American Revolution. In *Patriarcha*, Robert Filmer, an English theorist who promoted an absolutist monarchy, claimed the monarch's authority was comparable to a father's, and thus the divine commandment to "honor thy father" also meant "honor thy king." In refuting that political premise and setting forth ideas that the Founding Fathers would draw upon in establishing the new nation, John Locke described a different model for families. Parental power, he pointed out, lay equally with father and *mother*. Moreover, the subjection of children to parents was temporary and ceased when they came of age. In 1776 Thomas Paine's *Common Sense* applied to America the idea that a child became independent after his education was completed: "From the late rapid progress of the Continent to maturity, . . . independency of this Continent . . . cannot be far off" [*Rights of Man: Common Sense* (New York: Knopf, Everyman's Library, 1994), 273–74].

In contrast to the early colonial idea that a child's interests should be subordinated to the good of the household, Locke wrote that a major obligation of parents was to educate their children and form their character to prepare them for their eventual independence. According to Locke, children's minds are not formed at birth but rather are shaped by experiences, so impressions received by children had enormous and enduring consequences. As infants they were to be accustomed to hardship through fresh air, cold baths, and exercise, which precluded swaddling. When a child could talk, it was time for him to learn to read, which should be achieved by making it fun. "Children may be . . . taught to read," Locke counseled, "without perceiving it to be any thing but a sport, and play themselves into that which others are whipped for." He suggested that children could learn their letters by playing with balls or dice upon which the alphabet was pasted, "it being as good a sort of play to lay a stake who shall first throw an A or B, as who upon dice shall throw six or seven" ["Some Thoughts Concerning Education," in *The Works of John Locke*, Vol. 9, 10th ed. (London: Printed for J. Johnson [etc. by] T. Davison, 1801), 144–45].

But education also rested upon parental example, because a child would regard punishment for a practice he saw in his parent as "the peevishness and arbitrary imperiousness of a father" ["Some Thoughts Concerning Education," 60]. Unlike the early American emphasis upon inculcating external obedience to parental and community authority, the Lockean goal of a child's independence required internalizing habits of restraint and control. Parents' responsibility to educate and mold their children's unformed minds was heavy indeed. Locke, however, undercut the earlier notion that children should be made as adult-like as quickly as possible. "Never trouble yourself about those faults in them, which you know age will cure," he cautioned ["Some Thoughts Concerning Education," 50]. Running and playing, he declared, were natural to children and should be encouraged as long as these were guided to productive ends.

Throughout the eighteenth century various essayists, physicians, and novelists popularized and expanded on Locke's ideas, which by 1750 began to permeate America's elite families. Not needing their children's labor, wealthy families could afford to transform and lengthen childhood. Children's clothing signaled a significant change in the last quarter of the eighteenth century. Rather than dressing in adult clothing at age seven, boys between the ages of three to nine traded their baby petticoats for a hussar or skeleton suit: long trousers and a short jacket that permitted freedom of movement. At about eleven or twelve, they graduated into a relaxed version of man's apparel before, at about age fourteen, dressing in adult men's attire. A boy's childhood had lengthened from age seven to age fourteen. Female clothing indicated less change. A girl's infant costume was exchanged for a muslin frock, which she wore until sometime between ages ten and fourteen, when she was confined in her first corset to assure a ladylike bearing. Children's clothing was designed partly to allow for play. The appearance of a variety of toys—dolls, dominoes, balls, wagons, and sleds, for instance—manifested the new view of children's playing. As some forms of play became exclusively associated with children, the boundary between childhood and adulthood became more distinct.

Americans also embraced Locke's goal of children's independence when they had matured, a goal that, not surprisingly, appealed especially to the young. Parents' influence over their children's courtship and marriage declined as children claimed the choice of marrying whom and when they wished. After mid-century, the proportion of younger daughters marrying before their older sisters showed a noticeable increase. Similarly, whether or not the father was living no longer had an impact on the age the son married. In New England couples also hastened their marriages by conceiving a child out of wedlock. By the late eighteenth century more than 40 percent were pregnant when they wed, compared to fewer than 10 percent in the previous century. However, romantic love became increasingly important as the basis of marriage. In the thirty years before the Revolution, extant American periodicals averaged only one reference per four issues to romantic love as the proper basis of marriage; in the twenty years after the War the number of references tripled. Inundated by a barrage of literature decrying marriages based on property and lauding those based on love, parents conceded their children's right to choose their own marriage partners. John Adams disapproved of his daughter's being courted by a "reformed rake," for example. "I hoped to be at home and to have chosen a Partner for you," he wrote her but then softened, "Or at least to have given you some good Advice before you should choose" [L. H. Butterfield, Marc Friedlaender and Mary-Jo Kline, eds., *The Book of Abigail and John: Selected Letters of the Adams Family, 1762–1784* (Cambridge: Harvard University Press, 1975), 339–40]. Individual liberties were as important in families as in the nation.

Equality within families also was fostered by the Revolution. Before the War, the law of primogeniture, in force in the Southern states, stipulated that the eldest son would inherit all the property if the father left no will. Beginning with Georgia in 1777, all states abolished primogeniture during the Revolutionary period, replacing it with an equal distribution of property among all the children.

The movement away from hierarchical relationships that characterized society during the colonial period also typified families. Though most clearly shown by the changing relationships between children and parents, it also subtly affected husbands and wives. Many couples ceased calling each other mister and mistress, and husbands were less likely to address their wives as "dear child," while wives were more likely to call their husbands by their first names. Although the Revolution did little to expand women's political rights, women nevertheless adapted the ideology of civic virtue to their domestic situation. Because civic virtue was important in maintaining a republic and political socialization took place early, women claimed responsibility for training sons to be moral citizens who would uphold the newly established republic.

Born into a wealthy family, Eliza Lucas Pinckney was a model of Republican motherhood whose life in many ways illustrates the changed views about family. Educated in England, at age fifteen Eliza moved with her family to Wappoo plantation in South Carolina. Because her mother was an invalid, Eliza took over management of the household at an early age; and when her father left to fulfill his duties as lieutenant colonel in the British army during the War of Jenkins Ear, she took over managing the entire plantation when she was seventeen. The next year when Colonel Lucas proposed that she choose as a husband one of two men whom he had selected, she deferentially but firmly rejected both:

> As I know 'tis my happiness you consult [I] must beg the favour of you to pay my thanks to the old Gentleman for his Generosity and favourable sentiments of me and let him know my thought on the affair in such civil terms as you know much better than any I can dictate; and beg leave to say to you that the riches of Peru and Chili if he had them put together could not purchase a sufficient Esteem for him to make him my husband. As to the other gentleman you mention, Mr. Walsh, you know, Sir, I have so slight a knowledge of him I can form no judgement of him . . . But give me leave to assure you, my dear Sir, that a single life is my only Choice and if it were not as I am yet but Eighteen, hope you will [put] aside the thoughts of my marrying yet these 2 or 3 years at least [Eliza Lucas to Colonel Lucas, *The Letterbook of Eliza Lucas Pinckney, 1739–1762,* ed. Elise Pinckney, with Marvin R. Zahniser (Chapel Hill: University of North Carolina Press, 1972), 6].

Like more and more youth by the mid-eighteenth century, Eliza had her way. When she married four years later, it was to a man she, not her father, had chosen: Charles Pinckney, a widower with whose family she had been friends for several years.

From 1746 to 1750 Eliza bore four children: Charles Cotesworth, George Lucas (who died five days after his birth), Harriott, and Thomas. The energy and resourcefulness that Eliza had used to successfully manage her father's plantation was now focused on raising her children.

She planned to raise her children, she recorded, "according to Mr. Lock's [*sic*] method (w[hi]ch I have carefully studied)." When Charles Cotesworth was an infant, she wrote a friend requesting she buy a new toy so the infant could "play himself into learning." Her husband was also involved in teaching the baby: "Mr. Pinckney himself has been contriving a sett [*sic*] of toys to teach him his letters by the time he can speak, you perceive we begin by time for he is not yet four months old." Locke's methods worked. When Charles Cotesworth was twenty-two months old, his mother wrote that he "can tell all his letters in any book without hesitation." Eliza was equally concerned about her children's moral development. She resolved "to be a good Mother to my children . . . to carefully root out the first appearing and budings [*sic*] of vice, and to instill piety, Virtue and true religion into them" [Quoted in Constance B. Schulz, "Eliza Lucas Pinckney (1722–1793)" in *Portraits of American Women: From Settlement to the Present*, ed. G. J. Barker-Benfield and Catherine Clinton (New York: St. Martin's Press, 1991), 75–76].

Although Eliza was widowed only fourteen years after her marriage, she continued her plan for educating her children and instilled in them a love of their country. During the Revolution, both Charles Cotesworth and Thomas fought for the Patriot cause and were captured by the British. After independence, the two brothers continued to serve their country. Charles Cotesworth was a delegate to the Constitutional Convention of 1787, and the same year Thomas was elected governor of South Carolina. After serving a minister to France, Charles Cotesworth was the Federalist candidate for the Presidency in 1804 and 1808. Thomas, after successfully negotiating the Pinckney Treat with Spain in 1795, ran unsuccessfully as the Federalist candidate for Vice President in 1796 but served as a Congressman from 1797 to 1801. Using the new child-rearing methods inspired by Locke, Eliza had indeed been successful in instilling civic virtue in her family. When she died in 1793, George

Washington paid tribute to her devotion to the revolutionary cause by requesting to be one of Eliza's pallbearers.

Republican motherhood gave women a political role, as Eliza Pinckney's life demonstrated, but it also revealed the need for women to be educated. Benjamin Rush, signer of the Declaration of Independence, declared, "Our ladies should be qualified . . . in instructing their sons in the principles of liberty and government" [*Thoughts upon Female Education* (Philadelphia: Printed by Prichard & Hall, 1787), 7. (Woodbridge, Ct.: Primary Source Media, 1999, microfiche 28184)]. In the wake of the Revolution, the first female academies were established to prepare women for their expanded role as mothers. The political Revolution, then, was accompanied by familial alteration: changed ideas about the nature of children, longer period of childhood, increased independence of children, greater equality among siblings, and diminished formality between husbands and wives.

Victorian Families

Elite families were most likely to incorporate these changes, but those less wealthy soon followed. By the 1830s the middle classes had adopted these developments and were already expanding and modifying them. Alterations in family relationships are not surprising because the social and economic changes called the Industrial Revolution were rapidly transforming the northeastern United States, particularly urban areas. The household, once economically dependent on its own production or barter with neighbors, increasingly became tied into the market economy during the first half of the nineteenth century. The proliferation of economic institutions—factories, foundries, banks, mills, and railroad companies, to name a few—drew economic production away from households. Men, whose work had generally taken them further from home than women's, now followed their work into the new commercial enterprises. Their absence from home for many hours a day clearly changed their relationship to the remainder of the family. Husbands and fathers no longer supervised the work of the household or directed the education of their children. As providers and controllers of their households' financial resources, men, particularly those of the middle class, increasingly emphasized their economic role in supporting a comfortable lifestyle for their families. Freed from productive labor, middle-class women concentrated on their varied domestic and child-rearing duties in the home.

The ideal husband was a hard-working man who braved the competitive realm of economic activity; the True Woman was domestic, submissive, pious, and pure. Husbands and wives thus occupied, in the parlance of the day, separate spheres. Men were supreme in the public, insecure, dog-eat-dog world of work; women's domain was in the private refuge of the home. Women, untainted by a connection with the economic realm, were perceived as morally superior to men. "WOMAN is God's appointed agent of *morality*," wrote one leading woman editor [Sarah Josepha Hale, *Women's Record: or Sketches of All Distinguished Women, from "the Beginning" till A.D. 1850*, 3rd ed. (New York: Harper & Brothers, 1874), xxxv]. As moral guardians of the home, women created domestic refuges from the public world. The home was woman's domain, just as the economic world was man's, an idea that challenged men's superiority in some phases of family activity. A report of the U.S. Department of Agriculture chided farmers in 1862 for not making "the wife's authority in her domain as imperative as their own" [W. W. Hall, "Health of Farmer's Families," in *Report of the Commissioners of Agriculture for the Year 1862* (Washington, D. C.: Government Printing Office, 1863), 465]. The doctrine of separate spheres thus improved women's status within the family. Also enhancing women's position was the triumph of romantic love as the basis of marriage. At the core of nineteenth-century romantic love was the idea that one revealed one's true self to the beloved, and only to the beloved. Such intimacy mitigated against husbands' imperiousness. To be sure, coverture still constrained married women, but over the century laws were enacted increasing women's legal right to control their own property.

But much of a woman's augmented power within the household rested on her increased authority over her children. In colonial days child-rearing manuals had been addressed to fathers, but in the nineteenth century they were written for mothers. With the father away at work, the mother assumed primary responsibility for the children's education and formation of their characters. Children received much of their formal education in schools, which for middle-class children was increasingly prolonged. But to succeed in the precarious economic world, middle-class males learned from their mothers many essential traits of a self-made man: independence, industry, frugality, honesty, prudence, and self-control. Selfless mothers, then, helped nurture successful self-made men. This increased role in child-rearing was acknowledged by the courts, which by the 1820s began limiting fathers' customary custody of children in divorce cases and by the 1860s routinely gave custody of young children to mothers unless they proved themselves unfit.

Like the status of women, that of children also improved within the family. This was partly because middle-class families increasingly limited the number of children they had. The average number of children borne by white women fell from 7.04 in 1800 to 5.42 in 1850 and further to 3.56 in 1900. But children's status was also benefitted by the growing perception that they were innocent and pure rather than beset by original sin. To express that innocence, boys and girls were dressed alike in ankle-length dresses until about age three and then half-length petticoats and pantaloons until age seven. Children were also believed to be angelic with "the impress of divine nature . . . fresh and unsullied by contact with the breathing world" ["Childhood," *Godey's* 6 (June 1833): 268]. As such, they were even believed capable of perfecting their parents. In 1859 *Godey's Lady's Book*, the most popular women's periodical of its day, printed, "Men would be little better than savages but for women. With equal truth we may assert, both men and women would be hard and selfish beings but for children [who] refine and soften the best feelings of the parental heart" ["Children," 58 (December 1859): 506]. Such sentiments reveal a sea change in attitudes about men, women, and children.

The ideals of the nineteenth-century middle-class family were often only partially realized, as the Abraham Lincoln family shows. Lincoln fit the ideal as a self-made man who, through his intelligence, industry, and honesty, had moved from being the son of a hard-scrabble farmer to being a successful lawyer. He spent his days away from home at his law office, and during their early married years, he was gone three months of the year traveling the judicial circuit. As was typical of middle-class families, the home was the wife's sphere, and in it Mary Todd ruled. According to his law partner and biographer, Lincoln "exercised no government of any kind over his household" [William H. Herndon and Jesse W. Weik, *Herndon's Life of Lincoln* (Cleveland: World Publishing Company, 1930), 344]. Mary Todd managed the household budget and hired someone to help her with the many domestic tasks when the Lincolns could afford it; when they could not, she did all the cooking, cleaning, mending, and tending of the children herself. While she was domestic, however, she was not content to remain only in that sphere. She actively advised her husband on political matters, even recommending people for patronage jobs when Lincoln was President, much to the annoyance of his male political advisors. Nor was she submissive—her quick temper precluded that.

But she was completely devoted to her husband; and after his death, she cried that he was her "lover-husband-father & *all all to me*—Truly my all" [Justin G. Turner and Linda Levitt Turner, *Mary Todd Lincoln, Her Life and Letters* (New York: Alfred A. Knopf, 1974), 534].

Like most nineteenth-century middle-class couples, the Lincolns had fewer children than their colonial counterparts. Mary bore four sons—Robert, Edward, Willie, and Tad— within the first eleven years of marriage, giving birth to the last at age thirty-four. Having fewer children, the parents could devote more time to each. Lincoln was a concerned father, but it was characteristic of him that once, as he was pulling two sons in a wagon, he was so lost in his thoughts that he did not notice when one son fell out. Mary was just the opposite. Overprotective of Robert when he was young, she would often alert the whole neighborhood that he was lost if he disappeared momentarily. But her protectiveness could not spare two of her sons from early deaths: Edward died of tuberculosis before he turned four and Willie succumbed to typhoid at age eleven. After Willie's death, Mary wrote a friend:

> All that human skill could do, was done for our sainted boy, I fully believe the severe illness, he passed through, now, almost two years since, was but a warning to us, that one so pure, was not to remain long here and at the same time, he was *lent* us a little longer—to try us & wean us from a world, whose chains were fastening around us . . . Dear little Taddie who was so devoted to his darling Brother, although as deeply afflicted as ourselves, bears up and teaches us a lesson, in enduring the stroke, to which we *must submit* [Turner and Turner, *Mary Todd Lincoln*, 127–28].

Her words reflect the nineteenth-century view of children as not only saintly and pure but also as beings who teach and refine their parents. Unlike the death's head so typical of colonial tombstones, Edward's monument was graced with an angel, for the Lincolns thought of him as such.

Although working-class parents accepted many of the beliefs that underlay the middle-class families like the Lincolns, they rarely possessed the financial resources to emulate them. Working-class men were breadwinners; but with high unemployment and low wages, male industrial workers' earnings rarely sufficed to support a family, even in the last third of the century when real wages rose. As late as 1920 a worker in the Chicago slaughterhouses earned on average only 38 percent of the minimum needed to support a family of four. In the family-wage economy, most working-class children began earning money as early as possible to supplement the father's income, remaining with their parents until their late teens or early twenties and contributing most of their income to support the family. Although women's demanding domestic and child-rearing duties made working outside the home difficult—although some did so—most married mothers augmented their families' resources by doing piece work at home like making paper flowers, by taking in and cooking for boarders, by doing laundry for others, and by managing frugally their families' earnings to stretch them as far as possible.

Family financial strategies were, however, shaped by cultural values. Putting a high value on property ownership, the Irish and the Slavs, for example, put their children to work early to help reach that goal. Those immigrant groups were even more likely to purchase a house than were native-born families. On the other hand, Jews and African-Americans prized education and would forego the wages their children could earn to keep them in school longer. When Italian mothers had to work for wages, they favored finding hand work they could do at home. If they had to work outside the home, they chose workplaces where other Italians were employed. Jewish women avoided becoming domestic servants, preferring to work in factories, while Polish women's tastes were just the reverse.

Working-class families may have wanted to imitate the middle-class model of a close-knit nuclear family taking refuge behind thick walls and heavy draperies, but few could afford to do so. Many were able to buy a house or rent a larger apartment only by taking in lodgers, often kin or friends from the family's hometown, to help pay the cost. With intermittent unemployment and the risk of sickness and industrial accidents, working-class families relied on kin to help find jobs or to give assistance during difficult times. Industrialization did not weaken family ties; rather, relying on and assisting other family members were necessary to cope with the uncertainties of working-class life.

However difficult life may have been for working-class families, their family life was more stable than that of slaves. When slavery was first instituted in the seventeenth century, the high proportion of males and the small number of possible marriage partners known to any one slave thwarted chances of marriage. By the mid-eighteenth century, however, the native-born slave population was growing. Although their marriages had no legal standing and they had to gain their masters' consent to marry, many slaves formed stable, two-parent nuclear families. Among slaves in Louisiana during the nineteenth century, about three-quarters lived in nuclear families. About two-thirds of these households had husbands present, although in the upper South women headed about two-thirds of families. Parents sought to protect the young as long as possible, passing on knowledge and skills to their children, particularly the survival skills necessary to cope with the harsh conditions of slavery. Although slave women worked in the fields, men and women in their houses divided their tasks along traditional gender lines.

Ties to family members were strong, and slaves showed their familial bonds by naming children after their relatives, particularly male relatives who were more likely to be sold away. With a life expectancy of twelve years less than that for American whites, slaves were more likely to have their marriages disrupted early by death. Moreover, in the upper South where the need for slaves was decreasing, one marriage in three was disrupted by the sale of either husband or wife. Retaining contact with children was even more difficult, with about half of children being sold before maturity. Over the thirty-five years that slaves could expect to live, they were as likely to be sold as not and would experience the sale of at least some member of their immediate families. Despite the difficulties confronting their families, slaves managed to build meaningful family ties that helped them cope with the harshness of slavery.

Poverty continued to put pressure on Black families even after they gained their freedom. Nevertheless, in the Cotton South, a greater proportion of Black households than white were simple nuclear families, and Black families were almost as likely to have both husband and wife present. Revealing Black families' economic plight, however, more than 40 percent of Black married women listed jobs on the 1870 census, almost all as field laborers, while less than 2 percent of white women did. On the other hand, urban Black families were more than twice as likely to be headed by women as rural families, due in part to the number of widows who moved to cities but also to the lack of job opportunities there for Black males, who were relegated to low-paying, temporary jobs. The best jobs for young Black males were found in lumber camps, sawmill towns, steel mills, and large Delta plantations. Black women in towns also found only the lowest-paying jobs, as domestics and laundresses, but at least the work was steady. Low wages for all Blacks necessitated that more family members work. In the late nineteenth century, Black single women were three times more likely to work than their white counterparts, while five times more Black married women were employed than white. Faced with lack of opportunities and discrimination in employment, African-Americans rarely had the financial resources to emulate the white middle-class family.

Although from different circumstances, Mormon families were also under stress in the nineteenth century. To preach the gospel and build the newly-founded Church, men were asked to leave their families to go on proselyting missions. Moreover, families gathering with the Saints or driven from their homes by persecution often found themselves in meager circumstances. The need for mutual help among Saints, along with the Saints' strong cooperative ethic, overshadowed the middle-class values of competitiveness and isolation of the nuclear family. Lean years in Utah, as the Mormons brought the frontier under cultivation and suffered plagues of crickets and grasshoppers, further necessitated community cooperation, as did the large number of immigrants, who often sacrificed all they had to gather to Zion.

Like colonial households, those on the frontier needed both men's and women's work—interdependent hemispheres—for success. The frontier economy provided few economic niches for women to support themselves, so particularly widows and single women without fathers were dependent on community aid. Because Mormons believed in plural marriage and had introduced its practice on a limited basis in Nauvoo, it is not surprising that aid to economically disadvantaged women was extended in the form of proposals to become plural wives. Community aid thus came in the shape of an individual man committing himself to the care of the needy woman. To be sure, women who became plural wives believed in the doctrine of plural marriage; and although not all had been impoverished, the majority appears to have suffered from not having a man in the family to help economically. Moreover, a far greater proportion of women entered plural marriage in the famine-and-plague-stricken 1850s than in any other decade.

Like the middle class in nineteenth-century America, many Mormons valued romantic love with its corollary of an exclusive bond between a man and a woman. Valuing romantic love had always complicated living in plural marriage. As the Mormon economy improved, creating more economic opportunities for single women, fewer found plural marriage an attractive alternative. By the time the 1890 Manifesto curtailed future plural marriages, polygamy was already a waning institution among the Mormons. In fact, the nineteenth-century middle-class family type was more suitable to increasingly prosperous, urbanized, and mobile Mormon families. With more husbands away from home working and the surrounding community less likely to be exclusively Mormon, Latter-day Saint families more and more turned inward to insulate themselves from competing outside influences. Like middle-class women, who had the responsibility for inculcating the values necessary for their children to retain a middle-class lifestyle, Mormon women had the duty to instill in their children the religious beliefs and habits that would keep them in the faith and help them resist competing value systems. Conducive both to providing acceptance into American society and to reproducing devotion to the Mormon faith in children, the middle-class family type not only became the norm for Latter-day Saints but also received religious sanctions from Mormon authorities.

Twentieth-Century Families

Internalizing one's own system of values became more essential as the peer culture played a larger role in youth's lives. As the twentieth century dawned, no longer were the years from twelve to the early twenties seen as a period of growing maturity, but rather as a turbulent time of heightened self-consciousness, emerging sexual identity, and increased "repulsions" toward home and school. Recognition of this turbulent period, termed adolescence by G. Stanley Hall in 1904, produced a need for institutions to guide youths' development, such as junior high schools, the Boys Club of America, and the Boy Scouts. Nevertheless, youths gained more freedom from parental control and became more heavily influenced by popular culture and their peer groups. A distinct youth subculture flourished, stimulated by the lengthening time spent in school, by the proliferation of dance halls, movie theaters, and other places of entertainment providing social activities outside the home, and by the increased ability to get to these activities by public transportation or by automobile. With its own jargon, modes of dress, approved behavior and hierarchy, this subculture exerted considerable influence over teenagers.

The peer culture altered the relationship between guys and girls. Rather than being separated by formality and gender differences, they were to be "pals." This newly found familiarity was epitomized by the flapper. Short hair and clothing that de-emphasized her waist and chest gave the flapper a boyish look. Young women, who had joined the workforce in dramatically rising numbers since the 1880s, claimed the same independence as their brothers. The clock had, declared *Current Opinion* in 1913, struck "sex o'clock" in America. With premarital intercourse more than doubling from 1890 to 1920, with the divorce rate the highest in the world, with the drop in birthrate to an average of 3.56 children per woman by 1900, and with increased independence of women, some observers feared the family was in crisis.

Certainly, families were continuing to change. Among rural, immigrant, and American-born working families, the cooperative model, in which family members subordinated their interests to the general welfare of the family, continued to prevail, although even in such families older wage-earning children asserted their independence. Among middle-class families, the companionate model became the norm. Children and parents were pals, intimate and openly affectionate with each other, while parents allowed children greater independence. In the companionate marriage, first described by sociologists in 1925, husbands and wives were friends and lovers, a relationship based on emotional and sexual fulfillment.

However much the emotional quality of familial relationships had changed, gender roles had not. A study of Muncie, Indiana, in the 1920s showed that men defined their family obligations as providing economic resources and taking care of practical household matters like repairs. Love, not authority, characterized modern fatherhood. Providing discipline and moral guidance, part of a nineteenth-century father's role, had shifted to the mother, who now acquired almost sole responsibility for child-rearing and for organizing the household.

Child-rearing in the first quarter of the century became more difficult with the shift to "scientific mothering." Unlike their immediate predecessors who believed a child's character could be formed through the mother's example, early twentieth-century experts claimed that good habits must be inculcated through a strict schedule of feeding and sleeping. Moreover, according to one expert, mothers should not kiss and cuddle their children because that would make the child "totally unable to cope with the world it must later live in . . . won't you then remember when you are tempted to pet your child that mother love is a dangerous instrument?" [John B. Watson, *Psychological Care of Infant and Child* (New York: W. W. Norton & Company, Inc. 1928), 44.] Mothers not only bore the responsibility of rearing children but also the blame for their failures. It was a heavy responsibility indeed. Not surprisingly, mothers accepted new and opposite advice, beginning in the 1920s but becoming most influential after 1940, advocating infants' schedules based on "self-demand." While still stressing the crucial role of the mother, these new ideas emphasized that infants who experienced a minimum of frustration by having their needs met promptly would develop into well-adjusted individuals.

Shifts in child-raising advice, however, affected families much less than did the advent of the Depression. From 1929 to 1933 average family income plummeted 40 percent, a result of unemployment and pay cuts. In 1932, 28 percent of households were without any employed workers. Moreover, commodity prices fell by 55 percent from 1929 to 1932, shriveling farm income. Then wind erosion in the Dust Bowl forced 3.5 million people to abandon their farms and way of life during the Depression, most migrating to cities and especially to the west coast. With breadwinning their major role, unemployed husbands often lost their self-respect, and their status in the family was undermined. Wives struggled to make ends meet by buying less and producing more at home or by finding jobs, although some government agencies and school districts barred the employment of married women. Children assumed greater responsibilities, including earning income when they could, subordinating their interests to those of the family. As families tried to hide their declining standard of living, isolation of families from the surrounding community became even more pronounced, although kin often offered help or living space to needy relatives.

With economic conditions so difficult, fewer people tried to form new families, and the number of marriages during the thirties declined one-fourth compared to those of the twenties. The birthrate also dropped, falling below the replacement level for the first time since early colonial settlement. The divorce rate dropped too, but the number of desertions grew: divorce simply became too expensive. The majority of Americans who had lived at or below subsistence level even before the Depression suffered the most. Particularly hard hit were African-Americans. High unemployment among Black males, as high as 75 percent in some areas, and low wages prevented many from functioning as breadwinners. High mortality rates also disrupted Black families. Forty percent of Chicago's adult Black women had no husbands, mainly because of widowhood. For all Americans, not just the traditional poor, the Depression revealed how much families had changed from the self-sufficient households of the past. In the face of economic conditions far beyond individual families' control, the government began providing some protection against those conditions—old age, disability, and unemployment—which individual families could do little to change.

Even with a variety of New Deal programs, however, unemployment never dropped below 14 percent before 1941. American entrance into World War II ended the Depression but brought new stresses to American families. Nearly one-fifth of American families had one or more members serving in the armed forces. With sixteen million men in the military and the need for production expanding, women, including married women, were drawn into the workforce. In 1940 just 15 percent of married women were gainfully employed; by the end of the war five years later almost one-fourth were. To take advantage of new jobs in the armaments industries, many families, including southern Blacks, migrated to new areas of the country. The need for workers pushed wages up, although food, gasoline, and tires were rationed, reducing the goods families could finally afford to buy. Incomes of even the poorest families rose; for the poorest one-fifth of families, incomes increased 68 percent during the war, and for the next poorest fifth they rose almost as much. With incomes rising, the birthrate by 1943 soared to its highest rate in twenty years. The marriage rate also climbed, but rapid courtships before men left for military duty and pressures imposed by long absences also increased the divorce rate. In 1940 one marriage in six ended in divorce; in 1946 it increased to one in four.

Having experienced the deprivations of the Depression, the disruptions of the War, and then undergoing the insecurities produced by the rivalry with communism, the post-war generation sought protection in a family-centered culture. After the war marriage rates reached record highs: over 96 percent of women and 94 percent of men married. At the same time average marriage ages fell to all-time lows, 20 for women and 22 for men. With marriage almost universal and traditional gender roles in place, middle-class women attended college mainly to find suitable husbands. "What's college?" asked a Gimbel's department store ad in 1952. The answer: "That's where girls who are above cooking and sewing go to meet a man so they can spend their lives cooking and sewing." [Quoted in Steven Mintz and Susan Kellogg, *Domestic Revolutions: A Social History of American Family Life* (New York: Free Press, 1988), 181.] Not only were more women marrying and at earlier ages, they were also bearing more children and having them when they were younger. The baby boom was not created by women returning to colonial norms of seven or more children, but rather by more women having children and having three or four instead of two.

Post-war prosperity and pent-up demand greatly expanded the consumer culture, and expenditures on homes and domestic items skyrocketed. Suburbs' populations soared as families moved into new single-family dwellings there, a movement spurred by the GI Bill and other government programs. Mainly confined to wealthier families before the War, the ideal of the companionate family now was adopted by post-war, middle-class suburban families. With men spending much of their day at work and commuting to get there, these homes became mother-dominated and child-centered. Advice to be flexible in feeding and sleeping schedules dominated child care manuals, as did counsel to use love, reason, and example to instill discipline in children. Instead of molding a child by schedules and environment, as advised in the first decades of the century, mothers were told to meet the child's needs. A child's earliest years were still considered crucial, however, and the burden of successfully rearing children during them rested almost solely on the mother. As children grew older, mothers' responsibility changed to chauffeuring them to school, music lessons, and sport activities; but as children reached adolescence, parental supervision waned as the influence of youth subculture waxed. The companionate family also fulfilled the needs of husbands and fathers. For many men who felt trapped in the bureaucratic world of work, emotional and sexual intimacy with their wives and loving relationships with their children provided meaning and fulfillment.

The child-centered family of the fifties was prosperous, and some couples in this family-consumer economy found that a middle-class lifestyle necessitated two incomes. By 1960 the percentage of working mothers had grown considerably: over one-third of mothers with children between six and eighteen and almost one-quarter of those with children under six were in the work force. This trend intensified in the 1970s. Median family income had tripled between 1950 and 1970, but it peaked in 1972–73, and then started a steady decline, falling 15 percent by 1996. In 1972, only 14 percent of men aged 25 to 34 failed to earn incomes sufficient to keep a family of four above the poverty level; by 1994 that had risen to 32 percent. For African-American and Latino men the figure is almost 50 percent. About a third of two-parent families with children would live in poverty if both parents were not gainfully employed. Moreover, those with middle-class aspirations find reaching that goal more difficult; today fewer than half of men under thirty earn middle-class incomes.

To compensate for decreasing individual real wages and to maintain their accustomed standard of living, Americans employed four main strategies: going into debt, bearing fewer children, delaying marriage, and sending both husband and wife into the labor force. Birthrates, which reached an average of 3.8 children at the peak of the baby boom in the late 1950s, fell to 1.7 in 1976, though rising slightly to 2.0 by 1994. Conversely, marriage ages, after dropping to uncharacteristically low ages at mid-century, have risen to 24 for women and 26 for men. Also, by 1996 over 60 percent of married women and more than two-thirds of married women with children were employed. A majority of children, including preschoolers, had mothers in the labor force. Polls in the late 1990s show that about three-quarters of Americans believe that these changed relationships between men and women in families, the workplace, and society have made it harder to raise children and to have successful marriages. While over two-thirds thought it would be better for mothers to stay at home and take care of children, half indicated they would prefer to work fewer hours if they could live at the same standard without working, while only one-fifth would choose to stop working altogether.

To be sure, beliefs about roles in the family do shape choices men and women make. For example, believing that they have primary responsibility for the nurture of their children, committed Mormon women are more likely to work part time or spend fewer years in the labor force than American women in general, although the percentage of Mormon women who work is comparable to national percentages. Younger Latter-day Saint women are more likely to be employed than older women, an indication that they are experiencing the same economic stresses as other young Americans. Mormon beliefs are translated into behavior more clearly in their higher marriage rate and higher birth rate than national norms.

As the twentieth century closes, slightly less than half of all marriages end in divorce, partly because being divorced no longer carries a stigma but also because the emphasis on romantic love has raised considerably the expectations of personal and emotional fulfillment within marriage. The number of divorces has markedly increased the number of families headed by a single parent. While about half of American children live with both biological parents, about one-fifth live in a step-family, and another fourth live with a single parent. Single-parent households are more likely to be poor than two-parent households, not only because more families need two incomes to stay above the poverty line, but also because most single-parent households are headed by women and women's median income is about three-quarters of men's.

Composition of households has changed indeed over the past half century. Not only has the number of step-family and single-parent households increased, but also the number of nontraditional family and single-person households. Although the number of cohabiting couples has increased dramatically since 1970, there are still only seven such households for every one hundred ones with married couples. More dramatic has been the increase in the percentage of single-person households. The rising marriage age has increased the number of years young adults may live independently after leaving their parents' homes and before forming their own families. Also, with greater longevity more of the elderly are living alone after their two or three children have moved from home.

With longer life spans and fewer numbers of children, the average age of Americans is markedly older than even a century ago. Increasing longevity has been one of the most significant changes in family life. In 1870, 30 percent of female babies died before reaching marriageable age, while only slightly more than half of women survived to the end of their childbearing years. A century later a mere 2 percent died before age twenty, and only 5 percent failed to survive to age forty-five. A white American female today has a better chance of living to age sixty than her counterpart a century ago had of surviving to her first birthday. Such longevity for both men and women means that couples will be together much longer after their children have left home, that—barring divorce—they will have much longer marriages, and that in middle age they are more likely to be caring for both their own children and their elderly parents.

Longer life spans and fewer children, higher divorce rates and fewer families with both biological parents, more mothers working and lower incomes for young males—these are just some of the changes faced by late twentieth-century families. But, as this brief overview has shown, families have been adapting to economic and demographic changes since the beginning of European settlement in America. Successful adaptation to the manifold changes facing families will depend upon millions of individual decisions made within the context of loving commitments to parents, spouses, and children, just as it has for the past four centuries.

Suggested Readings

For a fine overview of the history of the family, see Steven Mintz and Susan Kellogg, *Domestic Revolutions: A Social History of American Family Life* (New York: The Free Press, A Division of Macmillan, Inc., 1989). Carl N. Degler, *At Odds: Women and the Family in America from the Revolution to the Present* (Oxford: Oxford University Press, 1980) emphasizes how the changing roles of women have had an impact on the family. An overview to 1900 that stresses economic issues is Stephanie Coontz, *The Social Origins of Private Life: A History of American Families 1600–1900* (London: Verso, 1988). For a demographic study as it applies to families, see Robert V. Wells, *Revolutions in Americans' Lives: A Demographic Perspective on the History of Americans, Their Families, and Their Society* (Westport, Conn.: Greenwood Press, 1982). Many original sources relating to the issues dealt with in this chapter may be found in Donald M. Scott & Bernard Wishy, eds. *America's Families: A Documentary History* (New York: Harper & Row, Publishers, 1981).

Many fine works deal with families in the seventeenth and eighteenth centuries. For New England see, for example, Edmund Morgan, *The Puritan Family: Religion and Domestic Relations in Seventeenth-Century New England*, rev. and enl. ed. (New York: Harper Torchbooks, 1966); John Demos, *The Little Commonwealth: Family Life in Plymouth Colony* (New York: Oxford University Press, 1971); Philip J. Greven, Jr., *Four Generations: Population, Land and Family in Colonial Andover, Massachusetts* (Ithaca, N.Y.: Cornell University Press, 1970); Kenneth A. Lockridge, *A New England Town, The First Hundred Years: Dedham, Massachusetts, 1636–1736* (New York: Norton, 1970); Laurel T. Ulrich, *Good Wives: Images and Reality in the Lives of Women in Northern New England, 1650–1750* (New York: Knopf, 1982). For the South see Daniel Blake Smith, *Inside the Great House: Planter Family Life in Eighteenth-Century Chesapeake Society* (Ithaca, N.Y.: Cornell University Press, 1980); Darrett B. Rutman and Anita H. Rutman, "'Now-Wives and Sons-in-Law': Parental Death in A Seventeenth-Century Virginia County," in *The Chesapeake in the Seventeenth Century: Essays on Anglo-American Society*, ed. Thad W. Tate and David L. Ammerman (Chapel Hill: University of North Carolina Press for the Institute of Early American History and Culture, Williamsburg, Va., 1979), 153-75. For the Middle colonies, see Barry J. Levy, *Quakers and the American Family: British Settlement in the Delaware Valley* (New York: Oxford University Press, 1988); Mary M.

Schweitzer, *Custom and Contract: Household, Government, and the Economy in Colonial Pennsylvania* (New York: Columbia University Press, 1987). David Hackett Fischer, *Albion's Seed: Four British Folkways in America* (New York: Oxford University Press, 1989) deals with colonial families in New England, in the South, in the Delaware Valley, and in the backcountry.

Changes in the family during the Revolutionary period are dealt with in several works. See Jay Fliegelman, *Prodigals and Pilgrims: The American Revolution Against Patriarchal Authority, 1750–1800 (*Cambridge: Cambridge University Press, 1982); Linda K. Kerber, *Women of the Republic: Intellect and Ideology in Revolutionary America* (Chapel Hill: University of North Carolina Press for the Institute of Early American History and Culture, Williamsburg, Va., 1980); Mary Beth Norton, *Liberty's Daughters: The Revolutionary Experience of American Women, 1750–1800* (Boston: Little, Brown and Company, 1980); and Daniel Scott Smith, "Parental Power and Marriage Patterns: An Analysis of Historical Trends in Hingham, Massachusetts," *Journal of Marriage and the Family* XXXV (August 1973): 419–428. For the early republic, an important and highly readable study is Laurel Thatcher Ulrich, *A Midwife's Tale: The Life of Martha Ballard, Based on Her Diary, 1785–1812* (New York: Knopf, 1990).

Works on the family in the nineteenth century have emphasized the middle class. See Nancy F. Cott, *The Bonds of Womanhood: "Women's Sphere" in New England, 1780–1835*, 2nd ed. (New Haven, Yale University Press, 1997); Mary Ryan, *Cradle of the Middle Class: The Family in Oneida County, New York, 1790–1865* (New York: Cambridge University Press, 1981); Ellen K. Rothman, *Hands and Hearts: A History of Courtship in America* (New York: Basic Books, Inc., 1984); Karen Lystra, *The Searching Heart: Women, Men, and Romantic Love in Nineteenth-Century America* (New York: Oxford University Press, 1989). For Southern families, see Bertram Wytatt-Brown, *Southern Honor: Ethics and Behavior in the Old South* (New York: Oxford University Press, 1982); Jane Turner Censer, *North Carolina Planters and Their Children, 1800–1860* (Baton Rouge: Louisiana State University Press, 1984); and Sally G. McMillen, *Motherhood in the Old South: Pregnancy, Childbirth, and Infant Rearing* (Baton Rouge: Louisiana State University Press, 1995). Robert L. Griswold, *Family and Divorce in California, 1850–1890: Victorian Illusions and Everyday Realities* (Albany, N.Y.: State University of New York Press, 1982) argues that middle-class values were permeating the working classes by the late nineteenth century. For changing family law, see Michael Grossberg, *Governing the Hearth: Law and the Family in Nineteenth-Century America* (Chapel Hill: The University of North Carolina Press, 1985). For slave families, see Herbert G. Gutman, *The Black Family in Slavery and Freedom, 1750–1925* (New York: Pantheon Books, 1976); and Ann Patton Malone, *Sweet Chariot: Slave Family and Household Structure in Nineteenth-Century Louisiana* (Chapel Hill: University of North Carolina Press, 1992). An overview of African-American families covering slavery to the present is found in Jacqueline Jones, *Labor of Love, Labor of Sorrow: Black Women, Work and Family, From Slavery to the Present* (New York: Basic Books, 1985). Immigrant families may be studied in Tamara Hareven, *Family Time and Historical Time: The Relationships between the Family and Work in a New England Industrial Community* (New York: Cambridge University Press, 1981); Virginia Yans-McLaughlin, *Family and Community: Italian Immigrants in Buffalo, 1880–1930* (Ithaca, N.Y.: Cornell University Press, 1977); Charles H. Mindel, et. al., *Ethnic Families in America: Patterns and Variations,* 4th ed. (Upper Saddle River, N.J.: Prentice Hall, 1998).

The literature on families in the twentieth century is extensive. See, for example, Stephanie Coontz, *The Way We Never Were: American Families and the Nostalgia Trip* (New York: BasicBooks, 1992) and her *The Way We Really Are: Coming to Terms with America's Changing Families* (New York: BasicBooks, 1997); Robert L. Griswold, *Fatherhood in America: A History* (New York: BasicBooks, 1993); Elaine Tyler May, *Great Expectations: Marriage and Divorce in Post-Victorian America* (Chicago: The University of Chicago Press, 1980) and her *Homeward Bound: American Families in the Cold War Era* (New York: Basic Books, Inc., Publishers, 1988); Joanne Meyerowitz, ed., *Not June Cleaver: Women and Gender in Postwar America, 1945–1960* (Philadelphia: Temple University Press, 1994); Ruth Schwartz Cowan, *More Work for Mother* (New York: Basic Books, 1983); Hilda Scott, *Working Your Way to the Bottom: The Feminization of Poverty* (Boston: Pandora Press, 1984). For changing courtship patterns in the early twentieth century, see Beth L. Bailey, *From Front Porch to Back Seat* (Baltimore: Johns Hopkins University Press, 1988).

For additional reading on children and child-rearing, see Robert H. Bremner, ed. *Children and Youth in America: A Documentary History,* 2 vols. (Cambridge: Harvard University Press, 1970); Karin Calvert, *Children in the House: The Material Culture of Early Childhood, 1600–1900* (Boston: Northeastern University Press, 1992); Philip J. Greven, Jr., *The*

Protestant Temperament: Patterns of Childrearing, Religious Experience, and the Self in Early America (New York: Knopf, 1977); Jacqueline S. Reinier, *From Virtue to Character: American Childhood, 1775–1850* (New York: Twayne Publishers, 1996; Bernard Wishy, *The Child and the Republic: The Dawn of Modern American Child Nurture* (Philadelphia: University of Pennsylvania Press, 1968); Elliott West, *Growing Up with the Country: Childhood on the Far Western Frontier* (Albuquerque: University of New Mexico Press, 1989); Glen H. Elder, Jr., *Children of the Great Depression* (Chicago: University of Chicago Press, 1974); John A. Clausen, *American Lives: Looking Back at the Children of the Great Depression* (New York: Free Press, 1993). For youth, see Joseph F. Kett, *Rites of Passage: Adolescence in America, 1790 to the Present* (New York: New York: Basic Books, 1977); John Modell, *Into One's Own: From Youth to Adulthood, 1920–1975* (Berkeley: University of California Press, 1989); Paula Fass, *The Damned and the Beautiful: American Youth in the 1920s* (New York: Oxford University Press, 1977).

POLITICAL PARTIES IN THE AMERICAN POLITICAL EXPERIENCE

Kelly D. Patterson
Department of Political Science

The political party system in America is largely the result of circumstance. Its existence is based more on the practical needs of the American republic as opposed to the institutions of government established by the Constitution. In this sense, the role and function of political parties has been much more of an evolution than a creation—with parties growing and adapting to new political climates and changing electoral needs. Political parties have come to embody the most current trends in government and society. They are one means for bringing about change in the American republic and one of the most versatile modes of voicing public opinion.

The Founding Fathers of our country never intended for political parties to emerge. In fact, they believed that parties were unruly and could destroy a republic. The Constitution of the United States, the document that united the fragmented colonies and created a central federal government, mentions nothing about the role or function of a party system. The prevailing attitude among the Founding Fathers was that parties were evils to be avoided. In their opinion, the citizens of the fragile, new republic could not withstand fragmentation or separation, with different groups of people breaking off into organizations or groups. The Founding Fathers felt these factions would quickly tear apart the already tenuous union they had so carefully put together. Factions had dangerous tendencies that had to be checked and contained. Thus, unlike the other facets of our government (Congress, voting, the civil liberties of citizens), political parties lacked any real philosophical foundation from the Framers to justify their existence.

James Madison, the "Father of the Constitution" and one of the co-authors of *The Federalist* (the classic commentary on and defense of the Constitution), was the most vocal about the evil of faction and division in a republic. He wrote extensively about faction in *The Federalist* 10, offering both a philosophical and practical opinion about why factions should be avoided. His classic treatise has become a starting point for scholars who debate the role of political parties in the American republic.

Madison argued that the greatest vice to which a republic is prone is the vice of faction because it "reduces public discourse on the common good to mere squabbling among private interests." He described a faction as a "number of citizens, whether amounting to a majority or minority of the whole, who are united and actuated by some common impulse of passion, or of interest, adverse to the rights of other citizens, or to the permanent and aggregate interests of the community" (*The Federalist* 10). Madison brings up the central dilemma of any democratic government—how to balance the interests of the majority against the interests of the minority. By nature, democratic government is directed by the will of the people. In theory, the people would choose a course that benefits the republic. But what if the majority becomes tyrannical in its motives? What if the majority seeks to crush the dissenting opinion of the minority? This suppression would violate every principle of democracy and resemble the dictatorships of Europe. Furthermore, Madison realized that a democracy could be prone to numerous competing interests that would never come together and compromise. If people were unwilling to unite and make concessions, the country would soon be ripped apart.

First among the concerns of Madison was the manner in which the Union could "break and control the violence of faction" (*The Federalist* 10). A republican form of government by nature would have different groups of people separating into blocks that shared common values or interests. The difficulty of the Union would be to "produce a plan that balances the principles of democracy and eliminates the evils of faction" (*The Federalist* 10).

Madison saw two methods of curing the potential mischief of faction: (1) by removing the causes of faction, or (2) by controlling the effects of faction. If a faction consists of less than a majority (a minority faction), it would be controlled by the democratic principle which allows the majority to defeat the faction in a regular vote. But what if the faction is a majority that could oppress the minority? This is the dilemma which the Framers encountered. How do you secure the public good and private rights against the danger of a majority faction, while at the same time preserving the spirit and the form of democratic government?

Part of the answer lies in the creation of a republic as opposed to a pure democracy. A republic contains representative government, with elected officials making major decisions on legislation and policy. Pure democracy, with government and policy being completely controlled by the will of the majority, could be prone to impulse and shortsightedness. Madison claimed that republics were less inclined to this problem because representation can "refine and enlarge the public views by passing them through the medium of a chosen body of citizens, whose wisdom may best discern the true interest of their country" (*The Federalist* 10).

Madison also identified one other means of combating a majority faction. He argued that the establishment of a large republic could combat the formation of a majority faction. Madison claimed, contrary to the traditional view that republics were appropriate only in small countries, that the use of federalism and representation made republican politics possible in a large country, and that a large territory made republican government less likely to succumb to the "mischiefs of faction" (*The Federalist* 10). A heterogeneous and diverse population "spread over an extensive region" is less likely to "be subject to the infection of violent passions or the danger of combining in pursuit of unjust measures" (*The Federalist* 63).

This was a novel idea for the world at the time. Never before had a republican form of government been instituted in a large country. Conventional wisdom dictated that large territories were unruly and must be contained by a powerful ruler who could control the populous. Madison, however, argued that not only were republics possible in a large territory, but that they were essential to sustain democracy. With an enlarged territory, "You take in a greater variety of parties and interest; you make it less probable that a majority of the whole will have a common motive to invade the rights of other citizens; or if such a common motive exists, it will be more difficult for all who feel it to discover their own strength and to act in unison with each" (*The Federalist* 10).

In *The Federalist*, Madison uses "parties" and "factions" interchangeably. More often than not, he views parties contemptuously. However, he never envisioned such an extensive party system nor the many goods such a system might achieve. The national conventions, the donkey and the elephant, the campaign platforms—these are all modern phenomena surrounding the American political party. But it is important to remember that such things were never in the minds of the Founders as they anticipated the role of political parties. Thus, to say that the Framers of the Constitution resented parties is rather misleading. What the Framers warned against were parties of interest (factions) rather than parties of principle (political parties).

But not even the Framers totally condemned parties of interest (factions). They accepted the proliferation and development of interest groups as inevitable features of a dynamic republic. Madison acknowledged that a great diversity of economic interests—"a landed interest, a manufacturing interest, a mercantile interest, a moneyed interest, with many lesser interests, grow up of necessity . . ." (*The Federalist* 10). The Founding Fathers had great hope that their experiment in republicanism would be more successful than those in the ancient world, where class warfare and opposing national goals had destroyed other representative governments. They did not think parties of interest (factions) could be avoided, but they did think rather optimistically that (1) the distance between interest groups and the new political institutions being set up by the Constitution could be great enough to allow adequate space for debate by politicians, relatively free from "the spirit of party and faction," and (2) although "a zeal for different opinions . . . concerning government" had been known to produce partisan conflict, parties of principle (political parties) would no longer be needed in America since everyone agreed on the principles of government (*The Federalist* 10). Thus, the Founders envisioned a Constitution that was not necessarily *against* parties (whether of interest or of principle), but a Constitution above parties or interest and untroubled by parties of principle.

However, as apparent from our current political landscape, both of these expectations were thwarted within a few years of the Constitution being put into operation. Some institutions were needed to organize government and to connect citizens to government and politics. This development took time, and by the first administration under George Washington in 1789, open party warfare was evident.

A Brief History of Political Parties

As stated previously, political parties were never completely anticipated. Their birth and evolution was mainly due to the current needs of the growing United States. Historians and political scientists generally divide the history of American political parties into five distinct party systems—

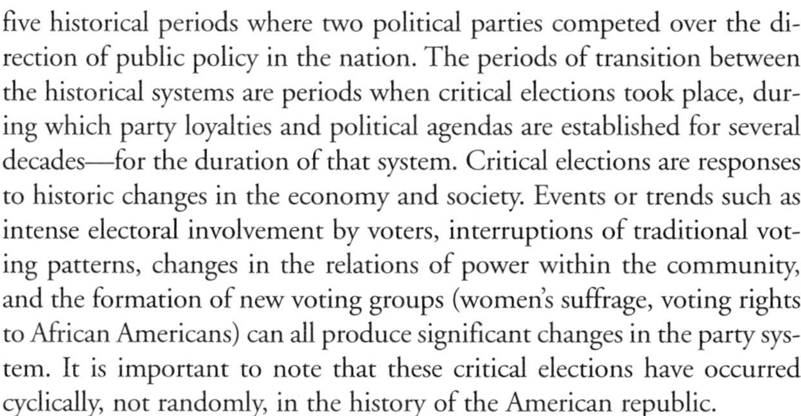
five historical periods where two political parties competed over the direction of public policy in the nation. The periods of transition between the historical systems are periods when critical elections took place, during which party loyalties and political agendas are established for several decades—for the duration of that system. Critical elections are responses to historic changes in the economy and society. Events or trends such as intense electoral involvement by voters, interruptions of traditional voting patterns, changes in the relations of power within the community, and the formation of new voting groups (women's suffrage, voting rights to African Americans) can all produce significant changes in the party system. It is important to note that these critical elections have occurred cyclically, not randomly, in the history of the American republic.

The First Party System (1790–1820s)

The first president of the newly formed union, George Washington, was a national hero and unifying force in government. His election as president in 1789 met nearly no resistance in any sector of society. However, this is not to say that Congress completely agreed on every policy the Washington administration advocated. In order to get his measures passed through the House of Representatives and the Senate, Washington had to develop a coalition of factions. But Washington was not a politician—he was a general that had little patience for bargaining and political maneuvering. The job of coalition building fell to Washington's secretary of the treasury, Alexander Hamilton, who was one of the co- authors of *The Federalist* with James Madison.

Hamilton felt that the new government was weak and unstable. In his opinion, the only way to develop a strong republic was to adopt policies that would attach certain powerful economic groups to the newly formed government. Hamilton wanted a strong central government that would be economically sound and united. Because he favored a powerful federal government, his coalition became known as the Federalists.

Washington's secretary of state, Thomas Jefferson, and James Madison, co-author of *The Federalist* and a congressman, disliked the philosophy of the Federalist coalition, believing that its policies would sow the seeds of destruction for the republic. In opposition, they organized the Republican Party—so named because it portrayed itself as the savior of the republic that Hamilton's policies were threatening to turn into a monarchy.

The Republican Party was stronger in terms of popular appeal and the number of interest groups it was able to mobilize. The agenda of Hamilton's Federalist Party was too narrow and complex for the average colonist to grasp. The Federalist ideology of an American government built on strong ties to big business and industrial interests was intimidating to a simple people that had just escaped the harsh economic intervention of Britain. The Republicans offered a less threatening vision of American development, a vision of virtuous farmers whose economic independence made them morally and politically independent. The Republicans advocated a simple, laissez-faire government as opposed to the stronger, Hamiltonian state.

The Second Party System (1820s–1850s)

Through popular presidential candidates and an agenda that resonated with the public, the Republican Party dominated national politics for three decades. However, the War of 1812 with Britain signaled the gradual weakening of its hold on government policy. By 1824, the Republican party was split in its choice for president between William Crawford, Andrew Jackson and John Quincy Adams. With no candidate receiving a majority of the electoral vote, it was left for the House of Representatives to choose among the candidates. Adams, who was second in both the popular and electoral vote, was chosen in a highly contentious political debate in the House. This dissidence in the Republican party caused splintering and division, to the point where a consensus in policy simply could not be reached. This led to the dissolution of the party and a turn to the popular Jackson as a nominee in the next presidential election. Andrew Jackson's election as president in 1828 signaled the arrival of a new majority party—the Jacksonian Democrats—which eclipsed the fading Republican Party. This party unified fragments of the Federalist and Republican parties by offering a new vision of government.

Consequently, the Whig Party succeeded the Federalists as the opposition party. By 1826, the National Republican opposition to Jackson, based in New England and the Ohio Valley, had allied themselves with those Southern planters who were dissatisfied with Jackson's acceptance of a high level of protective tariffs (Southern planters were interested in cotton exports to Europe). But this new alliance of Southerners with those in New England dictated a new name for the new anti-Jackson party. Southerners who advocated states' rights would never call themselves National Republicans. So, the name Whig was decided upon.

The Jacksonian Democrats defined themselves by a crusade against the Bank of the United States and federal money being allocated for internal development (roads, canals, bridges). Thus, Jacksonian Democracy was an updated version of the Jeffersonian Republican campaign against Hamiltonian Federalism. The Jacksonian Democrats called for the federal government to play a smaller role in society, while the Whigs advocated more federal regulation that sought to strengthen ties to business and commerce.

The Civil War Party System (1850s–1890s)

Slavery proved to be the contentious issue that molded the party system in the last half of the 19th century. Shortly before the Civil War, the Whig Party split between the northern Whig politicians who supported an abolition of slavery and the southern Whig politicians who wanted to ensure slavery's survival. These southern Whigs left the Whig Party and aligned themselves with the Democratic Party to advance the policies of slavery. The remaining divisions of the old Whig and Democratic parties eventually came together to form the Republican Party (not to be confused with the Jeffersonian Republicans sixty years earlier). The original tie that bound the elements of the party together was opposition to the extension of slavery and the "slave power" of the South. Their nominee for president in 1860, Abraham Lincoln, won the office with relative ease and helped make the party legitimate. The new Republican Party, the "Grand Old Party" (GOP), came to dominate American politics until the 1920s.

Many Whigs joined the new Republican Party and brought with them their philosophy that the federal government should play a more active role through funding internal improvements, promoting domestic manufactures, and aiding commerce. It is interesting to note that from just after the Civil War until the present day, the Republican Party has been generally known as the party of industry and business—a carryover from the influx of Whig policy into Republican thinking.

In the end, the slavery issue served to divide the Democrats and Republicans not only in terms of ideology, but in terms of geography as well. The Republican Party tended to cluster more in the North and West, with a strong urban base of support. Conversely, the Democratic Party congregated in the South and other rural enclaves.

1896: A Party System in Transition

The industrial revolution coupled with the resulting hard times for farmers transformed the Republican Party in the late 1800s. Western and Southern farmers, together with Western miners, sought an alliance with workers in the East and Midwest to combat the growing effects of industrialization. They wanted to re-focus the attention away from industry and back on the traditional needs of the farmer.

This dramatic shift in party constituency was more of a realignment of voters to the Republican Party as opposed to the creation of an entirely new party. In the realignment of 1896, party power did not change hands. The Republican Party was still the majority party in the United States. The influx of Western and Southern interests merely served to reinforce the Republican majority status that had been firmly in place since 1860.

The first two decades of the 20th century were dubbed the Progressive Era because of the intense political reform led by the Progressive wing of the Republican Party. The main focus of the Progressives was to root out the corruption in political parties. Their opposition to traditional party mechanisms helped pave the way for substantive change in American government. Civil service reforms shifted some of the power out of the hands of party officials and bosses. The direct primary election attempted to take control of nominations away from party leaders and place it in the hands of the rank-and-file voter. And in a number of cities, the role of party government was completely eliminated when nonpartisan governments replaced divided, partisan governments. Two constitutional changes also weakened the hold that parties had on the political system. With the ratification of the Seventeenth Amendment to the Constitution in 1913, U.S. senators came to be elected by the public, not state legislatures. And perhaps the greatest change in the political landscape came in 1920 when women obtained the right to vote with the ratification of the Nineteenth Amendment.

The New Deal Party System (1930s–1960s)

The Great Depression became the next great force in the evolution of the American party system. At the time of the stock market crash of 1929, the Republicans were led by President Herbert Hoover. Hoover responded very cautiously to popular pressure for the federal government to take action in relieving the poverty and unemployment caused by the

Depression. Political leaders made popular appeals for the government to reshape the structure of the economy and limit the impact that unruly business cycles would have on average citizens. However, the Republican Party took a laissez-faire stance, claiming that it was not the role of the federal government to play such a large role in the lives of private citizens. The Republican platform of 1932 illustrated this philosophy, stating that "the people themselves, by their own courage, their own patient and resolute effort in the readjustments of their own affairs, can and will work out the cure. The relief problem [is] one of State and local responsibility" (Johnson and Porter 1973, 339–41).

Franklin Delano Roosevelt, the Democratic nominee for president in 1932, took a more activist stance on the role of government in alleviating poverty and unemployment. The voters handsomely rewarded him for his positions: they continued to elect Roosevelt president until his death in 1945. Roosevelt's role in transforming the message of the Democratic Party in particular and of changing the role of the federal government in general cannot be over exaggerated. Roosevelt promised a "New Deal" to be brokered between the federal government and private citizens, a deal that ensured basic services and safety for all. No longer would the government stand idly by as its citizens tried to weather difficult times. Rather, the Democratic Party set out "humanizing policies of the federal government as they affect the personal, financial, industrial, and agricultural well-being of the American people" (Johnson and Porter 1973, 360).

The New Deal forever changed the role of government in modern American life. It endowed the federal government with new and significant responsibilities, from regulating corporate business to providing a social safety net through welfare, subsidized education, and a minimum wage. Consequently, because of the New Deal, the Democratic Party became known as the party that advocated a larger role for government, while the Republican party continued to be known as the party of smaller government.

The Current Party System: 1968 to the Present

The contours of the New Deal system remained largely unchanged until the turmoil of the sixties. Economic stagnation at home and war abroad produced a volatile political climate. These politics culminated in the 1968 Democratic National Convention in Chicago. Delegates and protestors alike converged on the city. Protestors camped out in Grant Park, only blocks away from the hotels in which the delegates to the convention stayed. Most of the protestors and many of the delegates resented the dictatorial fashion in which the party selected the presidential nominee. Senator Eugene McCarthy, the anti-war candidate, won more primaries than Vice President Hubert Humphrey. However, delegates were not selected to go to the convention according to the outcome of the primaries. Most of the primary events were "beauty contests"—they indicated to the party who the most popular candidate was but did little or nothing to determine how the delegates to the convention had to vote. Consequently, the large majority of delegates to the convention ignored the primary results and pledged their support to Vice President Humphrey. This decision to give Humphrey the nomination triggered the massive riots and protests that left one historian describing the streets of Chicago as a "sea of blood" (White 1970, 376).

In the wake of the disastrous 1968 convention, the Democratic Party undertook a series of reforms to make primaries more meaningful. The national party actually required states to adopt primaries and caucuses as the only means available for selecting delegates to the national convention. The candidate who received the most support in the primaries or the caucuses would then be guaranteed a substantial portion of the delegates from those states. The delegates would also be bound to vote for that candidate at the national convention, thus ensuring that the most popular candidate in the primaries and the caucuses would receive the party's nomination. The Republican party, without the impetus of protests in the streets, also adopted similar rules for selecting delegates to its national convention. Thus, social and cultural forces had a tremendous impact on political parties—not by the creation of a new party, but by molding the existing parties from within.

The current party system, ushered in on the heels of these reforms, has three distinct features. First, while most voters know about the two major parties and identify with either the Republican or the Democratic Party, voters today say they are more independent than voters in the past. They say they vote for the candidate and not for the party. Second, the party system is extremely competitive. Most party systems in the past usually saw one party dominate the other. However, elections for the presidency and for Congress are normally quite competitive. Republicans have enjoyed an advantage in presidential elections since 1968, while Democrats seemed to prosper in congressional elections. As of today those positions appear to have reversed. The two parties compete at all levels of the political system with only pockets of one-party dominance. Finally, most scholars characterize the modern party system as "candidate-centered." This means that the candidates, not the parties, control most of the electoral resources to run campaigns. Candidates file for the ballot, raise the money, and conduct the campaign. They use a party label, but rarely does the party dictate how the candidate should run for office or act once elected.

The Organization of Political Parties in America

The evolution of the party system in the United States has produced a rich variety of organizations at multiple levels of American society. The parties in these states and local areas have their own organizations which are distinct from the national party organizations. While the Framers never envisioned such an expansive system, the Constitution set the stage for its development. The federal system gives state and local governments power and autonomy over particular issues. Therefore, parties have a strong incentive to organize and capture the offices at these levels of government.

The Republican Party and the Democratic Party have local, state, and national layers of party organization. These include the elected representatives on the party's ticket at every level of government and the leaders who are not elected but who have a great deal of influence in how the party is organized and carries out its functions. Remarkably, this multi-layered system is not hierarchically organized, meaning that the national parties do not control or dictate what state and local parties do. For example, the Democratic Party's candidate-recruitment techniques, fund-raising tactics, and party policies can differ vastly from state to state. Each particular state and local organization adds its own flavor to how these party activities are performed.

I. Local Parties

The local parties have responsibility for several functions that are best accomplished at the grassroots level. They perform organizational tasks such as compiling current records on registered voters, laying the groundwork for membership activities like registration drives and fund raising, and help to mobilize their party's vote during elections by handing out literature and getting the vote out on election day. If you have contact with a particular party organization, it will most likely be with the local level of the party. There are no clear lines of authority for the party leadership at the state, district, county, city, ward-township, and precinct levels. This means the party leaders at the state and local level must rely on informal modes of association, where personality and persuasive ability can mean a great deal in how the party's work gets done. Chairman and committee leaders are periodically elected at each level, but these elected officials do not have the ability to control the lower levels in the party structure.

Local party organization is very important to the party system in America. The volunteers who work for the parties at this level are able to determine a great deal about how the party will look and be run in their area. Anyone can participate in a party at this level, which means there tends to be a diversity of backgrounds, interests, expertise, and incentives for those who volunteer. There is no formal screening of volunteers, so there is a looseness and a flexibility in how the local party operates.

Local parties used to have tighter forms of organization and more authority in the late 1800s and early 1900s. At this time, the parties were referred to locally as a "machine,"[1] controlled by a local party boss who dominated and controlled local politics by providing social welfare to the immigrants and the poor in the cities in return for their votes. For example, Chicago was controlled by the Democratic Party machine. Party supporters were given patronage jobs, and loyal communities received perks like free legal service, more police officers, and cleaner streets. In middle-class communities, the constituents' rewards came in the form of scholarships and summer jobs for students, having their tax bills appealed, and getting help with the bureaucracy. Parties have the ability to hand out several patronage jobs, which in those days paid a great deal of money in areas where jobs were hard to come by.

The party machines proved that patronage is a strong incentive for people to get involved in local party politics, but other incentives work as well. People are lured to local party politics to pursue the possibility of a career in public office, to receive special treatment or advantage from government, to obtain social and psychological satisfaction, or else to fulfill ideological goals. All of these incentives can motivate individuals to become involved at the local level. The incentive that is the strongest in a particular location can have a great deal to do with the shape and design of the local party structure.

II. State Parties

State parties perform slightly different functions than the local parties. Each state sets its own regulations for the operation of political parties so there is some variation in their shape and structure across the country. For the most part, each state party has a committee and a party chair. These officials set the policy for the party within the regulatory structure provided by the state, and they often assist the local organizations in the performance of their responsibilities. More often than not, the state party organizations take their cues from the highest elected official from their party. For example, the leader of the state Republican Party usually defers to the governor of the state when the governor is from the same party.

III. National Parties

The national party organizations are split into two categories: those organizations that exist in the Congress and those organizations that govern the affairs of the national party and plan the national conventions. These party organs at the national level have developed slowly in Washington, D.C. for the past two hundred years. Although these organizations are concentrated in the same geographic area, there is remarkably little collaboration between them. This lack of integration means the party components at the national level cannot cooperate enough to have effective control over the members of the party who are part of the government. There are no means available to national parties to discipline party members who do not vote a particular way in Congress.

There are five major components of the national party organizations: (1) national chair and staff, (2) House party organization (leader, whips, committee chairs, caucus), (3) Senate party organization (leader, whips, committees, caucus), (4) national committee and national executive committee, and (5) national party convention. A sixth component is added to the party that controls the White House. The president and his staff can exercise a great deal of influence on the conduct of the party's affairs.

There are no clear lines of hierarchy among these components of the national party; rather, they have a structure of equal power relationships. The different groups work together informally, and they recognize one another's influence and the importance of the function each performs. The chair and the staff provide management for the national party, the national committee provides the organization with a policy making and planning component, the Senate and the House party organizations provide the policy component and organize the Congress, and the national convention provides the plenary body or the representative component. The president and his staff provide the official decision making and patronage allocation components (Eldersveld 103–104).

In the past, presidents have attempted to gain some control over the way their parties operated. President Taft tried to use the Republican National Committee (RNC) to dictate who the chair would be and the rules for the national convention. President Franklin Roosevelt tried to block the re-nomination of anti-New Deal Democrats when election time rolled around. Both of these presidents failed at their attempts to control different aspects of the national party, underlining their diffuse power structures.

The leaders of the different party components must struggle for control and power through a bargaining system, where contacts and informal relationships often dominate the decision-making apparatus. The national parties must also attempt to appeal to a broad base of constituents, including women, minorities, and different age groups. This means parties may be comprised of groups with different, or even conflicting, points of view. American political parties must constantly satisfy the demands of these various factions to cobble together a broad base of electoral support.

The national party attempts to resolve the conflicts of the different groups that it represents by presenting a platform that can appeal to a large group of supporters and potential voters. The efforts of the national party to resolve conflicts are particularly noticeable when it tries to nominate a presidential candidate. Sometimes, however, the national party fails miserably to make peace among the various factions. For example, despite public declarations from Democratic leaders within Congress and from outside Congress, the Democratic leadership could do little to stem support among Democratic members of Congress for a budget proposal put forth by President Reagan in 1981. The Democrats controlled the Congress at this time, but 63 Democrats defected from the party policy and "crossed the floor" to vote with the Republicans. The Democratic National Committee (DNC) and the Democratic leaders in Congress did nothing to discipline those members who did not follow party policy.

This does not mean the national party committees do not play an important role in the party system; they do. The national party chair is the top official in the party and is formally elected by the national committee, even though the real appointment initiates from the party's pres-

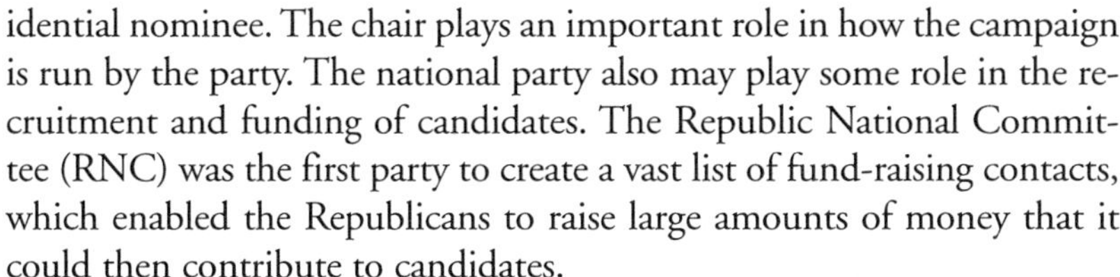

idential nominee. The chair plays an important role in how the campaign is run by the party. The national party also may play some role in the recruitment and funding of candidates. The Republic National Committee (RNC) was the first party to create a vast list of fund-raising contacts, which enabled the Republicans to raise large amounts of money that it could then contribute to candidates.

The Functions of Political Parties in a Republic

The large and diverse party system in the United States performs a number of crucial functions for the maintenance of a vast democratic republic. While the Framers never intended to create such a system, the functioning of modern democratic government is almost unthinkable without it. Political parties perform a variety of functions that make citizen participation and governance possible.

I. How Political Parties Help to Govern

Political parties act as intermediaries between the government and the public by serving as a conduit between the masses and those who govern. In this way, political parties institutionalize dissent and opposition. The party out of power acts as a check on the majority party and seeks to represent the opinions of the minority. The competition between parties works to the benefit of the general public. When the party in power makes a mistake, the minority party alerts the public. The minority party stands ready to court the dissatisfied public in order to gain electoral support. For this reason, a two-party system is much more desirable than a one-party system. In a one-party system, there is no mechanism to oversee the activities of the majority party. A competitive party system provides an alternative to the majority party, an alternative that can take office if the majority party should lose favor with the voters.

The party system also provides the means for the government to function and organize. Individuals with similar goals and ideologies assemble under the banner of a particular party, using this cohesion to manage the affairs of government. The party leadership in Congress can control what legislation comes to the floor of the House or the Senate because of their control over committees and other institutions within Congress.

It is important to note that there is a distinction between the presidential party organization and the congressional party organization. The presidential party is made up of a group of activists who choose to follow a particular candidate in pursuit of national goals. The congressional party only achieves unity in a limited number of areas because of the diversity and the differing interests of the party members at this level. The voters seem to reenforce this separation as they often elect a president from one party and a Congress from another. Traditionally Congress was dominated by the Democrats and the presidency by the Republicans, but that changed in 1994, two years after President Clinton started his first term in office, when the Republicans took over the House of Representatives for the first time in 40 years.

This separation of powers between the levels of the parties is important, as "[w]hat the Constitution separates our political parties do not combine" (Neustadt 26). The benefits of the separation of powers are strengthened because of the separation in the parties, but so are the weaknesses.

This separation has some adverse affects on governability. First, it is difficult to create an integrated national policy because the parties do not have the organization or the authority to provide this. If the parties in America were stronger, some would suggest that America would be more governable. The parties would be able to provide the voting public with a clearer political choice. As it stands now there are no true national policies put forward by the parties, and no real mechanisms to present coherent policies to the public.

Often during an election the presidential and congressional candidates from the same party will work together to try and maximize gains for the party. However, this congenial relationship usually ends after the election when the winners face the responsibility of fulfilling their constitutional duty to represent their own constituencies. Because of this constitutional division the president is forced to lobby the members of Congress directly, even members of his own party, in order to see his policies succeed. For example, modern presidents have sought and received authority from Congress to negotiate trade treaties on an all or nothing basis, an authority which makes passing trade legislation easier on the president and gives him wider latitude in the negotiations. However, President Clinton could not persuade enough Democrats in Congress to support Fast Track legislation, as it is commonly known, even though he had substantial support from the Republicans. He could not convince enough Democrats to support him because they had received pressure from various interest groups, including some powerful unions, from whom many

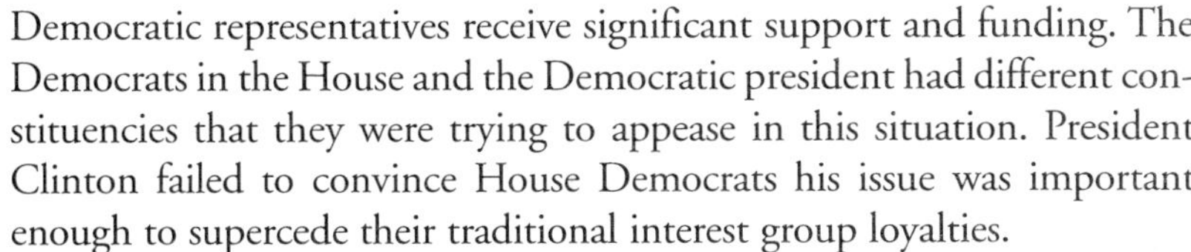

Democratic representatives receive significant support and funding. The Democrats in the House and the Democratic president had different constituencies that they were trying to appease in this situation. President Clinton failed to convince House Democrats his issue was important enough to supercede their traditional interest group loyalties.

II. Political Parties and Elections

Political parties help to organize electoral competition in this country and select the candidates who run for the numerous offices. One of the major tasks of American democracy—selecting the presidential candidates who desire to lead the country—could not occur without some assistance from the parties. The national conventions that select these candidates occur every four years and play a critical role in the electoral process. Today the conventions are events where the president and the vice-president are *formally* announced and chosen, even though the candidates have actually been designated prior to the convention.

The national party conventions first appeared in the 1930s, beginning as a small meeting of a few delegates, but now involve upwards of 5,000 delegates. Since so many delegates now attend the conventions they require a great deal of planning and coordination. In an attempt to make the conventions more representative, parties have moved away from the delegate selection system where convention delegates were appointed by the state party. Today the majority of delegates are chosen through a direct election by party members.

Conventions include a variety of groups including convention committees and the convention leadership, presidential candidate organizations that seek to mobilize voters, state delegations, and interest-group caucuses. The interest-group caucuses are groups of delegates who form various groupings according to a particular special interest, such as the labor union delegates, the black caucus, and the women's caucus.

Along with nominating the presidential candidates, the convention also convenes every four years so the party can draft its platform. Prior to the convention, a drafting committee is established and a chairman appointed, which receive the drafts of the "planks." The committee circulates and considers the planks, but this is usually a formality as the platform has ordinarily been assembled before the committee is convened. An incumbent president will often have the White House draft the party platform and give it to the committee chair to consider. The committee hears testimony on the platform, considers the draft, and then re-submits it to the drafting subcommittee. Before the platform can be presented at the convention for consideration, it must be sent back to the full committee for consent.

Conventions today are more representative then they have been in years past. Democrats use affirmative action principles to select convention delegates to increase the representation of women and blacks at the conventions. As the conventions become more representative, many delegates come to the conventions with a specific issue agenda, which leads them to assert that certain things be included in the platform. Prior to 1972, the conventions did not have an open-platform creation process. Party platforms today are the product of a more open and honest discussion between various interest groups within the party. The platform can be the basis for a unified party and can provide the gateway for the introduction of new ideas and policies. Yet one must ask how useful these platforms are since the party's candidates do not need to adhere to the ideas they express. Party platforms can be useful as national plans and play a role in the indication of future policy. Parties assume issue positions both to provide public alternatives and competition and to respond to public opinion and pressure.

Presidential nominees also apply pressure on the committee that drafts the platform so that their personal political agendas become the national party agenda. When President Reagan was first nominated to be the Republican candidate for president in 1980, he applied pressure on the party before the convention to drop support for the Equal Rights Amendment from the platform, even though the party had a history of supporting it. Reagan was able to maintain substantial support for this change, before and after it occurred, because of his ability to mobilize the conservative wing of the Republican party.

Another important function of parties is to help to mobilize the electorate and provide the public with political symbols around which it can rally during elections. Even though there is a large degree of individualism in American elections, meaning people vote for the candidate rather than the party, people still identify themselves with a particular party, especially during the early stages of an election. Furthermore, when Americans register to vote, they are able to identify the party with which they choose to affiliate. But unlike other nations, which demand dues and a membership card for those who wish to vote for party policies and candidate nominees, in the U.S. belonging to a party can be as simple as checking a box when registering to vote. These loose requirements for party membership cause some problems for American parties, because it eliminates any opportunity for them to control their membership.

Both the Democrats and the Republicans have traditional bases of support that they rely on during elections. However, both parties try to present a platform that is somewhat centrist so that they can capture the majority of the votes of the American public, whose opinions lie somewhere around the middle of the political spectrum.

Today most candidates are nominated to run for political office through a system of direct primaries, further limiting the party's ability to control completely how voters view the party. Candidates may be nominated who are hostile to the party, opposed to the party platform, not representative of the party's image, or simply candidates who may be weak and ineffective. During the 1998 Congressional elections a 76 year old Atlanta, Georgia resident, John H. Lewis, Sr., ran and won the Republican nomination even though he had been a Democrat his whole life. David Duke was poised to capture the Republican nomination for Senate in Louisiana and force the state into a further Senate election when top GOP officials asked the other top Republican candidate, Ben Bagert to withdraw from the race, and then backed his Democrat opponent, incumbent J. Bennett Johnston. Duke, who earlier had held a leadership position in the Ku Klux Klan, was an embarrassment to Republican officials, but they could do nothing to stop the voters from making him the Republican nominee in his state.

Parties can also play a role in elections today through fund raising. In the past few decades parties have been written out of the fund raising role for congressional and presidential candidates. Presidential candidates raise most of their money through a system of private and matching public contributions while congressional candidates receive most of their money from Political Action Committees (PACs). Parties lost control of campaigns because candidates could raise the money and spend that money to independently of the political parties. The financing system tilted control toward the candidates and away from the parties. However, new data suggests this pattern may be changing as parties develop sources of money that enable them to participate more significantly in the campaign process. The parties now seek to raise large amounts of "soft money" which they spend to bolster their party's candidates (Magleby and Holt 1998)[1] through the creation of issue advertising and "get-out-the-vote" activities. The parties' ability to spend money in this fashion diminishes somewhat the amount of control that candidates have over the election process.

The Future of Political Parties in America

Political parties are now an integral part of American politics. Even though public opinion polls consistently tell about the dislike of the American public for partisan politics, the nation needs political parties to accomplish certain functions.

Sometimes public dissatisfaction with the parties reaches particularly acute levels. In the 1992 election Ross Perot launched his own presidential campaign without the support of either major party. He felt neither the Democratic nor the Republican party had policies or platforms that he could support, so he ran independently. He was given copious amounts of attention during the election by the media and the voters, enabling him to determine some of the issues and the direction of the debates. He lost the 1992 election but had garnered enough votes to show the two major parties that people were dissatisfied with the traditional candidates. After the election, Perot started his own party, but it has not performed well in any election since 1992, as is the case with most minor parties that crop up in American elections. Other minor parties, including the Libertarians and the Green Party, run candidates in elections, but they do not receive enough support to challenge the current system.

Generally, people in America don't trust political parties, but they see them as necessary for the functioning of democracy. American citizens still overwhelmingly use their partisan attachments to evaluate candidates and cast their votes, and even occasionally contribute money to the parties.

Are the major American parties today weak and undisciplined? And if so, does that lessen their importance to the functioning of democracy? Individuals running for political office still need to identify themselves with a traditional party in order to gain enough support from the electorate to win an election, but because of direct primaries they do not need party support in order to gain this identification, weakening the parties and also confusing the voters ability to clearly identify a party with specific issues.

Direct primaries also play a role in the party's ability to discipline candidates after they are elected. There is less need for a member of Congress to follow party policy when the party has no control over the nomination process, as it lessens the member's responsibility and affiliation with the party. Individual candidates have also found more methods to fund raise, trying to eclipse the party's role in this vital area.

The mass media has also vastly changed the way campaigns work in America, thereby affecting how the party interacts with candidates and the electorate. Candidates step over the parties and interact directly with the public. This means that the mass media now provide information to the voting public in place of the parties, so the parties cannot control the flow of information the public receives about issues and policies. The intrusion of the media into the political arena also means that elections emphasize image rather than policy, and candidates must be marketed and raise huge amounts of money. The parties do little to discourage their candidates from running on image, instead they support it by providing money and access to the media. Parties have revised their recruitment techniques to include a candidate's ability to look good and perform well on TV. As a result, elections are more scripted, making it difficult for the electorate to determine what is genuine and what is not.

Despite all these problems parties are still an important component in our political system. The place for parties in our democracy must be rediscovered. We must ask whether or not parties are still necessary for the proper functioning of democracy, and whether or not a party's functions are now being performed by other institutions and organizations. The parties still play a particularly strong role in Congress. Members of the House and Senate define themselves largely by the party to which they belong. For example, the highly publicized votes on the articles of impeachment for President Clinton were divided down partisan lines in both the House and the Senate, despite public pressure and opinion.

Although the public dislikes voting according to party lines in Congress, the public benefits because parties set policy agendas and define issues. Parties simplify the means by which the public connects to the political process and gives it greater access to the institutions of government. Parties continue to play a substantial role in the election process. Parties create powerful symbols that make it easier for voters to identify major issues facing the republic and they provide the competition that makes it possible for citizens to hold their elected leaders accountable. Political parties provide the competition and debate so crucial to modern democracy, without becoming the factions so feared by Madison.

Whether reacting to changing cultural forces or nominating a candidate for office, whether advocating social change or getting a bill passed through Congress, the American party system has evolved to fit the progressive needs of the Republic. What will the future hold for our evolving party system? Will it continue to play an active role in our government and politics? From a brief look at history, it seems that a steady constant in our volatile political culture is the ever-changing, ever-evolving political party. Thus, whatever the form or structure, our party system will continue to be a viable force in the American experience of government.

Works Cited

Dye, Thomas R. 1999. *Politics in America.* 3d ed. Upper Saddle River, NJ: Simon & Schuster.

Eldersveld, Samuel J. 1982. *Political Parties in American Society.* New York: Basic Books, Inc.

Johnson, Donald Bruce, and Kirk H. Porter. 1972. *National Party Platforms 1840–1972.* Urbana, IL: University of Illinois Press.

Magleby, David B. and Marianne Holt, eds. 1998. *Outside Money: Soft Money and Issue Ads in Competitive 1998 Congressional Elections.* Provo, UT: Brigham Young University.

Neustadt, Richard E. 1980. *Presidential Power: The Politics of Leadership from FDR to Carter.* New York: John Wiley & Sons, Inc.

White, Theodore H. 1970. *The Making of the President 1968.* New York: Pocket Books.

Notes

[1] A machine is a "tightly disciplined party organization, headed by a boss, that relies on material rewards—including patronage jobs—to control politics."

[2] Soft money donations are given to the state or local party organizations or to PACs to be used for non- candidate election activities, and do not need to be reported according to the Federal Elections Campaign Act (1971) and also because of state and local tax laws that do not require disclosure.

FEDERALISM

Troy Smith
Department of Political Science

If a person standing in one State shoots and kills a person standing in another State, in which State did the crime occur? The question is not merely an academic riddle. In 1894, the North Carolina Supreme Court reversed the guilty conviction of a Mr. Hall on the grounds that while Mr. Hall stood in North Carolina when he squeezed the trigger, the crime occurred in Tennessee because that was where the bullet entered the victim. Subsequently, Tennessee's Governor requested that Mr. Hall be extradited to Tennessee to stand trial for murder. Again the North Carolina Supreme Court intervened, arguing that extradition was illegal in this case because Mr. Hall had never been in Tennessee and therefore was not a fugitive of justice (114 N.C. 900). Mr. Hall, consequently, got away with murder.

When the authors of America's Constitution divided power between the federal and state governments they created a unique form of government. They understood they were creating legalistic conundrums, like the one above, but they believed these problems would be worked out with time.[1] Through America's history, federalism has frustrated justice, protected slavery, made a mockery of civil liberties, and hampered political agendas. Many cite these problems as evidence that federalism should be abandoned. Furthermore, they continue, structures created during the horse and buggy era are no longer relevant for our era of global competition. Before the system is condemned as a set of compromises dictated by the colonial age and irrelevant to or incompatible with our modern era, we should understand the framers' purposes for creating "federalism" and evaluate how 200 years of tinkering has affected the founders' unique form of government.

In creating America's governmental system, two of the main questions faced by the founders were: Should America be one political community or many? If many, how much freedom should the different communities have to define and govern themselves?[2] While the founders devised answers to those questions, the questions themselves have not gone away. Each generation of Americans confronts those questions anew and each generation redefines the answers. In this chapter we look at how the founders answered those questions and how generations of Americans have reinterpreted them to give us our unique and very complex system of government. We will then consider what forces affect American federalism today and consider different directions American federalism may develop

The Constitutional Convention—Nationalists v. Confederalists

The delegates to Philadelphia in 1787 agreed that the end of government should be liberty. By liberty they meant the protection of individual rights, including the right to be governed by their consent.[3] They also agreed that the Articles of Confederation were less than ideal for preserving liberty. Under the Articles of Confederation each state was united only in a "firm league of friendship" (Articles of Confederation, Article III). Consequently, each State could abide by or disregard resolutions adopted by the Continental Congress. This proved dangerous to the union as the States ignored international law and treaties, waged war on the Indians and concluded peace with them contrary to the will of Congress, discriminated against citizens of other states, established protective trade policies which inhibited the flow of goods between states, and conceded to popular appeals for dangerous legislation. The delegates to Philadelphia perceived in these problems dangerous threats to liberty and agreed that rather than reform the Articles of Confederation, America required a new government.

When considering what should replace the Articles of Confederation, the delegates divided between those who wanted a national government (a single community) and those who preferred a confederal form of government (several communities). Those supporting a national form of government desired a government like the United Kingdom, where all governmental power resided in the central government. Those favoring a confederal form of government favored a central government that derived its authority from the state governments and possessed no authority over the individual citizens in the various states.

As the delegates debated the virtues of national and confederal forms of government, the confederalists were forced to concede that the problems confronting America were due not just to the Articles of Confederation, but are inherent to a confederacy.[4] A confederacy, James Madison argued, cannot protect individual rights, dispense justice or promote the national interest because the central government has no power to compel States' or individuals' compliance with national laws. Without some national control over State governments and individuals, Madison continued, liberty and the other ends of government favored by the delegates could not be protected.

The supporters of confederal government acknowledged the weaknesses of a confederation, but continued to oppose the creation of a national form of government. The confederalists believed liberty could be preserved only in a **small republic** because a national form of government possessed its own inherent dangers to liberty. The confederalists argued that government by the people requires a virtuous, informed and patriotic citizenry. By limiting government to a small area, government would be simpler, hence, the public would be attentive to and active in holding their government and elected representatives accountable to the public will. In a large republic, they reasoned, the issues, structures and processes of government would be too complex for the public to follow. Citizens, consequently, would feel disconnected from their government. Disconnected citizens soon become disinterested and apathetic, and then ignore or dismiss the public interest in favor of their own selfish interests. In this manner, the very foundation of a democratic government (a virtuous, informed and patriotic citizenry) would be eroded. Such citizens would also ignore their political leaders who, far away in the remote capital, could turn the powers of government to personal benefit and undermine the liberties of the people.[5] The arguments and fears expressed by the Anti-Federalists were shared by a significant portion of the American public at the time.[6]

James Madison turned the small republic argument on its head and argued that the best means to preserve liberty and government by the people was to extend government to a larger area. The danger of a small republic, Madison proposed, was that a powerful group could gain control of the government unopposed. Without a valid opposition, the dominant group could use the powers of government to benefit themselves and tyrannize the minority.

> "The only remedy [to tyranny of the minority]," Madison argued, "was to enlarge the sphere [of the republic], and thereby divide the community into so great a number of interests and parties, that in the 1st place a majority will not be likely at the same moment to have a common interest separate from that of the whole or of the minority; and in the 2nd place, that in case they should have such an interest, they may not be apt to unite in the pursuit of it."[7]

In other words, Madison argued that in an enlarged or **extended republic** no single group would gain control of the government because enough other interests groups would oppose them. Any governmental policy would therefore require a compromise agreed to by a number of different groups. In the rare case that a single majority did favor some proposal that violated the public good or individual liberties, however, they would be prevented from organizing and pursuing it due to the obstacles presented by the distance of a large republic. Madison and others also argued that extending the republic would increase the pool of potential legislators and thereby increase the probability that decent, capable men would be elected to serve in government. Madison, thus countered the small republic argument by claiming that liberty would best be preserved in a large republic.[8]

As the delegates in Philadelphia conferred on the merits and demerits of national and confederal forms of government, they forged many compromises and created a new form of government. Those compromises emerged not from stalemate but from vigorous analysis and intelligent discussions about the different options and consequences.[9] The delegates' support for the government they created is demonstrated by the fact that fifteen of the eighteen powers delegated to Congress were adopted without serious opposition, and the specific prohibitions placed on Congress and the States were adopted almost unanimously.[10]

The Constitution

The unique form of government created by the Constitution was neither confederal nor national, but contained a curious mixture of both. Unlike any government in the past, the Constitution gave two different and independent governments authority to pass laws and compel individuals to comply with those laws. Thus, the government created by the Constitution contained both confederal and nationalist elements.

The theory underlying the Constitution was to set institutions in competition with each other to prevent any one person or institution from gaining too much power and using that power to trample the liberties of the people. The only way to maintain the proper partition of power, wrote Madison is to "contrive the interior structure of the government as that its several constituent parts may, by their mutual relations, be the means of keeping each other in their proper places."[11] In order to accomplish this, the framers of the Constitution split power in two distinct ways. "In the compound republic of America," Madison continued, "the power surrendered by the people is first divided between two distinct governments, and then the portion allotted to each subdivided among distinct and separate departments. Hence a double security arises to the rights of the people."[12] The founders of the Constitution set ambition against ambition, not just within the federal government but also when they divided power between the federal and State governments.

Dividing power between two different governments was a unique characteristic of the Constitution. Under the old governments, either the national or the State governments had the authority to legislate and compel citizens to obey the laws. Under the Constitution, this power belongs to both the federal and state governments. While the two governments share authority to pass laws and compel citizen compliance, the federal and State governments were "constituted with different powers, and designed for different purposes."[13]

The powers identified by the Constitution can be divided into three categories: enumerated powers, concurrent powers and prohibited powers. The Constitution grants the federal government specific powers and divides them between the legislative, executive and judicial branches. These are the enumerated powers. The Constitution also prohibited the States from exercising certain powers, these are the prohibited powers. The concurrent powers are powers which both the federal and State governments may exercise.[14]

The fact that the powers of the federal government were enumerated (and the powers of the States were not) implies that the powers not assigned to the federal government belonged to the States or to the people. This implication was verified by the addition of the 10th Amendment to the Constitution which reads: "The powers not delegated to the United States by the Constitution, nor prohibited it to the States, are reserved to the States respectively, or to the people." Important as these words are, it should be clearly understood that the framers of the Constitution and the members of Congress who approved the 10th Amendment rejected using the word "expressly" to limit the federal government, as in "the powers expressly delegated to the federal government."[15] The framers of the Constitution and authors of the 10th Amendment understood the federal government to be a government of limited powers but not a government limited "expressly" to the Constitution's stated powers.

Table 1 The Constitution's Division of Powers, Including Amendments

Enumerated Powers	Prohibited Powers
The Federal Government:	The Federal Government:
To coin money	To tax articles exported from any State
To conduct foreign relations	To violate the Bill of Rights
To regulate interstate commerce	To change State boundaries
To levy and collect taxes	To suspend the right of *habeas corpus*
To declare war	To make *ex post facto* laws or *bills of attainder*
To raise and support the military	To subject officeholders to a religious test
To establish post offices	State Governments:
To establish courts inferior to the Supreme Court	To tax imports or exports
To admit new States	To coin money
State Governments:	To enter into treaties
To conduct elections	To impair obligations of contracts
To ratify amendments to the federal Constitution	To abridge the privileges or immunities of citizens or deny due process and equal protection of the laws
To establish a State militia	The Federal and State Governments:
Concurrent Powers:	To grant titles of nobility
To levy and collect taxes	To permit slavery
To borrow money	To deny citizens the right to vote because of race, color, or previous servitude
To make and enforce laws	To deny citizens the right to vote because of sex
To establish courts	
To charter banks and corporations	

In addition to dividing powers between the two governments, the Constitution creates structural barriers that guarantee the existence of the federal and State governments and prevents one level of government from subsuming the other. The Constitution prevents the States from dominating the federal government through the "supremacy" clause which declares that all laws and treaties approved by the federal government are the supreme law of the land (Article VI, paragraph 2). The Constitution protects the political integrity of the States in three ways. First, the Constitution guarantees the States equal representation in the Senate, which does can not be changed even by a Constitutional amendment unless the States agree to it (Article V). Second, a State's boundaries can not be changed except with the State Legislature's consent (Article IV, section 3). Third, the Constitution guarantees the States a "Republican Form of Government" and thereby requires federal assistance to protect the States from external and internal threats. These provisions protect the political integrity of each government and prevents one from obliterating the other.

Despite constituting the federal and State governments with "different powers and for different purposes," the Constitution's division of powers and responsibilities between the federal and State governments is neither systematic nor unambiguous. In fact, a close examination of *The Federalist Papers* reveals that neither Hamilton nor Madison envisioned completely separate governments operating independently. Rather, both expected a certain amount of interaction, even competition, between the federal and State governments. "The different governments," James Madison wrote "will control each other, at the same time that each will be controlled by itself."[16]

In fact, the Constitution institutionalized interaction between the federal and State governments. The Constitution provided the States two specific means to interact with and influence the federal government. First, each State's legislature elected the State's two United States Senators. State influence over Senators was minimized, however, by the Senators' six-year terms and the fact that the federal government paid the Senators' salaries rather than the respective State governments.[17] Second, the States determine how members of the presidential electoral college are selected. Theoretically, this would give the States significant influence in the election of the president. In these two ways, the founders hoped to insure that State governments' concerns figured prominently, but not decisively, in the president's and the Senate's deliberations.

The framers also expected that the federal and State governments would compete for power. Such conflicts, *The Federalist Papers* explained, would usually be resolved by the people. "Power being almost always the rival of power," Hamilton wrote in *The Federalist Papers* #28, "the general government will at all times stand ready to check the usurpations of the state governments, and these will have the same disposition towards the general government. The people, by throwing themselves into either scale, will infallibly make it preponderate."[18] Madison concurred in *The Federalist Papers* #46, "The ultimate authority . . . resides in the people alone" and neither the federal nor the State governments may enlarge its sphere of jurisdiction at the expense of the other without the support of the people.[19] Thus, in intergovernmental conflicts between the federal and state governments, the people would determine which level of government prevailed.

Yet what level of government would the public support in an intergovernmental conflict? Hamilton suggested two answers. First, the people would support the government in which they had the greatest confidence; and public confidence would flow to that level of government that was best administered.[20] Second, the government that is more familiar, that "touch[es] the sensible chords and put[s] in motion the most active springs of the human heart" will receive the "respect and attachment of the community."[21] In other words, in a conflict of power between the federal and State governments, the public would support the government that is best administered and that addresses the issues of most concern to its citizens.

For Alexander Hamilton, James Madison and others like George Washington who endorsed The Federalist Papers, the Constitution did not simply and cleanly divide governmental powers and responsibilities between two separate levels of government. A considerable amount of ambiguity remained. This ambiguity set the two levels of government against each other as checks against either's tyrannical usurpation of power or poor administration.

Constitutional Ambiguities

The Constitution's ambiguity in separating power and responsibility between the federal and State governments created a number of questions. The following four sections present questions or Constitutional phrases that are not clear and consequently have been interpreted in various ways. The different interpretations have profoundly influenced the relationship between the federal and state governments.

Imperia in Imperio

When the founders divided power between the federal and state governments "they split the atom of sovereignty," said Supreme Court Justice Anthony Kennedy.[22] Sovereignty can be understood as the supreme political authority. Some Anti-Federalists charged that the Constitution created an unstable regime by dividing sovereignty between the federal and state governments. This created an empire within an empire, or Imperia in Imperio, and set the two levels of government at war against each other. The final result, some Anti-Federalists claimed, could only be that one government would conquer and obliterate the other. The Federalist James Wilson countered that sovereignty belongs to the people who can distribute a portion of it to the State government and another portion to the federal government.[23] Not all accepted James Wilson's arguments that sovereignty resides in the people and the debate about where sovereignty resides continues to this day.

The question of sovereignty has expressed itself most forcefully in the question of who created the federal government? Some scholars suggest that the people as a whole created the federal government while others argue it was the people through each of their States. If sovereignty resides in the people as a whole, then they alone possess the authority to establish the federal government and change elements of the federal government. If the Declaration of Independence, however, made the states free and independent States bound together only in a confederation or "league of friendship," then the authority to establish the federal government and change elements of the federal government belonged to the people of each state.

A number of famous statesmen argued up to the Civil War that the Constitution was a compact of the States. The powers given to the federal government, therefore, were delegated it by the people through their States. This meant that the States could define federal powers, and **nullify** federal laws that violated states' rights. The logical conclusion of this line of reasoning was that a state could secede from the union if the State concluded its interests were no longer served as a member of the union. It was this argument the Southern States used to justify seceding from the Union and which provoked the Civil War.

President Lincoln responded to the Southern States' claims that they possessed a right to secede by arguing that the American union preceded the states. The union, Lincoln claimed, arose from the Declaration of Independence. The union thus preceded and, through the Constitution, created the States (Lincoln Message to Congress, July 4, 1861). Never having an independent existence, the states consequently never possessed any rights other than those given them by the Constitution. While Lincoln strenuously denied the states created the Union and have any rights exterior to the Constitution, his positions are silent on who created the federal government.

In our time, the question of who created the federal government, the people as a whole or the people through the states, still has profound implications. In 1995, the Supreme Court relied on the sovereignty argument to declare unconstitutional term limits imposed on members of Congress by individual States. The Court's majority argued that the United States was created by all the people and that changes to the qualifications of members of Congress therefore required the approval of all the people. The Court's minority argued that the people through their States had the authority to impose additional restrictions on their Congressional representatives because the Constitution did not specifically prohibit such restrictions.[24]

The question of sovereignty has long aggravated Constitutional interpretations. Advocates for a particular position base their arguments on sovereignty because decisions based on sovereignty are final. Yet, for most questions it is usually impossible to clearly determine where sovereignty resides. Perhaps we would be wise to heed the British Scholar Lord James Bryce's advice, given in 1896, and simply ignore the question of sovereignty because it is irresolveable.[25]

Enforcing the Division of Power

Alexander Hamilton and James Madison understood that there would be legitimate conflicts between the federal and State governments. These legitimate conflicts, they believed, would be resolved by the people. But what about the illegitimate conflicts, those conflicts where one level of government exceeds its Constitutional powers? Who would umpire these disputes to ensure that the Constitutional balance was not upset? In other words, who would interpret the meaning of the Constitution to insure that each level of government abided by but did not exceed its powers?

We have already discussed the idea that the States would serve as the umpires and nullify federal laws in those instances when the States' believed the federal government exceeded its authority. Relying on the States to serve as umpire, however, ignores the "supremacy" clause which explicitly declares that federal laws are the supreme law of the land and state officials and state judges must uphold federal law even if it contradicts State law. At the conclusion of the Civil War, the Supreme Court reaffirmed the supremacy clause when it declared "the United States is an indestructible Union, composed of indestructible States" and the States therefore do not have the right to secede (*Texas v. White* 74 U.S. (Y Wall.) 700 (1868)). This decision struck a lethal blow to the contract and States' rights theories for preserving the Constitutional balance.

Others argue that the federal government should strike and police the balance between the federal and State governments. Such a theory, however, is much like asking the fox to guard the henhouse. "Men are not angels," wrote Madison. Expecting federal officials to constrain themselves to the limits of a written Constitution requires a much more optimistic view of human nature than that endorsed by the framers and contradicts the founders' fundamental goal to check and balance government by creating opposing forces.

James Madison acknowledged in *Federalist* #39 that disputes could arise over the boundary between the different levels of government that, if unresolved, could end in war and dissolve the Constitution. In these instances, Madison wrote, "the tribunal which is ultimately to decide is to be established under the general government."[26] In other words, the federal judiciary would serve as the umpire defining the boundaries between federal and State powers. Madison acknowledged that while the federal judiciary is part of the federal government, he expected the Court to be unbiased because "the decision is to be impartially made, according to the rules of the Constitution."[27]

In *Marbury v. Madison,* the Supreme Court confirmed it possessed the authority to interpret the Constitution and thereby declare the constitutionality of all laws. This gave the Supreme Court the final say on what powers and responsibilities belonged to the federal government and which ones belonged to the States. As umpire between the federal and state governments, and also as the determiner of the Constitutionality of state laws, the Supreme Court has had a profound influence in shaping American government. More often than not, the federal judiciary has sided with the federal government in intergovernmental disputes and declared significantly more state than federal laws unconstitutional.[28] "One by one," complained Governor Tillman of South Carolina in 1894, "the reserved rights of the States are being absorbed by the federal judiciary."[29]

The great power of judicial review has been exercised primarily against the States.[30]

While the Supreme Court is generally responsible for defining the boundary between the federal and State governments, the reality is that in the last century the Supreme Court rarely limited the powers of the federal government. Consequently, the Executive and Congress have been fairly free to determine what powers belong to the federal government and, hence, what is and is not permissible. In the 1990s, however, the Supreme Court demonstrated a tentative willingness to limit federal authority.[31] The Supreme Court may further define the boundaries between the federal and State governments, but within those boundaries there will still be plenty of room for competition and conflict between the two levels of government.

The Necessary and Proper Clause of the Constitution

The Constitution's "necessary and proper" clause has also profoundly influenced federal-State relations. The Constitution authorizes Congress to "make all Laws which shall be necessary and proper for carrying into Execution the foregoing Powers, and all other Powers vested by this Constitution in the Government of the United States, or in any Department or Officer thereof" (Article I, Section 8). What exactly does "necessary and proper" mean in this context? The Anti-Federalist "Brutus" seized upon the "necessary and proper" and "supremacy" clauses of the Constitution to claim that the federal government would eventually overwhelm the States. According to Brutus, the federal government could pass any law under the "necessary and proper" clause and that law would be the supreme law of the land. These powers, wrote Brutus, could be used to overturn a particular state "at one stroke."[32]

A dispute over the meaning of the necessary and proper clause arose four years after the Constitution's ratification when Alexander Hamilton, the Secretary of the Treasury, proposed creating a national bank. Thomas Jefferson wrote to President Washington arguing that nothing in the Constitution authorized the federal government to create a national bank. In the letter, Jefferson cited the Tenth Amendment, and then wrote: "To take a single step beyond the boundaries thus specially drawn around the powers of Congress, is to take possession of a boundless field of power, no longer susceptible of any definition."[33] President Washington, however, accepted Hamilton's argument that the "necessary and proper" clause authorized the creation of a national bank.

The constitutionality of the national bank was then challenged in the courts. In *McCulloch v. Maryland* (17 U.S. (4 Wheat.) 315 (1819)), Supreme Court Chief Justice Marshall declared that while "the powers of the [federal] government are limited," the federal government may legitimately use the means to carry into execution its powers, even if those means are not listed by the Constitution as the powers of the federal government. "Let the end be legitimate, let it be within the scope of the constitution, and all means which are appropriate, which are plainly adapted to that end, which are not prohibited, but consist with the letter and spirit of the constitution, are constitutional."[34] Thus, to the list of powers identified by the Constitution must also be added the powers allowed by *McCulloch v. Maryland*. These have become known as the **implied powers.**

The Commerce Clause

A primary concern prompting the Constitutional Convention was the States' growing protective trade policies that inhibited the free flow of goods across State borders. In an effort to promote commerce between the States, the Constitution authorizes Congress "To regulate Commerce with foreign Nations, and among the several States, and with the Indian Tribes" (Article 1, Section 8, clause 2). What exactly did the framers of the Constitution mean by these words? Did they mean regulating only the transportation of goods across borders or did their meaning include the actual buying and selling of goods that had been transported across States' borders? Did they mean for Congress to regulate the production of goods bound for other states, or the production of goods using products from other states but meant for consumption within a state? Also, what about the production and consumption of goods within the state that have a secondary, but nonetheless real, impact on interstate commerce? The Supreme Court has provided many definitions of how the Constitution's commerce clause should be interpreted.

In *Gibbons v. Ogden* 22 U.S. 1 (1824), the Supreme Court rejected a "strict" interpretation of the Constitution's commerce clause and argued that commerce was more than transactions, it was intercourse. Congress, the Supreme Court ruled, had the authority to regulate any activity that interfered with that intercourse of goods, including any activity within a state. This case laid the cornerstone for an active federal government although the full impact of this decision would not be evident for another century.

Between 1835 and 1937, the Supreme Court withdrew from its expansive reading of the Commerce power and relied instead on what it called "dual federalism." **Dual federalism** is an idea developed by the Supreme Court.[35] Dual federalism posits that the federal and state governments possessed mutually exclusive powers and each is supreme and independent within its sphere. The federal government's commerce power thus did not extend to controlling production and manufacturing within states. Using this definition, the Supreme Court struck down federal laws prohibiting the use of child labor in the production or manufacturing of goods because, the Court argued, the federal government was trying to regulate an activity that was the sole responsibility of the States (see *Hammer v. Dagenhart* 247 U.S. 251 (1918)).

The Supreme Court also significantly limited the States' abilities to regulate commercial activities. The Supreme Court declared many state laws unconstitutional on the grounds that the Constitution prohibited the States from passing any "Law impairing the Obligation of Contract" (Art. I, Section 10, clause 1). State laws found to interfere with contracts between private citizens were declared unconstitutional. Thus, the Supreme Court struck down laws like New York's which limited the number of hours bakers could work during a week (*Lochner v. New York,* 198 U.S. 45 (1905)).

During the Great Depression, the Supreme Court suddenly shifted gears and authorized the federal government to regulate commerce "affected with a public interest" or with a substantial relation to interstate commerce. This allowed Congress to regulate just about any activity remotely related to interstate commerce. For example, in *Wickard v. Filburn* the Supreme Court ruled that federal law could regulate how much wheat a farmer could grow even if the farmer grew wheat on his own farm and fed it to his own cattle. The federal law, the Supreme Court ruled, was Constitutional because the farmer's wheat production decreased the overall demand for wheat traded through interstate commerce. If Congress can regulate a farmer growing and consuming his own wheat, then there is very little Congress cannot regulate.

For fifty years, the Supreme Court upheld every federal law and regulation that was based on the commerce clause. In 1995, however, the Supreme Court signaled a limit to the federal commerce power in *United States v. Lopez,* 115 S. Ct. 1624 (1995). In this case, the Supreme Court ruled that the commerce power did not authorize Congress to pass a law banning guns inside or near schools. It is not clear whether this case is an anomaly or signals a new willingness of the Supreme Court to limit the federal government's powers.

Contemporary Federalism

The Constitutional ambiguities outlined above create flexibility in our governmental system and allow American government to adapt to various circumstances. In the last century, America has risen from an island on the edge of the world to a global Superpower. We have moved from a rural society and economy to a service economy in the information age. Profound changes characterize our internal and external circumstances. American government has changed profoundly as well: Constitutional amendments have dramatically altered federal-State relations; and the federal and State government have both assumed new powers and responsibilities. Despite these changes, federalism persists and with it intergovernmental conflicts.

While public opinion and the federal judiciary have played important roles in changing our federal system, they are not the only factors determining the victor of an intergovernmental power grab. The federal judiciary is often silent on intergovernmental disputes, and public opinion is rarely expressed in such a manner as to give one level of government clear support over another.

Capacity and commitment are two other important factors to consider when evaluating which level of government will prevail in an intergovernmental conflict. Capacity refers to a government's resources and abilities. An important component of a government's capacity is the financial resources available to the government. The commitment of a government's officials determines how active and aggressive those officials are in protecting and promoting their government's power. In setting the federal and State governments against each other, the founders were hoping to counteract ambition with ambition. In order for this to work, officials from both governments must be ambitious and committed to protecting and promoting their government's interests. The commitment of soldiers to their cause is one of the most important determinants of success in a conflict. Officials committed to expanding their offices' authority and prerogatives have an advantage over those more timid or less interested in an intergovernmental conflict.

During the 20th century the federal government has assumed greater authority and responsibility over domestic affairs than at any time in the past. Federal authority prevailed because of the popularly perceived need for national authority, improved federal capacity and the commitment of federal officials to their causes.

The Progressive Era: 1890–1913

At the turn of the century, Americans felt threatened by social, economic and political upheavals. Big business, propelled by the railroads and industrialization, stormed across the land with apparent impunity for State regulations. Exploited workers organized into large unions and brought strikes and violence before realizing reform. New immigrants rallied around political machines whose political bosses were more interested in patronage and power than preserving liberty and the principles of American government.

Liberty—control over the political institutions and the decisions that affect one's life—appeared to flow to the few elites who controlled these mega-structures. In response, a generation of reformers crusaded to replace representative government with direct popular rule, end the political machines, strengthen the federal government, prohibit alcohol and make the world safe for democracy.[36]

These "progressive" reformers fundamentally altered the relationship between the federal and state governments in 1913 when they succeeded in adding the 16th and 17th Amendments to the Constitution. The 16th Amendment authorized the federal government to tax individual's incomes and thereby significantly enhanced federal capacity by giving the federal government a new and productive source of revenue.

The 17th Amendment changed the manner for electing United States' Senators. Prior to the 17th Amendment, Senators were elected by a State's Legislature. State Legislatures, with varying degrees of success, would occasionally instruct their Senators how to vote. Reformers claimed that allowing State legislatures to elect Senators gave the political parties too much power and encouraged corruption.[37] After the 17th Amendment, the people of each State elected their United States' Senators. Senators' allegiance and attention, consequently, shifted from their State governments to the public within their respective States and the United States Senate responded to public opinion quicker and with more sensitivity.[38]

The Great Depression and the New Deal

Demands for federal intervention increased dramatically after the stock market crashed in 1929 and plunged the United States into the Great Depression. At the time, responsibility for helping the poor and indigent fell to the State governments, but with 25 percent of the workforce unemployed the States lacked the fiscal capacity to provide for the destitute hordes.

In 1933, President Roosevelt assumed the presidency and pushed more than 15 major acts through Congress in his first 100 days. These acts gave the federal government considerable control over domestic issues previously considered the responsibility of State and local governments. Two years later, the Supreme Court declared many of President Roosevelt's policies unconstitutional on the grounds that they exceeded the federal government's power.

Despite the Supreme Court's rulings, public opinion favored increasing the federal government's power. In a 1936 opinion poll, 56 percent of the American public supported concentrating power in the federal government, only 44 percent favored concentrating power in the State governments.[39] The public also returned President Roosevelt to office in a landslide election.

Basking in favorable public opinion and the election win, President Roosevelt made two changes that gave the federal government authority to implement policies similar to those declared unconstitutional. First, upset by the Supreme Court's rulings, President Roosevelt threatened to "pack the court" by adding six new justices, all of whom would be appointed by him. Shortly after the proposal was made, the Supreme Court switched and began supporting President Roosevelt's programs.

Second, rather than implement the policies through the federal government, the States were given federal funds, called grants-in-aid, as an inducement to implement the federal government's policies. The grants were voluntary, that is the States could refuse them, but if the States accepted the grants they would have to abide by the conditions attached to the grants. The Supreme Court had ruled in 1923 that **grants-in-aid** were constitutional, as long as State participation was voluntary (*Frothingham v. Mellon,* 262 U.S. 447 (1923)). Grants-in-aid to the states rose from $217 million in 1932 to $744 million in 1941.

Public confidence, State capacity and State officials' commitment to their government reached a nadir during the Great Depression. Given the

States' fiscal crisis during the Great Depression and popular demand for government action, the States were not about to refuse federal monetary assistance even if the attached conditions contradicted State policy. One scholar noted: "From the viewpoint of the efficacy of state government, the states lost their confidence, and the people their faith in the states; the new media became cynical, the political scientists neglectful, and the critics became harsh."[40]

President Roosevelt's response to the Great Depression began a new era of federalism. By 1980 there were more than 500 categorical grant programs distributing $91.5 billion to State and local governments.[41] Former Utah Governor, Scott Matheson complained that these grants affected programs once considered "wholly State or local in nature, such as support for fire protection, libraries, police, sidewalks, noise control, solid waste disposal and others."[42] While federal intervention through grants-in-aid increased, state officials were reticent to engage in intergovernmental battles. One author referred to the governors of the 1950s and 1960s as "Goodtime Charlies," in office to enjoy the perks of office but not committed to protecting or promoting their State's interests.

The system of federalism that emerged from President Roosevelt's New Deal became know as **cooperative federalism.** Under cooperative federalism, the federal government cooperates with the states to implement and oversee public policy. The federal government may do this by providing money and other resources to help the states fulfill the programs' requirements. The federal government's influence stemmed from the fact that the federal government had a greater fiscal capacity, federal officials were committed to using federal powers to address popular ills, and public support for federal intervention.

Federal Deficits and the End of the Cold War

The tables began to reverse, however, in the 1980s and 1990s. Growing deficits and the national debt threatened the fiscal integrity and, consequently, the influence of the federal government. By 1995, 85 percent of the revenue collected by the federal government was already committed to pay for national defense, interest on the national debt, and entitlements (money committed to Social Security, Medicaid, Medicare and welfare programs). Only 15 cents of every dollar collected by the federal government was available to fund other programs. This severely limited the federal government's ability to create and fund additional programs. The federal government therefore lacked the capacity to fund new grants-in-aid for new programs. At the same time, States reformed their tax systems to make them more efficient. By the late 1990s, total revenues collected by State and local governments exceeded revenues collected by the federal government. The State governments' capacity gave them some independence from federal money and allowed them to refuse federal grant-in-aid programs.

Faced with increasingly independent State governments and lacking the money to induce the states to implement federal programs, the federal government turned to other means to control the States. The federal government may use **preemptions** to prohibit the States from taking specific actions and **mandates** to force specific actions from the State governments. During the 1980s, federal preemptions and mandates increased by 75 percent.[43] Some labeled this the era of **cooptive federalism.**

The States, however, are not powerless. Because the States implement the programs, the States have considerable power to determine how, and often what, programs and regulations will be implemented. For example, when the federal government deposited nuclear waste in Idaho against Governor Andrus's wishes, Governor Andrus ordered the state police to stop the trucks transporting the nuclear waste after they crossed the Idaho border. The state troopers then performed a safety inspection on the trucks. If they found anything slightly wrong with the truck, they declared it unsafe and ordered it to turn around and leave Idaho. Because Governor Andrus's plan forced a number of trucks to leave the State without depositing their load, Governor Andrus was able to force the federal government to negotiate with him over the disposal of nuclear waste.

State influence also increased as public confidence began shifting away from the federal government and towards State governments. During the 1980s, President Reagan's attacks on the evils of government focused public awareness on the problems of the federal government. The collapse of communism and the end of the Cold War in the early 1990s further weakened the justification for a strong national government. Meanwhile, many State governments implemented innovative and popular policies in such areas as welfare reform, education, environmental protection and pollution control. In 1995, 64 percent of those polled favored concentrating power in the State governments, compared to only 26 percent who favored concentrating power in the federal government.[44]

The Devolution Revolution

In 1994, Republicans won a majority in both houses of Congress. Almost immediately they proposed reducing the size of the federal government and sending power back to the States. Some commentators suggested that America was entering a ***Devolution Revolution*** with the pendulum of governmental power shifting from federal dominance back to the states.

Congressional attention to federalism in 1995 and 1996 stemmed less from a sincere desire to restore balance to the federal system than from the need for State expertise and support. In the 1994 elections, the Republicans ran on *The Contract with America* which outlined 10 reforms they would vote on if elected. None of those reforms mentioned federalism or returning power to the States. After being elected, the Republicans were faced with trying to find the means to accomplish what they had promised. The Republican Governors came to their assistance in two ways. First, the newly-elected Republicans were inexperienced with creating policy and governing. As the minority, their role was basically to attack proposals presented by the Democrats. As the majority, they had to create legislation that would actually govern the country. Lacking experience on how the programs worked and what reforms were possible, the Republican leaders of Congress turned to the Republican governors who knew the programs and had experimented with many of the reforms.

Second, the Republican Governors agreed to accept less federal money for programs like welfare and Medicaid in exchange for flexibility in implementing the programs. Theoretically this should have saved the federal government a significant amount of money and helped the Republicans achieve their goal of balancing the federal budget. While President Clinton and the Democrats in Congress prevented the Republicans from achieving all their objectives, significant elements were still approved.

By 1997 things had changed, yet again. A vibrant economy created budget surpluses, four years before even the most radical proposals projected. Two years as the majority party in Congress gave the Republican members of Congress experience governing Congress and the country and they relied less on the governors to help them write policy and build public support. Also, President Clinton's successful reelection (and later the 1998 election which decreased the Republicans majority in Congress) sent a signal that the public was not ready to send all power and responsibility back to the states.

The States v. the Federal Government—Today

In the last century, power has shifted in fits and starts to the federal government. In some areas of the country, there is a rising sentiment that the States are powerless to resist or restrain the federal government. This section compares the relative strengths and weaknesses of the two levels of government by looking at a few of the factors that will influence the different governments' capacity, commitment, and public confidence.

Capacity

The fiscal capacity of all levels of government is threatened by an American public that appears to have reached its tolerance-level for taxes. Rather than raising existing taxes, new types of taxes are proposed alongside sweeping tax reforms. New taxes and tax reforms could significantly alter the different governments' fiscal capacity and hence their odds in an intergovernmental conflict.

A fight is currently brewing over sales taxes. In 1994, only 8 percent of the federal government's revenue came from sales taxes, but 49 percent of State revenues came from sales taxes. Most States depend on the sales tax as their primary revenue generator. The States' ability to collect sales taxes, however, is threatened by the Internet because States do not collect taxes for most Internet transactions. If the Internet becomes a major source of revenue the States could see a serious decline in revenues. Some, like Utah's Governor Leavitt, have proposed mechanisms that would allow the States to collect taxes for sales conducted over the Internet. Congress is considering whether to place a moratorium on Internet taxes. Such a moratorium could devastate the states.[45]

The States' capacity to organize and confront the federal government is hampered by the fact that the States' interests differ. The Internet tax issue is a prime example. States like Massachusetts and Oregon do not have sales taxes, and states like California and New York would profit more from active Internet exchanges than they would lose in sales tax receipts. These states thus support a moratorium on Internet taxes. California, New York and Massachusetts represent over 20 percent of the seats in the United States House of Representatives. Thus, while a vast majority of States may oppose the Internet Tax Act, their voice is significantly degraded by a few select States pursuing their own interests rather than the collective interests of the States.

Commitment

In the 20th century, State officials' ambition to counteract the federal government has been weak. The problem is not that State officials aren't committed; it is that they are usually committed to promoting the interests of their own States rather than the common interests of all the States. For example, in the 1980s, Michigan's Governor Jim Blanchard wanted to enroll more poor people in Medicaid. Governor Blanchard lobbied Congress to mandate all States to increase the pool of Medicaid eligibles. Congress approved the mandate and Governor Blanchard got his program along with federal funding to cover a significant portion of the expenses.[46] In another example, California Governor successfully lobbied Congress to approve elements of his juvenile justice program after the California State Legislature rejected it. In both instances, individual governors benefitted from, and therefore lobbied for, the proposed federal mandates.

Besides asking for federal intervention, State officials may not oppose federal intervention for several reasons. State officials often fail to act because they are so busy with problems within their States they lack the time or energy to monitor and oppose federal activities. Federal intervention or mandates also allows State officials to shift blame and responsibility to the federal government. Also, State officials may rely on other States to oppose the federal government or they may get a special deal from the federal government to remain silent. The collective capacity of the States is great, yet, because of the problems of collective action, the States often fail to pool their resources, coordinate their activities and collectively oppose federal interventions.

A few governors have aggressively defended the States against federal intervention. These governors argue that the States can govern better, and are more innovative and efficient than the federal government. In 1995 and 1996, these governors risked the ire of their constituents and spent a lot of time in Washington, D.C. lobbying Congress to give the states greater authority to write and oversee social policy like welfare and Medicaid. This commitment helped a few governors in 1996 win Congressional approval for all States to reform their welfare programs.

While State officials' commitment to States' interests appears to be increasing, federal officials' commitment to using federal machinery to resolve problems is not decreasing. When federal officials observe a problem, they are less likely today to leave the problem to State or local governments. Representative Schumer (D-NY) explained the motives of many members of Congress when he said: "When my constituents have a problem, they expect me to fix it. They care if it's the responsibility of the State governments, they want it fixed." Members of Congress are quick to use federal machinery to solve problems championed by an all-pervasive media. Those same Republicans who were quick to tout devolution in 1995 and 1996 now search State laws to find successful policies they can implement through the federal government.

Confidence

While public confidence is not the determining factor Hamilton and Madison suggested it would be, it is nonetheless very important. A 1999 Gallup poll found 80 percent of the public expressing a high level of trust in State government (that is up from 63 percent in 1972). Only 61 percent of the American public expressed a similar level of confidence in the federal government's ability to handle domestic issues (compared to 70 percent in 1972).[47] Public perception of the States is also helped considerably by growing confidence that the Southern States will not violate the civil liberties of minorities if given the opportunity.[48] Despite public trust in State governments, the pendulum of power will not swing to the States' favor without ambitious State officials who are committed to protecting and promoting their governments' powers.

Federalism and the 21st Century

When the framers of the Constitution agreed to make America a federal system, they determined that America should be composed of many communities with considerable freedom. In the 20th Century, largely as a result of foreign threats and domestic upheavals, Americans willingly supported greater federal authority—a movement towards one community. America now stands at a crossroads. We are answering anew the question whether we want one community or many, and if many how much freedom should those communities have? The crossroads provides essentially two paths: diversity and innovation or uniformity and equality. Each path has its possible benefits and dangers.

Diversity and Innovation

Allowing many communities considerable freedom insures diversity in the laws that govern the different communities. Each community, through democratic means, can determine the laws that govern their society. One community may cho0se to set and enforce moral standards prohibiting X-rated material, other communities may consider such standards undesirable limits on individual freedom. Proponents of allowing communities significant latitude to determine the laws governing the society argue that individuals in the community who dislike the laws are free to move to communities with laws they support. This is called voting with your feet. Whether individuals will give up their jobs and families to move to a different community is debatable.

Diversity also allows the different communities to devise innovative policies. The States have long been called "the laboratories of democracy" because their experiments demonstrate for others what policies are successful and which are not. The welfare reform act that passed in 1996 grew largely from experiments in Wisconsin and Michigan and many of the educational reforms touted in Washington are successful State experiments. Successful State experiments can be adopted by other States or the federal government. National implementation of a successful policy insures that all qualifying recipients benefit from the policy. However, a policy that works in rural Vermont may not work in Los Angeles. Furthermore, if the federal government adopts the experiment and implements it nationally, the States are usually prohibited from conducting further policy experiments in that area. As conditions change, the federal policy may fail and no new policy experiments exist suggesting alternatives.

Opponents of diversity and innovation suggest four critiques. First, communities which define their own laws may infringe the civil liberties of individuals or groups they dislike. Second, communities may benefit from activities that harm others. For example, States benefit economically when rivers or winds carry pollution produced inside the State outside to other States. For example, coal burned in the Great Plains' States to produce electricity produces acid rain in the Northeastern States, which toxifies lakes and kills vegetation in that region. Forcing States to prevent or clean up pollution may require stringent pollution controls approved and enforced by the federal government

Third, some fear that allowing the States to create their own policies will lead to a "race to the bottom." According to this thesis, States try to keep taxes and public expenditures low to attract businesses. States, therefore, will not approve programs that increase their costs or attract unattractive elements. States with a generous welfare policy, for example, could become a welfare magnet, attracting poor people. More poor people equals higher costs, higher taxes and less chance that businesses will locate there. In order to prevent this from happening, States approve welfare policies less generous than those of the neighboring States. Neighboring States will consequently cut their welfare policies to maintain their competitive edge. This creates a **race to the bottom** as each State amends its welfare policy to insure that it provides less benefits than the surrounding States. Hence, the problem of allowing the states to innovate is that their innovations may actually have a negative impact rather than positive impact on society. This thesis is controversial and evidence exists supporting and countering it.

Fourth, diverse policies are inherently unequal. This is particularly evident in education. Some school districts are richer than others and can provide more programs and better quality than other school districts. Many feel that all Americans, and especially children, should have an equal opportunity to succeed. Gross inequities in education, they argue, reverberates through society and impairs America's ideal of equality for all.

Uniformity and Equality

The second path America may chose for the 21st century is to continue moving towards uniformity and equality. Uniform standards prevent one area from benefitting at the expense of others and insures that basic standards are upheld throughout the nation. For example, parents in Texas lobbied the federal government to force Louisiana to raise its drinking age from eighteen to twenty-one because many teenagers were driving to Louisiana for a night of drinking and then crashed and died on the way home. Many people also prefer that the federal government resolve such controversial questions as abortion or gay rights rather than leaving the question to the States. Businesses prefer that the federal government establish a single standard rather than allowing fifty different standards—one for each State .

Pursuing uniformity and equality gives the federal government the predominant voice in shaping the policies governing America. Shifting responsibility for making policy to the federal government removes that responsibility from the local communities. When citizens are but one voice in a sea of 250 million, they feel that they have little influence on the outcome. As a sense of powerlessness increase, citizen apathy for government grows as well.

Schools provide a cogent example of the tradeoff between activity and equality. Many parents are concerned about the education of their children and want to participate in the substantive decisions that affect how and what children are taught. Education is one of those issues that has remained largely in control of the State and local governments. Recently, however, commissions have suggested it is necessary that the federal government direct educational reforms to insure America's children learn what they need in order for America to be competitive in the 21st century. Should the decision over what children are taught be made by parents in a local or State community? Or should experts on the national level determine how and what schools teach? Giving the authority to the federal government will remove another local power of the citizens and place it in a complex and convoluted government. It will further promote citizens feelings of powerlessness regarding their government. Leaving the responsibility in the hands of the parents may risk teaching children outdated or even false information, and give those children a disadvantage in the competition of life.

Once again Americans are debating the fundamental questions that concerned the founders. The confederalists at the Constitutional Convention and the Anti-Federalists worried that giving the national government too much power would produce selfish individuals by undermining the people's desire and ability to participate in politics and shape the laws that governed them. The concerns of the nationalists and Federalists still echo that giving States and localities too much discretion will unnecessarily jeopardize civil liberties, undermine the national good, and produce unwise policies. The shape of federalism in the 21st century depends on how the American public and leaders answer anew our fundamental questions.

Related Reading

Storing, Herbert. *What the Anti-Federalists Were For.*

Notes

[1] In *The Federalist Papers* #82, Alexander Hamilton wrote that "questions of intricacy and nicety" would result from dividing sovereignty, but 'tis time only that can mature and perfect so compound a system, can liquidate the meaning of all the parts, and can adjust them to each other in a harmonious and consistent whole." All cites of *The Federalist Papers* in this chapter are from the 1987 Penguin Classics edition, edited by Isaac Kramnick.

[2] Martha Derthick, "Up-to-Date in Kansas City: Reflections on American Federalism," *PS: Political Science and Politics,* December 1992: 671–5.

[3] Samuel Beer, "Federalism, Nationalism and Democracy in America," *American Political Science Review* 72, 1 (1978), 10.

[4] See Martin Diamond, "What the Framers meant by Federalism," *As Far as Republican Principles Will Admit* (Washington, D.C.: The AEI Press, 1992).

[5] Ibid.

[6] These ideas were developed by the French political philosopher, Montesquieu in his *Spirit of the Laws.*

[7] James Madison, *Notes of the Debates in the Federal Convention of 1787* (New York: W.W. Norton & Company, 1987), Originally published in 1966 by Ohio.

[8] James Madison, *Notes of the Debates in the Federal Convention of 1787* (New York: W.W. Norton & Company, 1987), Originally published in 1966 by Ohio University Press, Notes from the convention, 75–77.

[9] Beers op. cit., 14.

[10] Joseph F. Zimmerman, *Contemporary American Federalism: the Growth of National Power* (Connecticut: Praeger, 1992), 23.

[11] *The Federalist Papers,* op. cit., 51:318–9.

[12] *The Federalist Papers,* op. cit., 51:321.

[13] *The Federalist Papers,* op. cit., 46.

[14] See *The Federalist Papers,* op. cit., 34:230 for a discussion of the concurrent powers.

[15] The House of Representatives rejected adding the word "expressly" to what became the Tenth Amendment on August 18 and 21. See Helen Veit, et al., *Creating the Bill of Rights: The Documentary Record from the First Federal Congress, B*altimore: John Hopkins Press: 33.

[16] *The Federalist Papers,* op. cit., 51.

[17] Malbin, Michael J. "Congress During the Convention and Ratification." *The Framing and Ratification of the Constitution* ed. by Leonard W. Levy and Dennis J. Mahoney. New York: Macmillan, 1987.

[18] *The Federalist Papers,* op. cit., 28:206.

[19] *The Federalist Papers,* op. cit., 46:297.

[20] *The Federalist Papers,* op. cit., 27:201.

[21] *The Federalist Papers,* op. cit., 27:203.

[22] *U.S. Term Limits, Inc. v. Thornton,* 115 s. Ct. 1842, 1872 (1995).

[23] Quoted in Gordon Wood, *The Creation of the American Republic, 1776–1787,* New York: W.W. Norton and Company, 530–1.

[24] *U.S. Term Limits v. Thornton* (115 S.Ct. 1842).

[25] In *The American Commonwealth,* James Bryce wrote: "The word "sovereignty," which has in many ways clouded the domain of public law and jurisprudence, confused men's minds by making them assume that there must in every country exist, and be discoverable by legal inquiry, either one body invested legally with supreme power over all minor bodies, or serval bodies which, though they had consented to form part of a larger body, were each in the last resort independent of it, and responsible to none but themselves. They forgot that a Constitution may not have determined where legal supremacy shall dwell. Where the Constitution of the United States placed it was at any rate doubtful, so doubtful that it would have been better to drop technicalities, and recognize the broad fact that the legal claims of the States had become incompatible with the historical as well as legal claims of the nation. In the uncertainty as to where legal right resided, it would have been prudent to consider where physical force resided."

[26] *The Federalist Papers,* op. cit., 39:258.

[27] *The Federalist Papers,* op. cit., 39:258.

[28] See Derthick, op. cit., 672.

[29] quoted by Scheiber 1996, 238.

[30] Derthick, op. cit., 672.

[31] See for example *New York v. U.S. or Lopez v. U.S.*

[32] Brutus, as quoted in Miroff's book, p. A-20.

[33] Jefferson, Thomas. 1975. *The Portable Thomas Jefferson,* ed. by Merrill D. Peterson. New York, New York: Penguin Books, 262.

[34] *McCulloch v. Maryland,* 17 U.S. 315. (p. 399 in the red con. law book).

[35] The Supreme Court uses the term "dual federalism" in the case *Abelman v. Booth,* 21 Howard 506 at 516 (1859).

[36] See Richard Hofstadter, *The Age of Reform,* New York: Vintage Books, 18.

[37] See Daynes, Byron W. 1971. "The Impact of the Direct Election of Senators on the Political System." Ph.D. diss., University of Chicago.

[38] Crook, Sara Brandes and John R. Hibbing. 1997. "A Not-so-distant Mirror: the 17th Amendment and Congressional Change." *American Political Science Review* 91 (December): 852.

[39] Rockefeller Institute Bulletin, p. 14.

[40] Terry Sanford, quoted by Larry Sabato in *Goodbye to Goodtime Charlie.*

[41] Matheson 1986, 20.

[42] Matheson 1986, 20.

[43] Conlan, Beam and Colella. 1993 *Federal Regulation of State and Local Governments: The Mixed Record of the 1980s.* Washington, D.C.: ACIR.

[44] The Rockefeller Institute Bulletin, p. 14.

[45] In this context it is interesting to note Alexander Hamilton's words on the importance of taxation for a government: "Money is with propriety considered as the vital principle of the body politic; as that which sustains its life and motion, and enables it to perform its most essential function. A complete power, therefore, to procure a regular and adequate supply of revenue, as far as the resources of the community will permit, may be regarded as an indispensable ingredient in every constitution . . . the "federal government must of necessity be vested with an unqualified power of taxation," and "the individual states should possess an independent and uncontrollable authority to raise their own revenue for the supply of their wants." (*The Federalist Papers*, 30–6).

[46] See also: Keith Boeckelman, "The influence of stats on federal policy adoptions," *Policy Studies Journal* 20, 3 (1992), 365–75.

[47] David W. Moore, "Public Trust in Federal Government Remains High," *Gallup News Service*, January 8, 1999; at: http://205.219.140.75/poll%5 Farchives/990108.htm.

[48] Martha Derthick calls this the "end of Southern exceptionalism" and means that "the case for the states can at last begin to be discussed on its merits." Quoted by Richard Nathan in "The 'Devolution Revolution': An overview," *Rockefeller Institute Bulletin*, 1996: 13.

MAJOR SUPREME COURT CASES

Gary Daynes

Marbury v. *Madison* (1803)

Thomas Jefferson began his first term of office in 1801. Jefferson had drafted the Declaration of Independence and well-remembered cutting ties with England. One of his principal goals had been to limit the power of government and rest that power in the people, avoiding the oppression which had caused them to flee England and fight the Revolutionary War. His time as president would test his devotion to limited government.

Just before handing the presidency over to Jefferson, President John Adams made some last minute appointments. Jefferson belonged to the Democratic Republican party and Adams, a Federalist, wanted to leave the government with as many Federalists as possible. He appointed 42 new justices of the peace in the District of Columbia, among them, William Marbury. Unfortunately, his secretary of state, John Marshall, failed to deliver the appointments to the justices before Jefferson took office. When the new secretary of state, James Madison, refused to deliver the commissions, William Marbury filed suit against him. Marbury requested a *writ of mandamus,* claiming that Section 13 of the Judiciary Act of 1789 gave the Supreme Court the right to issue such a writ.

The case was heard in 1803 in the Supreme Court by Chief Justice John Marshall. Ironically, it was Marshall (as Adams' secretary of state) who had failed to deliver the commissions in question in the case. President Adams had appointed him to the Supreme Court just before leaving office in 1801. *Marbury* v. *Madison* was one of his first cases.

In his ruling, Marshall reviewed the Judiciary Act of 1789. In Section 13 of the Act, Congress had given the Supreme Court the right to serve a writ of mandamus on an original jurisdiction only in specific cases, and in all other cases would only have appellate jurisdiction. In other words, since Marbury had started with the Supreme Court (original jurisdiction), Marshall declared the Court powerless to issue a writ. Had Marbury started in a lower court and appealed to the Supreme Court (appellate jurisdiction), Marshall would have been able to serve the writ on Madison, according to the Judiciary Act. Thus, the Jefferson administration won the case.

Marshall's ruling did not stop there. Citing Article III of the Constitution, Marshall voided Section 13 of the Judiciary Act of 1789. He stated that the Constitution of the United States did not specifically mention the right to issue a writ of mandamus and therefore, Section 13 of the Judiciary Act of 1789 was inconsistent with Constitutional law.

The significance of this decision was phenomenal. Chief Justice Marshall had given the Supreme Court the right of judicial review. In his function as a member of the judicial branch of government, he had assumed the right to void an action taken by the legislative branch. In defining judicial review he said, "It is, emphatically, the province and duty of the judicial department, to say what the law is." Marshall's ruling redefined Congress' power to pass laws only as far as they did not supersede the Constitution.

Marbury v. *Madison*

5 U.S. (1 Cranch) 137, 2 L.Ed. 60 (1803)

The opinion of the Court was delivered by the CHIEF JUSTICE [MARSHALL]. . . .

The first object of inquiry is—Has the applicant a right to the commission he demands? . . . [The court finds that as Marbury's appointment was complete he has a right to the commission.]

2. This brings us to the second inquiry; which is: If he has a right, and that right has been violated, do the laws of this country afford him a remedy? . . . [The court finds that they do.]

3. It remains to be inquired whether he is entitled to the remedy for which he applies? This depends on 1st. The nature of the writ applied for: and 2d. The power of this court.

1st. . . . This, then, is a plain case for a *mandamus*, either to deliver the commission, or a copy of it from the record: and it only remains to be inquired, whether it can issue from this court.

The act to establish the judicial courts of the United States authorizes the supreme court "to issue writs of *mandamus,* in cases warranted by the principles and usages of law, to any Courts appointed, or persons holding office, under the authority of the United States." . . . The constitution vests the whole judicial power of the United States in one supreme Court, and such inferior courts as congress shall, from time to time, ordain and establish. This power is expressly extended to all cases arising under the laws of the United States; and consequently, in some form, may be exercised over the present case; because the right claimed is given by a law of the United States.

In the distribution of this power, it is declared, that "the supreme court shall have original jurisdiction, in all cases affecting ambassadors, other public ministers and consuls, and those in which a state shall be a party. In all other cases, the supreme court shall have appellate jurisdiction." . . . If it had been intended to leave it in the discretion of the legislature, to apportion the judicial power between the supreme and inferior courts, according to the will of that body, it would certainly have been useless to have proceeded further than to have defined the judicial power, and the tribunals in which it should be vested. The subsequent part of the section is mere surplusage—is entirely without meaning, if such is to be the construction. If congress remains at liberty to give this court appellate jurisdiction, where the constitution has declared their jurisdiction shall be original: and original jurisdiction where the constitution has declared it shall be appellate; the distribution of jurisdiction, made in the constitution, is form without substance. . . . To enable this Court, then, to issue a *mandamus,* it must be shown to be an exercise of appellate jurisdiction, or to be necessary to enable them to exercise appellate jurisdiction. . . . It is the essential criterion of appellate jurisdiction, that it revises and corrects the proceedings in a cause already instituted, and does not create that cause. Although therefore, a *mandamus* may be directed to courts, yet to issue such a writ to an officer, for the delivery of a paper, is, in effect, the same as to sustain an original action for that paper, and therefore, seems not to belong to appellate, but to original jurisdiction. Neither is it necessary in such a case as this to enable the court to exercise its appellate jurisdiction. The authority, therefore, given to the supreme court, by the act establishing the judicial courts of the United States, to issue writs of *mandamus* to public officers, appears not to be warranted by the constitution; and it becomes necessary to inquire whether a jurisdiction so conferred can be exercised.

The question, whether an act, repugnant to the constitution, can become the law of the land, is a question deeply interesting to the United States: but, happily, not of an intricacy proportioned to its interest. It seems only necessary to recognize certain principles, supposed to have been long and well established, to decide it. That the people have an original right to establish, for their future government, such principles as, in their opinion, shall most conduce to their own happiness, is the basis on which the whole American fabric has been erected. The exercise of this original right is a very great exertion; nor can it, nor ought it, to be frequently repeated. The principles, therefore, so established, are deemed fundamental: and as the authority from which they proceed is supreme, and can seldom act, they are designed to be permanent.

This original and supreme will organizes the government, and assigns to different departments their respective powers. It may either stop here, or establish certain limits not to be transcended by those departments. The government of the United States is of the latter description. The powers of the legislature are defined and limited; and that those limits may not be mistaken, or forgotten, the constitution is written. To what purpose are powers limited, and to what purpose is that limitation committed to writing, if these limits may, at any time, be passed by those intended to be restrained? The distinction between a government with limited and unlimited powers is abolished, if those limits do not confine the persons on whom they are imposed, and if acts prohibited and acts allowed, are of equal obligation. It is a proposition too plain to be contested, that the constitution controls any legislative act repugnant to it; or, that the legislature may alter the constitution by an ordinary act.

Between these alternatives, there is no middle ground. The constitution is either a superior paramount law, unchangeable by ordinary means, or it is on a level with ordinary legislative acts, and, like other acts, is alterable when the legislature shall please to alter it. If the former part of the alternative be true, then a legislative act, contrary to the constitution, is not law; if the latter part be true, then written constitutions are absurd attempts, on the part of the people, to limit a power, in its own nature, illimitable.

Certainly, all those who have framed written constitutions contemplate them as forming the fundamental and paramount law of the nation, and consequently, the theory of every such government must be, that an act of the legislature, repugnant to the constitution, is void. This theory is essentially attached to a written constitution, and is, consequently, to be considered, by this court, as one of the fundamental principles of our society. It is not, therefore, to be lost sight of, in the further consideration of this subject.

If an act of the legislature, repugnant to the constitution, is void, does it, notwithstanding its invalidity, bind the courts, and oblige them to give it effect? Or, in other words, though it be not law, does it constitute a rule as operative as if it was a law? This would be to overthrow, in fact, what was established in theory; and would seem, at first view, an absurdity too gross to be insisted on. It shall, however, receive a more attentive consideration.

It is, emphatically, the province and duty of the judicial department, to say what the law is. Those who apply the rule to particular cases, must of necessity expound and interpret that rule. If two laws conflict with each other, the courts must decide on the operation of each. So, if a law be in opposition to the constitution; if both the law and the constitution apply to a particular case, so that the court must either decide that case, conformably to the law, disregarding the constitution; or conformably to the constitution, disregarding the law; the court must determine which of these conflicting rules governs the case: this is of the very essence of judicial duty. If then, the courts are to regard the constitution, and the constitution is superior to any ordinary act of the legislature, the constitution, and not such ordinary act, must govern the case to which they both apply.

Those, then, who controvert the principle, that the constitution is to be considered, in court, as a paramount law, are reduced to the necessity of maintaining that courts must close their eyes on the constitution, and see only the law. This doctrine would subvert the very foundation of all written constitutions. It would declare that an act which, according to the principles and theory of our government, is entirely void, is yet, in practice, completely obligatory. It would declare, that if the legislature shall do what is expressly forbidden, such act, notwithstanding the express prohibition, is in reality effectual. It would be giving to the legislature a practical and real omnipotence, with the same breath which professes to restrict their powers within narrow limits. It is prescribing limits, and declaring that those limits may be passed at pleasure. That it thus reduces to nothing, what we have deemed the greatest improvement on political institutions, a written constitution, would, of itself, be sufficient, in America, where written constitutions have been viewed with so much reverence, for rejecting the construction. But the peculiar expressions of the constitution of the United States furnish additional arguments in favor of its rejection. The judicial power of the United States is extended to all cases arising under the constitution. Could it be the intention of those who gave this power, to say, that in using it, the constitution should not be looked into? That a case arising under the constitution should be decided, without examining the instrument under which it arises? This is too extravagant to be maintained. In some cases, then, the constitution must be looked into by the judges. And if they can open it at all, what part of it are they forbidden to read or to obey?

There are many other parts of the constitution which serve to illustrate this subject. It is declared, that "no tax or duty shall be laid on articles exported from any state." Suppose, a duty on the export of cotton, of tobacco, or of flour; and a suit instituted to recover it. Ought judgment to be rendered in such a case? Ought the judges to close their eyes on the constitution, and only see the law?

The constitution declares "that no bill of attainder or *ex post facto* law shall be passed." If, however, such a bill should be passed, and a person should be prosecuted under it, must the court condemn to death those victims whom the constitution endeavors to preserve?

"No person," says the constitution, "shall be convicted of treason, unless on the testimony of two witnesses to the same overt act, or on confession in open court." Here, the language of the constitution is addressed especially to the courts. It prescribes, directly for them, a rule of evidence not to be departed from. If the legislature should change that rule, and declare one witness, or a confession out of court, sufficient for conviction, must the constitutional principle yield to the legislative act?

From these, and many other selections which might be made, it is apparent, that the framers of the constitution contemplated that instrument as a rule for the government of courts, as well as of the legislature. Why otherwise does it direct the judges to take an oath to support it? This oath certainly applies, in an especial manner, to their conduct in their official character. How immoral to impose it on them, if they were to be used as the instruments, and the knowing instruments, for violating what they swear to support!

The oath of office, too, imposed by the legislature, is completely demonstrative of the legislative opinion on this subject. It is in these words: "I do solemnly swear, that I will administer justice, without respect to persons, and do equal right to the poor and to the rich; and that I will faithfully and impartially discharge all the duties incumbent on me as———, according to the best of my abilities and understanding, agreeable to the constitution and laws of the United States." Why does a judge swear to discharge his duties agreeably to the constitution of the United States, if that constitution forms no rule for his government? If it is closed upon him, and cannot be inspected by him? If such be the real state of things, this is worse than solemn mockery. To prescribe, or take this oath, becomes equally a crime.

It is also not entirely unworthy of observation, that in declaring what shall be the supreme law of the land, the constitution itself is first mentioned; and not the laws of the United States, generally, but those only which shall be made in pursuance of the constitution, have that rank.

Thus, the particular phraseology of the constitution of the United States confirms and strengthens the principle, supposed to be essential to all written constitutions, that a law repugnant to the constitution is void; and that courts, as well as other departments, are bound by that instrument.

The rule must be discharged.

Scott v. *Sanford* (1857)

In 1836, Dr. John Emerson and his slave, Dred Scott, left Missouri and moved to Louisiana territory. In March 1820, the Missouri Compromise had outlawed slavery north of the 36* 30' line in that region. Scott returned to Missouri and later filed a suit claiming that his move to Louisiana Territory had made him a free man. The lower court ruled in favor of Scott, however, the Missouri Supreme Court reversed the decision. In the meantime, ownership of Dred Scott was passed to John Sanford who became involved in the federal and Supreme Court cases. In February of 1856, the case of *Scott* v. *Sanford* entered the court of Chief Justice Roger B. Taney.

The social and political atmosphere of the time are of great relevance in understanding this case. In 1852, *Uncle Tom's Cabin,* by Harriet Beecher Stowe, was released and sold 3 million copies in the United States alone. The book prompted widespread sympathy for slaves. Women's organizations and other abolitionist groups fought for the end of slavery. In contrast, the southern economy relied on slavery since mass production and industrialization had not yet provided other options. By 1856, even Congress was deeply divided by sectional conflict over slavery.

With this background in mind, we turn to the case itself. In his decision, Chief Justice Taney first answered the question of citizenship for slaves. He said: "We think . . . [the people of the Negro race] . . . are not included, and were not intended to be included, under the words 'citizens' in the Constitution . . . on the contrary, they were at that time considered as a subordinate and inferior class of beings, who had been subjugated by the dominant race." Dred Scott was, therefore, not entitled to free citizenship even in a territory. He was, in fact, not entitled to sue in the courts, according to Taney.

The second part of the verdict was monumental. The Missouri Compromise of 1820 (an act of Congress), had declared slavery illegal in the territories, and was the basis for Dred Scott's case. Chief Justice Taney maintained that the Constitution applied equally to territories and states. Further, he extended the 5th Amendment prohibition of unreasonable search and seizure to private property, in this case Dred Scott. He said, "It is the opinion of the court that the act of Congress which prohibited a citizen from holding and owning property of this kind in the territory of the United States . . . is not warranted by the Constitution and is therefore void."

The effects of the decision were far reaching. First, it limited the power of Congress to control the slavery issue which was deeply dividing the nation. Secondly, it gave the Supreme Court's stamp of approval to slavery. Lastly, the decision only intensified the conflict between the pro and anti-slavery groups, pushing the United States closer to the Civil War.

Scott v. *Sandford**

(60 U.S. (19 Howard) 393, 15 L.Ed. 691 (1857)

MR. CHIEF JUSTICE TANEY delivered the opinion of the Court.

. . . The question is simply this: Can a negro, whose ancestors were imported into this country, and sold as slaves, become a member of the political community formed and brought into existence by the Constitution of the United States, and as such become entitled to all the rights, and privileges, and immunities guarantied by that instrument to the citizen? One of which rights is the privilege of suing in a court of the United States in the cases specified in the Constitution.

We think . . . [the people of the Negro race] . . . are not included, and were not intended to be included, under the words "citizens" in the Constitution, and can therefore claim none of the rights and privileges which that instrument provides for and secures to citizens of the United States. On the contrary, they were at that time considered as a subordinate and inferior class of beings, who had been subjugated by the dominant race, and, whether emancipated or not, yet remained subject to their authority, and had no rights or privileges but such as those who held the power and the Government might choose to grant them. . . .

The question then arises, whether the provisions of the Constitution, in relation to the personal rights and privileges to which the citizen of the State should be entitled, embraced the negro African race, at that time in this country, or who might afterwards be imported, who had then or should afterwards be made free in any State; and to put it in the power of a single State to make him a citizen of the United States, and endue him with the full rights of citizenship in every other State without their consent? Does the Constitution of the United States act upon him whenever he shall be made free under the laws of a State. and raised there to the rank of a citizen, and immediately clothe him with all the privileges of a citizen in every other State, and in its own courts?

The court thinks the affirmative of these propositions cannot be maintained. And if it cannot, the plaintiff in error could not be a citizen of the State of Missouri, within the meaning of the Constitution of the United States, and, consequently, was not entitled to sue in its courts. . . .

No one, we presume, supposes that any change in public opinion or feeling, in relation to this unfortunate race, in the civilized nations of Europe or in this country, should induce the court to give to the words of the Constitution a more liberal construction in their favor than they were intended to bear when the instrument was framed and adopted. Such an argument would be altogether inadmissible in any tribunal called on to interpret it. If any of its provisions are deemed unjust, there is a mode prescribed in the instrument itself by which it may be amended; but while it remains unaltered, it must be construed now as it was understood at the time of its adoption. It is not only the same in words, but the same in meaning, and delegates the same powers to the Government, and reserves and secures the same rights and privileges to the citizen; and as long as it continues to exist in its present form, it speaks not only in the same words, but with the same meaning and intent with which it spoke when it came from the hands of its framers, and was voted on and adopted by the people of the United States. Any other rule of construction would abrogate the judicial character of this court, and make it the mere reflex of the popular opinion of the day. . . .

What the construction was at that time, we think can hardly admit of doubt. We have the language of the Declaration of Independence and of the Articles of Confederation, in addition to the plain words of the Constitution itself; we have the legislation of the different States, before, about the time, and since, the Constitution was adopted; we have the legislation of Congress, from the time of its adoption to a recent period; and we have the constant and uniform action of the Executive Department, all concurring together, and leading to the same result. And if anything in relation to the construction of the Constitution can be regarded as settled, it is that which we now give to the word "citizen" and the word "people." . . .

The act of Congress, upon which the plaintiff relies, declares that slavery and involuntary servitude, except as a punishment for crime, shall be forever prohibited in all that part of the territory ceded by France, under the name of Louisiana, which lies north of thirty-six degrees thirty minutes north latitude, and not included within the limits of Missouri. And the . . . inquiry is whether Congress was authorized to pass this law under any of the powers granted to it by the Constitution; for if the authority is not given by that instrument, it is the duty of this court to declare it void and inoperative, and incapable of conferring freedom upon any one who is held as a slave under the laws of any one of the States.

The counsel for the plaintiff has laid much stress upon that article in the Constitution which confers on Congress the power "to dispose of and make all needful rules and regulations respecting the territory or other property belonging to the United States," but, in the judgment of the court, that provision has no bearing on the present controversy, and the power there given, whatever it may be, is confined, and was intended to be confined, to the territory which at that time belonged to, or was claimed by the United States, and was within their boundaries as settled by the treaty with Great Britain, and can have no influence upon a territory afterwards acquired from a foreign Government. It was a special provision for a known and particular territory, and to meet a present emergency, and nothing more.

. . . The powers of the Government and the rights and privileges of the citizen are regulated and plainly defined by the Constitution itself. And when the Territory becomes a part of the United States, the Federal Government enters into possession in the character impressed upon it by those who created it. It enters upon it with its powers over the citizen strictly defined, and limited by the Constitution, from which it derives its own existence, and by virtue of which alone it continues to exist and act as a Government and sovereignty. It has not power of any kind beyond it; and it cannot, when it enters a Territory of the United States, put off its character and assume discretionary or despotic powers which the Constitution has denied to it. It cannot create for itself a new character separated from the citizens of the United States, and the duties it owes them under the provisions of the Constitution. The Territory being a part of the United States, the Government and the citizen both enter it under the authority of the Constitution, with their respective rights defined and marked out; and the Federal Government can exercise no power over his person or property, beyond what that instrument confers, nor lawfully deny any right which it has reserved. . . .

. . . An Act of Congress which deprives a citizen of the United States of his liberty or property, merely because he came himself or brought his property into a particular Territory of the United States, and who had committed no offense against the laws, could hardly be dignified with the name of due process of law.

Upon these considerations, it is the opinion of the court that the act of Congress which prohibited a citizen from holding and owning property of this kind in the territory of the United States north of the line therein mentioned, is not warranted by the Constitution, and is therefore void; and that neither Dred Scott himself, nor any of his family, were made free by being carried into this territory; even if they had been carried there by the owner, with the intention of becoming a permanent resident. . . .

MR. JUSTICE CURTIS, joined by MR. JUSTICE MCLEAN, dissenting:

. . . To determine whether any free person descended from Africans held in slavery, were citizens of the United States under the Confederation, and consequently at the time the adoption of the Constitution of the United States, it is only necessary to know whether any such persons were citizens of either of the States under the Confederation, at the time of the adoption of the Constitution.

Of this there can be no doubt. At the time of the ratification of the Articles of Confederation, all free native-born inhabitants of the States of New Hampshire, Massachusetts, New York, New Jersey, and North Carolina, though descended from African slaves, were not only citizens of those States, but such of them as had the other necessary qualifications possessed the franchise of electors, on equal terms with other citizens. . . .

Having first decided that they were bound to consider the sufficiency of the plea to the jurisdiction of the Circuit Court, and having decided that this plea showed that the Circuit Court had no jurisdiction, and consequently that this is a case to which the judicial power of the United States does not extend, they have gone on to examine the merits of the case they appeared on the trial before the court and jury, on the issues joined on the pleas in bar, and so have reached the question of the power of Congress to pass the act of 1820. On so grave a subject as this, I feel obliged to say that, in my opinion, such an exertion of judicial power transcends the limits of the authority of the court, as described by its repeated decisions and, as I understand, acknowledged in this opinion of the majority of the court. . . .

Nor, in my judgment, will the position, that a prohibition to bring slaves into a Territory deprives any one of his property without due process of law, bear examination. . . .

Civil Rights Cases (1883)

The end of the Civil War required the government of the United States to decide the status of freedmen and their former owners. This effort, known as Reconstruction, led to three Constitutional amendments. The 13th Amendment ended slavery, the 14th guaranteed due process and equal protection of the laws to all citizens, and the 15th extended the vote to black men. Each was a landmark step for former slaves. Congress went one step further by passing the Civil Rights Act of 1875. This act outlawed racial segregation in public transportation and public facilities (except schools). These Reconstruction efforts met immediate opposition.

In 1883, a collection of five cases arrived before the Supreme Court. In each case, a black plaintiff claimed discrimination in violation of the Civil Rights Act of 1875. The Court perceived a dilemma. In a nation healing from war, the national government could either use its power to alleviate problems but risk maintaining the divide between North and South. Or it could leave most decision-making power to the states and risk the disappearance of the rights of the freedmen. Chief Justice Bradley took the second option. He argued that the 14th Amendment gave states, not the federal government, the responsibility of protecting the rights of its citizens. Therefore, Congress did not have the power to pass the Civil Rights Act of 1875, since it infringed on the power of the states.

As well-intentioned as the decision may have been, it operated on the assumption that the states had adequate laws in place to protect the rights of citizens. This was clearly not the case in the South. And so, as a result of the Court's decision in the *Civil Rights Cases of 1883*, states no longer felt constrained to guarantee the rights promised to blacks in the Constitution.

Civil Rights Cases

(*United States* v. *Stanley*)
109 U.S. 3, 3 S.Ct. 18, 27 L. Ed. 835 (1883)

MR. JUSTICE BRADLEY delivered the opinion of the Court. . . .

The essence of the law is, not to declare broadly that all persons shall be entitled to the full and equal enjoyment of the accommodations, advantages, facilities, and privileges of inns, public conveyances, and theatres., but that such enjoyment shall not be subject to any conditions applicable only to citizens of a particular race or color, or who had been in a previous condition of servitude. . . .

Has Congress constitutional power to make such a law? Of course, no one will contend that the power to pass it was contained in the Constitution before the adoption of the last three amendments. The power is sought, first, in the Fourteenth Amendment. . . .

It is State action of a particular character that is prohibited. Individual invasion of individual rights is not the subject matter of the amendment. It has a deeper and broader scope. It nullifies and makes void all State legislation, and State action of every kind, which impairs the privileges and immunities of citizens of the United States, or which injures them in life, liberty or property without due process of law, or which denies to any of them the equal protection of the laws. It not only does this, but, in order that the national will, thus declared, may not be a mere *brutum fulmen,* the last section of the amendment invests Congress with power to enforce it by appropriate legislation. To enforce what? To enforce the prohibition. To adopt appropriate legislation for correcting the effects of such prohibited State laws and State acts, and thus to render them effectually null, void, and innocuous. This is the legislative power conferred upon Congress, and this is the whole of it. It does not invest Congress with power to legislate upon subjects which are within the domain of State legislation; but to provide modes of relief against State legislation, or State action, of the kind referred to. It does not authorize Congress to create a code of municipal law for the regulation of private rights; but to provide modes of redress against the operation of State laws, and the action of State officers, executive or judicial, when these are subversive of the fundamental rights specified in the amendment.

. . . Until some State law has been passed, or some State action through its officers or agents had been taken, adverse to the rights of citizens sought to be protected by the Fourteenth Amendment, no legislation of the United States under said amendment nor any proceeding under such legislation, can be called into activity: for the prohibitions of the amendment are against State laws and acts done under State authority. Of course, legislation may, and should be, provided in advance to meet the exigency when it arises; but it should be adapted to the mischief and wrong which the amendment was intended to provide against; and that is, State laws, or State action of some kind, adverse to the rights of the citizen secured by the amendment. Such legislation cannot properly cover the whole domain of rights appertaining to life, liberty and property, defining them and providing for their vindication. That would be to establish a code of municipal law regulative of all private rights between man and man in society. It would be to make Congress take the place of the State legislatures and to supersede them. . . .

If this legislation is appropriate for enforcing the prohibitions of the amendment, it is difficult to see where it is to stop. Why may not Congress with equal show of authority enact a code of laws for the enforcement and vindication of all rights of life, liberty, and property? . . . The truth is, that the implication of a power to legislate in this manner is based upon the assumption that if the States are forbidden to legislate or act in a particular way on a particular subject, and power is conferred upon Congress to enforce the prohibition, this gives Congress power to legislate generally upon that subject, and not merely power to provide modes of redress against such State legislation or action. The assumption is certainly unsound. It is repugnant to the Tenth Amendment of the Constitution, which declares that powers not delegated to the United States by the Constitution, nor prohibited by it to the States, are reserved to the States respectively or to the people. . . .

But the power of Congress to adopt direct and primary, as distinguished from corrective legislation, on the subject in hand, is sought, in the second place, from the Thirteenth Amendment, which abolishes slavery. This amendment declares "that neither slavery, nor involuntary servitude, except as a punishment for crime, whereof the party shall have been duly convicted, shall exist within the United States, or any place subject to their jurisdiction"; and it gives Congress power to enforce the amendment by appropriate legislation. . . .

. . . There were thousands of free colored people in this country before the abolition of slavery, enjoying all the essential rights of life, liberty and property the same as white citizens; yet no one, at that time, thought that it was any invasion of his personal status as a freeman because he was not admitted to all the privileges enjoyed by white citizens, or because he was subjected to discriminations in the enjoyment of accommodations in inns, public conveyances and places of amusement. Mere discriminations on account of race or color were not regarded as badges of slavery. If, since that time, the enjoyment of equal rights in all these respects has become established by constitutional enactment, it is not by force of the Thirteenth Amendment (which merely abolishes slavery), but by force of the Fourteenth and Fifteenth Amendments. . . .

MR. JUSTICE HARLAN dissenting . . . .

I am of the opinion that such discrimination practiced by corporations and individuals in the exercise of their public or quasi public functions is a badge of servitude the imposition of which Congress may prevent under its power, by appropriate legislation, to enforce the Thirteenth Amendment; and, consequently, without reference to its enlarged power under the Fourteenth Amendment, the act of March 1, 1875, is not, in my judgment, repugnant to the Constitution. . . . The assumption that this amendment [the Fourteenth] consists wholly of prohibitions upon State laws and State proceedings in hostility to its provisions, is unauthorized by its language. [Its] first clause. . . . "All persons born or naturalized in the United States, and Subject to the jurisdiction thereof, are citizens of the United States, and of the state wherein they reside"—is of a distinctly affirmative character. In its application to the colored race . . . it created and granted, as well as citizenship of the United States, citizenship of the State in which they respectively resided. It introduced all of that race, whose ancestors had been imported and sold as slaves, at once, into the political community known as the "People of the United States." They became, instantly, citizens of the United States, and of their respective States. Further, they were brought, by this Supreme act of the nation, within the direct operation of that provision of the Constitution which declares that "the citizens of each State shall he entitled to all privileges and immunities of citizens in the several States."

The citizenship thus acquired by that race, in virtue of an affirmative grant from the nation, may be protected, not alone by the judicial branch of the government, but by congressional legislation of a primary direct character; this, because the power of Congress is not restricted to the enforcement of prohibitions upon State laws or State action. It is, in terms distinct and positive, to enforce "the *provisions of this article*" of amendment; not simply those of a prohibitive character, but the provisions—*all* of the provisions—affirmative and prohibitive, of the amendment. . . .

It is said that any interpretation of the Fourteenth Amendment different from that adopted by the majority of the court, would imply that Congress had authority to enact a municipal code for all the States, covering every matter affecting the life, liberty, and property of the citizens of the several States. Not so. . . . The personal rights and immunities recognized in the prohibitive clauses of the amendment were, prior to its adoption, under the protection, primarily, of the States, while rights, created by or derived from the United States, have always been, and, in the nature of things, should always be, primarily, under the protection of the general government. Exemption from race discrimination in respect of the civil rights which are fundamental in *citizenship* in a republican government, is, as we have seen, a new right, created by the nation, with express power in Congress, by legislation, to enforce the constitutional provision from which it is derived. If, in some sense, such race discrimination is, within the letter of the last clause of the first section, a denial of that equal protection of the laws which is secured against State denial to all persons, whether citizens or not, it cannot be possible that a mere prohibition upon such State denial, or a prohibition upon State laws abridging the privileges and immunities of citizens of the United States, takes from the nation the power which it has uniformly exercised of protecting, by direct primary legislation, those privileges and immunities which existed under the Constitution before the adoption of the Fourteenth Amendment, or have been created by that amendment in behalf of those thereby made *citizens* of their respective States. . . .

Plessy v. *Ferguson* (1896)

On June 7, 1892, Homer A. Plessy bought a ticket on the East Louisiana Railway. In 1890, the state of Louisiana had passed a statute that both allowed for racial segregation on trains and provided for the enforcement of this law. Plessy, a black man, entered a "white" train car with the intention of being apprehended. Four years after his arrest, *Plessy* v. *Ferguson* entered the Supreme Court. *Plessy* challenged the Louisiana train law based on the rights granted him in the Thirteenth and Fourteenth Amendments.

In a nation still adjusting to post Civil War emancipation, many aspects of life were segregated. Signs designated "white" and "colored" restrooms, water fountains, and eating establishments. Although more concentrated in the South, where the majority of blacks lived, segregation was a nationwide custom.

Considering these social factors, Justice Brown faced a difficult decision. He began by denying any violation of the Thirteenth Amendment, which abolished slavery. However, the issue of the Fourteenth Amendment demanded further analysis. The Amendment reads: "No State shall make or enforce any law which shall abridge the privileges or immunities of citizens of the United States." Justice Brown affirmed that the Constitution protected the "absolute equality of the two races before the law." He then made a key distinction. Political and legal protection was distinct from *social* protection. He said: "If one race be inferior to the other *socially*, the Constitution of the United States cannot put them upon the same plane." (italics added). He further contended that social inequality must be remedied by legislation.

In what became known as the "separate but equal" decision, Justice Brown had institutionalized segregation. Many blacks were poorly educated and unable to vote, and were therefore powerless to defend their legal rights. Social rights were dependent on community and individual factors and unprotected by the Constitution.

The decision was not unanimous among the Supreme Court justices, however. Justice Harlan, a former slave owner himself, entered his dissenting opinion. He wrote:

> In my opinion, the judgment this day rendered will, in time, prove to be quite as pernicious as the decision made by this tribunal in the *Dred Scott* case . . . Sixty millions of whites are in no danger from the presence here of eight millions of blacks. The destinies of the two races, in this country are indissolubly linked together."

Voicing the other side of the nationwide argument, Harlan predicted that the decision would cause increased tension. Indeed, it would be more than 50 years of tension before Harlan's prediction would ring true. In 1954, the Supreme Court declared that separate educational facilities were "inherently unequal" *(Brown* v. *Board of Education)* and overturned the decision of *Plessy* v. *Ferguson.*

Plessy v. *Ferguson*

163 U.S. 537, 16 S.Ct. 1138, 41 L.Ed. 256 (1896)

MR. JUSTICE BROWN . . . delivered the opinion of the Court. . . .

The constitutionality of this act is attacked upon the ground that it conflicts both with the Thirteenth Amendment of the Constitution, abolishing slavery, and the Fourteenth Amendment, which prohibits certain restrictive legislation on the part of the States.

1. That it does not conflict with the Thirteenth Amendment, which abolished slavery and involuntary servitude, except as a punishment for crime, is too clear for argument. . . .

2. By the Fourteenth Amendment, all persons born or naturalized in the United States, and subject to the jurisdiction thereof, are made citizens of the United States and of the State wherein they reside; and the States are forbidden from making or enforcing any law which shall abridge the privileges or immunities of citizens of the United States, or shall deprive any person of life, liberty, or property without due process of law, or deny to any person within their jurisdiction the equal protection of the laws. . . .

The object of the amendment was undoubtedly to enforce the absolute equality of the two races before the law, but in the nature of things it could not have been intended to abolish distinctions based upon color, or to enforce social, as distinguished from political equality, or a commingling of the two races upon terms unsatisfactory to either. Laws permitting, and even requiring, their separation in places where they are liable to be brought into contact do not necessarily imply the inferiority of either race to the other, and have been generally, if not universally, recognized as within the competency of the state legislatures in the exercise of their police power. The most common instance of this is connected with the establishment of separate schools for white and colored children, which has been held to be a valid exercise of the legislative power even by courts of States where the political rights of the colored race have been longest and most earnestly enforced.

One of the earliest of these cases is that of *Roberts* v. *City of Boston* [1849], in which the Supreme Judicial Court of Massachusetts held that the general school committee of Boston had power to make provisions for the instruction of colored children in separate schools established exclusively for them, and to prohibit their attendance upon the other schools. . . .

. . . Similar laws have been enacted by Congress under its general power of legislation over the District of Columbia . . . as well as by the legislatures of many of the States, and have been generally, if not uniformly, sustained by the courts. . . .

The distinction between laws interfering with the political equality of the negro and those requiring the separation of the two races in schools, theatres, and railway carriages has been frequently drawn by this court. . . .

So far, then, as a conflict with the Fourteenth Amendment is concerned the case reduces itself to the question whether the statute of Louisiana is a reasonable regulation, and with respect to this there must necessarily be a large discretion on the part of the legislature. In determining the question of reasonableness it is at liberty to act with reference to the established usages, customs and traditions of the people, and with a view to the promotion of their comfort, and the preservation of the public peace and good order. Gauged by this standard, we cannot say that a law which authorizes or even requires the separation of the two races in public conveyances is unreasonable, or more obnoxious to the Fourteenth Amendment than the acts of Congress requiring separate schools for colored children in the District of Columbia, the constitutionality of which does not seem to have been questioned, or the corresponding acts of state legislatures.

We consider the underlying fallacy of the plaintiff's argument to consist in the assumption that the enforced separation of the two races stamps the colored race with a badge of inferiority. If this be so, it is not by reason of anything found in the act, but solely because the colored race chooses to put that construction upon it. The argument necessarily assumes that if, as has been more than once the case, and is not unlikely to be so again, the colored race should become the dominant power in the state legislature, and should enact a law in precisely similar terms, it would thereby relegate the white race to an inferior position. We imagine that the white race, at least, would not acquiesce in this assumption. The argument also assumes, that social prejudices may be overcome by legislation, and that equal rights cannot be secured to the negro except by an enforced commingling of the two races. We cannot accept this proposition. If the two races are to meet upon terms of social equality, it must be the result of natural affinities, a mutual appreciation of each other's merits and a voluntary consent of individuals. . . . Legislation is powerless to eradicate racial instincts or to abolish distinctions based upon physical differences, and the attempt to do so can only result in accentuating the difficulties of the present situation. If the civil and political rights of both races be equal one cannot be inferior to the other civilly or politically. If one race be inferior to the other socially, the Constitution of the United States cannot put them upon the same plane. . . .

The judgment of the court below is, therefore,

Affirmed.

MR. JUSTICE HARLAN, dissenting. . . .

. . . [I]n view of the Constitution, in the eye of the law, there is in this country no superior, dominant, ruling class of citizens. There is no caste here. Our Constitution is color-blind, and neither knows nor tolerates classes among citizens. In respect of civil rights, all citizens are equal before the law. The humblest is the peer of the most powerful. The law regards man as man, and takes no account of his surroundings or of his color when his civil rights as guaranteed by the supreme law of the land are involved." It is, therefore, to be regretted that this high tribunal, the final expositor of the fundamental law of the land, has reached the conclusion that it is competent for a state to regulate the enjoyment by citizens of their civil rights solely upon the basis of race. . . .

In my opinion, the judgment this day rendered will, in time, prove to be quite as pernicious as the decision made by this tribunal in the Dred Scott case. . . . The present decision, it may well be apprehended, will not only stimulate aggressions, more or less brutal and irritating, upon the admitted rights of colored citizens, but will encourage the belief that it is possible, by means of state enactments, to defeat the beneficient purposes which the people of the United States had in view when they adopted the recent amendments of the Constitution, by one of which the blacks of this country were made citizens of the United States and of the States in which they respectively reside, and whose privileges and immunities, as citizens, the States are forbidden to abridge. Sixty millions of whites are in no danger from the presence here of eight millions of blacks. The destinies of the two races, in this country, are indissolubly linked together, and the interests of both require that the common government of all shall not permit the seeds of race hate to be planted under the sanction of law. . . .

If evils will result from the commingling of the two races upon public highways established for the benefit of all, they will be infinitely less than those that will surely come from state legislation regulating the enjoyment of civil rights upon the basis of race. We boast of the freedom enjoyed by our people above all other people. But it is difficult to reconcile that boast with a state of the law which, practically, puts the brand of servitude and degradation upon a large class of our fellow-citizens, our equals before the law. The thin disguise of "equal" accommodations for passengers in railroad coaches will not mislead any one, nor atone for the wrong this day done. . . .

For the reasons stated, I am constrained to withold my assent from the opinion and judgment of the majority.

Brown v. *Board of Education of Topeka* (1954)

Thurgood Marshall became the first black Justice of the Supreme Court in 1967. Prior to his appointment, Marshall had won 29 of the 32 cases he argued before the Supreme Court, including *Brown v. Board of Education of Topeka.* In 1954, when he argued *Brown,* he was a lawyer in the Legal Defense Fund of the National Association for the Advancement of Colored People (NAACP). Both inside and outside of the courtroom, Marshall was an advocate of civil rights. *Brown* v. *Board of Education* required the Supreme Court to consider whether the "separate but equal" standard applied in *Plessy* v. *Ferguson* was constitutional. Marshall argued that it was not, and gathered a mountain of psychological and legal evidence to prove his contention.

Chief Justice Earl Warren had a substantial weight on his shoulders when *Brown v Board of Education e*ntered his courtroom. Education was a fundamental institution and served as one of the single most important influences on young minds. Declaring that separate facilities were not equal in education would set a precedent for every subsequent case against segregation. Chief Justice Warren began his ruling by focusing on "today." He was not concerned with the customs or reasons that made segregation possible in the past. He said, "In these days, it is doubtful that any child may reasonably be expected to succeed in life if he is denied the opportunity of an education." He continued by asserting that equal access to buildings and facilities, did not necessarily indicate equal opportunity for education. Taking into account the psychological damages inflicted by segregation, Warren asserted that "separate educational facilities are inherently unequal." The decision was based on Fourteenth Amendment rights which had been violated, according to the Warren court.

The decision was monumental. It called for a reorganization of schoolrooms, bus routes, and classroom roles. The adjustments seemed never ending. It was for this reason that the Warren Court issued the second half of *Brown,* in 1955, which dealt with the logistics of desegregation. Warren acknowledged that the process would move at different rates and face varying problems in some areas of the nation. After designating desegregation as a top priority, he gave jurisdiction to the lower, District Courts, to handle the details. He demanded that the changes be made "with all deliberate speed." This gave objecting states the excuse they needed to slow the process. Many Southern states protested the decision, crying for state sovereignty. Nearly all of the members of Congress from Southern states signed the "Declaration of Constitutional Principles" to resist desegregation. Many states implemented laws to slow the process. It would take the 1960s and more national government intervention to bring about real progress. Until then, the *Brown* decision stood as a symbol of a new era for black citizens. By attending school together, the children would break down the psychological and social barriers that had made segregation a viable practice in the past.

Brown v. *Board of Education*

(First Case)

347 U.S. 483, 74 S.Ct. 686, 98 L.Ed. 873 (1954)

MR. CHIEF JUSTICE WARREN delivered the opinion of the court.

These cases come to us from the States of Kansas, South Carolina, Virginia, and Delaware. They are premised on different facts and different local conditions, but a common legal question justifies their consideration together in this consolidated opinion.

In each of the cases, minors of the Negro race, through their legal representatives, seek the aid of the courts in obtaining admission to the public schools of their Community on a nonsegregated basis. In each instance, they had been denied admission to schools attended by white children under laws requiring or permitting segregation according to race.

This segregation was alleged to deprive the plaintiffs of the equal protection of the laws under the Fourteenth Amendment. In each of the cases other than the Delaware case, a three-judge Federal District Court denied relief to the plaintiffs on the so-called "separate but equal" doctrine, announced by this Court in *Plessy* v. *Ferguson*. . . .

The plaintiffs contend that segregated public schools are not "equal" and cannot be made "equal," and that, hence, they are deprived of the equal protection of the laws. Because of the obvious importance of the question presented, the Court took jurisdiction. Argument was heard in the 1952 term, and reargument was heard this term on certain questions propounded by the Court.

Reargument was largely devoted to the circumstances surrounding the adoption of the Fourteenth Amendment in 1868. It covered exhaustively, consideration of the Amendment in Congress, ratification by the states then existing practices in racial segregation and the views of proponents and opponent of the Amendment.

This discussion and our own investigation convince us that, although these sources cast some light, it is not enough to resolve the problem with which we are faced.

At best, they are inconclusive. The most avid proponents of the post-war Amendment undoubtedly intended them to remove all legal distinctions among "all persons born or naturalized in the United States."

Their opponents, just as certainly, were antagonistic to both the letter and the spirit of the Amendments and wished them to have the most limited effect. What others in Congress and the State legislatures had in mind cannot be determined with any degree of certainty.

An additional reason for the illusive nature of the Amendment's history, with respect to segregated schools, is the status of public education at that time. In the South, the movement toward free common schools, supported by general taxation, had not yet taken hold. Education of white children was largely in the hands of private groups. Education of Negroes was almost nonexistent, and practically all of the race was illiterate. In fact, any education of Negroes was forbidden by law in some states. . . .

As a consequence, it is not surprising that there should be so little in the history of the Fourteenth Amendment relating to its intended effect on public education. . . .

In approaching this problem, we cannot turn the clock back to 1868, when the Amendment was adopted, or even to 1896, when *Plessy* v. *Ferguson* was written. We must consider public education in the light of its full development and its present place in American life throughout the nation. Only in this way can it be determined if segregation in public schools deprives these plaintiffs of the equal protection of the laws.

Today, education is perhaps the most important function of state and local governments. Compulsory school attendance laws and the great expenditures for education both demonstrate our recognition of the importance of education to our democratic society. It is required in the performance of our most basic public responsibilities, even service in the armed forces. It is the very foundation of good citizenship.

Today, it is a principal instrument in awakening the child to cultural values, in preparing him for later professional training, and in helping him to adjust normally to his environment.

In these days, it is doubtful that any child may reasonably be expected to succeed in life if he is denied the opportunity of an education. Such an opportunity, where the state has undertaken to provide it, is a right which must be made available to all on equal terms.

We come then to the question presented: Does segregation of children in public schools solely on the basis of race, even though the physical facilities and other "tangible" factors may be equal, deprive the children of the minority group of equal educational opportunities? We believe that it does.

In *Sweatt* v. *Painter* . . . in finding that a segregated law school for Negroes could not provide them equal educational opportunities, this court relied in large part on "those qualities which are incapable of objective measurement but which make for greatness in a law school."

In *McLaurin* v. *Oklahoma State Regents* . . . the court, in requiring that a Negro admitted to a white graduate school be treated like all other students, again resorted to intangible considerations: ". . . his ability to study, engage in discussions and exchange views with other students, and, in general, to learn his profession."

Such considerations apply with added force to children in grade and high schools. To separate them from others of similar age and qualifications solely because of their race generates a feeling of inferiority as to their status in the community that may affect their hearts and minds in a way unlikely ever to be undone. . . .

Whatever may have been the extent of psychological knowledge at the time of *Plessy* v. Fer*guson,* this finding is amply supported by modern authority.*

. . . Any language in *Plessy* v. *Ferguson* contrary to this finding is rejected.

We conclude that in the field of public education the doctrine of "separate but equal" has no place. Separate educational facilities are inherently unequal. Therefore, we hold that the plaintiffs and others similarly situated for whom the actions have been brought are, by reason of the segregation complained of, deprived of the equal protection of the laws guaranteed by the Fourteenth Amendment. . . .

We have now announced that such segregation is a denial of the equal protection of the laws. In order that we may have the full assistance of the parties in formulating decrees the cases will be restored to the docket, and the parties are requested to present further argument on Questions 4 and 5 previously propounded by the court for the reargument this Term. [These pertained to that form of decree to be issued if segregated schools were outlawed.] . . .

It is so ordered.

Notes

* Citing: K. B. Clark, *Effect of Prejudice and Discrimination on Personality Development* (Mid-century White House Conference); Witmer and Kotinsky, *Personality in the Making* (1952), ch. VI; Deutscher and Chein, "The Psychological Effects of Enforced Segregation: A Survey of Social Science Opinion," 26 *J. Psychol.* 259 (1948); Chein, "What Are the Psychological Effects of Segregation Under Conditions of Equal Facilities?" 3 Int. *J. Opinion and Attitude Res.* 229 (1949); Brameld, "Educational Costs," in *Discrimination and National Welfare* (Maclver, ed., 1949), 44–48; Frazier, *The Negro in the United States* (1949), 674–681. And see generally Myrdal, *An American Dilemma* (1944).

Engel v. *Vitale* (1962)
Supreme Court Rules State Can Not Mandate Prayer in Schools

Throughout most of U.S. history, schools would begin their classes with the singing of the national anthem, recitation of the Pledge of Allegiance, or some readings from the bible. In New York, the Board of Regents mandated a universal prayer, for all religious groups, for the public schools. The parents, however, claimed that this was "contrary to the beliefs, religions, or religious practices of both themselves and their children." The state court then permitted the use of the prayer as long as it was not forced. Later, the Supreme Court was against the state's decision since it violated the First Amendment's ban against the establishment of religion.

According to the Engel decision of 1962, the Supreme Court held that the idea of the state to mandate prayer in schools was contrary to the First Amendment's ban against the establishment of religion. This case remains controversial, as the debate in defining what freedom of religion means today. Those opposed to the decision claim that the state should be in favor of, and therefore support, all religions. This means, the state should mandate prayer in schools. Those in favor believe that religion should be removed from the state's decision-making power and left to be determined outside of classes.

The following is Justice Black's opinion of the Court:

> The respondent Board of Education of Union Free School District No. 9, New Hyde Park, New York, acting in its official capacity under state law, directed the School District's principal to cause the following prayer to be said aloud by each class in the presence of a teacher at the beginning of each school day:
>
> Almighty God, we acknowledge our dependence upon Thee, and we beg Thy blessing upon us, our parents, our teachers and our Country.
>
> This daily procedure was adopted on the recommendation of the State Board of Regents, a governmental agency created by the State Constitution to which the New York

Legislature has granted broad supervisory, executive, and legislative powers over the State's public school system. These state officials composed the prayer which they recommended and published as apart of their "Statement on Moral and Spiritual Training in the Schools," saying: "We believe that this Statement will be subscribed to by all men and women of good will, and we call upon all of them to aid in giving life to our program.

We think that by using its public school system to encourage recitation of the Regents' prayer, the State of New York has adopted a practice wholly in consistent with the Establishment Clause. There can, of course, be no doubt that New York's program of daily classroom invocation of God's blessings as prescribed in the Regents' prayer is a religious activity. It is a solemn avowal of divine faith and supplication for the blessing of the Almighty. The nature of such a prayer has always been religious, none of the respondents has denied this and the trial court expressly so found. . .

The petitioners contend among other things that the state laws requiring or permitting use of the Regents' prayer must be struck down as a violation of the Establishment Clause because that prayer was composed by governmental officials as apart of a governmental program to further religious beliefs. For this reason, petitioners argue, the State's use of the Regents' prayer in its public school system breaches the constitutional wall of separation between Church and State. We agree with that contention since we think that the constitutional prohibition against laws respecting an establishment of religion must at least mean that in this country it is no part of the business of government to compose official prayers for any group of the American people to recite as a part of a religious program carried on by government.

It is a matter of history that this very practice of establishing governmentally composed prayers for religious services was one of the reasons which caused many of our early colonists to leave England and seek religious freedom in America. *The Book of Common Prayer,* which was created under governmental direction and which was approved by Acts of Parliament in 1548 and 1549, set out in minute detail the accepted form and content of prayer and other religious ceremonies to be used in the established, tax-supported Church of England. . . .

Griswold v. *Connecticut* (1965)

The "right to privacy" does not exist in the Constitution, at least not in so many words. However, privacy seems a natural human right. In a democratic government, the concept of privacy is a delicate balance between freedom and order. Individuals require the freedom to act in privacy, however, government must assert control over certain aspects of life to maintain order. This was the dilemma faced by the Supreme Court in 1965 with *Griswold* v. *Connecticut.*

A Connecticut law read, "Any person who uses any drug, medicinal article or instrument for the purpose of preventing conception shall be fined not less than fifty dollars or imprisoned not less than 60 days nor more than one year or be both fined and imprisoned." Although the law had existed since 1879, it was applied to Estelle Griswold in 1965. As the executive director of the Planned Parenthood League in Connecticut, she was convicted of aiding in contraception by giving information to married couples.

According to the 14th Amendment, it is principally the right of the State to enact laws for the protection of its citizens. If the State fails to protect the rights of its citizens, the Supreme Court then judges the case for constitutionality. Justice Douglas determined that the language of the Bill of Rights provided a "zone of privacy," although the words do not specifically appear. He contended that to prohibit the manufacture or distribution of contraceptives was one thing. To stop the use is to interfere in the relationship between husband and wife. The Connecticut law was determined unconstitutional.

The decision raised disagreement among the justices. Although none could deny the inherent right to privacy guarded by the decision, two justices denied the Court's right to impose such a judgment. More than 150 years earlier, the Supreme Court handed down a decision in *Marbury* v. *Madison*. It held that the Supreme Court had to change existing laws only insomuch as the Constitution permits. Since the "right to privacy" was not expressly provided in the wording of the Constitution or its Amendments, the dissenting justices contended that the *Griswold* v *Connecticut* decision was invalid. A majority of the justices supported the verdict, however, and the decision held. The Court had taken the liberty to interpret the Constitution more broadly in order to expand civil rights. Justice Douglas said, "We deal with a right of privacy older than the Bill of Rights. Marriage is a coming together for better or for worse, hopefully enduring, and intimate to the degree of being sacred." All of the justices, even those dissenting, recognized marriage as the supreme "zone of privacy."

Griswold v. *Connecticut*

381 U.S. 479, 85 S.Ct. 1678, 14 L.Ed. 2d 510 (1965)

MR. JUSTICE DOUGLAS delivered the opinion of the Court. . . .

Coming to the merits, we are met with a wide range of questions that implicate the Due Process Clause of the Fourteenth Amendment. Overtones of some arguments suggest that *Lochner* v. *New York* . . . should be our guide. But we decline that invitation. . . . We do not sit as a super-legislature to determine the wisdom, need, and propriety of laws that touch economic problems, business affairs, or social conditions. This law, however, operates directly on an intimate relation of husband and wife and their physician's role in one aspect of that relation. . . .

. . . [S]pecific guarantees in the Bill of Rights have penumbras, formed by emanations from those guarantees that help give them life and substance. . . . Various guarantees create zones of privacy. The right of association contained in the penumbra of the First Amendment is one. . . . The Third Amendment in its prohibition against the quartering of soldiers "in any house" in time of peace without the consent of the owner is another facet of that privacy. The Fourth Amendment explicitly affirms the "right of the people to be secure in their persons, houses, papers, and effects against unreasonable searches and seizures." The Fifth Amendment in its Self-Incrimination Clause enables the citizen to create a zone of privacy which government may not force him to surrender to his detriment. The Ninth Amendment provides: "The enumeration in the Constitution, of certain rights, shall not be construed to deny or disparage others retained by the people." . . .

The present case, then, concerns a relationship lying within the zone of privacy created by several fundamental constitutional guarantees. And it concerns a law which, in forbidding the use of contraceptives rather than regulating their manufacture or sale, seeks to achieve its goals by means having a maximum destructive impact upon that relationship. Such a law cannot stand in light of the familiar principle, so often applied by this Court, that a "governmental purpose to control or prevent activities constitutionally subject to state regulation may not be achieved by means which sweep unnecessarily broadly and thereby invade the area of protected freedom." Would we allow the police to search the sacred precincts of marital bedrooms for telltale signs of the use of contraceptives? The very idea is repulsive to the notions of privacy surrounding the marriage relationship.

We deal with a right of privacy older than the Bill of Rights—older than our political parties, older than our school system. Marriage is a coming together for better or for worse, hopefully enduring, and intimate to the degree of being sacred. It is an association that promotes a way of life, not causes; a harmony in living, not political faiths; a bilateral loyalty, not commercial or social projects. Yet it is an association for as noble a purpose as any involved in our prior decisions.

Reversed.

MR. JUSTICE GOLDBERG, whom the CHIEF JUSTICE and MR. JUSTICE BRENNAN join, concurring. . . .

The Ninth Amendment to the Constitution may be regarded by some as a recent discovery and may be forgotten by others, but since 1791 it has been a basic part of the Constitution which we are sworn to uphold. To hold that a right so basic and fundamental and so deep-rooted in our society as the right of privacy in marriage may be infringed because that right is not guaranteed in so many words by the first eight amendments to the Constitution is to ignore the Ninth Amendment and to give it no effect whatsoever. . . .

Nor am I turning somersaults with history in arguing that the Ninth Amendment is relevant in a case dealing with a *State's* infringement of a fundamental right. While the Ninth Amendment—and indeed the entire Bill of Rights—originally concerned restrictions upon federal power, the subsequently enacted Fourteenth Amendment prohibits the States as well from abridging fundamental personal liberties. And, the Ninth Amendment, in indicating that not all such liberties are specifically mentioned in the first eight amendments, is surely relevant in showing the existence of other fundamental personal rights, now protected from state, as well as federal, infringement. In sum, the Ninth Amendment simply lends strong support to the view that the "liberty" protected by the Fifth and Fourteenth Amendments from infringement by the Federal Government or the States is not restricted to rights specifically mentioned in the first eight amendments. . . ."

Miranda v. *Arizona* (1966)

We've all heard it. "You have the right to remain silent. Anything you say can and will be used against you in a court of law." Police action movies capitalize on the drama of these words. But what do they really mean? Why do all law enforcement agents say the same words after every arrest? The history dates back to 1966 and a landmark case called *Miranda* v. *Arizona.* Each of the four defendants claimed violation of Fifth Amendment rights in their arrests.

One man in particular, Ernesto Miranda, had been arrested in 1963 on charges of rape and kidnapping. After a positive identification by his accuser and two hours of questioning at the police station, Miranda signed a confession. A paragraph at the top of the paper explained that the confession was made willfully and "with full knowledge of my legal rights, understanding any statement I make may be used against me." In the trial that followed, one of the officers involved claimed he had read the paragraph to Miranda, although not before his oral confession.

The case considered Miranda's Fifth and Sixth Amendment rights. The Fifth Amendment reads: "No person shall be compelled in any criminal case to be a witness against himself," and the Sixth Amendment guarantees "the Assistance of Counsel for his defense." In delivering the decision of the Court, Chief Justice Earl Warren analyzed the police procedures in making arrests. He demanded that custodial interrogation (questioning while in police custody) be free from the possibility of involuntary self-incrimination. Warren affirmed the constitutionality of the "right to remain silent" and required federal and state officials to apprise suspects of their rights before commencing interrogation. In other words, by "pleading the Fifth" suspects are not required to speak. In cases where rights are not delineated, the evidence may be considered immaterial in a court of law.

Chief Justice Warren checked police manuals for procedures and described the results of his research. Regarding the interrogation process, he said, "Police then persuade, trick, or cajole [the subject] out of exercising his constitutional rights." It is in light of this procedure, called the "third degree," that Warren declared the right to the presence of an attorney "indispensable to the protection of the Fifth Amendment privilege."

It was not the intention of the Court to interfere with police procedure outside of insuring rights. Any voluntary confessions or statements were still admissible as evidence and conditions were dependent on individual situations. Although complicating court and police procedures, this sweeping decision protected the universal rights delineated in the Constitution.

Miranda v. *Arizona*

384 U.S. 436, 86 S.Ct. 1602, 16 L.Ed. 2d 694 (1966)

In *Escobedo* v. *Illinois* (1964), five justices overturned a conviction after police interrogated the defendant without first advising him of a right to remain silent and to consult with counsel in circumstances where police also denied his request to consult with counsel waiting outside the interrogation room. Two years later, the Court reviewed four cases from state courts that plainly raised the question whether police had an affirmative obligation to advise suspects of certain rights before interrogating them, if the fruits of the interrogation were to be admissible at trial. Although the interrogations in the four cases took place for varying lengths of time, none of the cases contained an allegation of violence or threat of violence to coerce the confession.

In one case, police in Phoenix, Arizona, arrested Ernesto Miranda at his home in 1963 on rape and kidnapping charges. The complaining witness identified him at the police station. Without advising him of a right to have an attorney present, two officers then questioned Miranda for two hours and obtained a signed confession from him. At the top of the statement was a typed paragraph explaining that the confession was made voluntarily, without threats or promises of immunity, and "with full knowledge of my legal rights, understanding any statement I make may be used against me." One of the officers later explained that he read this paragraph to Miranda, but apparently only after Miranda had confessed orally. The prosecution introduced the signed confession at trial, and Miranda was convicted of rape and kidnapping. On appeal, the Supreme Court of Arizona affirmed. Majority: Warren, Black, Brennan, Douglas, Fortas. Dissenting: Harlan, Clark, Stewart, White.

MR. CHIEF JUSTICE WARREN delivered the opinion of the Court . . . .

Our holding . . . briefly stated . . . is this: the prosecution may not use statements, whether exculpatory or inculpatory, stemming from custodial interrogation of the defendant unless it demonstrates the use of procedural safeguards effective to secure the privilege against self-incrimination. By custodial interrogation, we mean questioning initiated by law enforcement officers after a person has been taken into custody or otherwise deprived of his freedom of action in any significant way. As for the procedural safeguards to be employed, unless other fully effective means are devised to inform accused persons of their right of silence and to assure a continuous opportunity to exercise it, the following measures are required. Prior to any questioning, the person must be warned that he has a right to remain silent, that any statement he does make may be used as evidence against him, and that he has a right to the presence of an attorney, either retained or appointed. The defendant may waive effectuation of these rights, provided the waiver is made voluntarily, knowingly and intelligently. If, however, he indicates in any manner and at any stage of the process that he wishes to consult with an attorney before speaking there can be no questioning. Likewise, if the individual is alone and indicates in any manner that he does not wish to be interrogated, the police may not question him. The mere fact that he may have answered some questions or volunteered some statements on his own does not deprive him of the right to refrain from answering any further inquiries until he has consulted with an attorney and thereafter consents to be questioned.

The constitutional issue we decide in each of these cases is the admissibility of statements obtained from a defendant questioned while in custody and deprived of his freedom of action. In each, the defendant was questioned by police officers, detectives, or a prosecuting attorney in a room in which he was cut off from the outside world. In none of these cases was the defendant given a full and effective warning of his rights at the outset of the interrogation process. In all the cases, the questioning elicited oral admissions, and in three of them, signed statements as well which were admitted at their trials. They all thus share salient features—

incommunicado interrogation of individuals in a police-dominated atmosphere, resulting in self-incriminating statements without full warnings of constitutional rights.

An understanding of the nature and setting of this in-custody interrogation is essential to our decisions today. . . .

. . . [T]he modern practice of in-custody interrogation is psychologically rather than physically oriented. . . . Interrogation still takes place in privacy. Privacy results in secrecy and this in turn results in a gap in our knowledge as to what in fact goes on in the interrogation rooms. A valuable source of information about present police practices, however, may be found in various police manuals and texts which document procedures employed with success in the past, and which recommend various other effective tactics. [The opinion here surveys manuals and texts.]

From these representative samples of interrogation techniques, the setting prescribed by the manuals and observed in practice becomes clear. In essence, it is this: To be alone with the subject is essential to prevent distraction and to deprive him of any outside support. The aura of confidence in his guilt undermines his will to resist. He merely confirms the preconceived story the police seek to have him describe. Patience and persistence, at times relentless questioning, are employed. To obtain a confession, the interrogator must "Patiently maneuver himself or his quarry into a position from which the desired object may be obtained." When normal procedures fail to produce the needed result, the police may resort to deceptive stratagems such as giving false legal advice. It is important to keep the subject off balance, for example, by trading on his insecurity about himself or his surroundings. The police then persuade, trick, or cajole him out of exercising his constitutional rights.

Even without employing brutality, the "third degree" or the specific stratagems described above, the very fact of custodial interrogation exacts a heavy toll on individual liberty and trades on the weakness of individuals.

In these cases, we might not find the defendants' statements to have been involuntary in traditional terms. Our concern for adequate safeguards to protect precious Fifth Amendment rights is, of course, not lessened in the slightest. To be sure, the records do not evince overt physical coercion or patented psychological ploys. The fact remains that in none of these cases did the officers undertake to afford appropriate safeguards at the outset of the interrogation to insure that the statements were truly the product of free choice. . . .

Today . . . there can be no doubt that the Fifth Amendment privilege is available outside of criminal court proceedings and serves to protect persons in all settings in which their freedom of action is curtailed from being compelled to incriminate themselves. . . .

The circumstances surrounding in-custody interrogation can operate very quickly to overbear the will of one merely made aware of his privilege by his interrogators. Therefore, the right to have counsel present at the interrogation is indispensable to the protection of the Fifth Amendment privilege under the system we delineate today. Our aim is to assure that the individual's right to choose between silence and speech remains unfettered throughout the interrogation process. . . .

Our decision is not intended to hamper the traditional function of police officers in investigating crime. . . . General on-the-scene questioning as to facts surrounding a crime or other general questioning of citizens in the fact-finding process is not affected by our holding. It is an act of responsible citizenship for individuals to give whatever information they may have to aid in law enforcement. In such situations the compelling atmosphere inherent in the process of in-custody interrogation is not necessarily present.

In dealing with statements obtained through interrogation, we do not purport to find all confessions inadmissible. Confessions remain a proper element in law enforcement. Any statement given freely and voluntarily without any compelling influences is, of course, admissible in evidence. The fundamental import of the privilege while an individual is in custody is not whether he is allowed to talk to the police without the benefit of warnings and counsel, but whether he can be interrogated. There is no requirement that police stop a person who enters a police station and states that he wishes to confess to a crime, or a person who calls the police to offer a confession or any other statement he desires to make. Volunteered statements of any kind are not barred by the Fifth Amendment and their admissibility is not affected by our holding today. . . .

It is so ordered.

Roe v. *Wade* (1973)

A landmark case, *Roe* v. *Wade* appeared in the Supreme Court in 1973. Arriving in the middle of a sexual revolution, the abortion issue called political and social factions to arms. The 1960s and 70s had seen a dramatic easing of sexual restrictions and traditionally held moral standards. "Free Love" became a catchphrase of the day. The "Make Love Not War" slogan denounced the conflict in Vietnam. In the light of such sexual permissiveness, birth control became an urgent issue. By 1970, 12 million women were using "the Pill" with still others choosing different forms of birth control, among them, abortion.

"Jane Roe" was the fictitious name used to protect Norma McCorvey of Dallas, Texas. In 1970, Texas law prohibited abortion except in the case of circumstances threatening the life of the mother. Since this exception did not apply to her, Ms. McCorvey carried the baby to full term and attorneys arranged for an adoption. Norma McCorvey filed suit against the District Attorney of Dallas County, Henry Wade, claiming a violation of her constitutional rights. In 1973, 21 states had highly restrictive laws regarding abortion which dated back to the 19th Century. The issue of abortion saw very few fence-sitters. Whether expressed militantly or not, most knew where they stood. Such a divisive and far-reaching issue placed considerable responsibility on a Supreme Court ruling.

In rendering the Court's decision, Justice Blackmun first recognized the "sensitive and emotional nature of the abortion controversy." In his analysis of the historical basis of abortion legislation, Blackmun noted that early procedures of abortion were dangerous and entailed a great risk of infection. States had considered it their constitutional responsibility to protect prenatal life. In fact, the Court could have cited the 14th Amendment and handed jurisdiction in such matters back to the States for consideration. Instead, the Supreme Court provided a national definition of the conditions of abortion legislation. The decision considered the right to privacy "broad enough to encompass a woman's decisions whether or not to terminate her pregnancy." The decision legalized abortion through the first trimester of pregnancy, and nationalized the abortion issue.

The Court then turned to the constitutional definition of a "person." Since the language of the Fourteenth Amendment covers "All persons born or naturalized in the United States," the rights technically apply "only postnatally." With the *Roe* decision, state responsibility for the protection of life was extended to second trimester. Any state bans on abortions before that point were unconstitutional.

For the next two decades, *Roe* v. *Wade* entered courtrooms under many other names in an attempt to overturn the decision. Conservative groups picketed and protested outside abortion clinics and other arenas. "Pro-choice" groups were not without militancy and protests of their own. As predicted by opponents to legalized abortion, *Roe* clarified legislation but deepened the divide on the issue. As a demonstration of the ramifications of the 1973 decision, statistics show that 750, 000 women received abortions in 1973, a number which increased to 1.5 million in 1980.

Roe v. *Wade*

410 U.S. 113, 93 S.Ct. 705, 35 L.Ed. 2d 147 (1973)

In 1970, Norma McCorvey of Dallas, Texas, wished to terminate her pregnancy by abortion. Because Texas law prohibited abortions except those performed by a physician for the purpose of saving the life of the woman (an exception that did not apply to her), she filed suit against Henry Wade, District Attorney of Dallas County, in the U.S. District Court for the Northern District of Texas, claiming that the Texas law was unconstitutional and seeking an injunction against its enforcement. To protect her anonymity, she used the pseudonym of Jane Roe throughout the litigation. The district court held that the state statute was void on its face because it was unconstitutionally vague and overbroad and violated rights protected by the Ninth Amendment, but declined to enjoin further enforcement of the statute. (An attorney helped to arrange for the newborn's adoption later in 1970.) The Supreme Court twice heard oral arguments in the case—in December of 1971 and October of 1972. Majority: Blackmun, Brennan, Burger, Douglas, Marshall, Powell, Stewart. Dissenting: Rehnquist, White.

MR. JUSTICE BLACKMUN delivered the opinion of the Court.

. . . We forthwith acknowledge our awareness of the sensitive and emotional nature of the abortion controversy, of the vigorous opposing views, even among physicians, and of the deep and seemingly absolute convictions that the subject inspires. One's philosophy, one's experiences, one's exposure to the raw edges of human existence, one's religious training, one's attitudes toward life and family and their values, and the moral standards one establishes and seeks to observe, are all likely to influence and to color one's thinking and conclusions about abortion. . . .

The principal thrust of the appellant's attack on the Texas statutes is that they improperly invade a right, said to be possessed by the pregnant woman, to choose to terminate her pregnancy. Appellant would discover this right in the concept of personal "liberty" embodied in the Fourteenth Amendment's Due Process Clause; or in personal, marital, familial, and sexual privacy said to be protected by the Bill of Rights or its penumbras. . . . Before addressing this claim, we feel it desirable briefly to survey, in several aspects, the history of abortion, for such insight as that history may afford us, and then to examine the state purposes and interests behind the criminal abortion laws.

It perhaps is not generally appreciated that the restrictive criminal abortion laws in effect in a majority of States today are of relatively recent vintage. Those laws, generally proscribing abortion or its attempt at any time during pregnancy except when necessary to preserve the pregnant woman's life, are not of ancient or even of common law origin. Instead, they derive from statutory changes effected, for the most part, in the latter half of the 19th century. . . .

It is thus apparent that at common law, at the time of the adoption of our Constitution, and throughout the major portion of the 19th century, abortion was viewed with less disfavor than under most American statutes currently in effect. . . .

Three reasons have been advanced to explain historically the enactment of criminal abortion laws in the 19th century and to justify their continued existence.

It has been argued occasionally that these laws were the product of a Victorian social concern to discourage illicit sexual conduct. Texas, however, does not advance this justification in the present case, and it appears that no court or commentator has taken the argument seriously. . . .

A second reason is concerned with abortion as a medical procedure. When most criminal abortion laws were first enacted, the procedure was a hazardous one for the woman. This was particularly true prior to the development of antisepsis. . . . Abortion mortality was high. . . .

Modern medical techniques have altered this situation. Appellants and various amici refer to medical data indicating that abortion in early pregnancy, that is, prior to the end of the first trimester, although not without its risk, is now relatively safe. Mortality rates for women undergoing early abortions, where the procedure is legal, appear to be as low or lower than the rates for normal childbirth. . . . Of course, important state interests in the area of health and medical standards do remain. The State has a legitimate interest in seeing to it that abortion, like any other medical procedure, is performed under circumstances that insure maximum safety for the patient. . . . Moreover, the risk to the woman increases as her pregnancy continues. Thus the State retains a definite interest in protecting the woman's own health and safety when an abortion is proposed at a late stage of pregnancy.

The third reason is the State's interest—some phrase it in terms of duty—in protecting prenatal life. Some of the argument for this justification rests on the theory that a new human life is present from the moment of conception. The State's interest and general obligation to protect life then extends, it is argued, to prenatal life. Only when the life of the pregnant mother herself is at stake, balanced against the life she carries within her should the interests of the embryo or fetus now prevail. Logically, of course, a legitimate state interest in this area need not stand or fall on acceptance of the belief that life begins at conception or at some other point prior to live birth. In assessing the State's interest, recognition may be given to the less rigid claim that as long as at least *potential* life is involved, the State may assert interests beyond the protection of the pregnant woman alone. . . .

It is with these interests, and the weight to be attached to them, that this case is concerned.

The Constitution does not explicitly mention any right of privacy. In a line of decision however, going back perhaps as far as *Union Pacific R. Co.* v. *Botsford* (1891), the Court has recognized that a right of personal privacy, of a guarantee of certain areas or zones of privacy, does exist under the Constitution. In varying contexts the Court or individual Justice have indeed found at least the roots of that right in the First Amendment . . . in the Fourth and Fifth Amendments . . . in the penumbra of the Bill of Rights . . . in the Ninth Amendment . . . or in the concept of liberty guaranteed by the first section of the Fourteenth Amendment. . . . These decisions make it clear that only personal rights that can be deemed "fundamental" or "implicit in the concept of ordered liberty" . . . are included in this guarantee of personal privacy. They also make it clear that the right has some extension to activities relating to marriage . . . procreation, contraception, family relationships, and child rearing and education.

This right of privacy, whether it be founded in the Fourteenth Amendment's concept of personal liberty and restrictions upon state action, as we feel it is, or, as the District Court determined, in the Ninth Amendment's reservation of rights to the people, is broad enough to encompass a woman's decision whether or not to terminate her pregnancy. The detriment that the State would impose upon the pregnant woman by denying this choice altogether is apparent. Specific and direct harm medically diagnosable even in early pregnancy may be involved. Maternity, or additional offspring, may force upon the woman a distressful life and future. Psychological harm may be imminent. Mental and physical health may be taxed by child care. There is also the distress, for all concerned, associated with the unwanted child, and there is the problem of bringing a child into a family already unable, psychologically and otherwise, to care for it. In other cases, as in this one, the additional difficulties and continuing stigma of unwed motherhood may be involved. All these are factors the woman and her responsible physician necessarily will consider in consultation. . . .

We therefore conclude that the right of personal privacy includes the abortion decision, but that this right is not unqualified and must be considered against important state interests in regulation.

We note that those federal and state courts that have recently considered abortion law challenges have reached the same conclusion. A majority, in addition to the District Court in the present case, have held state laws unconstitutional, at least in part, because of vagueness or because of overbreadth and abridgment of rights. . . .

Although the results are divided, most of these courts have agreed that the right of privacy, however based, is broad enough to cover the abortion decision; that the right, nonetheless, is not absolute and is subject to some limitations; and that at some point the state interests as to protection of health, medical standards, and prenatal life, become dominant. We agree with this approach.

Where certain "fundamental rights" are involved, the Court has held that regulation limiting these rights may be justified only by a "compelling state interest," and that legislative enactments must be narrowly drawn to express only the legitimate state interests at stake. . . .

The appellee and certain amici argue that the fetus is a "person" within the language and meaning of the Fourteenth Amendment. . . .

The Constitution does not define "person" in so many words. Section 1 of the Fourteenth Amendment contains three references to "person." The first, in defining "citizens," speaks of "persons born or naturalized in the United States." The word also appears both in the Due Process Clause and in the Equal Protection Clause. "Person" is used in other places in the Constitution. . . . But in nearly all these instances, the use of the word is such that it has application only postnatally. None indicates, with any assurance, that it has any possible prenatal application. . . .

Texas urges that, apart from the Fourteenth Amendment, life begins at conception and is present throughout pregnancy, and that, therefore, the State has a compelling interest in protecting that life from and after conception. We need not resolve the difficult question of when life begins. When those trained in the respective disciplines of medicine, philosophy, and theology are unable to arrive at any consensus, the judiciary, at this point in the development of man's knowledge, is not in a position to speculate as to the answer. . . .

We do not agree that, by adopting one theory of life, Texas may override the rights of the pregnant woman that are at stake. We repeat, however, that the State does have an important and legitimate interest in preserving and protecting the health of the pregnant woman, whether she be a resident of the State or a nonresident who seeks medical consultation and treatment there, and that it has still another important and legitimate interest in protecting the potentiality of human life. These interests are separate and distinct. Each grows in substantiality as the woman approaches term and, at a point during pregnancy, each becomes "compelling."

With respect to the State's important and legitimate interest in the health of the mother, the "compelling" point, in the light of present medical knowledge, is at approximately the end of the first trimester. This is so because of the now established medical fact . . . that until the end of the first trimester mortality in abortion is less than mortality in normal childbirth. It follows that, from and after this point, a State may regulate the abortion procedure to the extent that the regulation reasonably relates to the preservation and protection of maternal health. Examples of permissible state regulation in this area are requirements as to the qualifications of the person who is to perform the abortion; as to the licensure of that person; as to the facility in which the procedure is to be performed, that is, whether it must be a hospital or may be a clinic or some other place of less-than-hospital status; as to the licensing of the facility; and the like.

This means, on the other hand, that, for the period of pregnancy prior to this "compelling" point, the attending physician, in consultation with his patient, is free to determine, without regulation by the State, that in his medical judgment the patient's pregnancy should be terminated. If that decision is reached, the judgment may be effectuated by an abortion free of interference by the State. . . .

With respect to the State's important and legitimate interest in potential life, the "compelling" point is at viability. This is so because the fetus then presumably has the capability of meaningful life outside the mother's womb. State regulation protective of fetal life after viability thus has both logical and biological justifications. If the State is interested in protecting fetal life after viability, it may go so far as to proscribe abortion during that period except when it is necessary to preserve the life or health of the mother.

Measured against these standards . . . Texas, in restricting legal abortion to those "procured or attempted by medical advice for the purpose of saving the life of the mother," sweeps too broadly. The statute makes no distinction between abortions performed early in pregnancy and those performed later, and it limits to a single reason, "saving" the mother's life, the legal justification for the procedure. The statute, therefore, cannot survive the constitutional attack made upon it here. . . .

To summarize and to repeat:

A state criminal abortion statute of the current Texas type, that excepts from criminality only a *life-saving* procedure on behalf of the mother, without regard to pregnancy stage and without recognition of the other interests involved, is violative of the Due Process Clause of the Fourteenth Amendment.

(a) For the stage prior to approximately the end of the first trimester, the abortion decision and its effectuation must be left to the medical judgment of the pregnant woman's attending physician.

(b) For the stage subsequent to approximately the end of the first trimester, the State, in promoting its interest in the health of the mother, may, if it chooses, regulate the abortion procedure in ways that are reasonably related to maternal health.

(c) For the stage subsequent to viability, the State in promoting its interest in the potentiality of human life may, if it chooses, regulate, and even proscribe, abortion except where it is necessary, in appropriate medical judgment, for the preservation of the life or health of the mother.

MR. CHIEF JUSTICE BURGER, concurring. . . [omitted).

MR. JUSTICE DOUGLAS, concurring . . . [omitted].

MR. JUSTICE STEWART, concurring . . . (omitted].

MR. JUSTICE WHITE, with whom MR. JUSTICE REHNQUIST joins, dissenting . . . [omitted].

MR. JUSTICE REHNQUIST, dissenting.

. . . I would reach a conclusion opposite to that reached by the Court. I have difficulty in concluding, as the Court does, that the right of "privacy" is involved in this case. Texas by the statute here challenged bars the performance of a medical abortion by a licensed physician on a plaintiff such as Roe. A transaction resulting in an operation such as this is not "private" in the ordinary usage of that word. Nor is the "privacy" which the Court finds here even a distant relative of the freedom from searches and seizures protected by the Fourth Amendment to the Constitution which the Court has referred to as embodying a right to privacy. . . .

If the Court means by the term "privacy" no more than that the claim of a person to be free from unwanted state regulation of consensual transactions may be a form of "liberty" protected by the Fourteenth Amendment, there is no doubt that similar claims have been upheld in our earlier decisions on the basis of that liberty. I agree with the statement of Mr. Justice Stewart in his concurring opinion that the "liberty," against deprivation of which without due process the Fourteenth Amendment protects, embraces more than the rights found in the Bill of Rights. But that liberty is not guaranteed absolutely against deprivation, but only against deprivation without due process of law. The test traditionally applied in the area of social and economic legislation is whether or not a law such as that challenged has a rational relation to a valid state objective. . . . But the Court's sweeping invalidation of any restrictions on abortion during the first trimester is impossible to justify under that standard, and the conscious weighing of competing factors which the Court's opinion apparently substitutes for the established test is far more appropriate to a legislative judgment than to a judicial one.

The Court eschews the history of the Fourteenth Amendment in its reliance on the "compelling state interest" test. . . . But the Court adds a new wrinkle to this test by transposing it from the legal considerations associated with the Equal Protection Clause of the Fourteenth Amendment to this case arising under the Due Process Clause of the Fourteenth Amendment. Unless I misapprehend the consequences of this transplanting of the "compelling state interest test," the Court's opinion will accomplish the seemingly impossible feat of leaving this treatment of the law more confused than it found it.

While the Court's opinion quotes from the dissent of Mr. Justice Holmes in *Lochner* v. *New York* . . the result it reaches is more closely attuned to the majority opinion of Mr. Justice Peckham in that case. As in Lochner and similar cases applying substantive due process standards to economic and social welfare legislation, the adoption of the compelling state interest standard will inevitably require this Court to examine the legislative policies and pass on the wisdom of these policies in the very process of deciding whether a particular state interest put forward may or may not be "compelling." The decision here to break the term of pregnancy into three distinct terms and to outline the permissible restrictions the State may impose in each one, for example, partakes more of judicial legislation than it does of a determination of the intent of the drafters of the Fourteenth Amendment.

The fact that a majority of the States, reflecting after all the majority sentiment in those States, have had restrictions on abortions for at least a century seems to me as strong an indication there is that the asserted right to an abortion is not "so rooted in the traditions and conscience of our people as to be ranked as fundamental.". . . Even today, when society's views on abortion are changing, the very existence of the debate is evidence that the "right" to an abortion is not so universally accepted as the appellants would have us believe.

To reach its result the Court necessarily has had to find within the scope of the Fourteenth Amendment a right that was apparently completely unknown to the drafters of the Amendment. As early as 1821, the first state law dealing directly with abortion was enacted by the Connecticut legislature. . . . By the time of the adoption of the Fourteenth Amendment in 1868 there were at least 36 laws enacted by state or territorial legislatures limiting abortion. While many States have amended or updated their laws, 21 of the laws on the books in 1868 remain in effect today. Indeed, the Texas statute struck down today was, as the majority notes, first enacted in 1857 and "has remained substantially unchanged to the present time." . . .

There apparently was no question concerning the validity of this provision or of any of the other state statutes when the Fourteenth Amendment was adopted. The only conclusion possible from this history is that the drafters did not intend to have the Fourteenth Amendment withdraw from the States the power to legislate with respect to this matter. . . .

For all of the foregoing reasons, I respectfully dissent.*

Note

* In *Doe* v. *Bolton,* decided the same day as Roe, the Court invalidated three parts of a Georgia statute patterned after the American Law Institute's Model Penal Code of 1962 which was the basis for the abortion laws in some of the states: 1) that the abortion be performed in an accredited hospital; 2) that the abortion be approved by a hospital committee; and 3) that the decision be confirmed by two other physicians. The Court sustained an interpretation of the Georgia law that permitted a physician to perform an abortion "based on his best clinical judgment that an abortion is necessary."—ED.

Regents of the University of California v. *Bakke* (1978)

In the wake of the Civil Rights Movement, the Civil Rights Act of 1964, and numerous clarifications of the Bill of Rights, affirmative action became part of America's response to racial discrimination. Focusing on the reversal of discrimination, affirmative action supported the establishment of programs aimed at a reversal of the history of racial repression. Many cases appeared in courts across the nation accusing such reverse discrimination of perpetuating prejudice.

In 1974, in the spirit of affirmative action, the University of California at Davis set aside 16 of the 100 seats for minority applicants at their medical school. Those applicants who checked the boxes designating "Blacks," "Chicanos," "Asians," or "American Indian" were sent to a special committee for consideration.

That same year, a white male named Allan Bakke was denied admission. He filed on grounds of violation of Title VI of the Civil Rights Act of 1964 (which protected against racial discrimination in federally funded programs) as well as his Fourteenth Amendment rights. Justice Powell found that Bakke's rejection from the medical school did indeed violate the Civil Rights Act and "set aside" the constitutionality issue altogether. Although the Supreme Court ruled in his favor, the decision was not considered a definitive victory against affirmative action.

The explanation of the verdict is significant for affirmative action and similar programs. Justice Powell did not issue a blanket statement prohibiting racial considerations in admission. Instead, he outlined the circumstances in which such considerations would be acceptable. First, the motivation would necessarily be focused on improving educational environment by incorporating diversity in the classroom. Secondly, the program could be established to provide future medical service to undeserved areas requiring racial specialization. Finally, the program could be instituted in an attempt to correct historically inflicted discrimination. Such programs would be required to provide specific rationale for preferential treatment. Above all, preferential programs would evaluate applicants *individually*, according to abilities and qualities.

It must be remembered that the applicants for admission in this time period were perhaps the first generation to enjoy a fully integrated educational experience. Educational opportunities were only just beginning to open up for these students. In fact, the dissenting justices in the *Regents* case provided statistics to verify the differences. Between the years of 1950 and 1970, black physicians comprised only 2.2% of the total number of physicians. In fact, according to the Court, "the number of Negro admittees to predominantly white medical schools had declined in absolute numbers during the years 1955 to 1964." Such statistics made a strong case for the preferential treatment called for by affirmative action to remedy these discrepancies.

Regents of the University of California vs. *Bakke*
438 U.S. 265, 98 S.Ct. 2733, 57 L.Ed. 2d 750 (1978)

MR. JUSTICE POWELL announced the judgment of the Court. . . .

Petitioner urges us to . . . hold that discrimination against members of the white "majority" cannot be suspect if its purpose can be characterized as "benign." The clock of our liberties, however, cannot be turned back to 1868. It is far too late to argue that the guarantee of equal protection to *all* persons permits the recognition of special wards entitled to a degree of protection greater than that accorded others. . . .

Once the artificial line of a "two-class theory" of the Fourteenth Amendment is put aside, the difficulties entailed in varying the level of judicial review according to a perceived "preferred" status of a particular racial or ethnic minority are intractable. The concepts of "majority" and "minority" necessarily reflect temporary arrangements and political judgments. As observed above, the white "majority" itself is composed of various minority groups, most of which can lay claim to a history of prior discrimination at the hands of the State and private individuals. . . . Courts would be asked to evaluate the extent of the prejudice and consequent harm suffered by various minority groups. Those whose societal injury is thought to exceed some arbitrary level of tolerability then would be entitled to preferential classifications at the expense of individuals belonging to other groups. Those classifications would be free from exacting judicial scrutiny. As these preferences began to have their desired effect, and the consequences of past discrimination were undone, new judicial rankings would be necessary. The kind of variable sociological and political analysis necessary to produce such rankings simply does not lie within the judicial competence even if they otherwise were politically feasible and socially desirable.

Moreover, there are serious problems of justice connected with the idea of preference itself. First, it may not always be clear that a so-called preference is in fact benign. . . . Second, preferential programs may only reinforce common stereotypes holding that certain groups are unable to achieve success without special protection based on a factor having no relationship to individual worth. Third, there is a measure of inequity in forcing innocent persons in respondent's position to bear the burdens of redressing grievances not of their making.

By hitching the meaning of the Equal Protection Clause to these transitory considerations, we would be holding, as a constitutional principle, that judicial scrutiny of classifications touching on racial and ethnic background may vary with the ebb and flow of political forces. . . .

We have held that in "order to justify the use of a suspect classification, a State must show that its purpose or interest is both constitutionally permissible and substantial, and that its use of the classification is 'necessary . . . to the accomplishment' of its purpose or the safeguarding of its interest." The special admissions program purports to serve the purposes of: (i) "reducing the historic deficit of traditionally disfavored minorities in medical schools and in the medical profession;" (ii) Countering the effects of societal discrimination; (iii) increasing the number of physicians who will practice in communities currently undeserved; and (iv) obtaining the educational benefits that flow from an ethnically diverse student body. It is necessary to decide which, if any, of these purposes is substantial enough to support the use of a suspect classification.

If petitioner's purpose is to assure within its student body some specified percentage of a particular group merely because of its race or ethnic origin, such a preferential purpose must be rejected not as insubstantial but as facially invalid. Preferring members of any one group for no reason other than race or ethnic origin is discrimination for its own sake. This the Constitution forbids. . . .

We have never approved a classification that aids persons perceived as members of relatively victimized groups at the expense of other innocent individuals in the absence of judicial, legislative, or administrative findings of constitutional or statutory violations. . . . Petitioner does not purport to have made, and is in no position to make, such findings. Its broad mission is education, not the formulation of any legislative policy or the adjudication of particular claims of illegality. . . . Petitioner simply has not carried its burden of demonstrating that it must prefer members of particular ethnic groups over all other individuals in order to promote better health-care delivery to deprived citizens. Indeed, petitioner has not shown that its preferential classification is likely to have any significant effect on the problem.

The fourth goal asserted by petitioner is the attainment of a diverse student body. This clearly is a constitutionally permissible goal for an institution of higher education.

. . . The diversity that furthers a compelling state interest encompasses a far broader array of qualifications and characteristics of which racial or ethnic origin is but a single though important element. Petitioner's special admissions program, focused *solely* on ethnic diversity, would hinder rather than further attainment of genuine diversity. Nor would the state interest in genuine diversity be served by expanding petitioner's two-track system into a multitrack program with a prescribed number of seats set aside for each identifiable category of applicants. Indeed, it is inconceivable that a university would thus pursue the logic of petitioner's two-track program to the illogical end of insulating each category of applicants with certain desired qualifications from competition with all other applicants. The experience of other university admissions programs, which take race into account in achieving the educational diversity valued by the First Amendment, demonstrates that the assignment of a fixed number of places to a minority group is not a necessary means toward that end. . . .

[R]ace or ethnic background may be deemed a "plus" in a particular applicant's file, yet it does not insulate the individual from comparison with all other candidates for the available seats. The file of a particular black applicant may be examined for his potential contribution to diversity without the factor of race being decisive when compared, for example, with that of an applicant identified as an Italian-American if the latter is thought to exhibit qualities more likely to promote beneficial educational pluralism. Such qualities could include exceptional talents, unique work or service experience, leadership potential, maturity, demonstrated compassion, a history of overcoming disadvantage, ability to communicate with the poor, or other qualifications deemed important. . . .

This kind of program treats each applicant as an individual in the admissions process. The applicant who loses out on the last available seat to another candidate receiving a "plus" on the basis of ethnic background will not have been foreclosed from all consideration for that seat simply because he was not the right color or had the wrong surname. It would mean only that his combined qualifications, which may have included similar nonobjective factors, did not outweigh those of the other applicant. His qualifications would have been weighed fairly and competitively, and he would have no basis to complain of unequal treatment under the Fourteenth Amendment. . . .

The fatal flaw in petitioner's preferential program is its disregard of individual rights as guaranteed by the Fourteenth Amendment. Such rights are not absolute. But when a State's distribution of benefits or imposition of burdens hinges on ancestry or the color of a person's skin or ancestry, that individual is entitled to a demonstration that the challenged classification is necessary to promote a substantial state interest. Petitioner has failed to carry this burden. For this reason, that portion of the California court's judgment holding petitioner's special admissions program invalid under the Fourteenth Amendment must be affirmed.

In enjoining petitioner from ever considering the race of any applicant, however, the courts below failed to recognize that the State has a substantial interest that legitimately may be served by a properly devised admissions program involving the competitive consideration of race and ethnic origin. For this reason, so much of the California court's judgment as enjoins petitioner from any consideration of the race of any applicant must be reversed. . . .

Joint opinion of MR. JUSTICE BRENNAN, MR. JUSTICE WHITE, MR. JUSTICE MARSHALL, and MR. JUSTICE BLACKMUN.

Texas v. *Johnson* (1989)

What kinds of emotions are summoned at the sight of a burning American flag? Amazement? Anger? Swellings of freedom? In 1989, *Texas* v. *Johnson,* would redefine the constitutionality of flag burning.

In 1984, a group of protesters gathered in front of Dallas City Hall, where the Republican National Convention was being held. President Ronald Reagan was a sure bet for the Republican nomination, a prospect that worried the demonstrators. Although enjoying enormous popularity, Reagan had chosen to attack communism in third world countries. He had already supported a 41 percent increase in defense spending and promised to add 17,000 nuclear weapons to the United States arsenal. The general consensus among American citizens, however, showed concern about increased aggression. Seventy percent of Americans favored "nuclear freeze" and 375,000 people had demonstrated in New York City to express their concerns.

Following the trend, Gregory Lee Johnson joined the protest in Texas. Taking to the streets of Dallas, the demonstrators entered buildings to stage "die-ins," emphasizing the human cost of nuclear warfare. A few protesters grabbed an American flag from one of the buildings and followed the group to the Republican National Convention at City Hall. While the demonstrators chanted, "America, the red, white, and blue, we spit on you," Johnson doused the flag in kerosene and set it ablaze.

Since Texas law prohibited such an act, Johnson was convicted for the violation and his case eventually reached the Supreme Court on appeal. Johnson claimed that his actions were protected by the First Amendment right to freedom of speech. The question at hand was whether or not the burning of a flag could be considered symbolic "speech." The Court decided that, "if there is a bedrock principle underlying the First Amendment, it is that the Government may not prohibit the expression of an idea simply because society finds the idea itself offensive or disagreeable." In other words, the flag does not symbolize one particular opinion or the status quo, but rather encompasses all views. The decision declared the flag nonpartisan.

Although *Texas* v. *Johnson,* overturned the Texas law, the Court was adamant in its view of the flag. While recognizing that the symbolic act of flag burning was covered by the First Amendment, the Court emphasized the sanctity of the flag as a symbol of national unity. The decision was not meant to undermine the meaning of the flag but to protect the freedoms it represented.

Texas v. *Johnson*

491 U.S. 397,109 S.Ct. 2533, 105 L.Ed. 2d 342 (1989)

Justice Brennan delivered the opinion of the Court.

While the Republican National Convention was taking place in Dallas in 1984, respondent Johnson participated in a political demonstration dubbed the "Republican War Chest Tour." As explained in literature distributed by the demonstrators and in speeches made by them, the purpose of this event was to protest the policies of the Reagan administration and of certain Dallas-based corporations. The demonstrators marched through the Dallas streets, chanting political slogans and stopping at several corporate locations to stage "die-ins" intended to dramatize the consequences of nuclear war. On several occasions they spray-painted the walls of buildings and overturned potted plants, but Johnson himself took no part in such activities. He did, however, accept an American flag handed to him by a fellow protester who had taken it from a flag pole outside one of the targeted buildings.

The demonstration ended in front of Dallas City Hall, where Johnson unfurled the American flag, doused it with kerosene, and set it on fire. While the flag burned, the protesters chanted, "America, the red, white, and blue, we spit on you." After the demonstrators dispersed, a witness to the flag-burning collected the flag's remains and buried them in his backyard. No one was physically injured or threatened with injury, though several witnesses testified that they had been seriously offended by the flag-burning.

Of the approximately 100 demonstrators, Johnson alone was charged with a crime. The only criminal offense with which he was charged was the desecration of a venerated object. . . .

Johnson was convicted of flag desecration for burning the flag rather than for uttering insulting words.* This fact somewhat complicates our consideration of his conviction under the First Amendment. We must first determine whether Johnson's burning of the flag constituted expressive conduct, permitting him to invoke the First Amendment in challenging his conviction. If his conduct was expressive, we next decide whether the State's regulation is related to the suppression of free expression. If the State's regulation is not related to expression, then the less stringent standard we announced in *O'Brien* for regulations of noncommunicative conduct controls. If it is, then we are outside of *O'Brien*'s test, and we must ask whether this interest justifies Johnson's conviction under a more demanding standard. A third possibility is that the State's asserted interest is simply not implicated on these facts, and in that event the interest drops out of the picture. . . .

In deciding whether particular conduct possesses sufficient communicative elements to bring the First Amendment into play, we have asked whether "[a]n intent to convey a particularized message was present, and [whether] the likelihood was great that the message would be understood by those who viewed it."

The State of Texas conceded for purposes of its oral argument in this case that Johnson's conduct was expressive conduct. . . .

In order to decide whether O'Brien's test applies here . . . we must decide whether Texas has asserted an interest in support of Johnson's conviction that is unrelated to the suppression of expression. . . . The State offers two separate interests to justify this conviction: preventing breaches of the peace, and preserving the flag as a symbol of nationhood and national unity. We hold that the first interest is not implicated on this record and that the second is related to the suppression of expression.

Texas claims that its interest in preventing breaches of the peace justifies Johnson's conviction for flag desecration. However, no disturbance of the peace actually occurred or threatened to occur because of Johnson's burning of the flag. . . . The only evidence offered by the State at trial to show the reaction to Johnson's actions was the testimony of several persons who had been seriously offended by the flag-burning.

The State's position, therefore, amounts to a claim that an audience that takes serious offense at particular expression is necessarily likely to disturb the peace and that the expression may be prohibited on this basis. . . . [W]e have not permitted the Government to assume that every expression of a provocative idea will incite a riot, but have instead required careful consideration of the actual circumstances surrounding such expression, asking whether the expression "is directed to inciting or producing imminent lawless action and is likely to incite or produce such action." To accept Texas' arguments that it need only demonstrate "the potential for a breach of the peace," and that every flag-burning necessarily possesses that potential, would be to eviscerate our holding in *Brandenburg.* This we decline to do.

Nor does Johnson's expressive conduct fall within that small class of "fighting words" that are "likely to provoke the average person to retaliation, and thereby cause a breach of the peace." No reasonable onlooker would have regarded Johnson's generalized expression of dissatisfaction with the policies of the Federal Government as a direct personal insult or an invitation to exchange fisticuffs.

We thus conclude that the State's interest in maintaining order is not implicated on these facts. . . .

The State also asserts an interest in preserving the flag as a symbol of nationhood and national unity. . . . The State, apparently, is concerned that such conduct will lead people to believe either that the flag does not stand for nationhood and national unity, but instead reflects other, less positive concepts, or that the concepts reflected in the flag do not in fact exist, that is, we do not enjoy unity as a Nation. These concerns blossom only when a person's treatment of the flag communicates some message, and thus are related "to the suppression of free expression" within the meaning of *O'Brien.* We are thus outside of *O'Brien*'s test altogether.

It remains to consider whether the State's interest in preserving the flag as a symbol of nationhood and national unity justifies Johnson's conviction. . . . The Texas law is thus not aimed at protecting the physical integrity of the flag in all circumstances, but is designed instead to protect it only against impairments that would cause serious offense to others. Texas concedes as much: "The statute mandates intentional or knowing abuse, that is, the kind of mistreatment that is not innocent, but rather is intentionally designed to seriously offend other individuals."

Whether Johnson's treatment of the flag violated Texas law thus depended on the likely communicative impact of his expressive conduct. Our decision in *Boos* v. *Barry* [1988] tells us that this restriction on Johnson's expression is content-based. In *Boos,* we considered the constitutionality of a law prohibiting "the display of any sign within 50 feet of a foreign embassy if that sign tends to bring that foreign government into 'public odium' or 'public disrepute.'" Rejecting the argument that the law was content-neutral because it was justified by "our international law obligation to shield diplomats from speech that offends their dignity," we held that "[t]he emotive impact of speech on its audience is not a 'secondary effect'" unrelated to the content of the expression itself.

According to the principles announced in *Boos*, Johnson's political expression was restricted because of the content of the message he conveyed. We must therefore subject the State's asserted interest in preserving the special symbolic character of the flag to "the most exacting scrutiny."

According to Texas, if one physically treats the flag in a way that would tend to cast doubt on either the idea that nationhood and national unity are the flag's referents or that national unity actually exists, the message conveyed thereby is a harmful one and therefore may be prohibited.

If there is a bedrock principle underlying the First Amendment, it is that the Government may not prohibit the expression of an idea simply because society finds the idea itself offensive or disagreeable. We have not recognized an exception to this principle even where our flag has been involved. . . . We never before have held that the Government may ensure that a symbol be used to express only one view of that symbol or its referents. . . .

To conclude that the Government may permit designated symbols to be used to communicate only a limited set of messages would be to enter territory having no discernible or defensible boundaries. Could the Government, on this theory, prohibit the burning of state flags? Of copies of the Presidential seal? Of the Constitution? In evaluating these choices under the First Amendment, how would we decide which symbols were sufficiently special to warrant this unique status? To do so we would be forced to consult our own political preferences, and impose them on the citizenry, in the very way that the First Amendment forbids us to do.

There is, moreover, no indication—either in the text of the Constitution or in our cases interpreting it—that a separate juridical category exists for the American flag alone. Indeed, we would not be surprised to learn that the persons who framed our Constitution and wrote the Amendment that we now construe were not known for their reverence for the Union Jack. The First Amendment does not guarantee that other concepts virtually sacred to our Nation as a whole—such as the principle that discrimination on the basis of race is odious and destructive—will go unquestioned in the marketplace of ideas. We decline, therefore, to create for the flag an exception to the joust of principles protected by the First Amendment.

It is not the State's ends, but its means, to which we object. It cannot be gainsaid that there is a special place reserved for the flag in this Nation, and thus we do not doubt that the Government has a legitimate interest in making efforts to "preserv[e] the national flag as an unalloyed symbol of our country." We reject the suggestion, urged at oral argument by counsel for Johnson, that the Government lacks "any state interest whatsoever" in regulating the manner in which the flag may be displayed. Congress has, for example, enacted precatory regulations describing the proper treatment of the flag, and we cast no doubt on the legitimacy of its interest in making such recommendations. To say that the Government has an interest in encouraging proper treatment of the flag, however, is not to say that it may criminally punish a person for burning a flag as a means of political protest. "National unity as an end which officials may foster by persuasion and example is not in question. The problem is whether under our Constitution compulsion as here employed is a permissible means for its achievement." . . .

The way to preserve the flag's special role is not to punish those who feel differently about these matters. It is to persuade them that they are wrong. . . . And, precisely because it is our flag that is involved, one's response to the flag-burner may exploit the uniquely persuasive power of the flag itself. We can imagine no more appropriate response to burning a flag than waving one's own, no better way to counter a flag-burner's message than by saluting the flag that burns, no surer means of preserving the dignity even of the flag that burned than by—as one witness here did—according its remains a respectful burial. We do not consecrate the flag by punishing its desecration, for in doing so we dilute the freedom that this cherished emblem represents. . . .

The judgment of the Texas Court of Criminal Appeals is therefore

Affirmed.

THE POLITICAL-ECONOMIC PROBLEM

Gary Daynes

No decision is ever a purely economic decision. Because all people live in a world of scarcity, where unlimited desires cannot be met by limited resources, people must decide what will be produced, how it will be produced, and who will have access to it. When a group of people have to make these sorts of decisions, they make the decisions through some sort of political process. Thus the effort to find a way in which goods and services can be exchanged efficiently, equitably, and with a considerable amount of freedom is a political and an economic problem.

No one would want to make all economic decisions through a political process (think of how hard it is to decide where you and your roommates are going to eat dinner). Instead, nations choose the type of economic system they wish to use, and then let others decide what to produce and what to consume. Although there are variety of economic systems from which a society may choose, nearly all decisions fall under one of two basic categories—the market economy or the planned economy. The former system is based on voluntary exchange under rules set by the market. The United States is an example of a nation that uses a market economic system. In a planned economy, the government decides what will be produced and who will produce it. The governments of China and Cuba plan a large portion of their nations' production. Neither system perfectly blends efficiency, equity, and freedom. And so, no economy today is based entirely on a market or planned system.

What follows are a series of essays that help to illustrate the political-economic problem and the difficulty of deciding between market and planned systems. Various strengths and weaknesses of each system can be seen in many of the case studies.

"From Each According to . . . , To Each According to . . ."?

Choosing the right mix of government and free enterprise involves questions of economics, philosophy, and politics. Economic incentives can lead to the success or downfall of political systems.

The *Communist Manifesto* was written by Karl Marx and Friedrich Engels in 1847 as a proclamation for the League of the Just, a secret international organization aimed at overcoming the exploitation of labor. The *Communist Manifesto* was a short book—little more than a pamphlet by today's standards. However, its influence in the field of political economy for a time rivaled Adam Smith's very lengthy *The Wealth of Nations,* first published in 1776. *Political economy* was the term used in the eighteenth and nineteenth centuries to describe the study of what we now call economics. Even today, some use the term to accentuate the close ties between economic analysis and public policy. Nowhere are these ties more apparent than in the two books just mentioned.

On the one hand, The Wealth of Nations provided the intellectual basis for the system of free markets found in the U.S. Constitution. James Madison, Thomas Jefferson, and the other founding fathers were well acquainted with Adam Smith's analysis of the virtues of competitive markets. On the other hand, the *Communist Manifesto* served as the intellectual basis for a very different kind of government, one founded on the notion of class warfare between owners of capital and labor resources. This idea was used to justify a strong central government that would allocate resources equitably. Equity was taken to mean, as Karl Marx stated in 1875, "from each according to his abilities, to each according to his needs."

The Communist Philosophy . . .

All I ask is a tall ship and a star to steer her by.
—John Masefield, 1878–1967, poet

What does a person need? A chicken in every pot? Will rice and beans do? A glass of wine and a loaf of bread? Love? Peace and quiet? We each have different ideas when it comes to fulfilling our personal needs. People want more, and yet make do with less. How is a government to know about diverse needs?

Partly because needs are so hard to pin down, the task of following Marx's philosophy has proved difficult in practice. The result is that Marxist governments have tended to expound a philosophy of **egalitarianism**, in which everyone is supposed to get the same access to everything from soap to medical care. If people can make do with what they get, they must be getting what they need, right?

. . . ignores Personal Incentives . . .

The problem with using egalitarianism as the rule to allocate a country's output is that egalitarianism provides no incentive for people to be productive. If a country distributes the same amounts to all, its people are not motivated to do their best. Since the Communist credo requires that each person produce according to that person's abilities, the lack of incentives to do so became a serious problem.

In a communist economy, smart people act stupid. The reason is simple. The smarter you act, the more will be expected of you. To live well, you are well advised to keep your head down and act as if you're no better than anyone else. It used to be said in the former Soviet Union that those whose heads stuck above the crowd got them chopped off!

. . . and Led to Its Own Collapse

With a central authority attempting to direct the what, how, and for whom of production, bad choices were made and resources were squandered. Everyone had a job, but productivity and purchasing power lagged badly. As put by disgruntled workers in Eastern Europe and the Soviet Union, "We pretend to work, and they pretend to pay us."

Actually, the USSR was quite effective at spurring economic growth when the problem was lack of physical capital, such as tractors. Indeed, the Soviet Union became known for its tractor factories. But a modern economy requires education, training, and the freedom and incentive to express creativity. On this score, communism failed badly.

It was small wonder that, over time, the comparatively free markets of the West led to a dramatically better standard of living than was available in the communist economies of the East. Exposed to this better way of life through the global reach of the media, residents of Eastern Europe and the Soviet Union became disillusioned with communism. Cynicism reigned. When the Communist apparatus was in jeopardy and it seemed safe to do so, there was a groundswell of support for its demise. Communism was not a philosophy worth fighting for, and so it collapsed with only a whimper.

Still, there is nostalgia for the relative order and security that was provided by the Communist State. While living standards were low, life was not crassly commercial. The stress of getting ahead in the job market or business world was absent, since opportunities were confined to the Communist party. Moreover, the advent of comparatively free markets has been rough, with many people finding their paltry living standards declining still further. Then, too, there is the matter of pride. With insufficient conviction to rally to the philosophy of communism, many former Communists have instead turned to the rallying cry of nationalism, risking its attendant danger of war. This risk was fulfilled in the conflict between the Serbs, Croats, and Bosnians in the former communist country of Yugoslavia.

The Marketplace Is Better at "from Each" . . .

Nationalism does not by itself answer the economic questions of resource allocation. Whatever their governmental leanings, nations can choose their own economic system. They are usually well served to allow relatively free markets, if their goal is to get the most value for their citizens from the resources they possess. Even China recognized this fact, leaving behind Mao Tse Tung's castigation of "Capitalist Roaders" in favor of moving in the direction of free markets.

Free markets offer people opportunity—the opportunity to get ahead or to fall behind. The market rewards people who use their abilities to satisfy their fellow citizens, so long as that satisfaction is embodied in a good or service that can be sold in the marketplace. "Build a better mousetrap, and the world will beat a path to your door."

The free market does not work through altruism. Rather, as Adam Smith put it, it is as though producers are guided by an invisible hand. The invisible hand of the marketplace means that people acting in their own self-interests will more effectively serve the public interest than could even the most well-meaning of governments or altruistic of philanthropists. In the marketplace, the myriad of decisions by individual customers determines what is and is not valuable enough to produce. The marketplace rewards those best able to offer goods and services of value to others. The better a person is at providing value to others, the more will be that person's income. In this way, each person has an incentive to develop his or her productive potential.

. . . but Lacks Compassion

Firms in the private marketplace offer products that people are willing to pay for or they go out of business. The money to pay for successful products comes from incomes or inheritances that depend upon people's abilities. The marketplace rewards ability with more income. That seems fair, to some extent.

The problem arises that, through no fault of their own, people do not all have the same potential. Furthermore, people may develop their potentials in ways that seem productive at the time, but turn out not to be. For example, elevator operators found their skills obsolete when the ingenuity of manufacturers created automatic elevators. That example reflects the changing opportunities in society, but hardly seems fair to many of the people whose livelihoods are involved.

In other cases people find themselves with disabilities that prevent them from reaching their full potential to provide for others. This situation does not mean that they are worth any less as humans, although the free market tends to pay them less. Again, that does not seem fair. Likewise, situations can arise in most people's lives that prevent them from following their desired paths. The free market appears not to care.

While not immoral, the market is amoral—it seems to turn a blind eye to questions of equity. Sometimes the market seems fair, such as by rewarding those who follow through on ideas that are of benefit to others. However, the free market is fair only by coincidence. Many issues of equity must be addressed through other means.

Attempts by Government to Correct Inequities . . .

Private charities are an attempt to correct inequities. Still, many people think that fairness requires help from all who have the ability. Enter government, with its ability to tax. Specifically, government imposes taxes that take from those who can afford to give and that give to those in need.

There's that word, again—need! What is a need? To the extent that government seeks to take from each in accordance with ability and give to each according to need, it finds itself back in the communist dilemma. Government becomes the arbiter of what people need. Government also becomes a drag on productivity, which leads modern economies to search for the mix in the middle. On the one hand, pure communism shrinks the economic pie badly. On the other hand, laissez-faire capitalism bakes a big pie, but may slice it very unequally.

. . . bring Tough Choices

How does a government decide where to draw the line on taxes and redistributional spending? In the political process, it may look to voters. Some voters will always want more redistribution; others will desire less. In many cases, the amount of redistribution depends upon the taxes that the individual voters expect to face. Low-income voters tend to want more and high-income voters less. It is the voters in the middle who usually decide elections. Where that middle lies will be affected by the extent to which those voters are paying burdensome taxes. It also depends on perceptions among those voters about whether high taxes along with generous spending make staying in poverty too easy and escaping it too difficult.

Rawls' Philosophy of the Original Position Can Illuminate . . .

Does political economy offer any help in making these choices? Perhaps economic philosophy can once more shed some light. In particular, imagine that we place ourselves in the **original position**. As described by twentieth-century political philosopher John Rawls, the original position occurs prior to when we have assumed identities as separate people. We do not know who we will become nor how much of those qualities that help us become wealthy we would have. From that position, we must contemplate the risk of becoming an individual the free market leaves behind. Of course, we could also be someone able to thrive in the marketplace.

. . . the Nature of the Trade-offs We Face . . .

The original position gives us a unique perspective. We might be at either the receiving or giving end of the tax system. What kinds of government policies would we support?

We would not want to be left out in the cold. For this reason, Rawls suggests that we choose a *maxi-min* philosophy, in which government attempts to maximize the well-being of the least well-off person in the economy, the person on the bottom rung of the economic ladder. The focus would be on improving the lot of those who are worst off, whoever they may be.

Alternatively, since the size of the economic pie is generally larger when government keeps taxes low, we might choose to take our chances. After all, while the risk is higher, so is the expected standard of living. We also might doubt government's ability to identify the needy. We might even mistrust government's will to fairly implement a policy to reward the neediest, even if identifying them were possible.

Most likely, we would choose a *safety net* to protect us from some but not all risks. This approach is the basis for such government programs as unemployment insurance and Social Security. We also figure that individuals are better positioned to know their own needs than government could ever be. Thus we want freedom and opportunity to go along with security.

. . . but We Will Still Argue

Exactly how much freedom and opportunity should we mix with exactly how much insurance against life's pitfalls? Debate will continue on and on and on. The issues are important to our lives, and we will have different perspectives. On that we can agree.

Crime and the Market for Drugs

The war on drugs causes expenditures on drugs to increase. Increased spending on drugs increases the crime and violence that the war on drugs is intended to fight.

The United States has the highest proportion of its citizens behind bars of any "first-world" country. Sixty percent of those prisoners are convicted on drug-related charges. It sometimes appears that recreational drugs are ripping apart our social fabric. Yet, the more we fight the problem, the worse it seems. How can this be?

Many images come to mind when the word *drugs* is mentioned. There are the wonder drugs that have helped the sick. There is the contrasting image of eggs in the frying pan—"your brain on drugs." The violence of the drug cartels involved in the production and sale of cocaine and the pathos of the cocaine babies born to addicted mothers both come to mind. There are the AIDS patients who have shared dirty needles and the thieves stealing to support their habits. Also woven in are the counterculture of the 1960s and the creativity of such classic writers and poets as Edgar Allen Poe and Samuel Coleridge.

We need to do some sorting. Suppose we put aside questions of whether drug use is moral and of where to draw the line on drug laws. Instead, let's employ economic analysis to solve the dilemma of why toughening up our enforcement of drug laws seems to make drug-related problems worse. Then we will examine the implications of changing the direction of public policy away from the so-called drug war.

The Market for Drugs . . .

Illegal drugs are sold in markets, in many ways much like the markets for other goods. One difference is that information is not readily available about sources of supply, since this information could be used by law enforcement agencies. Nor is product quality ensured by government regulation or legal recourse. In the drug market, it is truly **caveat emptor**—let the buyer beware!

One consequence is that drug users tend to connect with only one or two dealers, who then have an interest in maintaining quality standards to ensure the customer comes back. In turn, most dealers are connected to only one or two wholesalers. Since competition keeps prices down, this reduction of competition causes higher prices.

. . . Sees Violent Crime on the Supply Side . . .

On the supply side of the marketplace, government enforcement of drug laws pushes prices up even more dramatically by increasing the risk associated with dealing drugs. This will drive out the most *risk averse* suppliers and add a **risk premium** to prices. Who will remain? Some remaining suppliers will be those who shrug off the risk, perhaps because they enjoy it or have become accustomed to the lifestyle. For the most part, however, competition will select those suppliers who are best at circumventing the law. Usually that involves the insurance of hooking up with a powerful criminal organization.

From street gangs on up to the reputed drug Mafia, organized crime flourishes under tough drug law enforcement. These organizations offer both connections and firepower to the dealers. In addition, because the drug dealer cannot turn to the police for protection, that dealer becomes easy prey for organized criminals. Here is one source of crime associated with drugs—turf battles in which criminal organizations seek to dominate the sales of drugs in an area.

While having criminals killing criminals could be the subject of an intriguing debate, there are also unintended third parties who get caught in the crossfire. Furthermore, the survivors are those criminals who are best at violence. We see this in the violence of the drug trade along the U.S. border with Mexico and within Colombia, the major source of cocaine.

—Witness Colombia—

In Colombia, the dominance of the Medellin drug cartel came to an end with the gunning down of Pablo Escobar, the drug king. Although the dominance of the Medellin cartel merely gave way to dominance by the rival Cali cartel, most people breathed a sigh of relief. After all, the Cali cartel was known to be less violent.

Quickly after the Cali cartel came to prominence, the bosses of that cartel sought government clemency. After all, life had become dangerous for them, and they were already rich. Was this the end of drug violence in Colombia?

Unfortunately, a new generation of brutal gun-toting drug lords has replaced the old guard of the Cali cartel. The harsh law enforcement had driven out all but the most violence-prone from the top ranks of the leading cartel. Thus, while the new drug lords have teamed to avoid directing the wrath of the world at any one of them personally, the overall climate of violence in Colombia's drug-producing areas continues unabated.

. . . Crime for Cash to Buy Drugs, . . .

Why is there drug-related crime by drug users? Perhaps a small fraction has to do with the drugs impairing the user's judgment. Far and away the primary cause, however, is money. Tough enforcement of the drug laws makes it much more expensive to support a drug habit.

Drug users are often addicted to the drugs they use and would go to great lengths to avoid doing without. In other words, the demand for drugs is inelastic because the quantity purchased does not drop proportionally to increases in price. This means that, the tougher we enforce our drug laws, the more money drug users need. Moreover, the tougher we punish a convicted drug offender for the drug use itself, the less the user cares about adding other crimes to the list. Thus, while many addicts can support their habits with legally earned income, others think little of resorting to robberies, burglaries, and other crimes.

. . . and More Addictive Drugs

Tough enforcement of our drug laws has also had the perverse effect of increasing the popularity of the most highly addictive drugs. This effect occurs as users substitute more addictive drugs for less addictive ones. Why would users want to do this?

The answer has to do with bulk. The bulkier the drug, the more likely it is to be intercepted. This is why marijuana grown in the U.S. today is likely to be much more potent than that grown in the 1960s. More potent drugs cut down on bulk. Unfortunately, the least bulky drugs also tend to be the most addictive. For instance, "cracking" cocaine to form crack requires only a small amount of cocaine, a drug with very little bulk. The relatively lower cost and highly addictive nature of crack has led it to pervade the cities of our country.

Tough enforcement of drug laws causes more violence on the supply side, more money-related crime by addicts, and substitution of more addictive drugs. What about the alternative route of backing off on law enforcement efforts, or even of legalizing some or all drugs altogether?

There are Alternatives to the Current War on Drugs . . .

There are numerous possible drug control policies between the current war on drugs and a *laissez faire* hands off strategy. At the extreme, if all drugs were legalized, that would seem to suggest including prescription pharmaceuticals. Should drugstores allow the customer to point and buy "three of those green ones, one of those big red capsules, and twelve of the yellow ones with dots?" In this portion of the Exploration, we look at the implications of moving away from the current war on drugs without specifying the details of how far that movement goes.

Figure 3B1-1 depicts the market for drugs, where the model is deliberately nonspecific as to exactly what sort of drugs these are. The addictive nature of drugs leads to an inelastic demand curve. The market price and quantity of drugs in the free market, denoted Pfm and Qfm, is determined by the intersection of free market supply and demand. The drug war, denoted by subscript dw, causes the price to be higher and the quantity to be lower, *ceteris paribus.*

. . . that Might or Might Not Increase Usage

Relative to the outcome under the drug war, the free market would appear to offer both good news and bad news. The good news is that the quantity of spending, given by P multiplied by Q, would be lower without the drug war. This means less crime to raise money to buy drugs. Since drugs would be sold by legitimate businesses in the free market, the violent territorial crime of the drug rings would also largely disappear. The bad news is that drug use would rise, *ceteris paribus,* because demand always shows an inverse relationship between price and quantity.

Keep in mind that the demand curve keeps constant everything but price. But moving away from the drug war entails more than just a drop in price. For example, the entire demand curve would shift outward to the extent that users no longer fear being arrested, which would lead to greater usage. Alternatively, the demand curve might shift inward to the extent that drug usage constitutes less of an antiauthority rebellion and is seen more as a matter of responsible personal behavior.

Drug Pushers Would Lose Their Jobs at School . . .

There is another factor that would shift demand inward, one that obliterates one of the most disreputable groups in our society. Specifically, without the risk premium on prices to pay for their fancy cars and lavish lifestyles, drug pushers would be out of business. There would be no incentive to lure schoolchildren to drug use, because there would be no money in it. Without their wads of cash and the power it buys, pushers would lose their ill-bought status as role models for many of our children. Free from the pressure of pushers, and without drugs exemplifying rebellion against authority, fewer kids would turn to drugs. How far this change would shift the demand curve in, though, is anybody's guess.

Some people suggest legalization of many drugs, but only if we impose high sales taxes to discourage purchases and pay for drug-related problems. This policy would be akin to taxing cigarettes in proportion to their **external costs**—those not captured in the marketplace. While taxes can be reasonable, a prohibitively high tax would reopen the doors to criminal pushers and modern-day bootleggers.

Interestingly, some of the biggest unseen proponents of tough drug laws are the drug pushers and their suppliers. Do you know why? Without tough drug laws, these dealers would be out of business. Of course proponents include others with much purer intentions. As the saying goes, "Politics makes strange bedfellows."

. . . and Free Markets Would Keep Usage Down in the Workplace . . .

Moving away from the drug war toward legalization does raise many questions. Some people are concerned about whether quality would diminish in the workplace, especially when that quality involves personal safety. For example, with drug use legal, what would prevent aircraft maintenance and flight crews from being so "stoned" that it would be unsafe to fly in their planes?

The answer is that, without government prohibitions, the free market would provide its own incentives for a clear-headed workforce. The incredibly high cost of a plane crash in terms of replacing the equipment and settling lawsuits would give airlines strong incentives to screen their personnel for drugs, alcohol, or other judgment-impairing problems. In general, companies that employ workers with impaired judgment would lose out in the competitive marketplace to those firms that are more effective at screening out problem workers.

. . . but Problems of Addiction Will Persist

Legal or illegal, drugs do cause problems for both users and innocent victims. For example, driving-under-the-influence laws have reduced but not eliminated problems of drunk driving. Would a similar approach provide pedestrians and other drivers adequate protection from drivers hallucinating under the influence of LSD?

Questions of law aside, recreational drugs are the source of serious problems. For example, everyone's heart goes out to babies born addicted to cocaine. Viewing addicted babies and other heart-wrenching consequences of addiction can evoke a rage in which drug abuse becomes something to be wiped out at all costs. Should we act on that rage and escalate the current war on drugs? Alternatively, would backing off on the drug war lead to less addiction and more voluntary treatment? You be the judge.

Empowering the Consumer—Vouchers for Education

The market for primary and secondary education is both similar to, and different from, other markets. A school voucher plan can promote competition and choice at the levels of primary and secondary education.

For most goods and services, consumers know what they buy. With education, in contrast, the idea is to learn. Consumers cannot know exactly what that learning will be. If they did, they would not need to learn it.

To the extent possible, consumers do pick and choose when it comes to education. While most apparent at the college level, consumers also try to be selective at the elementary and high school levels. For example, consumers seek to live in public school districts with the best reputations, which drives up property values in those districts. Public schools also face competition from private schools. Private schools are frequently perceived as a **superior good.** Superior goods are normal goods that people buy more than in proportion to increases in their incomes. This explains why private schools are able to charge high tuitions and still attract students from the free public schools.

Efficiency in the marketplace comes about through competition. Competition would be more intense if private and public schools each had equal access to tax dollars. Should public policy promote competition in this way and let parents and students pick the winners?

The Demand Side and the Public Interest

Demand for education depends upon income and wealth. Thus, whatever the price of educational quality, the quantities chosen will be less in poor neighborhoods than in rich ones. Likewise, residents of poorer neighborhoods choose to buy lower quality cuts of meat and models of automobiles than do their counterparts in wealthier neighborhoods. This is the marketplace in action.

While most of us want others to have opportunities for adequate incomes, we do not usually focus our concerns on the types of vehicles they drive or on whether they choose hamburger or steak. In contrast, we do worry about variations in the quality of education between rich and poor districts. The reason is that, unlike most other goods that parents buy, education is likely to have a long-lasting impact on the prosperity of their children. Indeed, kids that are forced to make do with low-quality food and second- hand autos may be motivated to strive harder to succeed in life. In contrast, with defective educational tools and without being stimulated to learn more on their own, children with inferior educations possess less opportunity for future success.

Public schools are usually financed through local property taxes, which are at the discretion of local voters. Because demand for education is lower in poor districts, voters choose smaller budgets per pupils in those districts. In order to increase demand, poor school districts' resources are sometimes augmented with wealth transfers from elsewhere. These transfers can take many forms, such as grants from higher levels of government to low-income school districts, or even inclusion of some of the richer districts' property on the tax rolls of poorer districts.

Robin Hood plans that take from purportedly rich school districts and give to poor ones have some obvious appeal. Especially to those on the receiving end of the transfers, the plans seem fair. However, three cautions are in order. First, to the extent government transfers incomes from the haves to the have-nots, it is also taking away incentives to work hard and get ahead. If these policies are carried to the extreme of complete egalitarianism, in which everyone is guaranteed as much wealth as everyone else, there would be no incentive to work. National output would drop to nearly nothing, and we would all be equally impoverished.

A second caution has to do with the nature of collective choice. If most voters think that the level of spending they choose will be paid in part with money from elsewhere, they will choose to spend more because the price to them is lower. People are not as careful with other people's money as with their own.

The third caution concerns choice of family size. Again, the issue is one of price. To the extent that government helps pay for education, it is paying part of the cost of raising children. Parents then have less incentive to limit the size of their families. This is the law of demand in action. As the price of having children drops, the quantity chosen increases.

The Supply Side—Choice at a Price

Like all markets, the market for education is composed of a demand side and a supply side. As we have seen, the demand side is much like that of other markets, except that government has more interest in the amount people choose to purchase. On the supply side, however, the market for primary and secondary education in the United States differs dramatically from other markets. The reasons revolve around government.

The invisible hand of the free market achieves efficiency by allowing profit-seeking firms to compete for the affections of the consumer. Successful firms provide products that are the most valuable to consumers. Unfortunately, there is very little competition in the markets for primary and secondary education in the U.S.

While consumers are free to shop around for schools, the price is high. For instance, to switch from one "free" public school to another, parent-consumers must pull up their stakes and relocate. The monetary and nonmonetary costs of that action could be daunting. Alternatively, the parents could send their children to one of a handful of accessible private schools. Here too, considering tuition and transportation expenditures, the cost of choice is still quite high.

The result is that, rather than effective competition in the marketplace, primary and secondary education is provided largely through the "command and control" mechanism of government. This does not mean that those in education are not motivated to do right by the children in their classes. Still, because different people have different perspectives on educational quality, it is likely that the characteristics of education in America today would change if more competition were allowed.

Many educators point to the expertise of educational professionals as reason enough for them to call the shots. Other educators are more supportive, seeing competition as providing the checks and balances that keep expenses down and quality up. For evidence they point to statistics showing that public schools spend much more per pupil than do private schools, despite the private schools having a better reputation for quality. They say that parents should be allowed to shop for the best value in schools. Would parents shop well, or would the experts pick better?

School Vouchers Let the Parents Decide

To bring about more competition, government could issue vouchers for education—educational vouchers or school vouchers for short. **Vouchers** specify an amount that the holder can spend, but restrict that spending to a certain category of goods. For example, food stamps are vouchers that low-income recipients are allowed to use toward food purchases. School vouchers would be issued free of charge to parents on the basis of the grade levels of their children and would be spendable only on education for those children.

The amount of educational vouchers could vary, but might best be set equal to the estimated cost of providing a basic level of education for the appropriate grade level. Some parents, such as those of physically challenged children, would receive larger vouchers to compensate for their children's special needs. Vouchers could then be spent for education at the specified grade level in any accredited school. Parents would be free to supplement vouchers with extra money of their own. In this way, schools would compete to receive parents' vouchers. Schools could no longer count on politically defined school districts to provide them with a captive group of customers.

With a voucher plan in place, there would no longer be a necessity for the government to own any public schools. Not only would the operation of the schools be driven by market demand, but so too would their locations and designs. Despite its advantages, however, such a radical change from the status quo might prove difficult to get through the political process. Most actual legislative proposals for school vouchers retain support for publicly owned schools.

What of religion? Would allowing parents to spend their vouchers on church-run schools violate the separation of church and state that Americans hold dear? To answer this question, consider where the voucher money comes from. Under the present system, taxpayers pay for the public schools and get their money back only if they send their children there. In other words, the government takes taxpayers' money and offers to return it only if they keep their children out of religious or other private schools. That policy can be viewed as actively discouraging religion.

The basic notion of vouchers is much more evenhanded. With a pure voucher system, taxpayers are offered the opportunity to get their tax money back if they send children to any school, public or private. It would no longer be relevant whether the school is religious or sectarian.

Curiously, most existing and proposed voucher plans would explicitly restrict spending to government-owned public schools.

The Spectrum of Control

Some people worry that vouchers would lead to segregated, unequal schools. These critics imagine a collection of elitist schools filled with the most gifted. Alongside would be other schools for the "leftovers," those whose parents don't care, those with learning disabilities, immigrants with language difficulties, etc. Must vouchers lead to such a grim outcome?

The answer is that vouchers are very flexible and can be designed to meet a wide variety of objectives. For example, vouchers could be specified to apply only to schools meeting certain educational standards. Those standards need not be restricted to academic coverage, but could also include admission policies and actions to promote diversity. Indeed, anything required of our current system of public and private schools can be incorporated into vouchers, too.

While it is necessary to tie vouchers to some legitimate criteria of what schooling should consist of, there is a danger in going too far toward command and control. If we rigidly specify exactly what a school must do to qualify for voucher expenditures, then we lose the invisible hand of the marketplace that provides products consumers want. Choice has value to consumers. That value will be lost if the educational products must by law be identical.

As an example, consider mainstreaming, a philosophy that is currently popular among educators. Mainstreaming consists of placing physically challenged students in the same classes as everyone else, rather than isolating them in separate classes. Interpreters or other aides provide special assistance as necessary. The idea is to promote tolerance and prevent stigmatization. Opponents claim that the challenged are often better able to advance if grouped according to their special needs. Those holding this view would argue that the hard-of-hearing, for instance, perform better and feel better about themselves in classes designed exclusively for them.

Should we all debate this issue and then mandate one philosophy over another? The alternative is to let the marketplace make the decision. Some schools would offer one approach; others would offer the other. Parents, gauging their own children's experiences, would over time move their children to the schools offering what they perceive as the better way. This is what the marketplace does well, if allowed the opportunity.

Would a school voucher plan wreak havoc on school busing? After all, it would hardly make sense to have multiple bus systems crisscrossing one another so as to pick up scattered clusters of kids. That would mean more gas, wasted time, and a wastefully large number of buses. Someone would have to pay for that busing.

Again, the marketplace has the answer. Schools that locate near one another at relatively central locations could share the same bus routes. Third-party operators of school buses would contract their services to more than one school. Schools that save time and money in this manner would find themselves with a competitive advantage over those that do not. In short, rather than being wasteful, the marketplace is likely to offer an improvement over politically located schools. The invisible hand of the marketplace would position schools in areas that provide the most net value to their customers.

Who Should Do the Choosing?

The marketplace promotes diversity. When it comes to purely personal goods, such as what shows to watch and what to eat for dinner, diversity obviously promotes our wellbeing. However, education is not purely personal. To the extent that parents choose for their children, it is the children that bear most of the consequences of that choice. Allowing not-yet-educated children to choose on their own does not seem to offer much of an alternative. Yet, leaving school choice to the collective public sector raises the specter of unresponsive bureaucracies that trap the poor but not the rich. How much weight should be assigned to each concern is a matter of hot debate.

Adjusting to Technological Change—Lessons from the Family Farm

Despite costly subsidies paid to farmers, family farming has continued its steady decline. Rather than teach farmers how to survive, government might learn from farmers about how to cope with its own problems.

The country, indeed much of the world, is fed by crops grown on American farms. You might think that farmers would be handsomely rewarded for keeping the rest of us from starvation. Some farmers are wealthy. They are the survivors of an exodus from farming that has seen the farm population dwindle from 30 percent of the U.S. population in 1920 to less than 2 percent today. Even so, we have seen various events organized to raise money to ease the financial pain felt by the many smaller farmers who must struggle to stay afloat.

Competitive pressures in the marketplace have brought about this disturbing state of affairs. Have government policies helped or merely compounded the problems? There are lessons to be learned down on the farm, lessons that concern the adjustments of markets to technological change. Change is necessary, but disruptive. The sturdy farmer has faced it directly. Government, too, has learned from those experiences.

Farm Aid—Willie Nelson and Company Didn't Get There First

In recent years, singer Willie Nelson assembled the major stars of country music to perform concerts under the Farm Aid banner. The purpose of these shows was to raise money to promote family farming. It would seem that everyone admires such activities. Only the heartless could ignore the sight of farmers and their families packing up their belongings and moving from foreclosed farms. It's more than a job that is lost; it's a way of life, one that lots of city folks admire.

There is a puzzle, though. Aid for American farmers has been around for many decades. Franklin Delano Roosevelt's New Deal of the 1930s aimed to solve some of the same problems that continue to plague the farm sector today. Other farm programs even predate the New Deal era. Despite government farm aid, though, problems continue to plague the family farmer.

Fewer Farm Families, More Food

Sometimes markets work so well that old problems are replaced by new ones that are just as troublesome as the old. In fanning the problem is too much good land. It is easy, but not quite correct, to think of land as a fixed resource. After all, there are only so many acres of land. Unless the U.S. follows the example of the Netherlands and reclaims land from the sea, there is no possibility of increased supplies of land. Although it might seem as if the supply curve of land should be drawn as a vertical line, this reasoning ignores improvements to the quality of the land, its ability to produce crops. Achieving this improvement is what agricultural research, much of it sponsored by the federal government, is often about.

Such government-sponsored research has proven quite successful at raising crop yields. The supply of high-quality farmland can also be increased through the scientific application of modem fertilizers and through crop rotation practices. But technological change on the farm embodies much more.

Industry has also provided for the farmer. A generation or two ago it was the faithful mule that supplied the power to prepare soil for planting. Today, mules have largely been replaced by tractors. Other kinds of more specialized mechanical planting and harvesting equipment have also been introduced over the long run. The effect has been to increase the productivity of the farmer. The same number of hours spent farming result in more farm output as productivity rises.

Technological change has also included the development of new crop varieties. Better seeds mean more food even if nothing else changes on the farm. Every technological improvement shifts the supply curve of food to the right, *ceteris paribus.*

Many kinds of farming approximate **purely competitive** markets, in which all firms must sell at the same market price, despite some of them having cost advantages over others. The result of pure competition is that technological change affects farmers in varying ways. Some farmers will find it easy to adopt new techniques: others will not be able to do so without difficulty. The first group will profit, even as the second group suffers. Those farmers who are unable to sell their crops at the market price without suffering economic losses will, in the long run, be forced to leave their farms.

For example, farmers in the choppy hills of Tennessee are at a disadvantage to their counterparts in the Kansas plains when it comes to employing the modern technology of huge combines and other types of farm equipment. Yet, if they produce the same product, they must sell it for the same price. As technological change takes hold, that price drops. Farmers must adopt the changes or exit the industry.

Corporate Farming—Can Government Fight Economies of Scale?

Tragedy for one family can be opportunity for another. When one family stops farming or moves off the farm, an opportunity is created for another to expand its operations by buying or leasing the land. As evidence, the average number of acres per farm has been increasing steadily during the twentieth century, rising from 146 acres in 1900 to 461 acres in 1990. Other aspects of the farm problem can be understood by referring to data on farm income, population, and productivity, as shown in Table 1. Note the ups and downs in farm income. These fluctuations make it difficult for small farms to keep going. Also note the uptrend in productivity, reflecting technological improvements.

Even though farms disappear, farmland is usually not abandoned. Rather, it becomes part of someone else's farm. When one farmer loses money working a particular piece of acreage, why should another farmer be able to take it over and earn a profit?

An important reason is economies of scale in farming, such as those associated with the use of large-scale equipment, which causes the average cost of farm output to decrease as farms grow larger. For example, farmers waste less time maneuvering their combines when their fields are large. This means that a bushel of corn, wheat, or other commodity can be produced at a lower per unit cost on large farms. Economies of scale are identified with the downward sloping part of the U-shaped long-run average cost curve. Economies of scale do have limits, though. Since bringing in the crop and equipment uses time and fuel, fields that extend too far can lead to diseconomies of scale, in which average costs rise.

Table 1 Farm Income, Population, and Productivity, 1979–94

Year	Net Farm Income (billions of dollars)	Farm Population (millions of persons)	Productivity Index—Farm Output per Unit of Farm Labor
1979	$27.4	6.2	89
1980	16.1	6.1	89
1981	26.9	5.9	98
1982	23.8	5.6	100
1983	14.2	5.8	92
1984	26.1	5.7	104
1985	28.8	5.4	114
1986	31.1	5.2	117
1987	38.0	5.0	121
1988	37.5	5.0	111
1989	45.0	4.8	121
1990	44.8	4.6	126
1991	38.4	4.6	125
1992	47.9	NA	141
1993	42.1	NA	133
1994	46.7	NA	NA

Source: *1996 Economic Report of the President,* Tables B-93, B-95, and B-96, NA not available.

Then there is government aid to consider. Government programs to help farmers have had a triple focus. To put more income into the hands of farmers, government has (1) restricted the supply of farm output to drive up crop prices; (2) increased demand by seeking out new markets for agricultural commodities, especially overseas markets, to increase prices of those goods; and (3) set prices of farm outputs above market equilibriums through agricultural price supports, which are maintained through *deficiency payments* that compensate farmers for the difference between the support price and any lower market price.

To use agricultural price supports to keep every farmer in business would require a price of output that would provide even the highest cost producer with at least a normal profit. Consider the three graphs in Figure 1. Farmer A is the low-cost producer, farmer B the medium-cost producer, and farmer C the high-cost producer. Don't forget that each cost curve includes an allowance for the farmer's implicit opportunity cost.

Farmer C may be the high-cost producer because he or she has higher explicit costs arising from poorer quality of land or poor management skills. Farmer C might also have excellent opportunities for earning income off the farm. In that case, farmer C's higher costs result from higher

Figure 1 Low-cost, medium-cost, and high-cost farmers.

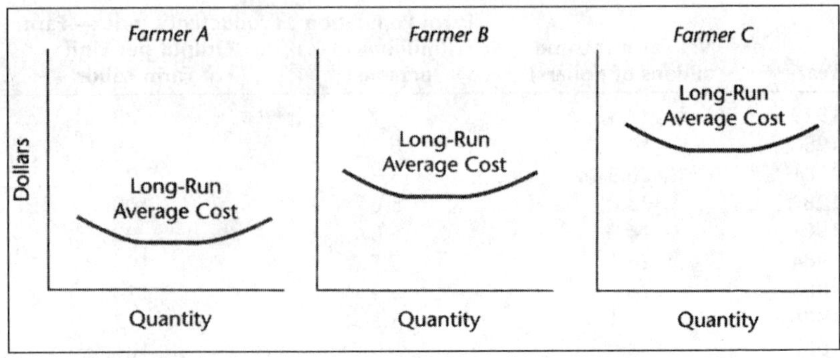

implicit opportunity costs. To keep farmer C farming, the government would have to manipulate prices so that all of farmer C's costs are covered by price. In the process, farmers A and B would grow wealthy on excess profits.

There are several objections to crop prices that keep all farmers farming. For one thing, consumers have to pay the higher prices. Since food is a necessity, high food prices hit the poor the hardest. For example, according to an analysis by Public Voice for Food and Health Policy, agricultural price supports added 33 cents to the price of a jar of peanut butter and 18 cents to the price of a gallon of milk in 1995. In total, price supports are estimated to have cost consumers an extra $4.5 billion dollars per year, most of which went to large operations rather than to small family farms.

Another problem concerns where to draw the line at government efforts to help people whose incomes are not enough to keep them in their present line of work. For example, many college professors find it difficult to support a family on their earnings. Should the government institute policies to increase college tuitions so that professors can be paid more? College students would be well aware of the costs. In general, the incomes of any category of producers cannot be raised without costs to others in society.

Since agricultural price supports are so expensive, why doesn't the government simply eliminate price supports, and replace them with subsidies to needy farmers? Actually, the Freedom to Farm Act of 1996 does just that. After 63 years, government has chosen to abandon most efforts to support prices and restrict supply. Farmers can grow what is most profitable and plant as much acreage as they wish, unlike under the system of price supports. However, supports for peanuts, sugar, and dairy products were left in place by the act. Furthermore, when the act expires in 2002, price supports are scheduled to be reimplemented, unless additional action is taken in the interim.

What Washington Has Learned from the Heartland

Over six decades of price supports failed to stop the exodus from the farm. For this, we should be grateful. If 30 percent of Americans were still to live on farms, as was true in 1920, many goods and services that we enjoy consuming would simply not be available. People would be growing food instead of, for example, assembling cars, building houses, and making movies. Besides, people frequently prefer to live in cities, suburbs, and small towns rather than on farms. We can take comfort that many of those who left farming did so because of attractive job opportunities elsewhere.

The history of government farm policy has been to fight the market, which has been telling us there are too many farmers. Until 1996, government chose to ignore the market's message. If government truly had wished to keep farmers on the farm, it would have been better served to outlaw all technological change in farming. If farmers were forced to stick with the farming techniques of a century ago, the country would need many more farmers today. That policy alternative is, of course, ridiculous. Still, government policies have prolonged the pain of market adjustment, and in the process forced us all to pay more for breakfast, lunch, and dinner.

In farm policy, as in the case of many other government policies, Washington has a choice to make. It can fight the market or work with it. Fighting the market means trying to stop or slow down the changes that occur as markets evolve. Working with the market means accepting change, but trying to ease the pain experienced by those who are adversely affected by that change. When to back off is a lesson learned the hard way by many onetime farmers. The recent changes in farm policy suggest that government lent an ear.

The United States Postal Service—Why Not Privatize?

The United States Postal Service holds a special place in our hearts and in our history. It has politics on its side. What of economics? This Exploration considers whether the delivery of first-class mail is a natural monopoly, and whether privatization and competition would better serve the public interest.

Neither snow, nor rain, nor heat, nor gloom of night stays these couriers from the swift completion of their appointed rounds.
Inscription on Manhattan Post Office, adapted from "The Histories of Herodotus"

No Madison Avenue advertising agency could think up a better slogan for the post office than the motto adapted from the centuries-old writings of Herodotus. The mails must go through. That has been true since the post office was established on September 22, 1789.

What is probably the oldest monopoly in America is rich in tradition. The first postmaster general was Benjamin Franklin. In 1995 the post office earned \$54.4 billion in revenue and had about 700,000 employees. That is big business, the 33rd largest company in the world according to *Fortune* magazine. Approximately 181 billion pieces of mail were sorted, routed, and delivered in 1995, 40 percent of the world's mail. Nonetheless, more and more, the following questions are being asked: Do we still need the post office? What could replace it?

The Postal Monopoly

All over the world delivery of mail is entrusted to governments. The U.S. Postal Service is a monopoly, guaranteed by the postal monopoly statutes and perhaps even the Constitution.

Critics of the post office have expressed disgust at how long it sometimes takes the mail to arrive, if it arrives at all. A few postal employees have even been known to dump mail into the garbage or take mail to their homes. Among the post office's other problems are occasionally rude employees and public worry over the rising costs of mailing a letter.

Will the delicate vase that we have mailed to Aunt Emma at Christmas arrive safely? What if she is at the doctor's office when delivery is attempted? Since the post office will not redeliver items and Aunt Emma no longer drives, how will she take delivery of the vase? The quality of service that consumers want is apparently not being delivered along with the mail. Could all these problems be related to the monopoly status of the Postal Service?

There is no private-sector firm exactly comparable to the U.S. Postal Service. Thus, legally and in practical terms, the Postal Service is a monopoly. Its colorful red, white, and blue vehicles rumble up and down the highways and byways of the country delivering mail to virtually every household and business in America. Full service to all communities is part of its tradition. No privately owned firm would deliver mail to communities if losses were the result. The post office must do so because of Congressional mandate.

Under penalty of law, deliveries to mailboxes are restricted to the Postal Service. Woe unto the youngster who unknowingly puts a hand-printed circular into a mailbox. That action, intended to help earn a little money from babysitting or mowing lawns, is a violation of federal law.

"Don't Fix What Ain't Broke"

Even if the postal monopoly laws did not provide barriers to entry, it is questionable whether a full-service competitor to the post office would enter the market. The reason is that, historically, the post office has required government appropriations to meet expenses. These appropriations have shrunk from 8.4 percent of total postal revenue in 1980 to 1.3 percent in 1991. The absolute dollar amounts are quite large, however, equaling $562 million in 1991, for example. Furthermore, the investment required to duplicate the fleet of vehicles, post offices, and equipment, and the recruiting and training of a work force, would mitigate against new competition.

Why does government deliver the mail, and not the private sector? Perhaps the best answer is that the public, while not entirely satisfied with the quality of service and its cost, has so far not pushed Congress to ex-

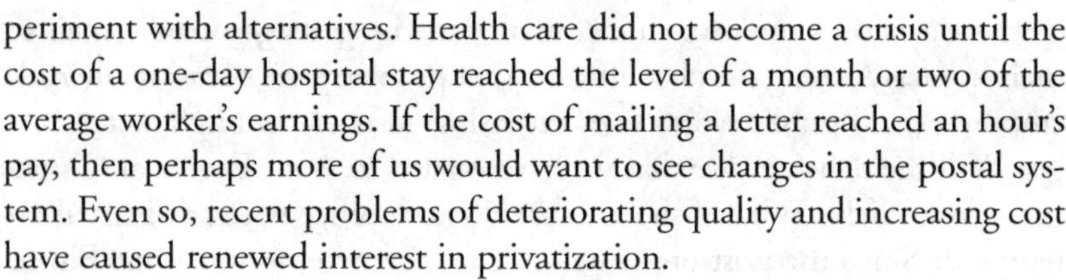

periment with alternatives. Health care did not become a crisis until the cost of a one-day hospital stay reached the level of a month or two of the average worker's earnings. If the cost of mailing a letter reached an hour's pay, then perhaps more of us would want to see changes in the postal system. Even so, recent problems of deteriorating quality and increasing cost have caused renewed interest in privatization.

The Promise of Privatization

The benefits of privatization are realized when operating efficiencies are captured and passed on to consumers along with improvements in service. Numerous studies have documented the benefits of providing services through the private sector. Take weather forecasting, for example. The government's National Weather Service provides weather forecasts to farmers, seafarers, pilots, and others for whom accurate weather forecasts are a matter of life, death, and livelihood. But many businesses find it is worth the cost to subscribe to one of the many private forecasting services, such as Accuweather. At a minimum, private forecasts provide a useful second opinion. Worse for the government is the hypothesis that private forecasts are more complete and more accurate than government forecasts.

Localities that have replaced government-provided garbage collection with private sector contracts have realized significant savings. Dozens of government-provided goods and services that have been turned over to the private sector show similar results. Towing of illegally parked cars, tree trimming along city streets, housekeeping and custodial services, forest management, private police protection, education, social services, family planning, and many more provide ample evidence. Furthermore, greater efficiency following privatization is a worldwide phenomena.

If the Postal Service were privatized—auctioned off to an owner who would run it on a for-profit basis—could consumers expect to benefit? Through cost savings and quality improvements, it would be possible to keep prices reasonable, make consumers happy with the service, and put profits into the pockets of the owner. However, it is also possible that a profit-maximizing monopolist would raise prices while allowing quality to deteriorate.

A privately owned post office monopoly would unquestionably raise public cries for regulation to provide incentives to operate with maximum efficiency while limiting profit to the level of normal profit. However, regulation is imperfect and is not likely to result in the capture of all efficiencies. Another possibility would be to repeal the postal monopoly statutes. There is plenty of competition in the market for package delivery. Without legal barriers preventing firms from delivering first-class mail, it seems likely that competition would emerge there, too.

Universal Access and Cross-Subsidies

If the postal service were privatized, would the public demand **universal access**? If universal access is preserved, the postal service would remain committed to the present practice of providing mail service to everyone. That adds to the cost. People who live in areas of sparse population are expensive to serve. An hour of a letter carrier's time and a gallon of gas can serve many more customers in a densely populated urban area than in a rural area. Would a privately owned postal service be tempted to cut off service to high-cost customers? Not if it were allowed to set a price that covered the cost of providing that service.

Certain services probably lose money for the Postal Service. In order to contribute to a higher level of national literacy, it reportedly delivers magazines and newspapers below cost. To reduce those losses, publishers agreed some years ago to standardize the size of their publications in accord with the desires of the Postal Service. That is why the *Ladies Home Journal* shrank in size, even as *Popular Mechanics* grew larger. A fully privatized post office would not continue to provide services at a loss. It would either raise prices, stop providing the service if profit proved impossible, or sell the facilities and equipment necessary to provide the service to another firm, which believed it could make a profit.

Postal authorities set prices on first class mail and on other services high enough to offset the losses on services that are underpriced. This practice is referred to as **cross-subsidization**. A problem is that these higher rates send customers searching for alternatives. As alternatives are found, the Postal Service loses customers. That means the remaining customers have to pay even higher rates. A vicious cycle is set in motion.

Stamping Out Innovation—At What Cost?

True monopoly involves the lack of close substitutes for a firm's product or service. Are there such substitutes for the services of the post office? Remember that the monopoly is a legal monopoly on first-class service, along with monopolization of the use of mail boxes. Private firms are allowed to compete against the post office on other kinds of service. United Parcel Service and Federal Express are examples of firms that have successfully taken on the competitive challenge.

Even with the rudimentary state of the information superhighway, snail mail, as the post office is derogatorily called by computer users, faces greater challenges in the future. Businesses are increasingly turning to their fax machines and e-mail because of lower cost and greater convenience. In this way, the market is circumventing the postal monopoly laws.

The choices facing the postal service are simple: (1) use its legal monopoly to eliminate innovative competitors, (2) innovate itself, or (3) do nothing and see its share of mail delivery continue to shrink. The first alternative is the simplest and possibly the most tempting. The result would be a twenty-first-century post office bearing a striking resemblance to its predecessor of the nineteenth century. The second alternative has been tried, but with mixed results. Competition is the spur to innovation, but with legal barriers to entry in first-class service, it remains to be seen how successful the Postal Service will be at remaking itself. One positive sign is that the Postal Service reduced its debt by $1.7 billion in 1995. The third alternative has little to recommend it, except for the power of the status quo. A national debate on the merits of privatization could help clarify alternatives and their costs as the information superhighway is expanded in the future.

The Power of Politics

Complicating privatization is the powerful postal workers' union. Postal workers are some of the nation's highest-paid unskilled workers. Privatization that increases the efficiency of delivery might involve layoffs, which would reduce the power of the union. Congress might find itself embroiled in controversy if privatization led to the loss of jobs.

One worry is that opening the Postal Service to competition would result in great rivalry in the most profitable segments of mail service, thus leaving the Postal Service with all the unprofitable segments. With unrestricted privatization, prices of each type of service would tend toward the marginal cost of that service. Prices would be efficient, but not necessarily fair. Politicians often worry about fairness rather than efficiency.

Perhaps the future will bring even newer technologies, which do away with postal services as we presently know them. Until that day, the economics of privatization paints a tantalizing picture of efficiency. Will that picture lose its allure? If privatization becomes a reality, time will tell.

Point/Counterpoint—
So Many Reasons Not to Trade!

There are many possible exceptions to the rule that free trade is desirable because it increases a country's consumption possibilities. However, objections to free trade frequently have limited applicability or are based on shaky assumptions.

Individuals, regions, and countries can specialize according to their respective comparative advantages and gain from trading with each other. We each do that—no one in modern society is self-sufficient. When we earn incomes that allow us to buy the things we want, we are specializing and gaining from trade. Regions specialize and trade with other regions within a country. Countries do the same with other countries. A country that specializes and trades with other countries will be able to consume more than it could produce on its own. As a general rule, then, restricting trade to protect either high-wage jobs or low-wage jobs is inefficient—it cuts down on the size of the economic pie.

Since the purpose of economic activity is to consume, not to produce for the sake of keeping busy, why restrict imports? Yet countries do impose restrictions on trade, especially on imports. Sometimes the reasons make economic sense. More often, the reasons have much more to do with politics than with sound economics. This Exploration examines some of the special circumstances under which trade restrictions have been justified. In each case, caution is in order.

Infant Industries—Where Are Investors?

Developing countries often try to nurture new industries they hope will one day become a source of export earnings. These infant industries, are thought to need protection in the rough world marketplace. The infant industry argument claims that government must first identify promising industries and then erect import barriers to protect them. When the infants grow strong enough to fend for themselves, government should remove the barriers.

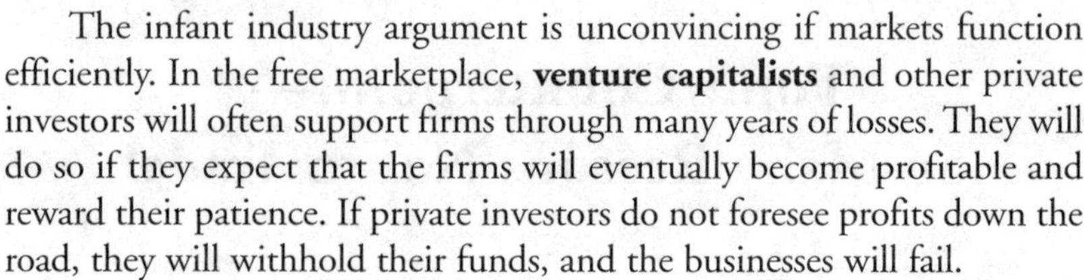

The infant industry argument is unconvincing if markets function efficiently. In the free marketplace, **venture capitalists** and other private investors will often support firms through many years of losses. They will do so if they expect that the firms will eventually become profitable and reward their patience. If private investors do not foresee profits down the road, they will withhold their funds, and the businesses will fail.

Unfortunately, there is much less assurance that government will pick industries that are likely to survive on their own. Governments often use political considerations to select "infant" industries. Even if governments do attempt careful economic analysis, such analyses are unlikely to match those of investors with their own money at risk. The result is that governments around the world have protected industries that never grew strong enough to withstand foreign competition. By requiring government subsidies to stay afloat, and by charging prices above prices in the rest of the world, such industries have proven to be expensive for governments and consumers alike.

National Defense—Valid but Overused

If imports or exports seriously threaten national defense, it makes sense to restrict them. No one denies this fact. However, translating national defense interests into policy is often not easy. When is the threat serious? For example, the U.S. Department of Defense has advocated restrictions on the export of computers and technology. However, if the U.S. is an unreliable supplier to other countries, will new technologies evolve elsewhere in places where the government allows producers to reap the profits from exports? Also, what weight should be put on civilian uses for products that could also be used in war? The judgments are often difficult.

On occasion, the judgments are easy. For example, is it necessary to protect the jobs of uniform makers and shoe makers in order to preserve the national security of the United States? If you work in or earn investment income from those industries, self-interest might prompt you to argue "yes!" That argument was indeed made to the U.S. International Trade Commission in the mid-1980s.

U.S. leather footwear manufacturing was in trouble, due to inexpensive imports from Brazil and Italy. It looked as if the leather footwear industry might follow the same route as the athletic shoe industry. With few exceptions, the athletic shoe industry had already abandoned the U.S.

in favor of manufacturing facilities in the Far East. The argument to protect remaining U.S. shoemakers went along the following lines:

> Without any shoe industry within its borders, what would the U.S. do in wartime if it were to run short of combat boots? Look what happened to the armies of Napoleon in Russia and to the Confederate armies in the U.S. Civil War. The soldiers of these armies marched so much that they wore out their boots. Unable to provide replacements, France and the Confederacy went down in defeat.

Yes, this argument is far-fetched. Few people envision that a modern war would pit the U.S. against Brazil, Italy, and countries of the Far East in years of ground warfare. Even if that were likely, a simple solution would be to stockpile extra boots. Nevertheless, when the security of an industry's profits and its workers' livelihoods are at stake, the more ammunition the better!

Energy Security—Drain America First?

While foreign armies are unlikely to threaten U.S. security, the U.S. might be susceptible to the threat of economic blackmail. Because the U.S. imports over half of the oil it uses, this seems to be its most vulnerable point. Despite having an abundance of coal and natural gas, the U.S. relies upon oil to provide most of its fuel and electricity. Oil is a critical energy source for transportation, heating, and production. Without energy, U.S. industry would grind to a halt.

The OPEC oil embargo of 1973 was an example of economic blackmail in action. The aim of the embargo was to punish the U.S. for its support of Israeli policy. While the embargo did not appear to affect U.S. policy, the U.S. paid the price of long gasoline lines and high energy prices. To prevent such blackmail in the future, some people argue in favor of an oil import tariff that would raise the price of imported oil and wean the U.S. from its dependency on that oil.

If the U.S. raises the price of imported oil, U.S. producers will substitute domestic oil, which increases the price of domestic oil. The higher price would prompt increased production from existing oil fields and increased drilling for new supplies. Since oil is a nonrenewable resource, opponents of oil import restrictions argue that they would "drain America first." This means that, as U.S. wells are pumped dry more quickly, the

U.S. would be forced to rely even more heavily on foreign supplies in the future.

Higher oil prices in the U.S. from import restrictions would cause additional undesirable effects. For example, while oil import restrictions would reduce the immediate risk of economic blackmail, it would shrink the economic pie over time. The economy can grow faster and stronger with cheaper energy and thus be better positioned to weather energy disruptions if they ever do materialize. In addition, higher oil prices would prompt the substitution of coal and nuclear power, both of which can harm the environment. For coal, the side effects are particulates, which lead to sooty air and acid rain. For nuclear power, the side effect is the risk of a catastrophic accident. These effects add up to a high price for a doubtful energy security.

Environmental, Health and Safety Standards—A Level Playing Field without a Game

Some U.S. industries cannot produce products as cheaply as products from abroad, because companies abroad do not have to pay for protecting the environment or the health and safety of their workers. Should the U.S. attempt to estimate the extra costs of producing in the U.S., and then add that cost to imports by imposing an appropriate set of tariffs? Some critics of current trade policy suggest that this approach is the only way to achieve a *level playing field.*

There is merit to this argument, insofar as the environmental or other damages reach U.S. territory or otherwise affect U.S. citizens. For example, the effect of chlorofluorocarbons—chemicals named by scientists as the culprit in creating a hole in the world's ozone layer—does not depend upon which country is the source of chlorofluorocarbon emissions. Likewise, the U.S. may have an interest in ensuring that the tuna it imports has been caught in a dolphin-friendly manner.

If carried to an extreme, leveling the playing field would remove the very basis for trade itself, comparative advantage. After all, if all firms have identical costs, there is much less reason to trade. For the U.S. to impose its own environmental standards upon other countries, when environmental effects are localized, would benefit neither the U.S. nor those countries. Such action could easily be interpreted by those countries' citizens as an act of U.S. arrogance or imperialism.

For example, environmental costs of production in poor countries are often less than in the U.S. because of weaker laws or law enforcement. Higher levels of pollution are likely to be efficient for these countries, because environmental quality is a normal good—as incomes rise, people demand more. Poor countries value extra income to spend on food, shelter, and other goods more highly than extra environmental quality. Thus, poor countries have a higher opportunity cost of environmental quality and might efficiently specialize in industries with a higher pollution content. In contrast, by valuing environmental quality highly, U.S. citizens are better off when those industries go elsewhere.

External Benefits—How Much and What Policy?

Sometimes the actions of an industry provide *external benefits,* meaning benefits that go to other individuals or industries. This concept has motivated many regions and countries to compete for high-tech industries in the hopes that there will be spinoff benefits. For example, entrepreneurs and innovators often have their start in high-tech firms. Promoting entrepreneurship and innovation has value to a country and can justify favorable treatment of such industries. By restricting imports of high-tech or other selected products, trade barriers may allow the domestic industries that produce similar products to flourish.

At least three cautions are in order, however. First, trade restrictions are likely to be inferior to other policies designed to target external benefits more directly. For example, if a firm creates external benefits that can be measured, those benefits would be promoted more effectively through direct payment for those effects in proportion to their value. In short, government could use a direct subsidy to pay for external benefits. Trade restrictions involve an implicit, indirect subsidy, with undesirable side effects upon consumers.

The second caution is closely related. Sometimes the amount of external benefits is highly questionable and easily manipulated in the political process. For example, high defense budgets were justified for many years on the basis of spillover benefits to the civilian economy. This policy was followed despite considerable evidence that external benefits per dollar of defense spending were likely to be much lower than external benefits from most other types of spending.

Third, benefits that appear to be external often are not. For example, if people think they can acquire valuable human capital by working at the

XYZ company, then the XYZ company can attract those workers for less pay. The lower wages make competing with imports easier. No policy action is needed, to the extent that external benefits are captured in wages. Thus, while external benefits can justify restricting trade, the justification is often unconvincing.

Dumping—Rarely Strategic

Dumping is defined as the selling of a good for less than its cost of production. A company may engage in dumping for various reasons. One common reason is that the company overestimates demand and produces too much. It then seeks to salvage what revenues it can from its bloated inventories.

A second common reason is that a company may be selling output at a price that covers wages, materials, and other operating expenses of production, but does not cover the cost of its capital and other *fixed costs* that it must pay whether it produces or not. Even though the company loses money, it would lose more by not selling.

A third reason, related to the second, revolves around different elasticities of demand in different markets. A company may dump a product in a country where its elasticity of demand is high, perhaps caused by intense competition from other companies in its industry. The company covers its capital costs by charging a higher price in markets where it faces less competition. Lower prices where competition is heavy are familiar occurrences within a country, as well as internationally. This is one reason why the same brand of gasoline sold along an interstate highway at the edge of a city is often priced much higher than when sold in the city itself.

Dumping for each of the above reasons occurs within a country, as well as in international trade. However, it is only in international trade that dumping is illegal, according to the GATT. If a company is charging a lower price in a foreign market than it does at home, and if that lower price does not cover its fixed costs, the company is guilty of dumping. Indeed, since a foreign company's capital costs are often hard to measure, the U.S. presumes dumping whenever a foreign company charges less in the U.S. than it does at home, irrespective of its costs. U.S. law allows for the imposition of antidumping tariffs, such as those imposed in the early 1990s on Japanese computer chips.

Why worry about dumping? After all, aren't U.S. consumers being offered a bargain? In most cases, the U.S. would be better off to accept the low prices and spend the savings on other products. The only time to worry is when there is **strategic dumping**—dumping that is intended to drive the competition out of business, so that the firms doing the dumping can monopolize output and drive prices up in the future. However, in most industries, the prospects for successful strategic dumping are highly questionable. After all, in a world marketplace, there are many potential competitors lurking in the wings. Even companies that have been driven out of a particular line of business can often reenter it in the future, should an increase in price make it profitable to do so.

Why All the Argument?

Sometimes objections to free trade are well-intentioned, and occasionally these objections are valid. However, mixed in with valid arguments to restrict trade are many arguments that can best be described as self-serving. It is in the interests of U.S. producers to restrict trade, if the goods and services they offer are in competition with imports. After all, this competition keeps prices and profits lower than they would otherwise be. Competition forces businesses to find ways to economize and become more efficient. They do not like this competitive pressure.

Of course, many U.S. companies have no interest in restricting imports, especially companies that use imported components or produce products for the export market. U.S. consumers are also poorly served by import restrictions, since these restrictions drive up consumer prices and thus reduce purchasing power. Curiously, consumers often seem unaware of their own interests. They may believe that importing products is somehow unpatriotic, since they perceive that importing products is equivalent to exporting jobs. Actually, this view fails to take into account the return flow of dollars—dollars return to the U.S. to buy exports and investments, thus creating other jobs.

If the arguments for and against free trade were to be counted, free trade would come up very short. However, the number of objections is not important. It is the validity of those objections that matters. In that respect, with minor exception, free trade offers the best chance of maintaining and improving the standard of living the world now enjoys.

EXPLORING MARKET WEAKNESSES

In the United States, economic tradition has favored a market economy. For many Americans, economic freedom and the opportunity for economic mobility are considered to be advantages which the market system provides. However, the free market does have its share of weaknesses. Among the most significant examples of market weakness, or failure, are: Monopoly Power, Recession or Depression, and Externalities. The following essays describe each weakness and show how the U. S. economic system attempts to deal with and correct market failure.

Income Distribution—$20-Million-Dollar Paychecks and the Big Squeeze in the Middle

This exploration examines the distribution of income between the rich, the poor, and the middle class. Explanations and possible solutions for income distribution problems are proposed.

What ever happened to economic security? It seems that most workers have to run faster and faster just to stay in place. Husbands were joined by their wives in the workplace in the 1970s and 1980s, but even with two incomes combined, median family income (half above and half below) has barely kept up with inflation. Even the booming economy of recent years did not always help. Inflation-adjusted median family incomes fell from $39,105 in 1991 to $38,632 in 1992 and to $37,905 in 1993 before rising to $38,782 in 1994. The behavior of family income over time is documented in Figure 2.

Two aspects of the problem of diminishing economic security must be disentangled. One is the slowdown in real income growth over the past two decades. The other is the increase in inequality in the distribution of income. The output of the economy is analogous to a pie. We first want to ensure that the pie keeps getting bigger, especially relative to population growth, and then we worry about the size of our slice of the pie relative to our neighbor's slice. While the pie has been growing, the pieces going to those at the top have gotten larger, leaving less for everyone else. These developments have financially squeezed the middle class.

So You're Gonna Be a Star

One way to solve your personal economic security problem is to become a star actor, athlete, or singer. Comic actor Jim Carrey of "Ace Ventura" fame solved his economic worries when the high demand for his unique services caused him to be paid $20 million per picture. Other celebrities

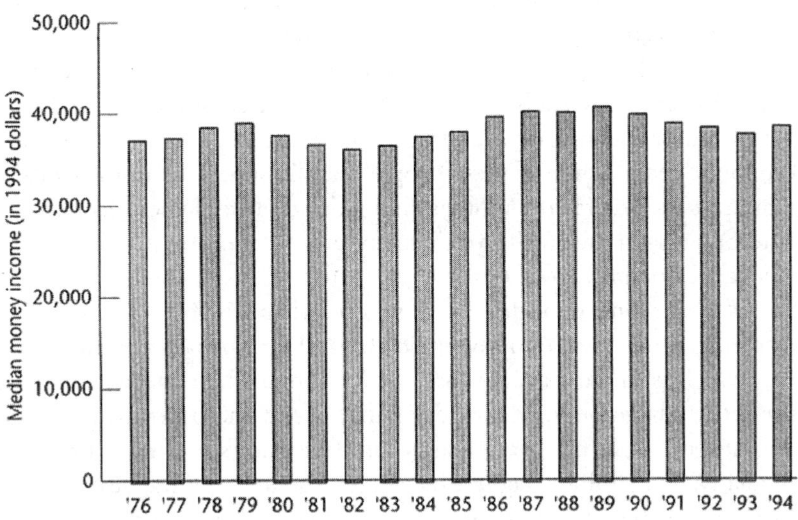

Figure 2 Inflation-adjusted median money income of families, 1976–1994.
Source: *1996 Economic Report of the President,* Table B-29.

whose multimillion-dollar incomes have made headlines in recent years include the Superbowl-winning quarterback Troy Aikman, basketball stars Michael Jordan and Shaquille O'Neil, and singers Michael Jackson and Madonna.

Economists have coined a term, **economic rent,** to describe earnings in excess of opportunity costs. Economic rent is responsible for the incredible earnings reaped by many celebrities. People whose talents and abilities are exceptionally scarce are sometimes able to earn much more than their next best alternative. For example, Michael Jackson's talent is uncommon and in fixed supply. The combination of fixed supply and great demand for his music and concerts results in sky-high earnings. Yet his opportunity cost, his best earnings opportunity outside the entertainment industry, is not nearly so spectacular.

Wage determination and economic rent for a superstar or other person with unique talents are illustrated in Figure 3. The fixed supply of superstar-quality talents results in a vertical supply curve of labor with that talent. For example, the quantity of Madonna's talent does not increase even if her earnings rise. The position of the demand curve for the star's talents determines earnings. When demand is large relative to supply, high earnings are the outcome. The portion of earnings representing economic rent is indicated by the blue shaded area in the figure.

This model applies to a spectrum of workers. Success in many fields requires exceptional skills. The most successful heart surgeons, stockbrokers, economists, attorneys, and business executives, among others, earn economic rents. Some of these people become superstars in their fields. Examples include former mutual fund manager Peter Lynch, economists Paul Samuelson and Milton Friedman, attorney Johnny Cochran, and Michael Eisner, head of Disney.

Not everyone, even those with unique talents, is able to earn significant economic rents. Your favorite club band may possess enormous talent, which is in fixed supply just like Madonna's. Nonetheless, without sufficiently large public demand for that talent, the band members are doomed to work for cover charges until the band's inevitable breakup. Similarly, many minor league athletes are close to major league quality in their talents, but the public is willing to pay high ticket prices only for major leaguers. Hence, a minor leaguer with 95 percent of the talent of a major leaguer may earn only 1 percent or less of the earnings of the major leaguer.

Clearly, the option of becoming a star is not open to most people seeking to boost their incomes. The theory of economic rent does, however, explain why some people end up in the group of highest paid workers, at the top of the income distribution. As predicted in 1981 by economist Sherwin Rosen, we increasingly live in a superstar economy, with a reward system of winner take all ever more common.

No More Middle Class?

The headlines bellow "More Layoffs Coming"; "Plant to Close"; "Inflation Up—Wages Fail to Keep Pace." Is the middle class dying a slow death? Some concepts related to the distribution of income can help clarify the answer to that question.

An income distribution reports the proportion of income each segment of the population receives. Since our biggest concern with the distribution of income is inequality, income distribution usually focuses on the fraction of total income received by different quintiles, where a quintile contains 20 percent of the population. If everyone's income were equal, each quintile of the population would receive 20 percent of total income. Where inequality exists, the quintiles show variation in the fraction of income received. A simple example will help. Consider a population of five persons, for which the total income received by the whole population is $100. In this example, each person represents a quintile, one-fifth of the population. If each person earned $20, each quintile would show a 20 percent share of income received. There would be perfect equality.

Suppose instead that there is inequality in the incomes received among our population of five. Beginning at the bottom of the distribution and moving up, the first person earns $5, the second $10, the third $15, the fourth $20, and the top earner $50. The total is still $ 100, but now there is inequality. The lowest quintile receives 5 percent of income, the next quintile 10 percent, and so forth up to the highest quintile, which receives 50 percent of income.

In Table 2, data on the income distribution for the U.S. in 1977 is contrasted with similar data for 1989 and 1992. The lowest quintile of the population has seen its share of income fall from 5.7 percent of the total to 4.1 percent. At the same time, those Americans in the top 1 percent of the income distribution have seen their share increase from 7.3 percent to 12.1 percent. Middle America, those in the three middle quintiles, garnered 46.8 percent of the income, down from 50.7 percent in 1977. Between 1989 and 1992, there appears to have occurred a slight reversal of the trend to growing inequality, but nonetheless the average American remains uneasy over whether the rich are getting richer and the poor poorer.

How Equal Should Equal Be?

Is the income distribution in Table 2 good or bad? That is unclear. Two important points are not apparent from the data. The first is that in spite of growing inequality, the distribution nonetheless exhibits significant stability. The changes are slight in absolute terms. The second is that there

Table 2 Shares of Total After-Tax Incomes (in percent)

Year	Total	Lowest Quintile	Second Quintile	Middle Quintile	Fourth Quintile	Highest Quintile	Top 1 Percent
1977	100.0	5.7	11.6	16.3	22.8	44.0	7.3
1989	100.0	4.3	10.1	15.1	21.5	49.9	12.4
1992	100.0	4.1	9.9	15.2	21.7	49.8	12.1

Source: *Center on Budget Policy and Priorities,* based upon Congressional Budget Office data.

is substantial movement within the distribution. Some people move up and others move down with the passage of time. For example, many younger workers who were at the bottom of the distribution in 1979 had moved up by 1993 after acquiring education and job experience. Meanwhile, many older workers who were at the top in 1979 had moved down because they retired. This dynamic movement in the distribution means that most people are not permanently stuck at the bottom. A final point can also help put inequality in perspective. The average estimated 1996 after-tax income of families in the top 1 percent is $438,000; that of families in the bottom quintile is $8,230. Without upward mobility, such a stark contrast would be hard to justify.

Income distribution is the outcome of a complex process involving numerous forces and depends heavily on what is counted as income. For example, there would be much less inequality apparent if in-kind government assistance to the poor were included in income. Nevertheless, it is reasonable to be concerned about the income distribution. If those who live in poverty come to believe that aspiring to the middle class is an impossible dream, then the frustration created could alienate potentially productive workers, thereby reducing their motivation to obtain schooling and work hard.

The income distribution can be made more equal. Indeed, changes in federal tax policy are capable of reducing the share of the well-to-do. Such policy changes must be tempered, however, by recognition that incentives to acquire human capital and be productive may be reduced by higher taxes. The problem is how to keep the pie growing while ensuring that everyone receives a fair slice.

Stumbling through the Culture of Success

Not everyone measures success in terms of money. For those many who do, perhaps the most encouraging fact is that the monetary returns to education have apparently been increasing in recent years. That is part of the reason the rich have been getting richer and the poor poorer. Those with more education have prospered; those without have suffered.

To what do economists attribute the premium placed on skilled labor? The most compelling argument seems to be the impact of technological change on the workplace, best exemplified by computerization during the 1970s and 1980s. Today's workers are forced to work smarter, not harder. Brain power has replaced muscle power as the most important determinant of success in the labor market, which suggests that education and job training could provide the answers to stagnating wages and income inequality.

The Tax Man Cometh . . . With a Postcard?

The income tax is complicated by many exemptions, deductions, and other so called loopholes that lower tax revenues, but often have economic justifications. Replacing the complex tax code with a simple flat-rate tax also has a basis in economics, but would limit government's ability to accomplish social aims.

The Simple Tax
How much money did you make? $____ . __
Send it in.

"Too complicated!" We hear that complaint every spring, as Americans once more delve into their financial records to prepare their tax returns. Why is it necessary to compute all the exemptions, deductions, exclusions, alternative minimum taxes, and so forth? Is it just a jobs program for tax accountants, tax lawyers, and Internal Revenue Service agents, or just breaks for special interests wanting to escape paying their fair share? Yes, many people long for a flat and simple tax. Such a tax would have a single rate, applicable to all income. Tax returns could be filled out on a postcard, although not quite the one represented above.

The flat tax has appeal for its simplicity, but there are other considerations that are argued to justify a more complicated system of taxation. These can be seen by asking the most basic question of all: What is the goal of an income tax? The goal is for government to raise revenues for its many programs and to do so in the most equitable and efficient manner possible.

A tax is efficient only if it does not *distort* relative prices within the economy, since price signals are what allocate resources to their highest-valued uses. By taxing all income equally, distortions are minimized. Efficiency thus calls for a *broadly based* tax, meaning one that it is difficult to escape. Much of the complexity of the current income tax code stems from innumerable provisions that remove income from taxation, thus narrowing the tax base.

The ability-to-pay principle of equity suggests that some income should be taxed more than other income, depending on how needy the person is. Exempting low incomes concentrates the tax base and leads to inefficiencies. Thus, the personal income tax is a compromise between efficiency and equity. Unfortunately, the compromise accomplishes neither goal fully and is also complicated.

Taxing Personal Income, with Lots of Exceptions

The concept of income is not altogether easy to pin down, since income is more than money. For example, if you drill a water well in your back yard and inadvertently strike oil, your wealth spikes upward. That change in wealth is income, even if you do not sell any of that newly discovered oil until next year or beyond. A **comprehensive measure of income** would subtract a person's wealth at the beginning of the year from wealth at the end of the year, and then add back in the person's consumption during the course of that year. Consumption is added because it represents income that is spent.

Government does not use this comprehensive measure of income in computing the amount of personal income taxes to collect. It would be too complicated and intrusive for government to attempt assessing how valuable each person's assets are at the end of each year. After all, assets include homes, cars, stocks, stamp collections, and much more. Moreover, even if the government could assess these values, there is the problem of *liquidity*—of converting assets into cash. Liquidity is necessary to pay taxes. The federal government does not want to be responsible for kicking Grandma out of her house, just because property values around her have increased and she does not have the liquidity to pay the taxes on her rising comprehensive income.

The result is that the tax code looks at only a subset of comprehensive income, that which is liquid. If people sell their illiquid assets, they obtain liquidity and are subject to taxation on their **realized capital gains,** the increase in the value of assets between when they were bought and when they were sold. Even here, however, there are exceptions. For example, Grandma would fall under an exemption for the elderly, were she to sell her house. Throughout the tax code, there is special treatment for special interest groups. Yes, Grandma has a special interest loophole.

So-called *loopholes* include the various exemptions, deductions, exclusions, and credits that complicate the tax code. Despite their notoriety, there are often economic principles behind these **tax expenditures,** so termed because they sacrifice tax dollars. The basis of tax expenditures often revolves around equity.

For example, the concepts of vertical equity and horizontal equity are two ways to judge whether a tax meets the ability-to-pay principle. **Vertical equity** is hard to pin down, because it concerns the proper tax burden for people of differing abilities to pay. **Horizontal equity,** which suggests that people with equal means should pay equal taxes, is more straightforward. Yet, even ignoring differences in wealth, equal monetary incomes do not necessarily imply an equal ability to pay. Differences in the ability to pay explain why there are tax exemptions for children, major medical expenses, and other facets of life that hit some people harder than others.

The search for equity complicates the tax code and makes it less efficient. This inefficiency hurts us all by reducing our standard of living. Thus, in trying to allocate the tax burden fairly, government winds up increasing it for the average citizen. These efforts to be fair cause price distortions within the economy and waste our labor resources because of the paperwork, accountants, and tax lawyers associated with a tax code that often seems like an imponderable murky morass to the average citizen. Is it worth it? Has government even accomplished its fairness goals?

The Flat Tax Sounds Appealing

Some people argue that a truly flat tax is not only efficient, but also quite fair. A tax that is truly flat would apply the same tax rate to everyone. As your income rises, you would still pay more taxes. However, as a percentage of income, each person would pay equally. Thus, if the tax rate is 15 percent and your income is $16,000, you would owe $2,400 in taxes. If your income is $160,000, you would owe $24,000 in taxes. A flat tax designed in this way is entirely proportional.

There is still the question of what constitutes income. Proponents of the flat tax often favor exempting income from savings and investment, since such income is generated by other income that has already been taxed. Such an exemption would be efficient, since it avoids penalizing income that is directed to savings and investment relative to that which is directed to consumption.

The biggest appeal of the flat tax is that it is transparent and easy to comply with. *Transparency* means that its operation is easily monitored. We know the rules, and those same rules apply to everyone. Thus we need not worry about clever tax dodges that we suspect others use to avoid paying their fair share of taxes. Moreover, we need not concern ourselves with keeping records and adjusting our behavior in ways that will minimize our own tax burdens. With the flat tax, we pay it when it comes due and ignore it for the rest of the year. That is appealing!

How Flat Is Flat?

In practice, flat tax proposals are not as simple as "Report your earned income, and send in 15 percent." Flat tax proposals usually include some exemptions and deductions. Most prominently, these proposals are made to be progressive by exempting the first many thousands of dollars from taxes altogether. For example, under some proposals, the first $16,000 of income would be exempted. By exempting some income from taxation, the tax rate must be higher because the tax base is smaller. While proposals for flat taxes differ in the amount of income they exclude, some would require rates over 20 percent to bring in as much revenue as the current personal income tax.

There are two reasons that some income is exempted from taxation. One reason concerns equity. For example, since low-income citizens are more needy, many people view it as unfair to take any of their money through taxation. The other reason is politics. Because changing the tax code results in both gainers and losers, care must be taken that more people gain than lose, or the change is not likely to happen. For these reasons, flat tax proposals typically exempt some income and certain popular deductions, such as the deduction for home mortgage interest payments. While there is no obvious economic reason for the tax code to favor homeowners over renters, the idea is to gain the support of special interests that pay attention—in this case, the homeowners.

Low-income citizens comprise another large group of potential voters. Since these people do not provide much tax revenue anyway, why not just promise them a zero tax burden? Exempting income at the low end of the scale has the potential to buy a great deal of public support at a relatively low cost. Of course, the higher up the income ladder those exemptions go, the higher the cost will be.

Not everyone supports the idea of exempting income. Even without exemptions, taking the same percentage of income from the rich and poor alike means that wealthier citizens pay a much higher price for government than is paid by the poor. Moreover, the poor receive benefits from redistributional programs, which are not offered to the more well-to-do. If the poor receive a totally free ride, will they still be responsible citizens? It would be rational for them to support inefficient and excessive government spending, since the costs are borne by others.

There is also a concern over what might be termed psychological issues. If low income households pay no taxes whatsoever and are on the receiving end of government programs paid for by others, how will they view themselves and their country? Paying taxes denotes participation, being a part of the process.

In contrast, those who receive benefits without paying a dime in taxes may rationalize this situation by viewing themselves as disadvantaged victims of an unfair economy. That way, they can feel good about receiving back from society some part of what was rightfully theirs all along. After all, the powerful people who craft the tax code seem to be saying that those with more money owe amends to the poor, who owe nothing. The message is that the poor are victims and are not responsible for their plight. This message is probably true for some of the poor, but certainly not for all. We might prefer to avoid ensconcing that message in the tax code.

Should the Tax System Be the Tool of Government Policy?

Taxes are the price we pay for living in our country. Government needs the money, so it seems fair to pay. However, because government has a monopoly on the power to tax, it can practice price discrimination. In other words, it can charge some people more than others, irrespective of how much government service they consume. Government can price discriminate on the basis of its citizens' characteristics, such as income or family size, although supposedly not by race, color, or creed. Government makes use of this power to vary the prices it charges, just as the theater owner charges higher prices for adults than for children.

A truly flat tax without exclusions takes away from government much of its power to price discriminate. Its hands are tied. Would this loss of a government policy instrument be the country's loss as well? Perhaps the answer comes down to this: When the government adjusts the tax code to right social injustices, does it do a good job? Do the benefits outweigh the costs? If so, the current tax system is justified. If not, perhaps we should order up a flat tax and direct our attention to other matters.

Social Security—Questions of Savings and Investment

Social Security is subject to stresses that bring its future into question. There are likely to be changes that affect national savings and economic growth, as well as individuals' incentives to be productive.

According to a recent survey, college students today are more likely to believe in alien visitors from outer space than in the future of Social Security. What is wrong with Social Security that its very existence is called into question? What does the future really hold? While time will tell, we can nonetheless make some intelligent predictions. We can see the stresses, as well as suggestions on how to relieve those stresses. The consequences are significant, both for individuals and the country. Choices about Social Security will affect productivity for years to come.

The Pay-As-You-Go Puzzle

The fundamental problem with Social Security is that it is pay-as-you-go, meaning that current workers pay for people who are currently retired. This arrangement was fine when the program was first established in the 1930s. At that time, the ratio of workers to eligible retirees was quite high. Now that ratio is down to about three workers per retiree. By the year 2030, the ratio is predicted to drop to only about two workers per retiree. Advances in medicine and the aging of the baby boom generation take the blame for these demographic trends.

If the present structure of Social Security were to be offered by any private business, the owners of that business would be prosecuted for fraud for running an illegal **pyramid scheme**, in which the money from current investors is used to finance paybacks to longer-term investors. Pyramid schemes are very risky; if new investors ever stop coming, the most recent investors lose their money.

Social Security has a significant advantage over the typical pyramid scheme. New investors are forced into the system by government and its power to tax. However, if government changes its mind down the road, investors who have yet to receive a payback could lose out. Even if Social Security were fully financed, though, the low returns it offers would dissuade potential investors. Figure 3 illustrates these returns. Note that the return to those born before 1945 greatly exceeds the return to those born in later years. For this reason, Social Security is said to be redistributional across generations, in addition to being redistributional within each generation.

Social Security collects taxes on all payroll income, and allots the proceeds for *OASDHI,* which stands for old age, survivors, disability, and hospitalization insurance. As of this writing, the combined employer and employee Social Security tax rate is 15.25 percent of the first $61,200 of that income, where the threshold is adjusted upward over time for inflation. For income over that threshold, the Social Security tax is eliminated except for the 2.9 percent hospitalization insurance.

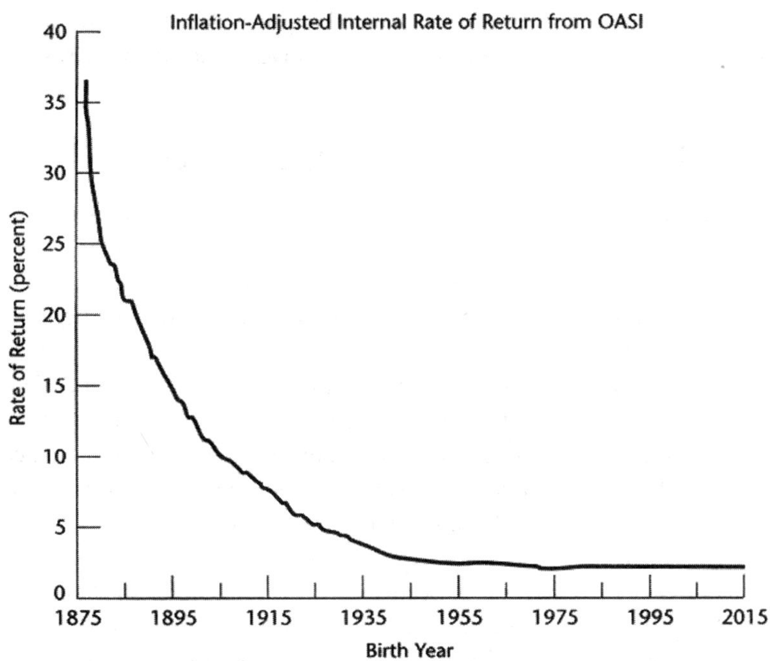

Figure 3 The rate of return for Social Security participants is significantly lower for those born after 1945 than for those born in earlier years.
Source: *Economic Trends,* Federal Reserve Bank of Cleveland, April 10, 1996, p. 13.

If population projections are correct, and if no changes are made in the structure of Social Security itself, the combined payroll tax rate of 15.25 percent would have to rise to over 22 percent in the next twenty years. However, workers might balk at redistributing nearly a quarter of their incomes to the elderly, especially when there is no guarantee that they will see equivalent benefits when they retire. That's why people mistrust the staying power of Social Security.

There is a **Social Security trust fund,** which collects excess revenue and *earmarks* it for the payment of benefits in the future. However, the approximately $400 billion size of that trust fund is quite small relative to the demands against it. The trust fund would run out in a little over one year if not continuously supplemented by the Social Security tax payments of current workers and the firms who employ them. Moreover, if the trust fund is to become a meaningful resource for the future, Social Security tax rates would need to be increased in the present. This action would leave current workers paying not only for current retirees, but also for themselves as well. Few workers would support this double taxation. They would rather save their money themselves, instead of entrusting those savings to government.

No Real Savings—No Real Alternative?

The issue of savings is quite troublesome in a macroeconomic sense. As it stands, all savings held in the Social Security trust fund take the form of special government bonds. Since a bond is merely a promise to pay in the future, savings within the Social Security trust fund are nothing more than government IOUs.

To pay those IOUs, government must either create extra money via the Federal Reserve or collect extra tax dollars in the future. Either way, future taxpayers pay. If the government increases the monetary base, taxpayers pay the tax of inflation that eats away the value of their earnings. Otherwise, the trust fund bonds would be redeemed out of general tax revenues, which would require higher personal income taxes or other general taxes. Even if the Social Security trust fund were to stack a warehouse full of its special government bonds, it would still be up to future taxpayers to pay them off. Thus, for the macroeconomy, balances in the Social Security trust fund are not real savings.

Not only does the Social Security system fail to augment the country's savings, it actually lowers national savings to the extent that people expect to receive Social Security checks in the future. Workers substitute government's promises for their own savings. Moreover, because the Social Security tax reduces take-home pay, current workers have less money that could be saved. The reduction in the national savings rate because of Social Security implies less money for investment, and thus less capital formation. With less capital, the country's production possibilities grow more slowly. The result is that, when current workers retire, the economic capacity of the country to support them will be smaller than if Social Security never existed in the first place.

For the Social Security trust fund to represent real savings, it must generate real capital that will increase the country's production possibilities in years to come. The amount of savings needed for the Social Security trust fund to be **fully funded**—able to pay off all its future obligations without recourse to future taxation—would be well over a year's worth of GDP. In other words, the buildup of savings in the Social Security trust fund must represent more than a doubling of the country's current productive capacity.

If government were to invest the Social Security trust fund into the production of real capital, it could take one of two routes. It could produce the necessary capital itself. Government production may be justified to the extent that the needed investment applies to the provision of public goods, such as highway infrastructure needed for smoothly flowing traffic. Beyond this, however, direct government investment would lead the economy in the direction of command and control. Alternatively, government could invest the money in the marketplace, perhaps buying stock offerings of private companies. Imagine the consequences of that!

If the government were to enter the private marketplace, politics would undoubtedly affect the direction of its investment. Thus, we could expect to see politically correct industries and those with powerful constituencies thrive, while other industries would be denied access to government coffers. The result would be an industrial policy, in which government picks the industries in which to stake the country's future. Workers interested in real savings for their retirements might prefer that such investment choices be left to private investors guided by profit rather than by politics.

Personal Security Accounts—Who Holds the Reins of Investment and Growth?

Individuals do save for their own retirement. *Individual retirement accounts (IRAs)* promote that savings by allowing tax-free contributions of up to $2,000 per year, depending upon income. Government has been reluctant to increase that limit, since any increase in tax-free savings would deplete current tax revenues. Government has also been content to accumulate bonds in the Social Security trust fund, because selling those bonds to the trust fund transfers any extra money collected by Social Security taxes into general revenues that can be spent elsewhere.

If government so chooses, it can promote private savings for the future. It can do this in varying degrees. It could start by increasing or eliminating the contribution cap on IRAs. It could go further by eliminating the taxation of all savings. It could even go so far as to require that individuals save some fraction of their earnings for their own retirement. This savings would be placed into *Personal Security Accounts (PSAs),* which would be financed by a payroll tax but be under the individual's own control and ownership. Because Social Security depends upon current workers to support current retirees, PSAs could only supplement, not replace, Social Security as it now stands.

Workers who get to keep control of their own savings might be more inclined to accept the double tax of paying for current retirees and also building up savings for their own retirement. Such an approach has the economic advantage of maintaining a freemarket allocation of investment. Companies that offer mutual funds and other forms of investment would compete for savings, and the winners would be those companies that offer the best services and investments.

Coming Welfare for the Aged

The strategy of promoting savings and investment by inducing individuals to save for their own retirements does not provide for income redistribution from wealthier workers to poorer ones. As Social Security now stands, it is highly redistributional in this respect. The ratio of payments to retirees relative to the amount they contributed in their working years is much higher for the low income than for the high income. Payments are also adjusted on the basis of need, such as indicated by the number of dependents. Thus, even though the Social Security tax took out the same portion of each person's income when they were working, the percentage that Social Security gives back is much higher for the poor.

On an after-tax basis, Social Security may even pay the retired low-income worker more than he or she earned when working. A worker at the maximum income subject to Social Security tax, in contrast, is likely to receive only about 30 percent as much as when employed. The upshot is that, when Social Security taxes and payments are combined, the Social Security system is highly progressive. Low-income workers have money redistributed their way from the tax dollars paid by higher-income workers.

The redistribution from higher-income workers to lower-income workers is one reason participation in Social Security is required by law. If it were optional, workers with above-average incomes would all quit, leaving no money to redistribute. Workers would also be deterred from joining voluntarily by intergenerational redistribution, which gives current retirees a much better deal than can be expected by current workers.

If individuals are poor, suffer financial misfortune, or for any other reason have little savings when they retire, what are they to do? It seems clear that society will demand some safety net to prevent indigent retirees from a life of abject poverty. Thus, there will continue to be redistributional Social Security taxes. However, as people are forced to save for their own retirement, and as Social Security as we know it becomes merely a fallback for those in need, Social Security becomes ever more a welfare program.

In the past, Social Security has been viewed as something that people deserve to have, because they have been forced to pay Social Security taxes all their life. The more redistributional Social Security becomes, however, the less sense this view makes. If workers see their payroll taxes rise in order to pay for the rising proportion of the elderly, there is likely to be an outcry against paying for those who can afford to pay for themselves. The better-off Social Security recipients will be cut from the roles, and the taxes they paid will not save them. As Social Security advances down this road, it will become known as welfare for the aged. The question will be asked: "Why is there a separate tax earmarked for this welfare?" If this scenario is correct, the country will probably see the demise of the Social Security payroll tax, and its replacement by higher income taxes and other taxes.

Whether to Work or Not to Work—That is the Question

This prediction of the future suggests that workers have some serious thinking to do. Do they struggle to acquire human capital and increase their earnings? If they do, they will face paying for the Social Security welfare of others. The alternative is to live it up and avoid the hard work necessary to earn a high income. After all, living into retirement years is not ensured. Those who live for the moment, acquire little human capital, and save nothing for retirement would have the safety net of Social Security to cushion their fall. If that cushion is too appealing, the future of the U.S. economy will not be appealing at all.

Preventing Workplace Negligence—The Price of Life and Limb

For the sake of cost-benefit analysis and lawsuits over negligence, economists are often called upon to place a value on human life. Different techniques are appropriate, depending upon the use to which the estimate is put.

A worker in an aluminum refinery falls into a vat of molten metal. Later, the company offers the grieving family $100,000 in compensation. Is that a fair settlement? An oil refinery explodes and burns, killing three employees. The employer accepts responsibility, but is not sure what fair compensation to offer the families of the deceased. An airliner crashes killing all aboard. Are all the lives lost of equal value?

These are examples of the issues facing economists who are called upon to place a dollar value on life and good health. Often these economists serve as expert witnesses in court proceedings that grow out of wrongful death lawsuits. Well-established and accepted methodologies exist for valuing life. It is these methodologies, explained below, that economists bring to bear.

Health and safety are regulated by government in an effort to save lives and reduce injuries. How much of such regulations is enough? This question also requires the application of economic principles to answer.

Ex post versus *Ex ante*—Can Placing a Monetary Value on Human Life Be Justified?

Some feel it is immoral to place a monetary value on human life. Indeed, few of us would fail to object if someone tried to tell us what our lives are worth or that some lives are worth more than others. We intuitively feel that the value of our life is beyond economic calculation and that it is just as valuable as that of the next person. For these reasons, economists do not place a monetary value on the life of any living human being.

When individuals suffer wrongful death, however, their survivors are deprived of the income that the deceased could have earned. At that point economics comes into the picture. Economists also recognize that the loss of loved ones goes beyond dollars and that economic analysis is not well suited to delve into the emotional costs attached to losses of loved ones. However, most would agree that restoring the incomes lost to those who have suffered the wrongful death of a loved one is equitable. Analyzing how much that reimbursement should be is aided by economic analysis.

The concept of human capital is used to place a value on lost earnings. Individuals invest in education and job training in the expectation that they will live long enough to reap the return from those investments. Investments in education often involve financial sacrifice for the individuals making them. The wrongful death of an individual prevents those returns from being realized. It thus seems fair that the loss should be compensated.

It may not seem as fair that the human capital approach discriminates among persons. Those with the most human capital are worth more than those with less human capital. That means children are worth less, because they have no labor market experience. The elderly are worth less, because their prime earning years are behind them. The physically and mentally challenged are also worth less because of their relative lack of earning power. The reason for these differences is that economic analysis of specific lives lost does not truly value that life; it only values productivity received by others. Valuing a human life in this way has a long history. For example, English common law has traditionally permitted the practice in court proceedings.

Measuring and Interpreting the Value of Lost Earnings

When a life ends, all that can be said about the future unfolding of that life must be based upon past evidence. When valuing that loss of life, the starting point is an examination of the record of the individual's past earnings.

The trend in earnings can be projected into the future. Such projections must be carefully crafted, however, because past earnings growth depended partially upon past inflation rates. If future expected inflation is lower or higher than past inflation, the projections must be adjusted accordingly.

When going to court, the economist brings a set of yearly net income projections, based upon expectations about future inflation and upon estimates of future promotions and other factors relating to the best guess about future earnings. These are sums of money that would have been received in the future. As such they must be placed in *present value* terms, which adjusts for the time value of money. The calculation of present value allows the economist to state the value of future net earnings as a single lump sum, payable today. Unfortunately, many court cases have been known to omit the concept of present value, thus overstating the value of lost earnings.

Earnings projections take account of the *life cycle,* which refers to the typical pattern of earnings over the course of a person's life. An individual who is young and inexperienced is at a point in the life cycle where current earnings are low. As the years go by, earnings typically increase, peak out in middle age, and decline slightly as health and other problems associated with advanced age become apparent. By making assumptions about the age a person would have retired, economists can estimate the number of remaining years of earning power.

Another component of loss is also estimated. This is the value of services provided to the household by the deceased. Examples include housework and child-rearing services. Courts accept the notion that survivors should be compensated for this loss as well.

Offsetting the loss of wages and household services is the value of the consumption the deceased would have undertaken. Examples include food, clothing, and medical services the deceased would have consumed. These sums of money are subtracted by the economist from the estimated value of wages plus household services.

There are problems with arriving at an indisputable value for a human life. Much of the economist's work is speculative, even when the economist attempts to be objective. Attorneys would not normally attack the methodology, which is well established, but could disagree with the earnings projections. It is left to the judge or jury to decide who is more persuasive.

Valuing the Chances We Are Willing to Take

Just how dangerous the workplace is can be gauged by referring to Figure 4. The data show the on-the-job death rate has been falling for some thirty or more years. Even so, in 1993, the death rate reveals an average

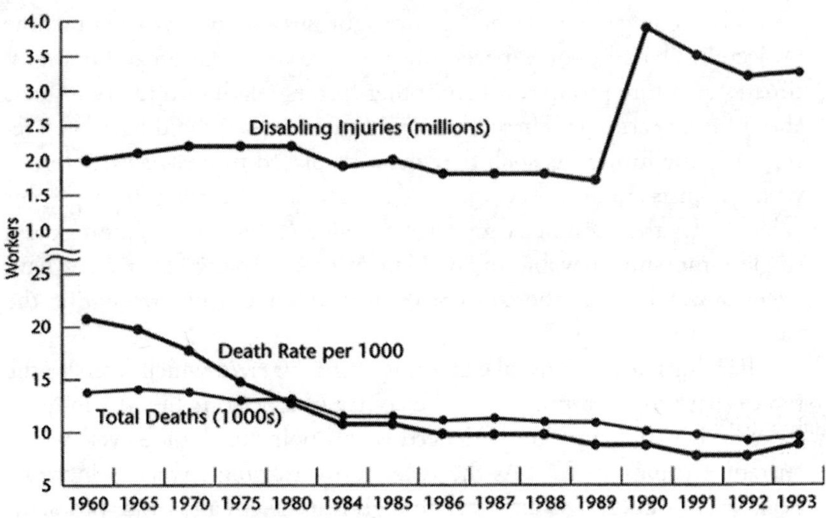

Figure 4 Workers killed or disabled on the job,m 1960–1993.
Source: *1995 Statistical Abstract of the U.S.,* Table No. 688.

of eight of every 1000 workers were killed on the job. On top of those 9,100 deaths, 3.2 million workers suffered disabling injuries. Some jobs are clearly more dangerous than others. Obviously, the workplace can never be made perfectly safe. If employers are willing to spend enough money, though, the risk of injury and death can be reduced.

Alternatively, the employer can offer higher wages to compensate workers for workplace dangers. The theory of compensating wage differentials posits that employers will be forced to pay higher wages when jobs are dangerous. Higher wages are necessary to attract a sufficient supply of workers and to compensate them for the risk to life and limb. We can impute a value of life by observing the behavior of workers who willingly take the hazardous jobs in exchange for higher pay.

Suppose, hypothetically, that the risk of death among police officers is increased by one in one hundred over the risk of death among security guards. Also suppose that police officers are paid $10,000 in additional income to accept that risk. What value do police officers place on their lives in this example? An approximate answer can be had by dividing the additional income by the additional risk. $1,000,000 (10,000/.01) is the value that officers themselves place on their lives. Another way of looking at this calculation is to note that each group of 100 police officers employed costs $1,000,000 in extra wages ($10,000 multiplied by 100 police). That $1,000,000 in wage costs "pays" for the death of one police officer. Since no individual officer knows for sure who will die, the $1,000,000 reflects the value of a *statistical life.*

How much would you be willing to pay to reduce your risk of death on the job? Suppose that you hold a job on an offshore oil rig that is dangerous, but that the risk of death can be reduced by 1 percent if you are willing to spend $100 for the purchase of a hard hat and steel-toe boots. Good deal? You bet. If you and your co-workers refused to make the purchases, then your statistical life is valued at less than $10,000 ($100/.01).

In reality, the Occupational Safety and Health Administration (OSHA), the Federal agency charged with enforcing health and safety rules, will probably force the oil rig operators to pay for your hard hat and boots and force you to wear them. How is safety regulation justified? Cost-benefit analysis is the key. An important benefit of safety regulation is the value of lives saved. Suppose a new regulation imposes safety measures that cost employers $100 million and is expected to save ten lives. Economic analysis suggests that the safety measures are worthwhile only if lives are worth at least $10 million each. If statistical lives were worth that much, the average worker would be willing to pay $100,000 for the hard hat and boots in the previous paragraph.

Safety in the Marketplace—What Role Government?

The search for profit motivates firms to implement numerous safety measures, even when no regulation forces them to do so. The rationale is that unsafe working conditions lead to various costs, such as costs associated with interruptions in production and higher costs of labor compensation. For example, a dangerous firm must offer higher wages and better benefits to attract workers. It would also be forced to pay higher insurance premiums to cover health care expenses and liability. If these costs exceed the cost of the safety measures, a profit-maximizing firm will undertake the safety measures.

There is also a role for government. The most clear-cut role for government occurs when there are external costs, costs borne by others. For example, highway speed limits and drunk driving laws can be justified on the basis of saving the lives of careful drivers who have the misfortune of being hit by a vehicle driven recklessly. To achieve economic efficiency, government must weigh costs and benefits of alternative regulations. Lowering the speed limit on interstate highways to twenty miles per hour, for example, would undoubtedly save lives. However, people are willing to accept some extra risk of injury or death voluntarily in order to receive the benefits from saving time in traveling.

Figure 8B2-2 shows in principle how to choose an efficient amount of safety. The idea is to keep adding safety measures so long as the marginal benefit exceeds the marginal cost. For example, the value of the statistical lives saved by lowering a speed limit from eighty to seventy miles per hour would usually exceed the cost of the extra time spent traveling. However, the marginal cost of lowering the speed limit from thirty to twenty would usually exceed the marginal benefit.

Figure 8B2-2 also applies to the firm. This section started by noting that profit motivates the firm to implement safety measures. However, there are questions about whether all of the benefits from safety improvements are captured in the firm's profits. If they are not, then firms will not choose to be safe enough. This situation might occur if workers have insufficient information about the value of safety improvements. For example, the workers might not realize how risky a job actually is and thus be unwilling to sacrifice much pay or other benefits in order to receive extra safety. In this case, the firm perceives less than the true marginal benefits from safety and implements too few safety measures. Figure 8B2-2 illustrates this possibility.

If firms do not undertake an efficient number of safety measures, there is a role for government regulators. Specifically, government regulators might estimate the efficient amount of safety and force firms to achieve that amount. However, it is difficult to estimate these marginal costs and benefits of extra safety, especially since different workers have different preferences when it comes to how much risk they are willing to accept in exchange for extra income.

It is impractical for government safety regulations to be tailored to the wants of different groups of workers. The result is that both firms and workers often complain about rigid work rules and safety measures. However, throwing the rules out risks that the marketplace might surprise workers with how unsafe their jobs can be.

There is an ongoing controversy over whether government should cut back its regulation of workplace safety. In that case, government could still make information on workplace safety available to workers so that they could choose more efficiently. On the other hand, backers of government safety regulation point out that there are economies of scale in evaluating information about safety. From that perspective, it seems sensible to let experts in government evaluate the information and make choices more efficiently than most workers could do themselves.

Borderlands of the Southwest—Whose Pollution? Whose Solution?

Trade between the U.S. and Mexico intensifies preexisting problems of transborder pollution. This Exploration looks at the very imperfect options available to resolve this issue.

The American Southwest

Wide open spaces, broad vistas, a freshening breeze—our vision of America's Southwest is one of expansiveness and freedom. It is a place to do and be as we please. The Southwest is part of our psyche; it's a state of mind. It's also a real place with real problems. As ever more people live in the vicinity of the Southwest, unlimited personal freedom comes into conflict with preservation of the environment that attracts them there. The environment of the Southwest is ill-suited to accommodate unrestricted pollution.

As in other parts of the country, citizens of the Southwest must abide by U.S. environmental laws, which means driving cars or operating factories with emission controls in place. The special problem of the Southwest, though, is that those controls apply to only a fraction of the sources of pollution. Much of the air and water pollution has its source in Mexico, an industrializing country with a rapidly growing population and less stringent control over pollutants.

An American Medical Association group depicted parts of the U.S.–Mexico border as "a virtual cesspool and breeding ground for infectious diseases." (Council on Scientific Affairs). Exemplifying the problem of border air pollution, the city of El Paso, Texas, is in noncompliance with guidelines set by the U.S. Environmental Protection Agency (EPA). However, the EPA allows this noncompliance to continue without penalty. There is a reason.

If you have ever flown into El Paso and looked out the airplane window as you approached the city, you may have a good idea as to why the EPA makes exceptions for El Paso. On the south side of the Rio Grande is a polluted haze that greatly restricts visibility. The haze on the north side is much lighter. El Paso is on the north side and its twin, Ciudad Juarez, is on the south side. Ciudad Juarez has nearly triple the population and generates proportionally much more pollution than does El Paso. Unfortunately for El Paso, pollution knows no borders.

Transborder Pollution

Transborder pollution is a problem of growing magnitude around the world. The problems are worsening for two reasons. On the one hand, economic growth in the less developed countries does not emphasize pollution control. Of greater concern to those countries are such tangibles as food, clothing, and shelter. On the other hand, the increased wealth of the developed countries has allowed them the luxury to focus beyond immediate necessities toward the quality and long-term sustainability of lifestyles. Environmental quality is important to both of those lifestyle goals.

Transborder pollution problems come in many forms. Some are global in nature, such as concerns that emissions of chlorofluorocarbons are depleting the earth's ozone layer. The pollution problem of most concern in America's Southwest is more local in nature. Here we have two countries, each of which feels the effects of the other's pollution. What trouble does this cause?

The problem of localized transborder pollution centers on incentives. There is much more incentive to control pollution that affects your own residents than there is incentive to control pollution absorbed elsewhere. For instance, cities along rivers routinely locate sewage treatment plants downstream and city dumps downwind from the city itself. When cities are all governed by one state or country, there are limits to how much pollution exporting is allowed. For example, while sewage from U.S. cities may be discharged downriver, at least U.S. law requires that it be treated. Given an absence of a world government, is there some other incentive for neighboring countries to be sensitive to each other's concerns?

Pollution Control Policies

It would be very difficult for the U.S. to apply any particular pollution control strategy to firms in Mexico. Options that work well within a jurisdiction don't work as well across jurisdictions. For example, one option long advocated by economists is for government to impose a tax on emissions of pollutants, such that the *external costs* of pollution are *internalized* into the production process. The idea is to make firms pay for environmental services. In other words, firms would be forced to pay for the waste-removal services of the air above or the river next door in the same way they pay for other types of services. In that case, you can rest assured firms would find ways to economize on smoke emissions and discharges into waterways.

A *second-best,* less desirable, alternative would be to tax the output of the firm. This approach would not give firms any incentive to reduce the amount of pollution per unit of output, but it would at least drive up the price of that output. Higher prices would mean fewer sales and thus less pollution. Could we apply either of these tax ideas to transborder pollution?

The answer is the U.S. probably could not effectively use pollution taxes on Mexican polluters. The U.S. could not tax pollution emissions effectively, because it lacks the authority to monitor pollution in Mexico and lacks the authority to impose taxes even if it could monitor that pollution. In principle, the U.S. could levy a pollution tax on output crossing the border. However, that tax could not effectively differentiate where in Mexico that output was produced. Furthermore, that tax would be politically unpalatable and violate international treaties.

Other policy instruments, such as pollution permits or mandated pollution control technologies, would also be infeasible for the same reasons taxes would not work. Where does that leave us?

Cooperation, Not Contention

The best solution may be voluntary cooperation between the U.S. and Mexico based on mutual self-interest. While both the U.S. and Mexico gain from trade between the two countries, the gains to Mexico are proportionally larger because it is the smaller country. This cooperative spirit is attested to by the 1994 implementation of the North American Free Trade Agreement (NAFTA), which incorporated Mexico into a revised and expanded free trade agreement between the U.S. and Canada.

NAFTA broke new ground in international trade by writing environmental safeguards directly into the treaty and side accords. For example, NAFTA signatories are obligated to maintain effective enforcement of their own environmental laws, even when the affected pollutants spill over the border. While NAFTA does not itself solve the problems of border pollution, it does provide a framework for cooperation on that issue.

What kind of cooperation can the United States legitimately expect from Mexico? Should we expect Mexico to maintain environmental standards equal to our own? Beware of environmental imperialism. The U.S. cannot expect the world to follow its standards, at least not without granting the rest of the world's citizens voting rights in U.S. elections. Moreover, uniform environmental standards would not make sense across all countries. After all, maintaining those standards is expensive, and incomes in some countries are much lower than in the U.S.

Mexico's per capita income is under $5,000 per year. Relative to the average U.S. citizen, the average citizen in Mexico thus consumes less in the way of high-quality food, clothing, shelter, medical care, and so forth. For Mexico to upgrade its control of pollution to match that in the U.S. would require further reductions in the quality of those goods.

One of the best ways for the U.S. to see greater control of pollution in Mexico is to see greater per capita income in Mexico. The reason is that environmental quality is a normal good, meaning that people want more as their incomes rise. The growth in income has been occurring in recent years and will be spurred along as NAFTA continues to be phased in. We are already seeing an increased interest in environmental improvement in Mexico. Over time, we can expect this interest to translate into concrete policy action.

In the meantime, there remain pollution problems along the U.S.–Mexico border. For example, sources of air pollution in the El Paso-Juarez airshed include the burning of tires to fuel brick kilns, dusty unpaved streets, and open-air spray painting of automobiles. The citizens of El Paso want action to clean this up sooner rather than later. So too do citizens of Juarez. Is effective action possible?

To answer that question, it must be noted that the environment is a *common property resource*, meaning that we can all use it, but that no one really owns it. This gives us no incentive as individuals to maintain it in the present or invest in its future. The way that government solves pollution problems is, in effect, to lay its own claim to the common property environment. Government then seeks to represent the interests of present and future users of the environment. Policy is implemented via such tools as carefully designed pollution charges, allocation of pollution permits, or mandated pollution controls.

Along the border, local governments have an incentive to cooperate in order to address the common pollution problem jointly. That is exactly what El Paso and Juarez have done. Specifically, those governments have formed a single international air quality management district for their region. This district is empowered with the authority to set air quality goals and employ market mechanisms to meet those goals.

For example, the market mechanism might grant limited emission rights to local polluters, but allow them to buy and sell these rights in the marketplace. In this way, overall pollution would be reduced and the firms that actually undertake pollution reduction would be those who can do so least expensively. The idea is for government to allocate property rights to the quantity of pollution that is permitted, and then let the free market determine which firms actually use those rights. For this approach to work, though, firms must not fear losing future allocations of pollution rights if they do not use those rights in the present. That has been a problem that has bedeviled such programs in the past. Markets function efficiently only when property rights are clear and reliable.

Conclusion

This Exploration has not dealt with all aspects of the transborder pollution problem. For example, much pollution is left over from the past, especially when it comes to toxins on the land and in the water. Therefore, controlling the flow of new pollutants is not enough; there is the stock of old pollutants to clean up. Who will pay for that cleanup? Part of the answer may be found in the recently established *North American Development Bank*, financed by the governments of Mexico and the United States to fund border cleanup projects. Yes, the hands of government and the pockets of taxpayers are likely to be major parts of any final resolution to the transborder pollution problems of the American Southwest.

GE Brings Good Things to You

The world of electrical turbine generators would not seem to be prime material for Robert Ludlum mystery novels. One doubts that the Mafia would ever try to control that hotbed of corruption, the circuit breaker business. The television programs "Dallas" and "Dynasty" are believable because they are about oil, not electrical insulators, right?

In the 1950s, however, the business of electrical equipment sales very much resembled a Ludlum novel or an episode of "Dallas." There were secret meetings in hotels and country clubs during which business executives plotted how to cheat competitors, consumers, and the government. There were code names for products and aliases for conspirators. There were phony documents and paper shredders. Between 1950 and 1960, twenty-nine major suppliers of electrical equipment engaged in one of the most extensive price-fixing and bid-rigging schemes of the modern American economy. Their conspiracy bilked Americans out of millions of dollars, and demonstrated that even in a free-market economy the markets aren't always very free. The five major conspirators were General Electric, Westinghouse, Allis-Chalmers, Federal Pacific, and ITE Circuit Breakers. General Electric was eventually fined more than $425,000 and three of its executives were thrown in jail, albeit for only thirty days.

The methods those twenty-nine companies used were strange and definitely anticompetitive. Their main objective was to divide up the electrical equipment market which kept the competition from lowering prices and profits. Electric utilities regularly requested the companies to submit sealed bids for equipment, the objective being to get the lowest possible price. However, the electric companies agreed in advance which company would submit the low bid, and just how high the low bid would be.

The companies devised three plans to decide which company would win which bid. The most bizarre was known as the "phases of the moon" scheme. Although it sounded strange, it merely meant that the companies rotated turns submitting the lowest bid. Another company would get its turn once the moon changed phases. This scheme was considered safe since it required no communication between the different companies. The second and third plans were a market-share theory and a geographical theory. Under the market-share theory, General Electric was to get 39 percent of the contracts, Westinghouse was to get 31 percent of the contracts, etc. The geographical plan divided the nation into different sectors, and each company received one sector over which it was to exercise control. Each company was free to divide the contracts as it saw fit.

Keeping the bid-rigging scheme secret was no easy matter. Meetings were held on a regular basis in swanky New York hotels, but the companies' representatives never acknowledged each other in restaurants or lobbies. Indeed, as a joke, the Barclay Hotel later advertised itself as an excellent host for having price-fixing meetings. "Antitrustcorporation secrets are best discussed in the privacy of an Executive suite at the Barclay," the advertisement read. In addition, the conspirators always called each other by their first names, all phone calls were made from pay phones to each other's home phones, company letterhead paper was never used for memoranda, and even the companies' own lawyers were kept completely in the dark. All of the companies had express policies against price fixing, but obviously, those policies were more form than substance.

How was the pricing scheme uncovered? Slowly, reports of bizarre pricing began to filter down to the United States Justice Department. When the Tennessee Valley Authority complained that it was getting identical bids on insulators and transformers, the Justice Department began to search hotel registers for electrical company employees. Once it became clear that executives from all the companies were meeting in the same hotel at the same time, and that indictments would follow, the Justice Department was able to convince some of the perpetrators to tell the whole story in return for clemency. Amazingly, it seems evident that the very top officials of the different companies were unaware of what was going on. The corporations' structures were so decentralized, and the pressure on division managers to generate profits so intense, that lower-level executives masterminded the schemes without ever telling the corporation bosses. Nevertheless, under the legal theory of vicarious liability, the corporations were held liable for the wrongs of their employees and were forced to pay millions of dollars in reparations in the government and to utility companies.

One of the great ironies of the story is that ten years after Westinghouse pled guilty to the antitrust charges, it nearly went bankrupt as the victim of a price-fixing scheme by uranium producers. Westinghouse held a number of contracts to supply uranium to utility companies at a certain price. When the price of uranium escalated because of a successful price-fixing plan, Westinghouse found itself with hundreds of losing contracts. Westinghouse sued to renegotiate the contracts, but a court, perhaps with a long memory, held that Westinghouse would have to take its lumps.

Price fixing is just one example of how markets are subject to abuse. Normally, cartels die of their own weight, since the incentive for companies to break out of the cartel and grab a large share of the market is great. However, when they don't break up, cartels can wreak havoc with the free enterprise system. "What is really at stake here," said Judge J. Cullen Graney, who presided over the government's suit against the electrical conspirators, "is the survival of the kind of economy under which this country has grown great, the free-enterprise system." Market economies are based on the notion that prices and profits determine production and resource allocation. Price fixing skews the market and causes distortions. Conspirators argue, of course, that price fixing is sometimes necessary just to survive. "We need protection from buyers," said F. F. Loock of Allen-Bradley, one of the defendants. Obviously, the government and the judge did not agree.

Profile of a Recession

Living in a market economy can be harsh. Like so many sports heroes, when a market economy is good, it is very, very good, and when it is bad, it is very, very bad. In 1981 and 1982, the American economy was very, very bad. In the early years of Ronald Reagan's first term, the United States experienced a typical recession; it wasn't a pleasant experience, but it was familiar.

In its April 6, 1981 issue, *Time* heralded a new eight year high in the Dow-Jones average at a value of 1015 and decided that the economy was more healthy than many supposed. The economy had been growing since 1975 with the exception of the election year, 1980. But inflation had been at double digit rates for three years and interest rates were at historic highs. Unlike *Time*, some analysts thought a recession was coming. They were right. In the summer of 1981, the Fed stepped on the monetary brake—money growth stopped and interest rates went still higher to 20 percent. In the last three months of 1981, GNP fell at an annual rate of nearly 5 percent. Unemployment increased by over a million workers. By December 14, 1981, *Time* had changed its optimistic tune of the spring, "With each passing day, the industrial landscape is increasingly marred by padlocked factory gates and smokeless smokestacks." Fortunately for the Reagan administration, the economic slump had come soon enough that they could blame it on the Carter administration.

Through most of 1982, the economic slide continued. The recession was now worldwide. Canadian Prime Minister Trudeau warned, "We are moving from crisis to catastrophe." (He was right for he would soon be "moving from" office.) In the U.S., unemployment continued to climb and topped 10 percent in the fall of 1982. Comparisons were made (stupidly) to the Great Depression.

Unemployment rates above 10 percent meant that more than three million Americans had lost their jobs, most of them in the high-paying automobile, steel, mining, and general manufacturing industries. In shocking comparison, the unemployment rate had been as low as 3.4 percent twelve years earlier, and had been 5.8 percent just three years earlier. The unemployment rates for minorities were particularly stunning. The rate for black workers reached 18.6 percent, and for black teenagers, an astronomical 46.1 percent; for single women with children, 13.3 percent. Since government expenditures on income support programs had been cut, at least nominally, unemployment translated into economic suffering for millions.

All during the fall, the evening newscasts were filled with stories of discouraged unemployed workers. Pessimism and gloom were everywhere. The media always like to personalize economic news. There is nothing as boring as an economist pontificating about the latest unfathomable economic numbers. At the end of 1982, the media were everywhere looking for real people to personify economic troubles. They found just the right person.

Reginald Andrews was a twenty-nine-year-old father of eight from Manhattan. In December 1982, Andrews was among the 10.6 percent who didn't have a job. His phone was disconnected, he didn't have a car, and food was scarce. That Christmas there would be no presents for the children. He had, by his own estimates, filled out more than one thousand job applications in the past year.

On December 20, 1982, Andrews was waiting for a subway in downtown Manhattan after a job interview. As he waited for the right train, a blind man, seventy-five-year-old David Schair of the Bronx, attempted to board a different train. Schair got confused, and instead of walking into the car he walked right between two cars. He fell down the crack and lay moaning as the subway car prepared to depart. If the train departed before he moved, it would have crushed him. Andrews leaped to save him even though the train was only seconds from starting to roll. He climbed down the crack, grabbed Schair, and pulled him into the narrow crawl space under the edge of the train platform. Unless the train stopped, Andrews would now be crushed, because there was only room for one body. Fortunately, a screaming woman caught the conductor's attention, and the train was stopped just after it had started to roll. "I wasn't thinking about the danger," said Andrews, "just that, hey, somebody needs help." He tore ligaments in his leg in the process.

The next day Andrews became a hero. He had to limp down five flights of stairs every time someone called, since the nearest phone was in a grocery store at the bottom of his building. One of his congratulatory

Table 18.1 Statistical Profile of a Recession

Year	Months	GNP Growth	Unemployment	Consumption	Investment	Gov't. Spending	Money Growth	Interest Rate
1980	Oct–Dec	4.3%	7.4%	$941	$210	$283	1.0%	17.5%
1981	Jan–Mar	9.0	7.4	954	220	286	2.0	19.5
	Apr–Jun	0.7	7.4	957	221	284	1.0	18.7
	Jul–Sep	3.6	7.4	963	220	287	0.7	20.0
	Oct–Dec	- 5.9	8.3	958	216	290	2.2	17.6
1982	Jan-Mar	- 4.6	8.7	954	205	290	1.7	16.3
	Apr–Jun	- 0.8	9.3	959	200	287	1.1	16.5
	Jul–Sep	- 0.9	9.8	964	194	293	2.1	15.0
	Oct–Dec	0.5	10.5	976	178	301	3.2	12.5
1983	Jan-Mar	3.3	10.2	983	191	294	4.0	11.0
	Apr–Jun	9.4	10.0	1006	213	292	2.8	10.5
	Jul–Sep	6.8	9.2	1016	231	292	1.0	10.7
	Oct–Dec	5.9	8.4	1032	250	289	0.8	11.0
1984	Jan–Mar	10.1	7.8	1044	286	289	2.7	11.2
	Apr–Jun	7.1	7.4	1064	284	302	2.0	12.3

Note: Percentages are in annual rates. Dollar amounts are in billions of 1972 dollars.
Source: Economic Reports of the President.

calls came from Ronald Reagan, who wanted to thank him "for all Americans." "I thought he was Rich Little," Andrews said. When Reagan found out that Andrews had been coming from a job interview, he asked for the name of the employer. "Give me their phone number," he said, "I want to call and give you a reference from me."

With that kind of high-powered support, Andrews got the job working for a frozen foods business. But recessions show no respect for heroes. Within a month, the business lost its lease and Andrews was again unemployed. When the *New York Times* checked on Andrews three months later, he was earning $100 a week, hanging out at grocery stores helping unload produce trucks. "I'm still behind in my rent. I'm back right where I was before," he said. "I'm not uncomfortable in this position, because I'm so used to being there."

In 1983, the economy slowly improved. Over the spring and summer, GNP grew at a very high rate as it often does at the end of a recession. By fall, unemployment was down to 8 percent and interest rates were half what they had been two years earlier. At the end of 1983, *Time* headlined "Cheers for a Banner Year." Reginald-Andrews found work in 1984.

The 1981–1982 recession was like many others of the past-not anticipated by most, very costly to some, and blamed on the other guy by politicians. Most Americans were just glad it was over.